Mastering
Sibelius® 5

Marc E. Schonbrun

Course Technology PTR
A part of Cengage Learning

COURSE TECHNOLOGY

Australia • Brazil • n • United States

COURSE TECHNOLOGY
CENGAGE Learning™

Mastering Sibelius® 5
Marc E. Schonbrun

Publisher and General Manager, Course Technology PTR: Stacy L. Hiquet

Associate Director of Marketing: Sarah Panella

Manager of Editorial Services: Heather Talbot

Marketing Manager: Mark Hughes

Acquisitions Editor: Orren Merton

Development Editor: Cathleen D. Small

Project Editor/Copy Editor: Cathleen D. Small

Technical Reviewer: Dave Budde

PTR Editorial Services Coordinator: Erin Johnson

Interior Layout Tech: ICC Macmillan Inc.

Cover Designer: Mike Tanamachi

CD-ROM Producer: Brandon Penticuff

Indexer: Larry Sweazy

Proofreader: Kim V. Benbow

For product information and technology assistance, contact us at
Cengage Learning Customer & Sales Support, 1-800-354-9706

For permission to use material from this text or product, submit all requests online at **cengage.com/permissions**
Further permissions questions can be emailed to
permissionrequest@cengage.com

Sibelius is a registered trademark of Sibelius Software, a part of Avid Technology Inc. All other trademarks are the property of their respective owners. "Holy, Holy, Holy" by John Bacchus Dykes (1823–1876) used according to the Free Art License at artlibre.org/licence/lal/en. Song acquired from www.cipoo.net.

Library of Congress Control Number: 2007936138

ISBN-13: 978-1-59863-426-6

ISBN-10: 1-59863-426-7

Course Technology
25 Thomson Place
Boston, MA 02210
USA

Cengage Learning is a leading provider of customized learning solutions with office locations around the globe, including Singapore, the United Kingdom, Australia, Mexico, Brazil, and Japan. Locate your local office at:
international.cengage.com/region

Cengage Learning products are represented in Canada by Nelson Education, Ltd.

For your lifelong learning solutions, visit **courseptr.com**

Visit our corporate website at **cengage.com**

Printed in the United States of America
1 2 3 4 5 6 7 11 10 09

This book is dedicated to the memory of Julius Bick.

Foreword

For his entire professional life, my dad was a mechanical engineer at a prestigious international firm headquartered on Park Avenue in New York City. One day, senior management brought in a consultant to help the top-level engineers learn to "think outside the box." My father, along with a half dozen colleagues, was ushered into a conference room. There were the predictable fluorescent lights, the never-empty coffee pot in the corner, as well as the typical pad of paper and pencil in front of each seat. When all were settled, the consultant issued a challenge.

"You are locked inside a cement bunker with an overhead light, a door, and no windows. In the middle of the floor is a two-and-a-half-foot length of pipe sticking straight out of the floor. The solid iron pipe is approximately one-and-a-half inches in diameter. A common ping-pong ball has been dropped down the pipe and is resting at the bottom.

"You gentlemen have the following materials with which to work: a box of Wheaties cereal, a wire coat hanger, a light bulb, and a two-foot length of nylon rope. Your job is to retrieve the ping-pong ball in good condition without damaging the pipe or the floor. The first engineer who comes up with a viable solution gets a paid day off. Good luck."

For the next few minutes, my dad's buddies were abuzz, concocting the most amazing contraptions. Using the coat hanger, making a loop on the end, creating a poultice or mucilage out of masticated Wheaties, and then gently lowering the wire above the ball, hoping to affix it to the sticky glop and lift it out, was but one of the many solutions. Stabbing the ball with a piece of shattered light bulb pinched between a pair of makeshift coat-hanger tweezers was discounted as it ruined the ping-pong ball.

My dad listened in silence.

Finally, after he'd heard enough, my dad asked the consultant a question: "Do we have to use the given materials in order to extricate the ball?"

"Not necessarily, but what else have you got to work with in an empty bunker?"

My dad replied, "Well, with six guys who've been drinking coffee all morning in the room, I figure we could each take a turn filling the pipe as the need arose. Seems to me the ball would eventually float to the top in perfect condition."

My dad got the paid day off—for thinking outside the box.

Marc Schonbrun thinks outside the box. As a longtime Sibelius user, I consider his book a gem of elegant and creative thinking, and I'm honored to have been asked to write this foreword.

The Brothers Finn, Daniel Spreadbury, Michael Eastwood, and their development team have done a wonderful job in writing the Sibelius handbook and the reference guide. Both are excellent volumes with different purposes. The handbook gives you a quick tour and then has a very useful how-to section that is greatly enhanced by way of graphic examples that direct you to the appropriate section of the reference guide for further in-depth information.

The only problem with this approach, in my opinion, is that not all people learn Sibelius (or anything else, for that matter) in the same way. Some are visual learners; some learn most efficiently by listening. Others need to read instructions and mull them over. Some folks yearn for step-by-step progressive instruction, and others like to dive in and splash around using a trial-and-error approach. Some procedures might be more efficacious than others, but all are valid methods.

Marc's marvelous new book fills in the gap between the two excellent Sibelius volumes—especially if you are a hands-on kind of learner (as I am). Whereas the Sibelius reference covers its subjects by topic, Marc's book takes more of a step-by-step approach, much like the handbook. His book follows a similar and logical "quick tour" progression but covers each subject with the in-depth detail of the Sibelius reference.

Lastly—and most importantly if you are a visual, or hands-on, learner—Marc includes a CD of projects for each and every subject covered. By completing a given exercise, you have not only the satisfaction of intuiting the answer, but that of actually solving the problem yourself. This has an amazing benefit, which I'm sure many readers have experienced: In six months, having not used the program on a daily basis, you nonetheless stand a fighting chance of remembering what you did to solve a problem because you originally worked through it step by step using Marc's CD examples.

The only problem with the Sibelius reference (which seems endemic to all reference volumes) is that often you have to know what to ask—sometimes even before you know precisely what it is you're looking for! Allow me to cite but one example. Let's say you are looking for a way to create so-called "feathered beams" (or eighth notes, which become sixteenth notes, which become thirty-second notes—a valiant, though not altogether precise, method of notating an accelerando). If you look under accelerando, beams, splayed ligatures, or any other logical description, you won't find them—unless you know and remember that in Sibelius, they are called *feathered beams*.

Yes, you can eventually find the information. The problem is, in six months when you have to retrieve it again, will you remember what you did? Not usually, I have found. Even with book-marks, Post-its, and margin notations in abundance, the search begins anew: "How *did* I do that?"

What is so valuable about Marc's book is that, having gone through a number of hands-on exercises, there is a strong likelihood you will remember what you did because you have a tactile memory of having produced it. These "etudes," together with Marc's Essential Tips and occasional workarounds, are sage and priceless.

Creating and manipulating lyrics and grappling with MIDI issues, page layout, layers and multiple voices, stemless noteheads, harmonics, notating arrhythmic recitative, correct and accurate playback of unpitched percussion instruments—these are just some of the myriad quagmires and bugaboos with which notation programmers must contend. As a longtime Sibelius user, I can boast with firsthand experience that Sibelius, more than any other available notation program, has stayed current with these and countless other issues and has continued its undaunted improvement by leaps and bounds. The Sibelius programmers and engineers are musicians them-selves. They continue to listen to the needs of rockers, orchestrators, copyists, choral directors, educators, publishers, film score composers—and they often implement their requests elegantly and astonishingly quickly!

A musician keeping up with these myriad developments is tantamount to an accountant keeping up with IRS tax law. Marc Schonbrun is such a musician, who has used and knows Sibelius at the molecular level. He understands with an engineer's insight and yet is able to translate this highly esoteric information through a musician's filters. Marc writes in an informal style, yet is never pedantic, never patronizing; searching for information is logical and intuitive. Marc writes *as* a musician *for* the musician; he thinks about and explains concepts backed up by a wealth of practical hands-on experience and his own trial-by-error frustrations. Beginner or seasoned veteran, you will easily find the solution you're looking for in Marc's book.

Starting with the basics and advancing through the most arcane concepts, I predict you will never again boot up Sibelius without this indispensable book by your side! And it is my personal hope that Marc's book will someday join the Sibelius canon of information.

J. Owen Burdick, Ph.D., F.R.S.C.M., A.A.G.O., Ch.M.
17th Organist and Director of Music
Trinity Church, Wall Street

Acknowledgments

This book would not have been possible without the help and support of the following people:

My family for all of their continued support.

Jeremy Silver, Alison Kerr, Ben Moore, Ben Hodson, Sam Butler, David Harvey, and Richard Payne at Sibelius UK for all their assistance in making this project a reality.

Philip Nicol, Lisa Speegle, Dr. Lee Whitmore, Peter Maund, Gabe Cobas, John Kline, Jill Schaub, Michelle Springmeyer, Judy Tomsovic, Tom Betts, Maribel Aveno, David Christiansen, Alan Steel, and everyone else at Sibelius USA for their continued support of everything I do.

Thanks to Orren Merton and Cathleen Small for being much more than editors—you guys are my friends.

Jonathan and Ben Finn for creating the software that made all of this possible.

John Bienvenue at Sibelius Australia.

Jeff Horton and Tobias Thon at Native Instruments.

Eric Lindemann at Synful.

Michael Good for his help with MusicXML information and his donation of a piece to this book.

Jim Casella at Tapspace.

Martin Tichy at VSL.

Arjen van der Schoot at Audio Ease.

Dr. Owen Burdick for his wonderful foreword and keen insights.

James Humberstone for his help and wisdom on formatting, layout, and Sibelius in general.

Mary Elizabeth for her time and knowledge of so many different disciplines related to this book.

Dr. Sandi MacLeod for having the faith and vision to bring composition to children with the Vermont MIDI Project though Sibelius.

Ron James for his donation of the video file used in this book.

Robin Hodson for reading every chapter, making suggestions, sharing his music, and being a great teacher.

Thanks to Richard Boukas, Robin Hodson, and Gabe Cobas for the use of their scores in this book and the accompanying examples.

And finally, Daniel Spreadbury for taking the time to read every word to ensure accuracy and give great suggestions to make this book the best it could be. This book would not be what it is without your help. Thank you, Daniel.

About the Author

Marc Schonbrun is one of the top Sibelius trainers in America. A highly respected clinician, he travels extensively, teaching musicians of all types how to use Sibelius and its related products, as well as presenting at trade shows and special events worldwide. Marc graduated magna cum laude from the Crane School of Music. He is an active educator, writer, and performer. Marc's musical resume ranges from classical guitar concertos to jazz trios and rock concerts. He is also the author of numerous books and articles on music theory, guitar playing, and music technology. Marc is the author of *The Everything Rock & Blues Guitar Book*, *The Everything Home Recording Book*, *The Everything Reading Music Book*, *The Everything Guitar Chords Book*, *The Efficient Guitarist: Book One*, *The Efficient Guitarist: Book Two*, *The Everything Music Theory Book*, *The Everything Guitar Scales Book*, *Digital Guitar Power!*, and TrueFire.com's *Geek Guitar*. He is endorsed by Godin Guitars, D'Addario Strings, Planet Waves, and Flite Sound Speakers and is a professional training specialist for Digidesign/Avid/M-Audio, Native Instruments, and Korg USA. More at www.marcschonbrun.com.

Contents

Chapter 5
Creating Everything Else   127

Chapter 6
Instrument-Specific Notation   159

Chapter 7
Properties, Editing, and Filtering   195

Chapter 8
House Styles and Engraving Rules   227

Chapter 9
Document Layout and Formatting   251

Chapter 10
Dynamic Parts   287

Chapter 11
Ideas   303

Chapter 12
Playback and Virtual Instruments
321

Chapter 13
Composing to Video in Sibelius
363

Chapter 14
Scanning and the Arrange Feature

Chapter 15
Worksheets and the Worksheet Creator

Chapter 16
Using Plug-Ins

Chapter 17
Customizing Sibelius   437

Chapter 18
Importing and Exporting   455

Introduction

Welcome to *Mastering Sibelius 5*! Sibelius music software has been around since 1993 (though development started as early as 1987) and was developed by twin brothers Ben and Jonathan Finn shortly after they left Oxford and Cambridge Universities. The original Sibelius ran on a computer platform called the Acorn computer, which was a RISC-based computer system. From the onset of the Finns' programming efforts, the software was designed to be as easy to use as it was powerful. Sibelius continued to run on Acorn systems until 1998, when the company debuted its first major release for Macintosh and Windows computer systems: Sibelius 1. From that point on, Sibelius and Finale would jockey for the title of most popular score-writing software. Sibelius has gained considerable market share and popularity since its inception, something which continues to grow to this day. In 2006, Sibelius became part of the Avid family of companies and now joins Digidesign and M-Audio as sister companies.

Regardless of your background or what you used in the past to engrave music (even the good old pencil and paper), you've now come to Sibelius, and we're happy to show you how to get the most out of your software and truly "master Sibelius."

Who Uses Sibelius?

The question of who uses Sibelius is as open-ended a question as one could ask. Notation is the written language of music, and anyone who wishes to speak the language of music needs to write it down in some way. You can think of Sibelius as a musical word processor, much like Microsoft Word (the program I'm writing this very book in!). So, who uses Sibelius? Here is a list to get started:

- Composers
- Songwriters
- Music educators
- Copyists
- Engravers
- Music publishers

- Arrangers
- Musicians

Within that distinguished list of potential Sibelius users, we can further break down what Sibelius can actually output as a musical score:

- Simple single-note melodies
- Grand staff piano music
- Symphony orchestra scores
- Choral scores with lyrics
- Chamber music
- Big-band jazz scores
- Jazz "lead" sheets
- Solo music for any instrument
- Opera
- Avant-garde graphical notation
- Guitar tablature
- Percussion notation
- Much, much more

Sibelius has the monumental task of notating these diverse styles of written music by an equally diverse group of composers, engravers, and other musicians. The point is that Sibelius is what you make of it. Its true power is in its ability to adapt to whatever you throw at it, no matter what kind of music floats your boat.

The Approach

The way we're going to approach this book is not to single out any one area of musical engraving (the art of musical notation). There's not going to be a distinct section for choral music, which is separate from instruction for orchestral music. This book is going to progress in a linear fashion through the program, gaining depth as we build foundation. The beauty (in my mind) of Sibelius is that once you get grounded in the basics of how Sibelius works—and more importantly *where to look to find things you haven't learned yet*—then no matter what style of music you want to produce with it, you're able to get about 95 percent of the way there. There is always that small percentage of Sibelius that remains elusive unless you, for example, set choral music every day and encounter the proper way to space lyrics vertically on a page. This is true of every Sibelius user I've ever met—we all get into our little niches in the program and earn our last five percent. Again, we come back to the same 95 percent that we all have to know. That's how this book is going to progress; we're going to show you how the program works and where to look for the rest. Along the way, you'll learn the skills to work with any style of music you could ever need.

The CD

Along with the book, you'll find an accompanying CD, which contains tons of files for you to practice with. The files are Sibelius 5–formatted files and will open on a Mac or a PC.

Throughout the book you'll find these special markings interspersed within the chapters:

CD Go to the CD and practice with Example *X*.

Each CD example is a full Sibelius file intended for you to work on. In each chapter, after you learn something, you'll go right to the CD and try your hand at a real score. In the Sibelius files themselves, you'll have specific instructions on what to do. This kind of hands-on instruction will help you learn Sibelius so much faster! Don't just read about features—get your hands dirty right away and learn by doing (and let the book get you there faster than you ever thought possible).

More   You'll also find more examples on the CD than are called out in the chapters. These are for folks who'd like some additional practice with the various tasks. As always, the instructions are inserted as text within the Sibelius files.

Common Ground

The only common ground we can start with is the beginning so if you already have some experience with Sibelius, feel free to move to the sections that interest you. However, you may gain some great tips from reading this book as a whole, from beginning to end. Many Sibelius users have learned ways to get around Sibelius, and sometimes this isn't the best or most efficient way to work. If you've got the time (heck, you bought the whole book), make sure you don't fly through the early chapters!

Essential Tips

Throughout the book, we'll use special notes and sidebars that point out important and necessary information for you as you go along. In reality, some notes are more important than others, so we'll call some of them "Essential Tips," because if you learn them, you'll be much better off. In addition to just calling out these tips as we go along, each chapter will begin with a short Essential Tips section, basically outlining the most important things you'll learn in that chapter. Consider them as reminders that if you don't learn anything else in this chapter, learn these. Hopefully, all of these elements together will help make your experience of mastering Sibelius that much better. Let's just start with a set of Essential Tips—ones that I want you to come back to when you've finished this book. By the end of the book, everything you see in these Essential Tips should make total sense to you.

Here are the Essential Tips for Sibelius:

1. Escape, escape, escape, or you'll be sorry.

2. If something is selected, that's where the action is.

3. Sibelius wants to know where you'd like to do that.

4. Leave KONTAKT PLAYER alone; let Sibelius do it for you.

5. Panorama is a better way to work. Write in Panorama and worry about layout later.

6. Paste using Alt-click/Option-click.

7. Please never, ever drag a stave. If you want more room, there's a proper way to make it.

8. Learn the Filter menu; it's your friend.

9. Stop doing that 1,000 times in a row; there's a plug-in that does that.

Installing Sibelius

This section is broken down into two subsections: one for brand-new users of Sibelius 5 who have never had a copy of Sibelius installed on their machines and the other for those who are upgrading from an earlier version. If you have already installed Sibelius, feel free to skip over this part!

System Requirements   Before you install, have a look at the system requirements for your computer and make sure you can run Sibelius comfortably.

For Windows users, you'll need XP Service Pack 2 or Vista with a minimum of 512 megabytes of RAM, a DVD-ROM drive, and about 350 megabytes of free space. To use the new Sibelius Sounds Essentials, you'll want 1 gigabyte of RAM, 3.5 gigabytes of free space on your hard drive, and a soundcard that supports ASIO.

For Macintosh users, the big news is that Sibelius 5 is a Universal Binary, allowing it to run on both PowerPC-based Macs (G4, G5) and the new Intel chips Apple is currently shipping. The RAM, soundcard, and hard drive space remain the same as the Windows requirements. To run Sibelius 5 on a Mac, you need to run OS X 10.4 or later. It will not work on any earlier version of OS X.

Installing Sibelius 5 for the First Time

Rather than rehash the user guide provided for you in your Sibelius 5 box, I'll give you some tips for installing Sibelius so you can work with this book. Install Sibelius 5, but make sure that you install the following components so you have a complete installation to work with:

- The Sibelius 5 program

- Sibelius Sounds Essentials

- Sibelius Scorch

- PhotoScore Lite

After you've taken the time to run the full installer (which should take a bit of time because you're copying the large sample library), run the software for the first time and go through the authorization process.

Authorizing Sibelius   To protect their intellectual property from software piracy, Sibelius uses a copy-protection scheme called *challenge and response*. Their system is far less invasive than that of other companies. In short, your computer generates a unique code that is called a *challenge*. This number, along with your serial number, will generate a unique response that will unlock Sibelius on your computer. Sibelius allows you to install legally on two different computers at the same time. This is typically for laptop and desktop computer setups.

Sibelius' authorization system runs through the Internet and should work for 99.9 percent of users. If you're not on the Internet or you have an issue, you can contact their super-friendly technical support, which will sort you out in a jiffy!

At this point, you're installed and ready to go, so feel free to go right on to the section about what's new in Sibelius 5 (just a bit further on in this chapter).

Upgrading to Sibelius 5 from an Earlier Version

If you're upgrading from an earlier version of Sibelius, make sure that your previous version of Sibelius is installed and registered. You'll also want to consult the handy "Upgrading to Sibelius 5" handbook provided in the box (you really should read those things) for some particular details about upgrading, especially if you're upgrading from Sibelius 1.x.

Install the upgrade to Sibelius 5, but make sure that you install the following components so you have a complete installation to work with:

1. The Sibelius 5 program

2. Sibelius Sounds Essentials

3.   Sibelius Scorch

4.   PhotoScore Lite

After you've taken the time to run the full installer (which should take a bit of time because you're copying the large sample library), run the software for the first time and go through the authorization process. Sibelius will ask you to locate your previous copy of Sibelius and then prompt you for an upgrade code. At that point you will go through the registration process, which should take no time at all, and then you'll be ready to roll in Sibelius 5.

Most Recent Versions   Even great software changes! At the time this book was started, Sibelius 5.0 was just being released. Midway through the writing, Sibelius released 5.2, which added some additional features and a few bug fixes. Make sure that you go to the Help > Check for Updates menu and ensure you have the most recent version of Sibelius. At the time of this writing, the most recent version was Sibelius 5.2.

What's New in Sibelius 5

It goes without saying that if you're new to Sibelius, then *everything* is new in Sibelius 5. However, here is a list of the major new features introduced with Sibelius 5:

- Drastically improved playback system (Sibelius SoundWorld) that searches for the most appropriate sound under all playback conditions.

- A 3.5-gigabyte sample library culled from sample manufacturers, such as Sibelius, Garritan, Tapspace, and M-Audio.

- Sibelius now hosts VST/AU instrument and effect plug-ins, greatly expanding the type and quality of sounds Sibelius can produce.

- A newly redesigned Mixer for controlling your playback levels and sounds.

- The Panorama view, which displays your music on a continuous, endlessly wide page.

- The Ideas feature, which allows you to capture musical fragments, recall them, and copy and paste them into your score at any point. Sibelius includes a library of Ideas for you to start working with right out of the box.

- Automatic instrument changes: You can now specify an instrument change within a part, and Sibelius will add automatically the appropriate clef and transposition for you.

- Hundreds of other small improvements that will make your life easier.

Now that you're installed and excited about the new features, let's get into the heart of the program and learn how to start working with Sibelius from the ground up.

1 Setting Up Sibelius 5 for the First Time

Essential Tips for Chapter 1

1. When setting up Sibelius for the first time, you'll want to get all of your MIDI input and output devices set up first. (MIDI devices are now in Sibelius > Preferences, unlike in older versions of the program.)

2. Sibelius 5 relies on virtual instruments for playback through a new system called *Sibelius Sounds Essentials (SSE)*. To hear your work, make sure SSE is installed from the installation DVD.

3. The Quick Start menu provides easy access to Sibelius functions, such as starting new scores, importing MIDI files, or scanning music.

4. The Create drop-down menu is the central hub for creating objects in your Sibelius score; check out its contents.

5. The toolbar contains shortcuts to the most used functions in Sibelius. You can hover your mouse over any button, and Sibelius will share a tool tip that lets you know what the currently selected button does.

When you're installed and ready to roll, you need to start the process of getting Sibelius set up for your own personal working style. To begin with, you'll set up the following parameters within Sibelius:

- Detecting and activating your external MIDI instruments/interfaces

- Activating the Sibelius Sounds Essentials plug-in

- Fine-tuning the audio system options for your computer

These essential tasks only need to be set up the first time you run Sibelius. As long as you don't change your working style too much, these settings will remain intact for as long as you run Sibelius. Thankfully, they're not hard to change at any point, if you should need to.

An important note: We're going to dive into these parts of the program first to ensure that as soon as you truly enter the world of Sibelius, things simply "work" for you (scores play back, your soundcard is found, your MIDI input device works as expected, and so on). To do this, I have to jump around to a few different parts of the program before I actually explain the interface or why you're doing what you're doing. Have no fear! We will cover each of these elements again in more detail. For now, I want to simply get Sibelius working for you so that when you take your first steps with the program, you get all you expect. Sound good?

Windows and Mac Sibelius is a cross-platform application, which means that it runs on both Windows- or Mac-based computers. More importantly, Sibelius looks remarkably similar when running on Windows or Mac. The only obvious differences are in the key commands. On the Mac, the Command key is used instead of the Ctrl key on a Windows keyboard. Because these keyboard shortcuts will run throughout the book, I will list shortcuts for Windows first, followed by the equivalent Mac shortcut.

Files created on the Windows version of Sibelius can be opened on the Mac version of Sibelius and vice versa. More often than not, if you simply substitute the Command key for the Ctrl key when using Sibelius on a Mac (or vice versa when using a Windows PC), you should find almost everything else the same. Any differences will be clearly pointed out throughout the text.

Starting Sibelius

Once Sibelius has been launched and successfully registered, you will come to the Quick Start dialog box shown in Figure 1.1.

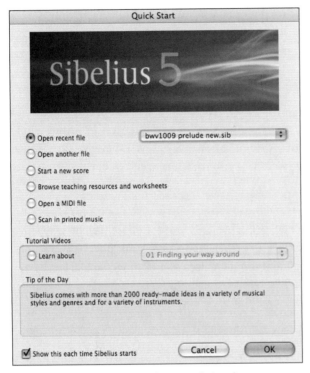

Figure 1.1   Sibelius's Quick Start dialog box.

The Quick Start dialog box provides you with a portal into the most commonly used tasks when you start Sibelius. These tasks include:

- Opening a recently created document

- Opening any other file

- Starting a new score

- Browsing the teaching resources and worksheets built into Sibelius

- Opening a standard MIDI file

- Scanning in printed music with PhotoScore

- Watching some tutorial movies

All of the items in the Quick Start dialog box are there to speed up your entry into any Sibelius score by consolidating the most frequently used commands into one screen. You can gain access to any of the functions in the Quick Start dialog box from the drop-down menus across the top of the Sibelius window as well.

For now, close the Quick Start dialog box by clicking once on the Cancel button. Don't worry; we'll come back to the Quick Start dialog box. But now you're ready to start setting up Sibelius for your own personal needs.

Activating MIDI Input Devices

Sibelius communicates with external MIDI input devices (such as keyboards or guitar synths) for its note input. Although you can input notes into a Sibelius with a combination of mouse clicks and computer keyboard entries, many musicians still enter notes using MIDI keyboards. To set up Sibelius to listen to your external MIDI sources, you need to set up the input device preferences.

Changed in Sibelius 5 If you're an experienced Sibelius user, it's worth noting that the way you set up your input devices has changed in v5. In previous versions, input devices were managed through the consolidated Playback and Input Devices menu. In v5, Sibelius has moved the input device setup to the Sibelius Preferences dialog box.

You first need to access the Preferences dialog box within Sibelius, which you can find in Windows by choosing Preferences from the File menu or by using the key command Ctrl+, (comma). On Mac, you will find it by choosing Preference from the Sibelius 5 menu or by using the key command Command+, (comma). Figure 1.2 shows the default Preferences dialog box.

As you can see, Sibelius has a lot of preferences you can set. The window is divided into two sides: The left side has a list of categories, while the right side shows you all the preferences for the selected category. To access your MIDI devices, on the left side, scroll down to Input Devices and highlight it to bring up its preferences. Figure 1.3 shows the Input Devices Preferences dialog box.

This dialog box is Sibelius's way of dealing with and controlling any external MIDI devices you may have attached to your system. Any MIDI devices that are installed on your computer will show up in this dialog box, and you can activate them, tell Sibelius what types of devices they are, and define the input map (which maps extra controllers, such as knobs and sliders if your keyboard has them, to different mixer and playback functions within Sibelius).

Driver Setup Sibelius will only detect MIDI devices that are already installed and working on your system. This typically involves the installation of a driver of some sort that enables your device to function within the operating system. Please check with the documentation that came with your MIDI device for instructions on how to install it in your system. Remember, Sibelius will only manage and see devices that are already installed on your system. The exception is a *class-compliant* device that does not require a driver to function. Your product's documentation will tell you whether your device needs a driver. Sibelius can't install a driver file for you. You will always need to do this through your operating system. The best way to ensure that you have an up-to-date driver is to download one from the manufacturer's website.

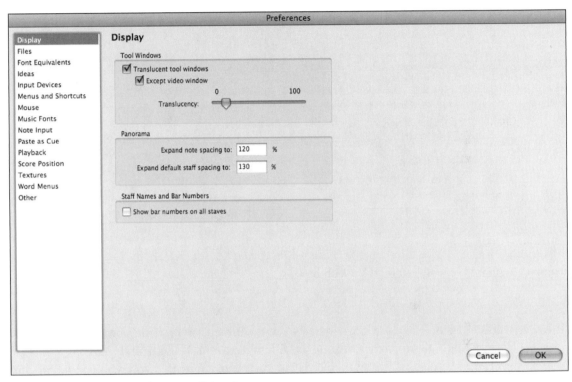

Figure 1.2   Sibelius's Preferences dialog box.

Installed devices will automatically show up in the list on the left side of the window. To enable a device for use with Sibelius, you must check the Use column directly to the right of the name of the device. When you've done that, tap a few keys on your device to see whether it's working. If everything is working, the Test indicator will light up with a green activity meter to signify a successful connection.

Next to the name of your device, you will see a column for Type, which sets the type of MIDI device you're using. There are a limited number of choices: Keyboard or Guitar. Unless you're one of the brave few who use a MIDI guitar input device, choose Keyboard (which is the default anyway).

If you are using a MIDI guitar, choosing Guitar in the Type column will activate the guitar-specific MIDI Guitar Channels, which will make note entry with a guitar much easier. In the

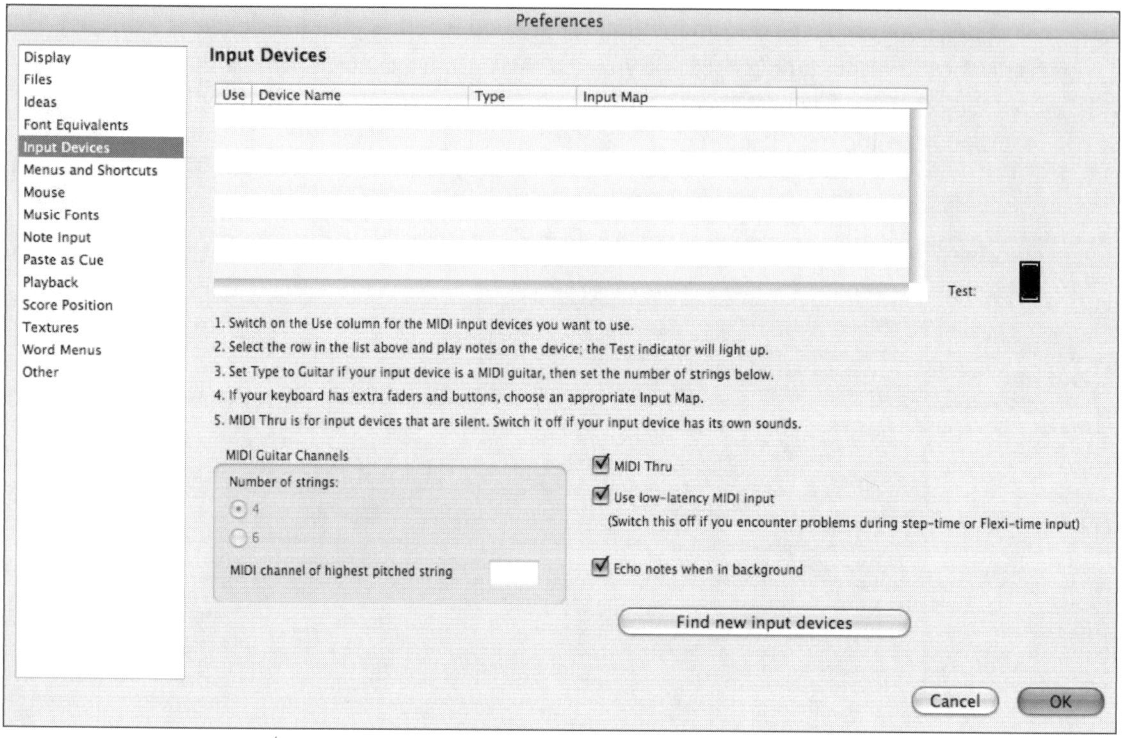

Figure 1.3 Input Devices Preferences dialog box.

lower-left corner, simply choose how many strings your guitar has and specify which MIDI channel your first (highest pitched) string is. On all current Roland and AXON guitar-to-MIDI converters, the default is Channel 1. Setting up your guitar this way will enable Sibelius to automatically create tablature at the correct location on the guitar's neck when using a guitar-to-MIDI converter.

The last column in the Input Devices window is the Input Map column, which is useful if your MIDI controller has an array of knobs and sliders for controlling functions in Sibelius (Playback, Mixer Levels). The default "keyboard" should work for you, but if you see the model of your device listed in the Input Map drop-down menu (which is seen when you click on the word Keyboard), please choose it to enable that functionality on your device.

The MIDI Thru check box should only be enabled (checked) if your MIDI keyboard has built-in sounds that you want to use instead of the software sounds that Sibelius provides through Sibelius Sounds Essentials. Some keyboards are only "controller" (or dummy) keyboards and don't provide any sounds of their own. In this case, you need to have MIDI Thru enabled.

The last preference is whether to engage low-latency MIDI input. Most MIDI inputs have a short delay, or *latency,* and this check box is useful in combating that when you're playing live into

Sibelius using Flexi-time, Sibelius's real-time note input method (detailed in Chapter 2, "Note Entry").

Figure 1.4 shows an example screen, fully set up for an M-Audio Oxygen 8 MIDI controller keyboard. Because this keyboard is a controller (thus, it makes no sound of its own), I made sure to select MIDI Thru for that device.

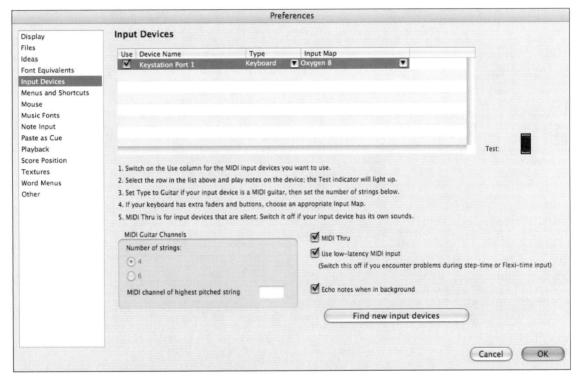

Figure 1.4 A completed Input Devices window.

The good news is that you're finished setting up MIDI devices (unless you buy a new one). It only takes a few minutes, but it's well worth the time to get Sibelius talking properly to your devices.

Activating Sibelius Sounds Essentials

One of the major new features in Sibelius 5 is its expanded playback capabilities. If you're not interested in playback (you just want to score music), then you can skip this entire section. The included sound system (new in Sibelius 5) is Sibelius Sounds Essentials. SSE is a collection of samples from leading sample manufacturers that guarantee you the most realistic playback from

Sibelius. If you've used the built-in engine in previous versions of Sibelius, there is simply no comparison.

To run this system, Sibelius utilizes a VST/AU plug-in by Native Instruments called KONTAKT PLAYER 2. You'll want to set up Sibelius to play back through this new system. To do so, in the top Sibelius menu bar, select Playback Devices from the Play menu. (The procedure is the same in both Mac and Windows.) This will bring you to the screen shown in Figure 1.5, the Playback Devices window.

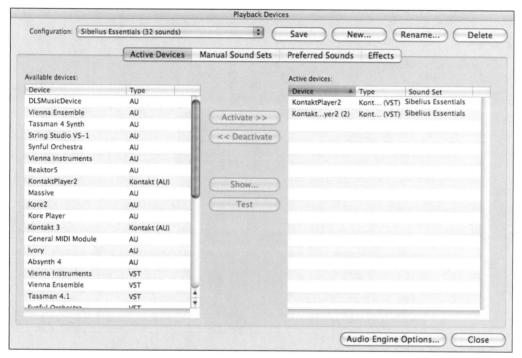

Figure 1.5 The Playback Devices window.

Install it! Sibelius Sounds Essentials is not installed by default. You have to install it from a separate installer on your installation DVD. If you can't find the KONTAKT PLAYER 2 in your devices list, check and see whether you've installed the SSE library.

The Playback Devices window is a four-part window that configures how Sibelius plays back to its included KONTAKT PLAYER 2 plug-in, your third-party VST/AU plug-ins, or external hardware. The window is fairly extensive, and we will cover it in more detail later in the book. For now, you are going to activate Sibelius Sounds Essentials. To do so, in your Playback

Devices window, find the Configuration menu and select Sibelius Essentials (32 Sounds) from it. Doing so will automatically activate a pair of KONTAKT PLAYER 2 devices in the Active Devices section on the right side of the Playback Devices window.

Know Your Slot The "32" in Sibelius Essentials (32 Sounds) refers to how many sounds the plug-in can play back at any one time. Each instance of KONTAKT PLAYER 2 can support up to 16 sounds, or *slots*. It's easy to add more instances of KONTAKT PLAYER 2 to enable more channels of playback. Thirty-two channels will get you through most playback situations. If for some reason you need more instances of KONTAKT PLAYER 2, Sibelius 5 will tell you that you need additional instances and will even add them for you.

Once that's finished, you can close the window, and Sibelius will automatically play back your scores with the new SSE sound engine.

Virtual Instruments KONTAKT PLAYER 2 is a virtual instrument. Simply put, a *virtual instrument* is a piece of software (called a *plug-in*) that produces sound on your computer. In the past, MIDI keyboards, or MIDI sound generators, generated all of the sounds we heard. Nowadays, sounds are living within the computer as plug-ins. This requires that the computer itself generate the sounds that you hear, and this is done through a virtual instrument.

Virtual instruments have one thing in common: They require a relatively fast computer to run. The more instruments you run simultaneously, the more stressed your computer will become. Sibelius itself has no limit on the number of sounds you can play back. The limit depends on the speed of your computer. This is easily managed when you learn about the mixer and its CPU utilization display in a later chapter. For a complete listing of Sibelius's computer requirements, check out www.sibelius.com/products/sibelius/features/requirements.html.

Fine-Tuning Your Audio Settings

Sibelius 5 also boasts a new playback engine that integrates with built-in and external soundcards (USB or FireWire). Go back to the Play menu and select Playback Devices. On the resulting screen, click the Audio Engine Options button (see Figure 1.6).

To get the best possible performance from Sibelius, make sure you have a soundcard that supports low latency. Latency is a measure of the time it takes for sound to become audible as it runs through your computer system. For a program like Sibelius, which allows you to enter notes along to a click track (called *Flexi-time*) input, high latency can be a real challenge for accurate

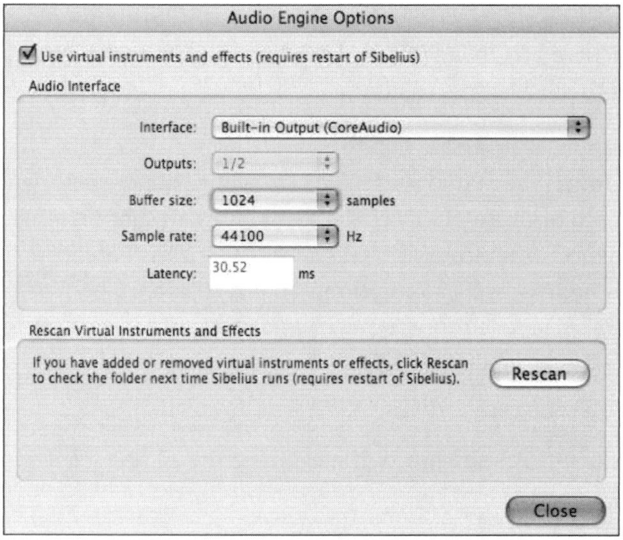

Figure 1.6 Audio Engine Options window.

transcription. Because of this, Sibelius supports a few different ways to interact with soundcards. On the Mac, audio is very straightforward: Every device that runs off OS X 10.4 or later needs to have a CoreAudio driver in order to run. Sibelius takes advantage of this, and if you're a Mac user, you'll see your choices are all CoreAudio devices.

On a PC, there are three different drivers that Sibelius supports: ASIO, DirectSound, and MME. ASIO will give you the lowest latency, and Sibelius will try to use an ASIO device if it can. If it can't find one, it will try a DirectSound device, followed by an MME device. ASIO is the way to go, and you should see whether your built-in soundcard supports ASIO for low-latency operation. In the unlikely event that it doesn't support ASIO, there is a free third-party driver available at www.asio4all.com that will allow most embedded soundcards to use ASIO and gain lower-latency options.

The Audio Engine Options screen provides you with the following options:

■ **Use Virtual Instruments and Effects.** This allows you to shut off Sibelius's ability to use instruments and effects. This could help if you have a very old computer and you just need a program to engrave music on (and you don't care about playback). But the vast majority of users will want this switched on.

■ **Interface.** Here is where you can select the audio interface you want activated.

■ **Outputs.** Sibelius uses only a stereo output. If your device has more than two outputs, you'll need to tell Sibelius which two outputs to use—Sibelius defaults to Outputs 1 and 2.

- **Buffer Size.** The buffer size (measured in samples) is in direct proportion to the amount of latency on your system. A low buffer will result in low latency, but with higher CPU taxation. Higher buffers will incur more latency, but will allow your CPU to do more (such as play back more instruments), so the magic number for your buffer size will always vary depending on what you're doing. Use lower buffers for Flexi-time and higher buffers for playback.

- **Sample Rate.** This is the frequency of the output audio and should remain at 44.1 unless you have a specific reason or need to change it (for example, when using third-party samples that are sampled at 96 kHz).

- **Latency.** This window is not editable; it's calculated by the sample rate and your latency buffer. It shows you how long it will take (in milliseconds) from the time you press a note on a MIDI keyboard until you actually hear it.

- **Rescan.** This rescans your computer for new VST and AU effects and instruments. Only use this if you've added or removed plug-ins from your computer.

Figure 1.7 shows some sample settings to get you started. The buffer has been set fairly low to allow you to enter notes with lower latency.

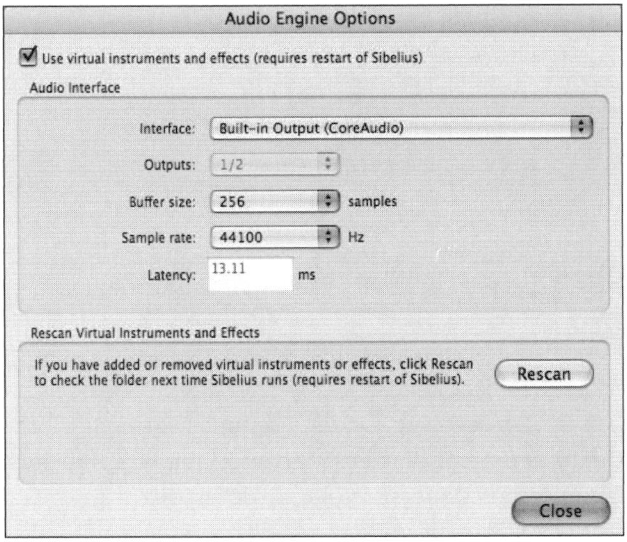

Audio Engine Options

☑ Use virtual instruments and effects (requires restart of Sibelius)

Audio Interface

Interface: Built-in Output (CoreAudio)

Outputs: 1/2

Buffer size: 256   samples

Sample rate: 44100   Hz

Latency: 13.11   ms

Rescan Virtual Instruments and Effects

If you have added or removed virtual instruments or effects, click Rescan to check the folder next time Sibelius runs (requires restart of Sibelius).   Rescan

Close

Figure 1.7 Sample audio engine settings.

You can always come back to this window and change the buffer size (which is generally the only thing you would change in this window) to balance between lower latency for note input and higher latency to allow playback or more simultaneous virtual instrument sounds.

Now that you have these vital settings configured, you can start using Sibelius.

Quick Start to a New Score

Remember that Quick Start dialog box that you dismissed earlier in order to set up your program preferences? It's time to bring it back and use it. You can get it back in one of two ways. The first method is to quit the program, and the Quick Start dialog box will come back up by itself. But you certainly don't have to do that! The other way is to go to the File menu and select Quick Start to reshow the dialog (see Figure 1.8).

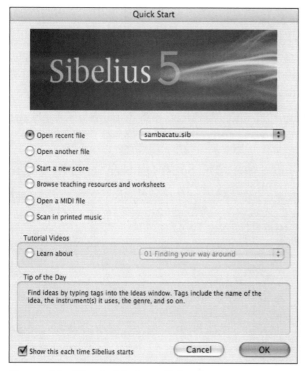

Figure 1.8   The Quick Start dialog box.

We're going to let the Quick Start dialog set up a new score for us, taking us through all the various options for setting up a new score. This is a great place to start working with Sibelius, because it will take you through some very important steps in a logical, ordered way.

More Than One Way The Quick Start dialog box is just a collection of shortcuts to various functions within Sibelius. We're going to create a new score, which can also be accomplished by simply selecting New from the File menu. The Quick Start dialog box is just a portal to important functions that exist in the menus at the top of Sibelius's screen.

From the first Quick Start screen, select the radio button for Start a New Score, and then click OK. Clicking OK takes you to Figure 1.9, where you'll select your manuscript paper, add additional instruments, and change your paper size and orientation (if necessary).

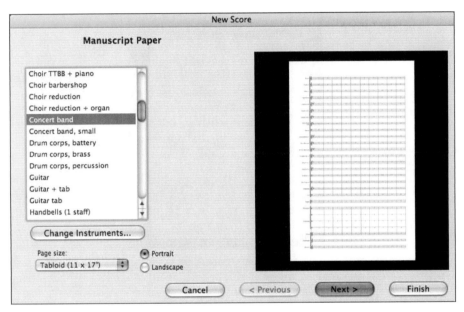

Figure 1.9 Start a new score.

Manuscript Paper

The Manuscript Paper screen contains pre-made groupings of instruments that come with Sibelius. If you scroll through the long, distinguished list on the left side of the window, you'll see quite a few choices. Hopefully, the group of instruments you want to write for will be available to you already. If not, no big deal—you can always add instruments in a second. Find the manuscript paper that is closest to the ensemble for which you want to write.

Custom Manuscript The manuscript papers that Sibelius ships with make up a generous list to get you started. If you find that the ensembles you typically write for aren't showing up and you have to add instruments each time, have no fear. You can create your own manuscript papers that will show up in the list whenever you create a score. We will cover that in Chapter 17, "Customizing Sibelius."

For our purposes, select String Quartet from the Manuscript Paper list. You'll notice that as soon as you do so, you get a preview (a very small one) of the paper on the right side of the window, as shown in Figure 1.10.

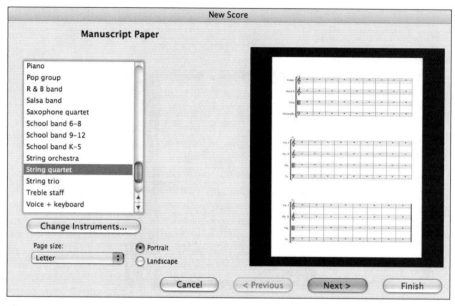

Figure 1.10   Manuscript preview.

Adding Additional Instruments to Any Manuscript Paper

To show you how easy it is to add an additional instrument to any manuscript paper, choose the Change Instruments button, directly below the list of available manuscript papers on the left side. Figure 1.11 shows the Instruments dialog.

This dialog box shows you all of the selected instruments in your score (or manuscript paper). The window is divided up between the left side, where you can choose instruments; the middle controls, where you can add, remove, or reorder instruments in your score; and the right side, where the instruments in your score are organized.

To add instruments, first select from the broad category of instrument types at the top-left of the screen, and then select the proper family of instruments directly below that. To the right of those lists will be the final list of instruments. Once you've found and highlighted the instrument you want, you can either double-click the instrument name or click the Add to Score button to add the instrument to the score. When you've done that, you'll see that your instrument is now added to the Staves in Score list, with a small + next to its name. When Sibelius adds instruments to

Available Instruments
to Add

Currently Added Staves
in Your Score

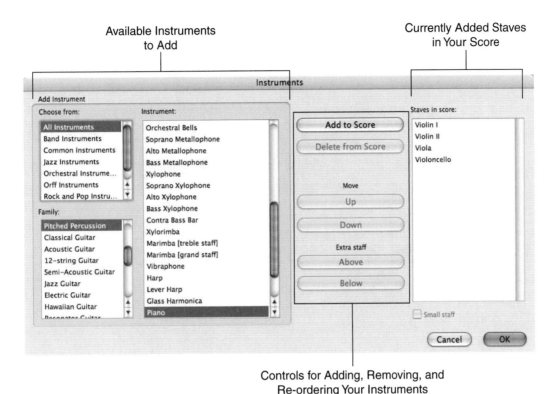

Controls for Adding, Removing, and
Re-ordering Your Instruments

Figure 1.11   The Instruments dialog.

your score, it does so in proper score order. You can also reorder the instruments using the Move
Up or Move Down button, which will move the currently selected instrument up or down.

Add a flute to your string quartet by choosing All Instruments > Woodwinds > Flute and add it
to your score. Figure 1.12 shows the result.

When you're finished, you can select OK to get back to the Manuscript Paper screen. Because
you don't necessarily need to change paper size or orientation yet, click Next to progress to the
next screen: House Style.

House Style

House Styles are Sibelius's set of engraving rules for any particular score. House Styles encompass the type of music font used, the staff margins, the appearance of bar numbers (or the lack
thereof), and many other visual changes. In short, a House Style is the look and feel of your
score. Popular choices within the House Style are changes to the musical font—the default

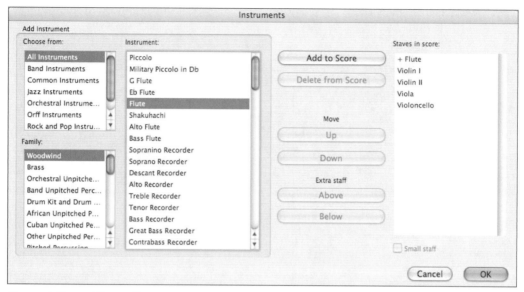

Figure 1.12   Adding a flute.

Sibelius font (Opus), the plate engraved style (Helsinki), the handwritten style (Inkpen), or the popular West Coast–styled font (Reprise). Figure 1.13 shows the House Style window. You can also change the main text font used in your score to any font installed on your computer system via the Main Text Font drop-down menu.

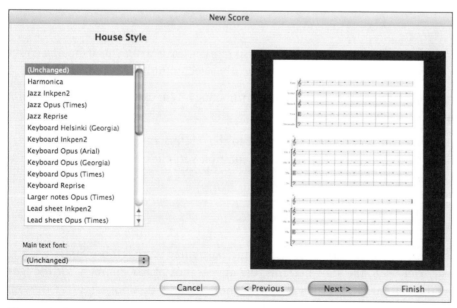

Figure 1.13   House Style choices.

Feel free to experiment with the House Styles to give your scores a different visual look. For now, choose Unchanged as the default House Style for the selected manuscript paper (based on the Opus font). It looks very good and is sufficient for learning.

Click Next to progress to the next screen in the score setup.

Time Signature and Tempo

The next screen in your score setup is the Time Signature and Tempo screen. From this window, you can set up your initial time signature, define your beam and rest groupings, add a pick-up measure (anacrusis), add tempo text, and even add a metronome marking! Figure 1.14 shows the Time Signature and Tempo screen.

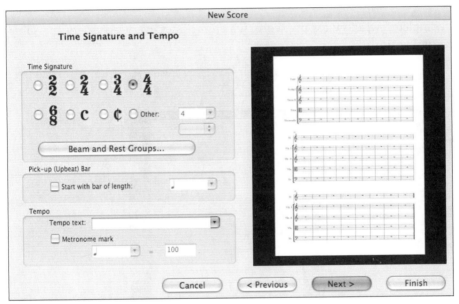

Figure 1.14   Time Signature and Tempo options.

Let's start off with the time signature. The popular choices are listed for you, and if you need to write an asymmetric or a special time signature, you can select Other and choose your top and bottom values for the time signature.

If you have special requirements for how your beam and rests groups need to be set up, you can access options via the Beam and Rest Groups button. The default should be fine, and we will come back to this at a later point in the book. If you absolutely know you need to change it, go ahead and tweak it to your heart's content—you can always change it later!

Pick-up measures, or *anacrusis bars,* are easily set here. To add one, make sure the check box next to Start with Bar of Length is selected. Doing so will allow you to enter values into the drop-down box. The value of the pick-up bar always defaults to a quarter note. To change this, click in the field that contains the quarter note. You can either backspace (or delete) to get rid of the quarter note, or you can add notes to equal the required length. There is a drop-down menu to the immediate right of the quarter note (or the spot where it lived if you deleted it) that will expose note values. Clicking on any note duration will add these together. For example, if you wanted a dotted quarter note, you could start with the quarter note they provide and add an eighth note, or add the dot (.).

You can add tempo text to your score either by choosing one of the default Italian and English texts, or creating your own in the dialog box.

To add a metronome mark, deselect the check box, and choose your main pulse and the number of beats per minute you'd like automatically added to the score.

Figure 1.15 shows a completed window for my score, which includes every feature of the Time Signature and Tempo dialog box.

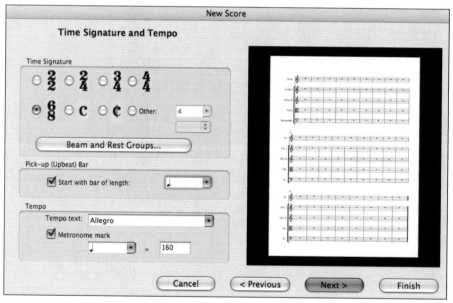

Figure 1.15 Completed Time Signature and Tempo dialog.

Now that those important details are filled in, let's progress to the next screen: Key Signature.

Never Too Late During the setup of your score, you can always go back a screen in the new score setup by clicking the Previous button. You can do this only when you're in the new score setup—once you've pressed Finish and actually started your score, you will have to change elements of your score in other ways.

Key Signature

The Key Signature dialog box shown in Figure 1.16 is a fairly easy screen to explain; it lets you set the initial key signature for your score.

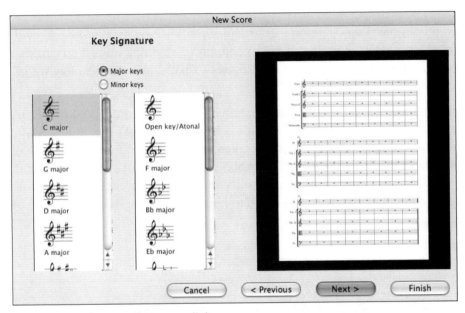

Figure 1.16   The Key Signature dialog.

Select the desired signature by using the sharp signatures in the left column and the flat signatures in the right column. The boxes for Major Keys and Minor Keys indeed make a difference! When Sibelius takes MIDI input and has to decide which accidental to use, it chooses the accidental based on which key signature was listed (choosing a C sharp instead of a D flat in D minor, for example). If you're not using MIDI input, don't worry too much about it—you can easily re-spell an accidental at any time. Once you've selected the proper major or minor key signature, click the Next button to take you to the Score Info page, the final screen in the new score setup.

Score Info

The final screen is the Score Info screen, which lets you add the following information to your score:

- Title
- Composer/songwriter
- Lyricist

- Copyright information
- The ability to create a separate title page based on this information
- Other information about your score

This screen helps you fill out the most common text headings you'll see on most scores. As with any window in the new score setup, you don't have to commit to anything now. You can skip this altogether and add all the information later via Create > Text, which I'll detail as we get rolling.

When you've filled in the information for your score and decided whether you'd like a title page, you'll see that there's no Next button to click, but now a Finish button. At this point, you're finished with the new score setup, and you'll now be taken to your newly created score. If all went as planned, you should be greeted by a completed blank score in Sibelius in which you can start writing music. As your new score loads, you'll notice that the sounds for your new score will preload as the score comes up. This will enable you to hear notes as you input them, and, of course, play back when asked!

Figure 1.17 shows a newly created score.

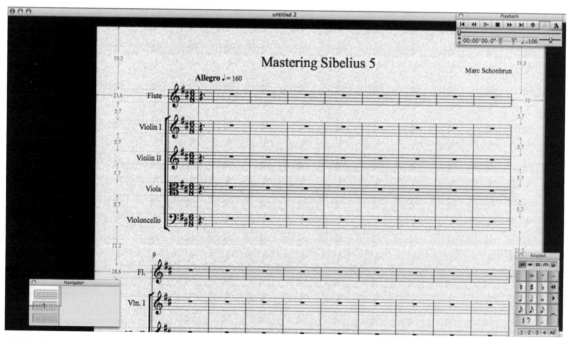

Figure 1.17 A fully set-up score.

Essential Tip: New Score Setup Just to remind you: Everything we set up in this score can be easily changed at any point. The new score setup helps you automate the most commonly configured parts of your score. This is the basis of Sibelius's score setup, but you can do everything in the New Score window directly from any Sibelius score, and really easily!

Now I'd like to take some time to go over the Sibelius interface so that you can understand the functions of the visual user interface presented to you.

Interface Tutorial

Sibelius has the marketing catchphrase of "The fastest, smartest, easiest way to write music." I'll go through its interface and show you that it is indeed easy to understand. Figure 1.18 illustrates the major elements of the Sibelius interface.

Figure 1.18 A guide to Sibelius's interface.

You can break the interface into the following three parts:

- Drop-down menus
- The toolbar
- Tool windows

Drop-Down Menus

Drop-down menus are a consistent visual feature in almost every software application you can imagine. In Sibelius, the drop-down menus give you access to the plethora of features and power within the program. Knowing your menus is a huge step to fully understand a software program; Sibelius is no exception. Figure 1.19 shows the available drop-down menus in Sibelius.

Figure 1.19 Sibelius's drop-down menus.

Keyboard Access Learning the key commands to any software program will make you a faster, more efficient user. To this end, I designed a keyboard cover that slips right over your existing Mac keyboard. This cover provides direct access to all the important key commands in Sibelius. The covers are inexpensive and even protect your keyboard from dirt and wear and tear. If you want to accelerate your learning process with Sibelius, pick one up today at www.kbcovers.com. These covers are only available for Mac users due to the wide variety of PC keyboard types and the few Mac ones. You can also purchase a full keyboard from www.sibelius.com that will work on Mac or PC (via USB) and that will replace your current keyboard.

Here are some basic descriptions of what each menu contains:

- **Sibelius.** On the Mac, home to your Preferences and window-based controls.

- **File.** Anything to do with creating, saving, opening, printing, and exporting files.

- **Edit.** Standard editing (cut, copy, and paste), along with music-specific editing, such as hiding or showing elements, flipping stems, deleting bars, filtering music, changing voices, and capturing ideas.

- **View.** The visual menu! Change the view from standard to Panorama, show or hide the rulers, color notes, and zoom.

- **Notes.** Input notes, Flexi-time record (record to a click), use automatic arrange styles, and transpose music.

- **Create.** The central repository for basically anything you can do or add to a score in Sibelius. It's the most used menu in Sibelius, so they have provided an easy shortcut: Right-click (Control-click on a Mac) to access the Create menu anywhere. When you want to add something to your score, chances are that you can find it here!

- **Play.** Everything that's related to the playback and video features with Sibelius. This includes the new virtual instrument support introduced in Sibelius 5.

- **Layout.** Your score's document setup and layout controls. Tweak the appearance and layout of your scores here.

- **House Style.** This controls how your score will print out; these features are also commonly referred to as *engraving rules*. You'll find elements such as the appearance of text and musical fonts here.

- **Plug-Ins.** These are extremely helpful automated "widgets" within Sibelius. There are literally hundreds of plug-ins within Sibelius that will do a variety of things for you. Plug-ins start with simple commands, such as checking for missing repeat bar lines or unattached ties, and go as far as finding errors in your voice leading! There are more than 100 additional plug-ins free for download at www.sibelius.com/download/plugins.

- **Window.** Access to the many tool windows within Sibelius. These include your keypad for entering notes, the Playback window, Sibelius's properties, and many more. If you're working with multiple scores at the same time, the Window menu will show you a list of your open scores so you can switch between them.

- **Help.** When you're stuck, you can access the full 600-page Sibelius reference and access other helpful guides and websites that relate to Sibelius. You can also check for program updates and manage your Sibelius registration from this menu.

My goal here was not to take every menu down and describe each entry—that would be tedious and quite boring. Now that you have a general idea of what each menu does, you'll have a better chance at finding what you want at this early stage. As you get going through the book and access all the commands within Sibelius, you'll be calling upon these menus quite often.

Essential Tip: The Create Menu As for ease of use, check this out: I said that the Create drop-down menu was very useful. I also said that all the elements of the new score could be replicated easily within Sibelius. That's right, you guessed it—the Create menu provides access to key signatures, time signatures, instruments, and text. (It also does more!) Consider it your central hub for creating score elements in Sibelius 5

The Toolbar

Directly below the drop-down menus is Sibelius's toolbar, which is a collection of shortcut buttons for various important tasks within Sibelius. Because the toolbar itself is quite large and does so many things, for the sake of illustration, I'm going to break it into two parts, starting with the left side of the toolbar, shown in Figure 1.20.

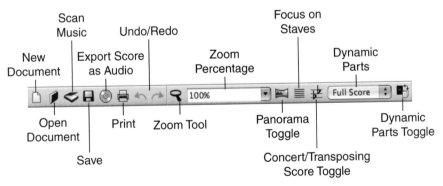

Figure 1.20 Sibelius's toolbar part one: the left side.

Here is a breakdown of the functions that you can access from the left toolbar. Keep in mind that this is just an illustrated overview. You don't need to memorize or learn these right now. As you progress through this book, these shortcuts, when applicable, will be utilized in context.

- **New.** Create a new score.

- **Open.** Open a saved score.

- **Scan.** Scan music into Sibelius through PhotoScore.

- **Save.** Save your score to hard disk.

- **Export Audio.** Render your score to an audio file, suitable for burning to a CD or posting on a website.

- **Print.** Print your score.

- **Redo.** Redo the last action in Sibelius.

- **Undo.** Undo the last action in Sibelius.

- **Zoom.** Turn your pointer into a magnifying glass and click to zoom in or out of your score.

- **Zoom Box.** This shows the current level of zoom in your score. You can click in the box to enter a specific zoom percentage.

- **Panorama.** This changes from the default score view to Panorama view, which lays your score out on a single, never-ending page.

- **Focus on Staves.** This amazing button lets you select the staves you want to edit by clicking on them, and automatically hides the rest.

- **Transposing Score.** This allows you to toggle the view of your score from transposing instrument view to concert pitch.

- **Dynamic Parts.** This drop-down menu lets you switch between the full score and an individual part. (In Sibelius, you never need to extract a part, because you can always switch to a part from this menu.)

- **Switch to Part/Score.** This button takes you either from a full score to the selected part (stave), or from a part window back to the full-score view.

Figure 1.21 shows the rest of the Sibelius toolbar (the right side).

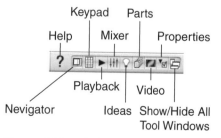

Figure 1.21 Sibelius's toolbar part two: the right side.

- **Help.** Access Sibelius's built-in help by accessing the full Sibelius reference in PDF form.

- **Navigator.** Show or hide the onscreen score navigator.

- **Keypad.** Show or hide the keypad view.

- **Playback.** Hide or show the VCR-style playback controls.

- **Mixer.** Hide or show Sibelius's virtual instrument and effect mixer.

- **Ideas.** Show or hide the Ideas hub.

- **Parts.** Show or hide the Parts window. (These are not the dynamic parts; rather, they are preferences and other controls for the parts that are created automatically in your score.)

- **Video.** Show or hide the Video window.

- **Properties.** Show or hide the Properties window. This window provides access to a myriad of important onscreen properties that affect general aspects of Sibelius, text, playback, lines, bars, and notes.

- **Show/Hide.** This button will show or hide the currently active tool windows. Active tool windows will be shaded blue in the toolbar and, of course, appear on the screen.

As you can see, the toolbar is chock full of important shortcuts and tools within Sibelius. It contains visual links that you can find just by mousing around the interface.

Essential Tip: Tool Tips Sibelius will show you the function of any toolbar icon if you simply hover your mouse over the button. Once you've dragged your mouse over the icon or control, a small yellow box will emerge, telling you what the control or button will do.

The toolbar is very important, but you should try as hard as you can to learn the keyboard shortcuts whenever possible. It's no surprise that everything on the toolbar can be duplicated as a keyboard shortcut. Why would you want to use keyboard shortcuts rather than just using your mouse? For starters, the mouse is simply very slow—keyboard shortcuts are faster. Secondly, in Sibelius, you may want to use the mouse for other things, so taking the cursor away from your current working area just to save your file is inefficient when you could have simply pressed Ctrl+S (PC) or Command+S (Mac) without having to move. The other benefit is that standard keyboard shortcuts (Save, Open, Close, Print, Undo, Redo) are found in almost every program on your computer! The most experienced computer users rely on keyboard shortcuts.

Onscreen Helpers (Tool Windows)

The toolbar showed you a collection of shortcuts. The last area of the toolbar is composed of a larger group of windows called *tool windows*. When Sibelius starts, you will see three of these windows by default. Because they are central to the functionally of Sibelius, you'll want to know as much as you can about them. Don't worry; we'll use the rest of the tool windows when they're needed—these three windows are just the ones to start with.

The Navigator

The Navigator window, shown in Figure 1.22, usually resides at the bottom-left corner of your screen (although you can move it wherever you need to).

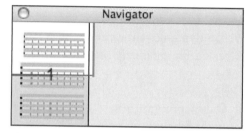

Figure 1.22   The Navigator window.

The Navigator has the single job of allowing you to move your score around. It consists of two parts. The first part is the Navigator itself, which shows a very small view of the visible score. The exact amount of the score you can see in the Navigator depends completely on your zoom level. You can show as few as one page or as many as thirteen pages (at 12.5% zoom). The mini-score that it displays will never contain notes, only bars and systems as an overview.

The second part is the white rectangle, which allows you to select what's visible on the Sibelius screen. You can do the following things with the Navigator:

- Click anywhere in the Navigator window, and the score will jump to the spot you click!

- Drag the rectangle around to move the visible area of the screen.

- If you drag the rectangle to the left or right edge, the score will navigate to the pages you can't currently see. As you drag the rectangle more to either side, the score will scroll faster.

Lost your Navigator? Never had it in the first place? You can show the Navigator in one of three ways. The first is by using keyboard shortcuts (which are mirrored in the Windows pull-down menu): Ctrl+Alt+N (PC) or Command+Option+N (Mac).

Panorama It's worth mentioning that if you're in Panorama view, you can't use or see the Navigator. You'll also notice that the Navigator's button is grayed out in the toolbar.

You can drag the Navigator window itself by clicking on the title bar of the window (where it says Navigator) and moving it to an inconspicuous spot in your score.

You can also show the Navigator by clicking on the Navigator button on the toolbar.

The Keypad

The Keypad is a central window in Sibelius. It provides access to note values, rests, articulations, and a slew of other important commands. Rather than just being a window you can click to access, the aptly named Keypad window is a re-creation of the keypad on your desktop computer's keyboard. Figure 1.23 shows you the relationship of the Keypad window to your computer's keypad.

Figure 1.23   Keypad with overlay.

The Keypad window has five different views. The default view is the first keypad layout, which takes care of basic note values, accidentals, and simple articulations. Figure 1.24 shows the first keypad layout.

Figure 1.24   First keypad layout.

The keypad is an overview of your real keypad. In the first keypad view, a whole note is taken by the number 6, while a quarter note is taken by the number 4—these two keys should center your brain for the rest of the keys. As you use these more, you'll memorize their locations. There are other keypads that you should look at, and you can access them by clicking on the top row of the keypad view, as shown in Figure 1.25.

Figure 1.25   Changing keypad views.

Each keypad has specific features for specific tasks; you'll want to check through each one to see what lives where. From your computer's keypad itself, you can change the current keypad view by pressing the + key to go up a keypad view and the – key to go down a keypad view. There are a total of five keypad layouts, and Figure 1.26 shows you all five.

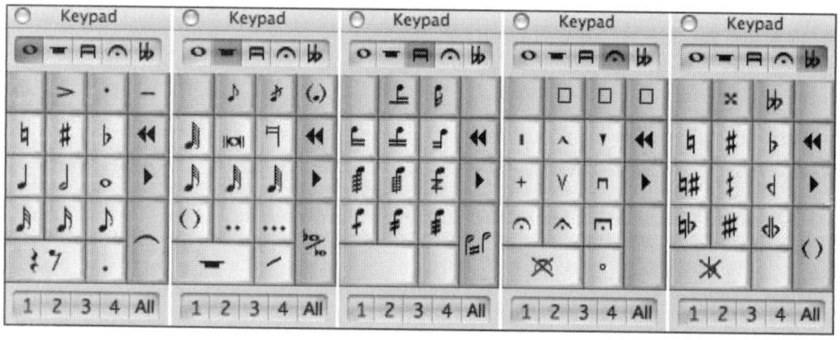

Figure 1.26   The complete keypad layouts.

You'll spend the majority of your time using the first keypad. The others are definitely useful, but you'll call on them less often. The final visual aspect of the keypad is voice. Sibelius allows you to enter notes in up to four different voices. Voices are used on polyphonic music, piano music, and any time you need more than one musical layer sharing the same stave. Across the bottom of the keypad is a selector for the four voices. Voice 1 is the default choice (of course). You can change voices by clicking on the voice number you want, as shown in Figure 1.27.

Figure 1.27   Voice selection.

Voices do all sorts of neat stuff that you'll learn about as you proceed. One important thing about voices is that each has its own color. There is blue for Voice 1 and green for Voice 2. This helps you keep track of which note is in which voice as you navigate through your score.

Laptop Users Laptop users, look down at your keyboard. Do you see a keypad? At first blush, no—you don't have a keypad because most laptops try to shrink their overall size down as much as possible for the sake of portability. However, the engineers did give you the functionality; it's just hidden. If you stare at the J, K, L keys, you'll see a small 1, 2, 3 on each key, respectively (only on a laptop, of course). You have a hidden keypad!

To access this keypad, you'll have to press the Function key, which is typically shortened to FN on your keyboard. When you press the Function key, your J key turns into a 1 on the keypad, and the rest of the keys that have dual personalities will follow suit. This enables you to access Sibelius's keypad. Unfortunately, it also cuts off a few other Sibelius shortcuts (most importantly, the K shortcut for changing a key signature). So, what should you do? Either plug in a full-size USB keyboard (they usually cost about $20) or get a USB keypad, which, as you'd guess, fills in the missing keys on your laptop keyboard. Several companies make plug-and-play USB keypads. If you're going to use Sibelius, you'll want/need a proper keypad, so go to your local office supply store and grab one.

Playback Controls
Playback controls, as shown in Figure 1.28, make up the last window shown by default in Sibelius.

Figure 1.28   The Playback window.

The Playback window is a sandwich of three layers. The first layer has the basic controls. The basic controls act like a VCR or standard sequencer, allowing you to rewind, fast-forward, and play your music. There are keys to move the playback to the start of your score, move the playback to the end of your score, and even enter a real-time recording mode, in which you can record from an external MIDI source. There are other buttons that we'll get into in our playback chapter. For now, you can start and stop your score whenever you need to. A couple of useful keyboard shortcuts include:

- P: Start playback from the currently selected note

- Spacebar: Stop or start playback from the currently selected point/note

- [: Rewind

-]: Fast-foward

If you rewind or fast-forward while playback is engaged, you'll hear the music while you scrub around the score. The longer you hold down fast-forward or rewind, the faster those functions work.

The middle layer is a playback bar, which follows the playback head as it goes. It's laid out from left to right, and you can think of it like the needle of a record player. You can "drag" the slider to the middle of its range, and it will play back exactly from the middle of your score. It's very handy for starting playback from general spots in the score.

The bottom layer shows the time readout of your score. It displays where you are in the score in the following format: hours:minutes'seconds.milliseconds. It displays these exact timings because Sibelius can synchronize to video, and it's also useful to know how long your piece may be when played. To the right of that are the bar and beat displays that read out where you are during playback. (When playback is stopped, this shows the location of the playback head so that when you press spacebar, you'll know where to play back from.) There is also the current metronome mark or tempo of your piece. There is even a tempo slider here for changing the playback tempo (either while playing or while stopped).

Amazingly enough, that's all you need to understand to get going. It's time to start your first score and learn how to get notes from your creative mind into Sibelius.

2 Note Entry

1. When you enter notes, Sibelius will play them back as you enter them. Make sure that you have something (preferably Sibelius Sounds Essentials) set up to play back.

2. Use the new Panorama view when entering notes; it will save you a great deal of time scrolling around your score.

3. There are more note values than just the ones you see on the default keypad. Additional note values are found on the second keypad layout, which you can access by pressing F9.

4. Note snap: When you enter notes with the mouse, you can only access quarter-note values by default. (You can't enter on the "and" of any beat unless you go to Sibelius > Preference > Mouse and change the Snap Positions field to a smaller note value.)

5. The Escape (Esc) key is very important in Sibelius. No matter where you are or what you're doing, it will "unload" the mouse, quickly leave note entry mode, and deselect all objects in your score. You'll use the Escape key often.

6. Don't forget about Re-input Pitches, which lets you enter new note names and keep the existing rhythms. This is great for copying music from stave to stave when the rhythms are the same, but the notes are not.

7. Shortcut keys: Don't forget these critical shortcut keys for this chapter:
    - N: Enter/leave note entry mode
    - R: Repeat selected item(s)
    - P: Play back
    - M: Launch the Mixer
    - X: Flip a stem

- Enter/Return: Respell an accidental enharmonically
- A–G: Add notes A–G
- Esc: Deselect, cancel an action, leave note entry mode, and, in general, lets you get you out of trouble

It's time to put the pen to paper! No, that's not right. It's time to put dots on your screen! Sibelius is flexible. When it comes to note entry, it's extremely flexible. There are currently four ways to enter notes into Sibelius (not counting scanning, which would make five). This chapter will detail how to enter notes, regardless of which way you prefer. One of the hallmarks of Sibelius's flexibility lies in the fact that you can change from any of the note input methods to any other, totally at will. There's no button you have to press and no setting to configure; you can just switch. With that being said, you'll want to read about all four methods of note entry, even if you browse the Table of Contents and say, "I have a MIDI keyboard, so I'll be using Step-time entry." Sure, you may use that the majority of the time, but there are times when you'll want and/or need to use just the computer keyboard. Plus, there are some tips that only apply to certain note input methods (such as tuplet entry), so make sure that you read this important chapter in its entirety!

Options Even though I will describe four different ways of entering notes, a lot of the detail will go into the mouse entry section because it's the first section that you'll read. The meat of the chapter will lie in that section, so please spend some time on the mouse input section, even if you don't plan to make extensive use of it.

The Four Input Methods

There are currently four ways to enter notes in Sibelius 5:

- **Mouse input.** Click your way (albeit slowly) along.

- **Computer keyboard entry.** One hand takes care of rhythms, while the other keys in notes using the A through G keys on your computer's keyboard. This method is actually surprisingly fast.

- **Step-time MIDI input.** One hand takes care of rhythms, while the other hand plays notes from a MIDI device.

- **Flexi-time entry.** You play in real time to a click track, and Sibelius transcribes what you play into notation. The accuracy of the notation depends on the accuracy of your playing.

Before we begin, start up a new score. (You know how from last chapter.) It honestly doesn't matter what kind of score or how many instruments you choose, because note input is applicable to any kind of score. Make sure your time signature and key signatures are in there as well. (They are set up in the New Score dialog box.) Let's start with the most basic form: mouse input.

Essential Tip As you enter notes, Sibelius will play back for aural feedback. For it to do so, you need to have your playback set up properly. If you skipped over the introductory chapter, now is the time to go back and set up Sibelius Sounds Essentials so you can hear what you're doing!

Mouse Input

The mouse is a necessary evil on a computer system. It's fairly handy for some things, but very slow at others. Mouse input in Sibelius is a pretty good case study in "it works okay, but it's not the best tool for the job." In any event, it's where you should start.

To get started, you should configure your screen to show the Navigator, Keypad, and Playback windows, as shown in Figure 2.1.

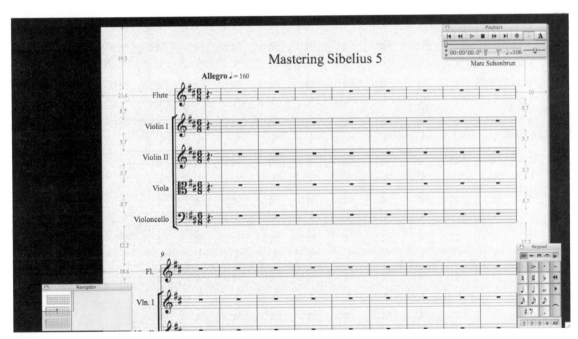

Figure 2.1 Window configuration for note entry.

The first pro tip you'll receive is that while you're working on inputting notes, especially with a mouse, you'll want to zoom in a bit so you can see where you are and what you're doing. This is a good time to remind you that you can zoom in via the toolbar either by selecting the Zoom tool and clicking on your score or by accessing the Zoom controls and selecting a preset magnification value (or typing in your own). Alternatively, you can use the super-fast keyboard shortcuts:

- Zoom in (Windows): Ctrl++ (holding down Ctrl and the + key on your keyboard)

- Zoom out (Windows): Ctrl+− (holding down Ctrl and the − key on your keyboard)

- Zoom in (Mac): Command++ (holding down Command and the + key on your keyboard)

- Zoom out (Mac): Command+− (holding down Command and the − key on your keyboard)

Which Keys? For ultimate clarity, there are two plus and minus keys on a full computer keyboard. The keys you're interested in are *not* on the keypad. They are the keys just to the right of your horizontal number row (next to the 0). The + and − keys on the keypad have different functions—but then, you already knew that!

Zoom in to a comfortable level—you may find that being able to see three to four measures at a time is a good zoom level.

Transposing Score If you have transposing instruments, you can toggle between transposing and non-transposing view either by clicking on the Transposing Score button (which has two flats) on the toolbar (it will be shaded blue when you're in transposing view) or by using the key command Ctrl+Shift+T (Windows) or Command+Shift+T (Mac). Note that you can switch back and forth between transposing and non-transposing scores at any point during your note entry.

First Steps

Essential Tip Use Panorama view when entering notes. It's new in Sibelius 5, and it's a much faster way to work, especially when you are composing. You can turn Panorama view on from the toolbar or by using the shortcut Shift+P (both PC and Mac). You'll leave Panorama view only when you need to look at the final layout of the score.

Here's the flow you'll use while inputting with a mouse: First, you'll select where you want to enter notes. Then, you'll select a note value from the keypad. Finally, you'll click into the stave to enter notes.

Essential Tip Not seeing the note value you want on the first keypad layout? Try the second keypad layout, which contains faster note values and other symbols you might need.

Click once on the measure in which you want to start entering notes. You'll notice that a single blue box is drawn around the measure, as shown in Figure 2.2.

Figure 2.2 Measure selection.

The single blue box is called a *measure selection*. Now, press the N key on your keyboard to start in note entry mode. You'll notice that the blue box is gone, and now the whole rest is selected in blue. That's good! This is another way to get into note entry node: You can select the note or rest where you want to begin entry and press N. When you press N, you'll get the *caret*, which is shown in Figure 2.3.

Figure 2.3 The caret.

The caret is like the blinking line you see in word processing programs such as Word. It shows you where you'll be entering notes, and it's also how you'll know that you're in note entry mode.

Now that you're in note entry mode, you'll want to select your rhythmic value. This is done from the first keypad layout. You can either click on the keypad value you want with your mouse or use the corresponding key on your real computer keypad. (They do exactly the same thing, and *not* using the mouse to grab each note value is faster.) After you've selected a note value, you'll see that the mouse has shifted to be a deep shade of blue. Keep note of this; we're coming back to it in a minute.

Move your mouse pointer to the bar. You'll notice that as you get it over the staff, you'll see a gray shadow cast onto the score. This gives you a slight preview of where you're going to land if you click, which is very handy for ensuring that the correct note goes in. Click a note in where Beat 1 would occur (to the left corner of a bar). This should give you something that looks like Figure 2.4.

Figure 2.4 Your first note entry.

This brings up an important point: Sibelius is sensitive to where in the bar you click. It does not just take your first entry as Beat 1. It divides the bar up into imaginary zones, so if you click in the middle of the bar, you will input into the middle of the bar! You can see this in action as you drag your gray "ghost" note around a measure. You'll see that it "snaps" into four places: Beats 1 through 4.

Essential Tip By default, the note snap is set to the quarter note, dividing your mouse input into four zones. If you access Sibelius's Preferences (File > Preference on Windows or Sibelius > Preference on Mac), under the Mouse window you'll see a control for changing how the mouse snaps. By default it's a quarter note, but you might prefer a different value, such as an eighth note. Changing this will allow you to "shadow" in eight places on the bar.

As you enter a note, notice how the caret automatically goes to the next note so you can keep entering note values. The note values you select will stick as long as you keep entering notes, so if you have a long section of eighth notes, you only need to select it once and just continue entering notes into your score—the value will stay an eighth note until you decide to change it.

Watch the Mouse As you enter notes into the score, you may accidentally make a mistake or for some reason leave note entry mode and need to re-enter it. To do so, make sure that you press the Escape key so that your mouse is no longer active for adding or editing a selected note, then click on the place you want to start entering notes (usually a rest) and press N to bring back the caret to re-enter notes.

Of course, you can only enter the correct amount of notes based on your time signature; Sibelius follows all the rules your music teacher taught you.

Leaving Note Entry When you're finished entering notes, remember to press N again to leave note entry mode. Doing so will allow you to select other parts of the score without accidentally entering notes. The N key either activates or deactivates note entry—it just depends on where you are!

CD: Go to the accompanying CD, and you'll find a bunch of melodies to copy with your mouse input skills! Examples 2.1, 2.2, and 2.3 will give you some good practice.

Arrow Keys

Because note entry with a mouse isn't an exact science, it's reassuring to know that you can step notes up and down using the arrow keys after you've entered them into your score. For example, suppose you want to enter an F#, and you get an E by accident, as shown in Figure 2.5.

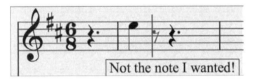

Figure 2.5 The accidental click.

Even thought the caret has moved on, the note you entered is still active and highlighted. You can use the arrow keys on your computer's keyboard to move it up or down by diatonic steps. This is handy when you make a mistake or simply want to change a note.

Ctrl=Big Action If you ever feel the need to move a note one octave up or down, hold down Ctrl (Windows) or Command (Mac) while you press the arrow key, and the note will jump via octaves!

CD: Go to the accompanying CD and work with Examples 2.4 and 2.5, which have some errors that you can fix with a combination of arrow keys and octave jumps.

In the Red

As you enter notes, you might notice that some of your notes are shaded red. I'd show you a screenshot to demonstrate, but because the book is black and white, you wouldn't notice it. But if and when you encounter a red note, you should know that this is Sibelius's subtle way of telling you, "Excuse me! The last time I checked, the instrument you're writing for couldn't easily play that note. Are you sure you want to write that?" Mind you, Sibelius won't print the notes in red; it's simply a reminder that you may be out of range. You can also change the range later. This is handy if you're writing for virtuoso players who can hit notes in the stratosphere!

Range Sibelius determines the range of any given instrument via the Edit Instrument Properties in the House Style. You can freely edit any instrument if you want to change its attributes, especially the range! This will be covered in Chapter 8, "House Styles and Engraving Rules."

Accidental Order

As you enter notes, you'll need to use accidentals. When you're entering notes without a MIDI keyboard, there is a slight paradigm shift when you enter an accidental. In your head, you think, "I'd like an F sharp," but with Sibelius, you have to specify an accidental before you click a note into your score. So, when you want an F sharp, you have to select the rhythmic value from the keypad, and then select the accidental you need, and *then* click it into your score. So, just get used to thinking in that slightly reversed order.

Entering Rests

Entering a rest is a simple act in Sibelius. On the keypad, there is one key that corresponds to a rest. You have to ignore the fact that it has a quarter and an eighth rest printed on the 0 key. Pressing the rest key on the keypad will turn the currently selected note value into a rest, so the button itself just shows you that a rest is active; the actual duration of the rest is chosen by the keypad rhythmic values.

As you are entering notes in note entry mode, you'll be pleased to find that a rest takes the place of a note and automatically advances you to the next note; so as you're entering notes, you don't have to stop what you're doing.

Starting Mid-Measure

You can also use rests to break up the bar and allow yourself to begin a musical phrase mid-measure. Suppose you need to enter the passage shown in Figure 2.6 into Sibelius. By default, any new measure will show up with a whole-measure rest. If you want to break up a measure, you can do so with the keypad. To get your bar to look like Figure 2.6, follow this logic: To make the last eighth note active, you could break the rests down by clicking on the rest, changing it to a half rest, changing that rest to a quarter, changing that one to an eighth, and then progressing to the note you want. That's also a ton of unnecessary work.

Figure 2.6 Mid-measure notation.

In this instance, you'll want to visit Sibelius's Preferences dialog box and access the Mouse panel. Under Snap Positions, change the value to an eighth note. This will allow you to click into the "off" beats and access eight snap positions in each bar. Now, select the whole-measure rest, enter note entry mode (by pressing N), and change your note value to an eighth note (by pressing 3). Now snap your mouse where you think the last eighth note should appear (which is the fifth to the right of the bar because you're in 6/8, and there are six possible spots to click in) and click! Magically, your bar appears just as it should.

CD: Play with Example 2.6 on your CD; it contains a few measures to copy in which your melodies start mid-measure.

Zoom When you're dealing with snapping to eighth notes and precision is a must, make sure you're zoomed in close enough. Trying to mouse precisely when the bar is small will prove difficult.

You can see that as you drag the mouse over any bar, you now have eight spots to snap into. If you need to access sixteenth notes like this, go back to the Preferences dialog box and change the mouse snap position to a sixteenth note. Fortunately, you can change this preference at any time.

Renotating Rests

If you're copying music and you have to get your rests to look a particular way, it's helpful to know that you can notate your rest however you need to. If you select any rest, you can change its value by clicking on a new rest value in the keypad. You can break down a beat into as many parts as you need to this way. Conversely, you can take rests and consolidate them by changing their value via the keypad. All the magic happens in the keypad. Consider the example shown in Figure 2.7.

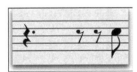

Figure 2.7 Simple measure.

This measure was made by inserting a single eighth note into the last beat of the bar. Doing so gave us a dotted quarter note followed by two eighth rests, which may not be the way you want your bar of 6/8 notated. If your music needed to look like Figure 2.8 you'd have to go about it via the keypad.

Figure 2.8   Quarter rest.

To change the appearance of the rest, make sure you're not in note entry mode (press N to leave note entry mode, or press Escape a few times), and click on the first eighth-note rest (see Figure 2.9). On the keypad, press the 4 key to change to a quarter rest. The bar will automatically renotate itself as a dotted half note, followed by an eighth-note rest.

Figure 2.9   Renotating a rest.

Essential Tip It's worth mentioning that the rest button on the numeric keypad can be *any* rest! Even though it has a quarter note printed on it, it simply means "rest," and you choose the duration from the other numeric keys.

CD: Play with Example 2.7 on your CD and renotate a few rests that need to be broken into smaller values.

Augmentation Dots and Ties

As you are entering your rhythms, you can add an augmentation dot at any time by hitting the period (.) on your keypad; this will dot the currently selected note value. In those rare instances when you need double dots, you'll find them in the second keypad layout along with a host of other symbols, as shown in Figure 2.10.

Figure 2.10 Second keypad layout.

The second keypad layout has the whole-rest symbol, second from the left. You can get to the second keypad layout in a few ways. You can select the different layouts in the top bar of the Keypad window. You can also access the second keypad layout on the keypad itself by hitting the plus (+) button on the right side of the keypad to navigate up one keypad. Then, use the minus (−) to navigate back to the first layout. (Mac keyboards have this button—not all PC keyboards do. See the "Attention Mac Users" Note in a moment.) Another way to get to the second keypad is to use the function keys on your computer's keyboard. Function keys F8 through F12 correspond to the five keypad layouts, so you can press F9 to get to the second keypad layout and then F8 to get back to the first keypad (where you'll hang out most of the time).

Attention Mac Users Starting in OS X 10.4 and continuing into 10.5, Apple assigns the function keys F9 through F12 to specific functions within the operating system, which takes over control of those keys. By default, you won't be able to access the second, third, fourth, and fifth keypad layouts on a Mac using function keys. To remap this, you'll have to go to System Preferences, and then Dashboard and Expose. There, you can remap the function keys to other keys, or you can simply not use them. This is up to you—Dashboard and Expose are pretty handy if you have a Mac.

Remember that you can access the keypad layouts using the plus (+) and minus (−) buttons on the right side of your keypad. Keep in mind that some, not all, Windows-based PC keyboard lacks the minus (−) button. Mac keyboards have an extra button.

Ties are no problem, either. After you've entered a note, you can tie it forward by pressing the tie on the numeric keypad (the Enter key), which will tie the note forward to the following rest. You'll still have to add the next note, because Sibelius has no way of guessing whether you want a note of the same rhythmic value, but the following note entry will be automatically tied. You can, of course, enter ties in after the fact when editing (just enter the notes without ties), but you'll want to grab them all while entering notes because it's another step to go back.

Quick Tie! Choosing a note value longer than the bar will produce an instant tie! Try entering a half note on Beat 4 in a 4/4 measure and see what happens!

Tuplet Entry

Entering tuplets requires a bit of forethought when you enter notes by any other means besides Flexi-time. Because you won't find any means of entering a tuplet from the numeric keypad, you'll need to access it with a different key command. To enter a tuplet, follow these simple steps:

1.   Add in the first note and note value of your tuplet. (For an eighth-note triplet, enter an eighth note, and so on.)

2.   After you've entered the first note, press the Ctrl key (Windows) or the Command key (Mac), along with the number of notes the tuplet will contain (for this exercise, use 3). You'll need to use the numbers across the top of your keyboard because the keypad is reserved for keypad layout functions. So, in this case, the key command would be Ctrl+3 (Windows) or Command+3 (Mac). The original note will be converted automatically to the first note of a triplet, and you'll have two rests in which to enter more notes.

3.   The caret will automatically move to the next note so you can complete the tuplet.

4.   When you've completed the tuplet, Sibelius will take you back to non-tuplet mode for the next whole beat you reach.

If all went well, you should end up with something like Figure 2.11.

Figure 2.11   A triplet!

Keep in mind that you can create any length of tuplet that will fit in the bar by choosing another number from the keys across the top of your keyboard. As long as it will rhythmically work in the spaces allotted, you'll be fine, and Sibelius will warn you when you've broken the musical laws, as shown in Figure 2.12.

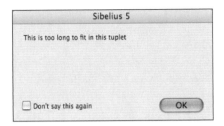

Figure 2.12 Too many notes!

More Options If you'd like to create more advanced tuplets, such as ratio-based tuplets, you can go to Create > Tuplet and use the advanced options there in lieu of the method just described.

CD: Play with Example 2.8 on your CD and copy a few tuplets. You'll be using both methods, from the keyboard and from the Create menu, to make your tuplets.

Intervals

You've primarily dealt with single-note entry, so you may be wondering about entering intervals/chords into Sibelius using just your mouse. After you've entered a single note in note entry mode, Sibelius allows you to go back and click an interval above or below the original note to create chords. What's great is that Sibelius allows you to do this without moving the caret.

Here are some important things to remember when entering chords/intervals with the mouse:

- You can add any interval above or below your note.

- You can change the accidental of the note you're going to input by selecting the accidental *before* you click into the score.

- You can't change the rhythmic value of an interval or chord because it will change the value of the note you've already entered.

The other way to add intervals above any note is to use the number keys on the top of your keyboard. The numbers correspond to intervals. If you want to add a third, press 3, and a third will be created automatically. The same rules for accidentals apply here: If you've entered a C as your first note, and you need an E flat entered, pressing 3 will only give you the diatonic third from the currently selected key signature. For an E flat in this case, you'll enter the C normally, select the flat sign from the keypad (the number 9), and then press 3 on the horizontal row of numbers to produce Figure 2.13.

Figure 2.13   Adding an interval with an accidental.

By default, the intervals you add with the horizontal number keys will be ascending intervals. If you want to add a descending interval, it's easy enough—just hold the Shift key along with the number you want.

Caret Moves It's important to remember what you can do before the caret moves to the next note in mouse entry. You can add any number of ascending or descending intervals, make any of the notes show an accidental, tie a note, and dot the note. All of these actions take place on the currently selected note. The next *actual* click you place in the score will move the caret.

Want a really quick triad? Press 3 twice, and you'll get an instant triad!

Interval Clicking You can't go back and click intervals in with the mouse; it will replace the music that's already there. If you want an interval, use the method just discussed, or you can Alt/Option-click, and it will add the interval without taking away the original note.

CD: Example 2.9 on your CD contains a few examples using intervals from the number row.

The Mighty R
Here's a super-useful tip for dealing with repeated notes. Pressing the R key will repeat the last note you entered, so anytime you have to enter the same note in succession, press R instead of repeating the note. You'll hear about the Repeat command many times in this book because it's useful for repeating more than just the last thing you did—you can repeat anything you'd like, from small selections of notes to whole sections of selected music.

CD: Example 2.10 on your CD is a perfect example of when to use the R key for the Repeat command.

Voices

Because you're entering notes, you need to understand voices. *Voices* are multiple notes within the same measure, each abiding to the rules of the key signature. You'll see this in any and all contrapuntal music and divisi sections where two instruments share a single part, as shown in Figure 2.14.

Figure 2.14   2 voices/divisi.

Sibelius very nicely color-codes its voices. You've been dealing with the blue voice, which is Voice 1. Each additional voice has its own color. Voice 2 happens to be green. You can access a second voice in one of two ways. The first way is to click on the second voice button on the keypad, as shown in Figure 2.15. (The keypad notes will glow green as a result.)

Figure 2.15   Changing to Voice 2 from the keypad.

The second way to change voices is through a key command: Alt+voice number (1 2 3 4) (Windows) or Option+voice number (1 2 3 4) (Mac).

Follow the simple example shown in Figure 2.16.

Figure 2.16   Two voices.

Start by entering the top row of quarter notes in Voice 1, as you always have. Then, press N to leave note entry mode.

Select the bar again by clicking on it so that a blue box appears around it. Press N to enter note entry mode. To enter Voice 2, use Alt+2 (Windows) or Opt+2 (Mac) on your keyboard or click on the number 2 at the bottom of the keypad view. Now, place the next row of quarter notes below the notes you already have. When you're finished, press Escape.

Notice that as soon as you added a second voice, the stems flipped up for Voice 1 and down for Voice 2. This is normal notational practice, but it's nice that Sibelius knows to do this for you. Sibelius takes care of spacing the notes accordingly, and if rests are involved, it will move a lower voice's rest lower on the page so it doesn't conflict with the line of music. For most things, you'll never need to use the third and fourth layers. Voices 1 and 2 are usually sufficient. When you need more voices, 3 and 4 are there for you.

CD: Example 2.11 on your CD is perfect practice for adding an additional voice to some preexisting music.

Understanding the State of the Mouse

So far, you've been told very carefully to press N after you've finished entering notes. In general, this escape is a good idea. However, it might be a good time to go back and explain a bit more about why this is so important. In the last chapter, we talked about moving the score around by using the Navigator window. That's a good way to move the score, but it's not the only way. You can simply click onto a blank part of your score (the paper, not the staves), and a hand will appear. As you click and hold with your mouse button, you can drag the music to and fro.

There are a few reasons why I didn't tell you this yet. First, being able to grab the paper is fine, but it's not a terribly efficient way to move around. The Navigator is much better, and key commands are better still—but we'll get to that. Second, if you haven't left note entry mode (your mouse is still glowing a color, based on what voice you're currently in), then when you click on the score to move it, you'll end up adding notes—usually horribly high-pitched notes that you didn't intend. Those errors are always fun to fix. That's why I'm advocating pressing Escape; no matter what "mode" you're in (Sibelius doesn't have modes, but it's a good analogy), you can get back to the nondestructive cursor using a single, easy-to-hit key.

If you wanted to drag the paper, you'd need to have the non–note entry cursor to do so. The last reason I didn't advocate dragging the paper is because you can change the behavior of the mouse via a preference, which will let you drag a selection box around multiple objects. This is extremely handy, and we'll look at it when we get to editing. For now, leave the dragging to the Navigator; you can do better things with the mouse.

The state of the mouse is always dictated by color. The default mouse cursor is black. When you enter note entry mode, it will turn the color of the currently selected voice (and it will face the other direction). Because of this, it's pretty easy to tell what your mouse is ready to do. As you progress through learning Sibelius, you'll be mindful of the color of the mouse; it will tell you that Sibelius is ready to do something....

Computer (Alphabetic) Keyboard Input

After all that ragging on the mouse, telling you how slow it is, you finally get a better alternative—computer keyboard entry, or *alphabetic input,* as the Sibelius reference calls it. Simply put, you use the keys on your computer's keyboard to enter pitches. Your right hand will hang out on the keypad, and your left will man the keyboard. The beauty about this kind of input is that the A through G keys correspond to the musical pitches from A through G. This makes life very simple. Plus, it's much faster than using a mouse. If you don't have a MIDI input device, this is as good as it gets!

Starting Keyboard Input

Starting keyboard input is no different than starting mouse input. You still need to select your starting point by selecting the entire measure, selecting the whole-bar rest, or clicking on a mid-measure rest and pressing N to start entering notes—you'll get the familiar caret, as you have in the past. With your right hand situated on the numeric keypad, choose the note duration you want from either Keypad 1 (common notes) or Keypad 2 (more note choices). To start entering a pitch, use the A through G keys on your keyboard to enter a note. As you enter notes, Sibelius will place the notes in the closest relative octave as you go. For example, if you type in FGABC, you will get an ascending F scale, as shown in Figure 2.17.

Figure 2.17 Automatically ascending notes.

As you keep progressing, there's no need to touch the mouse at all. Your right hand can take care of all the rests, ties, articulations, and accidentals you need, while your left hand takes care of the notes.

Here are some similarities between keyboard input and mouse input:

- Accidentals and articulations must be entered before you type A through G. Even though you might want a C sharp, you'll have to enter a sharp C.

- If you want to move a note diatonically up or down, you can use the arrow keys to move the note.

- You can still enter rests with the keypad. Remember that doing so will force the caret to the next available beat.

- You can still move notes by octave by holding down the Ctrl (Windows) or Command (Mac) key while you press the arrow key to move the note up or down an octave.

- Adding intervals/chords is still done using the row of numbers across the top of your keyboard. Intervals will ascend by default. To add a descending interval, hold down Shift before you press the number of the interval you want.

- Tuplets are still added the same way: Enter the first note of the tuplet, hold down Ctrl (Windows) or Command (Mac) along with the number of the tuplet, and Sibelius will create an automatic tuplet for you (as long as it fits in the bar/time allotted by the time signature).

- You can tie a note forward after it has been created by hitting the Enter key on the first numeric keypad layout.

The only very small difference that mouse entry has over alphabetic entry is that the mouse doesn't have to guess your octave entry; you specify it with your click. Unfortunately, that's about all mousing around saves you time on. Fortunately, you can change the octave of a note you enter in alphabetic mode with this simple shortcut, which is worth repeating. To change/transpose a note by octave, hold down the Ctrl key and use the up or down arrow key (Windows) or hold down the Command key and use the up or down arrow key.

You'll want to change the octave before you enter your next note. If you forget to do this, you can always highlight a section of notes and transpose the selection of notes down or up an octave with one key command.

A Little Hint Because you just learned about using the alphabet keys to enter notes and you heard how sluggish the mouse is, it's worth mentioning that nothing is stopping you from using a combination of mouse and alphabetic input. For example, if your melody starts on the last eighth note of the bar, it's much faster to start that rhythm by using the mouse to enter the first note (only the first). Once you're in note entry mode and you've engraved the special bar, you can switch to alphabetic input without telling Sibelius anything. You can simply go back and forth at will.

That's pretty much all there is to alphabetic input. Because alphabetic input is quite similar to mouse input, the majority of detail was put into that section. The only difference is that you're typing notes into the keyboard instead of clicking in with the mouse. You will be surprised by how fast you can get with this input method. If you have a laptop and you haven't looked into getting a USB keyboard or a USB keypad, please do so; it will make you more efficient, and it will make your Sibelius experience better on the whole.

CD: Example 2.12 on your CD has some examples that you should copy using alphabetic input on your keyboard.

Step-Time MIDI (Keyboard) Input

Because you've learned so much about note entry, this section will be fairly short. The only thing that changes with Step-time MIDI input is the fact that you're using a MIDI keyboard or guitar to enter notes instead of a mouse or alphabetic input.

Here are some things to keep in mind about Step-time entry:

- Make sure your MIDI device is set up properly in Preferences > Input Devices.

- You'll still pick your note values via the keypad. One hand will still select the rhythmic values.

- You'll still enter note entry mode via the N key.

- You'll still have to enter articulations before you enter the notes.

- You can tie notes after you've entered them.

- If you want to move a note diatonically up or down, you can use the arrow keys to move the note.

- The MIDI input device takes care of octave selection for you. There's no need to shift octaves as in alphabetic input.

- Accidentals are also taken care of automatically via MIDI. Sibelius knows which accidental to choose based on the key signature you've chosen. This is why it's important to specify major/minor key signatures when appropriate.

- You can enter intervals/chords by entering notes simultaneously.

- Tuplets are started the same way as in mouse input and alphabetic input: You enter the first note of the tuplet and hold down Ctrl (Windows) or Command (Mac) along with the number of the tuplet, and Sibelius will create an automatic tuplet for you, as long as it fits in the bar/time allotted by the time signature.

- You can only enter notes on one staff at a time in Step-time entry. That means that piano music will be entered one hand at a time.

If you have a MIDI controller available and you're handy with it, this is a great way to go because it takes care of octave and accidentals automatically. Since you are picking the rhythms ahead of time, you'll find that this should be as error-free as possible (because Sibelius isn't transcribing anything but note names).

CD: If you're using Step-time entry with a MIDI source, Example 2.13 has some examples to copy, including chords.

There are a couple of things worth mentioning about entering notes using Step-time input. First, I'll talk about guitar.

Guitar Input

You can use a guitar to enter notes into Sibelius! You'll need to use an external guitar-to-MIDI converter, such as those made by Roland and AXON, but it works really well! Sibelius will even tab out what you play in the correct spot (assuming you have it set up correctly). To make sure that your guitar is set up correctly, you'll need to visit the Preferences > Input Devices screen (Ctrl+, [Windows] or Command+, [Mac]), as shown in Figure 2.18.

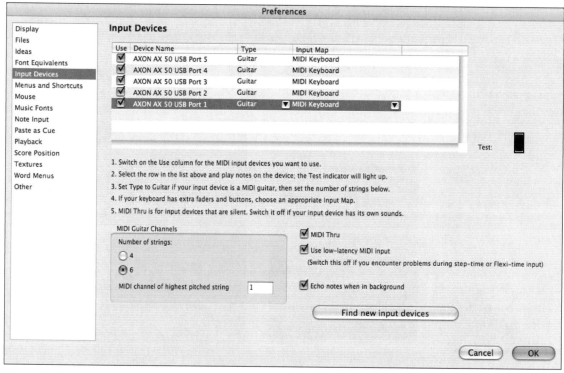

Figure 2.18 Input Devices > guitar settings.

There are a few things you'll need to set up correctly before you go any further:

- Under the Type column of your input device, make sure you select Guitar.

- In the MIDI Guitar Channels section, make sure you select the number of strings (6 for guitar or 4 for bass).

- You need to specify which MIDI channel your high E string comes in on. (This is almost always Channel 1.) This will help Sibelius automatically tab out your notes for you.

There's one more Preferences screen to look at, as shown in Figure 2.19: Preferences > Note Input (Ctrl+, [Windows] or Command+, [Mac]).

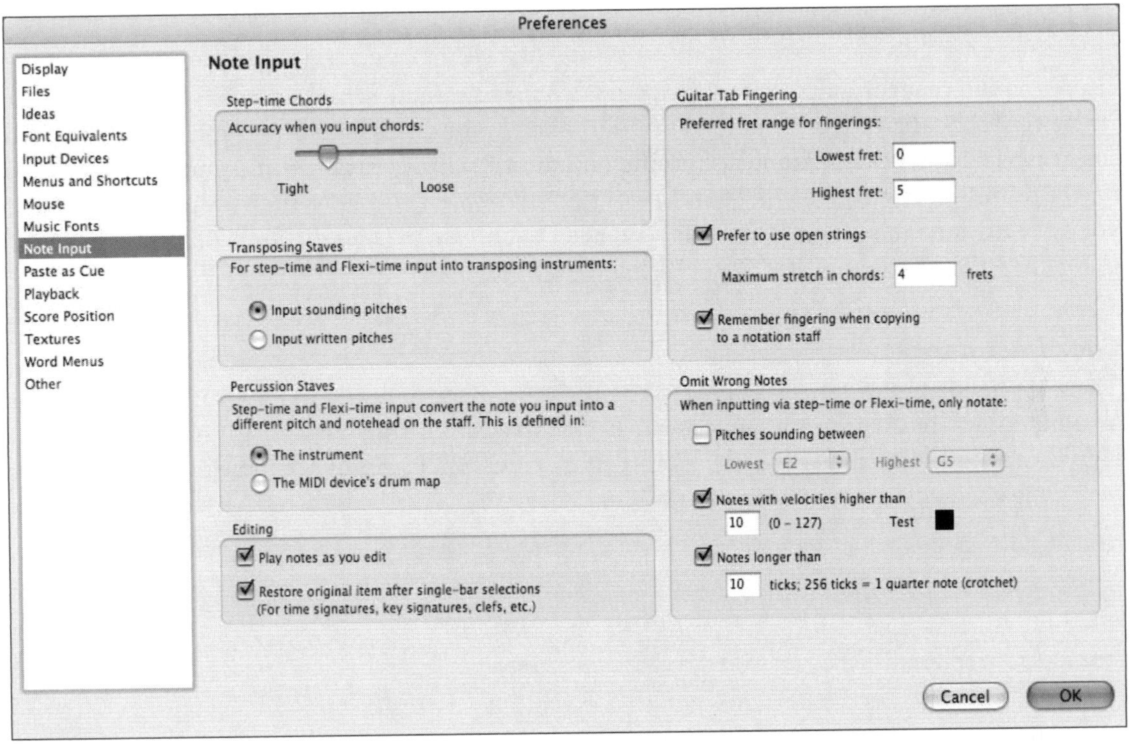

Figure 2.19 Note input options.

Here is a description of the relevant options in the Note Input page of Preferences.

- In the Step-Time Chords section, the slider controls how tightly or loosely Sibelius interprets chords. Because the majority of guitar chords are strummed (and lightly rolled) rather than hit at the same time, you'll find that setting this slider toward the loose side will allow you to enter chords with greater accuracy.

- Under the Guitar Tab Fingering section, make sure there's a check next to the Remember Fingering When Copying to a Notation Staff option.

- The options in the Omit Wrong Notes section are vital for MIDI guitar players. Sibelius can automatically omit notes that are considered "wrong" based on their duration and velocity. Since the majority of errant guitar input pitches are short notes that you didn't intend to play, setting the velocity and duration of this section is vital. A small green test light will light up when a note "passes the test" and is longer and louder than the minimum. The default values are fine for most players, but because guitar is so deeply personal and everyone's touch is so different, you may have to tweak these to taste. The green test light is clearly your friend.

Keep in mind that for guitar entry, as long as you set up these screens correctly, you can enter into either the tablature or notation staff and copy and paste to the other, including tablature fingerings! Chapter 6, "Instrument-Specific Notation," will cover guitar and guitar tablature, so if you're into guitar entry, you'll find everything you need to know there. Shameless plug: If you're really into guitar and computers, you need to check out *Digital Guitar Power!: The Comprehensive Guide* (Thomson Course Technology PTR, 2006).

Chord Accuracy

There's a handy preference that pertains to how accurately you need to play chords in order for Sibelius to notate them in the same beat. If you navigate to Preferences > Note Input (Ctrl+, [Windows] or Command+, [Mac]), as shown in Figure 2.20, you'll see the slider that controls Step-time accuracy when playing chords.

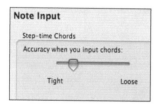

Figure 2.20 Chord accuracy.

The Step-Time Chords slider is a simple setting that tells Sibelius how loose or rigid to be about chords. Not everyone plays chords at *exactly* the same instant. By moving this slider to the right or left, you can control how strictly Sibelius will enforce this. It's actually much easier to test this in a score. Try entering some chords and see whether Sibelius takes them all in one stroke or spills them into the next beat. If you're getting a split chord across a few beats, you'll want to set the control "looser" to allow for this. Toggle back and forth until the chords appear as you expect them to.

That's actually it for using a MIDI device with Sibelius for Step-time input. It's pretty easy. Just remember that Sibelius doesn't care which input method you choose, and you can switch back and forth between methods at will, without having to change a single setting within the program.

Essential Tip Don't forget about Re-input Pitches! When you have sections of music in which each instrument plays the same rhythm, but has different pitches, you can simply copy that music from stave to stave and use Notes > Re-Input Pitches as a note entry method. This will only change the note names and take you to the next note, automatically jumping over the rests. It's a huge timesaver.

Flexi-Time Input

Flexi-time input is Sibelius's way of recording and transcribing your performance in real time, playing to a click track. Real-time transcription is no simple task, so for it to work as invisibly and reliably as possibly, there are many things you'll want to set up within the program to make it work for you.

Flexi Flexi-time is named "Flexi" because Sibelius has engineered the ability for tempo flexibility as you enter notes. That is, you can select whether you'd like Sibelius to speed up and slow down with you. For some this cleans up the performance, and for others it makes the performance worse. Thankfully, you can turn this setting off and play to a strict click.

Before we discuss setup, I want to talk about the merits of Flexi-time over the other forms of note entry described previously.

- There is no need to access the keypad at all; Flexi-time transcribes both your notes and their durations at the same time.

- You can keep two hands on the MIDI device at all times.

- If you're an accurate player, you can produce clean notation very simply.

- Ties are notated automatically (assuming you hold down the keys for long enough).

- Articulations are notated automatically (assuming you set them up beforehand—you'll see how to do this shortly).

- Velocities are stored for live playback if you want a more sequencer-like performance of your note entry. (You can switch back and forth between these as necessary.)

- Sibelius automatically quantizes your performance dynamically to avoid messy notation.

- You *can* record into two adjacent staves (for example, piano) at the same time in Flexi-time.

- Tuplets are created automatically.

- Sibelius records and plays back controller messages (for example, sustain pedals).

- You can record into multiple voices at the same time.

- The new Renotate Performance plug-in lets you re-quantize your performance after you hit Stop.

Of course, this isn't a perfect system. There are a few things to be aware of:

- If you're playing back using software-based sounds (virtual instruments), latency and real-time transcription simply don't always mix well. (This is the nature of latency, and you can work around this.)

- There's a difference between what you play and what you'd publish in a transcription book. You will get a clear transcription, but you still might want to change your notation for simplicity.

- If you let Flexi-time "follow" your tempo and your time isn't very tight, you might end up with slightly messy notation. That's easy enough to fix; just set the Flexibility of Tempo to Non-Rubato, and it will stay strict to the click. The burden is on you to play in time.

Click Playing to a click track (or metronome) isn't everyone's strength. Music is largely expressive, and we tend to ebb and flow naturally as we play. A computer is a computer, and as clever as they are, they still need to figure out what you're doing. In this way, Sibelius is an instrument, and it would behoove you to spend a few minutes getting used to playing something as simple as quarter notes absolutely in time. Then move to eighth and sixteenth notes. Playing to a click takes a bit of practice, but is well worth the effort.

You engage Flexi-time recording in much the same way you do regular input methods—you still have to locate where you want to start by selecting the measure or specific rhythmic rest. You can engage Flexi-time in one of two ways. The first is by pressing the Record button on the Playback window, as shown in Figure 2.21.

Figure 2.21 The Record button.

The other way to engage Flexi-time is through the key command Shift+Ctrl+F (Windows) or Shift+Command+F (Mac). You'll find the same function in the Notes drop-down menu.

Before you engage Flexi-time, make sure your settings are suitable in the Flexi-Time Options.

Flexi-Time Options

Flexi-time boasts an impressive list of options for you to set up (as there should be with a system as sophisticated as this). Taking the time to set Flexi-time up correctly will make your work with it that much more enjoyable. To navigate to the Flexi-Time Options, pull down the Notes menu and select Flexi-Time Options. You can also use the key command Shift+Ctrl+O (Windows) or Shift+Command+O (Mac). It's worth memorizing that key command because you may need to manipulate your Flexi-time settings differently depending on the musical task at hand. The dialog box you open will look like Figure 2.22.

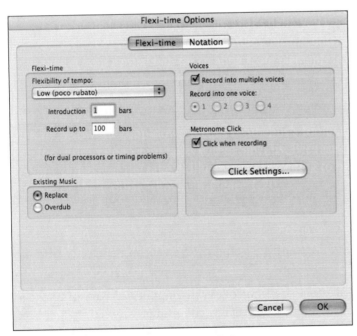

Figure 2.22 The Flexi-Time Options dialog.

This dialog box has two panes, which you can access at the top of the window. The two panes are Flexi-Time and Notation. Each window deals with different aspects of real-time notation. To switch from one window to the next, simply click on Flexi-Time or Notation at the top of the dialog box.

Let's break down what each of these important windows does!

The Flexi-Time Window

The Flexi-Time Options window, shown in Figure 2.22, contains the settings discussed in the following subsections. I'll break the window into the four visually segmented areas, each discussed in the appropriate subsection.

Flexibility of Tempo. The Flexibility of Tempo menu (see Figure 2.23) lets you select the four different levels of Flexi-time flexibility.

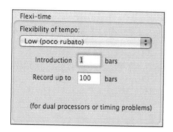

Figure 2.23   The Flexibility of Tempo area.

- **None (No Rubato).** Sibelius will play a steady click that refuses to slow down or waver.

- **Low (Poco Rubato).** Sibelius will allow you a small amount of rubato in your note entry and will follow you.

- **Medium (Rubato).** Sibelius will allow you even more rubato in your note entry and will follow you.

- **High (Molto Rubato).** Sibelius will allow you the maximum rubato in your note entry and will follow you.

By all means, please experiment with the different levels and their effect on the clarity of notation as you use Flexi-time.

Below that menu are important numeric boxes for controlling the number of bars of count-in and how many bars Flexi-time will record before it stops. The count-in is essential. You'll need at least one bar (and maybe more, depending on your tempo) or click/count-off after you hit Record and get onto your MIDI device. Set this to as many bars as you need—you can always change it later.

Opinions on Flexibility If you want to use Flexi-time, I suggest that you limit the rubato to low if you want to use it at all. Most musicians do best with no rubato and play to the steady click track. As always, please experiment and see what works best for you.

The number of bars Sibelius records is not inconsequential. If you don't have enough bars in your score, Sibelius will add extra bars up to this amount automatically for you. The downside is that if you set this to too many bars, you may end up with a plethora of unused, blank bars. You can easily delete them later, but if you know you're only recording a smaller number of bars, set this control to the requisite number.

The Internal MIDI Time Stamps control is for Windows users only (see Figure 2.24). It allows Sibelius to correct some mistakes with hyperthreaded CPUs (Pentium 4) and dual-processor computers that negatively affect MIDI input. If you're on a dual-processor machine or a Pentium 4 and you notice that Flexi-time is a train wreck, selecting this box should make everything better. Remember, this is for Windows only!

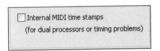

Figure 2.24   The Internal MIDI Time Stamps option.

Existing Music. The Existing Music control (see Figure 2.25) lets you choose whether you'd like to replace music or "overdub" it. This is only useful when you are re-recording music into already used bars. If you select Replace, Sibelius will delete the old as you enter the new. The Overdub option will merge the new music onto the old music. This is handy if you're recording multi-voiced music one voice at a time.

Figure 2.25   The Existing Music area.

Voices. The Voices area (see Figure 2.26) controls how Sibelius will deal with polyphonic input. You have the option to record into multiple voices, in which case Sibelius will bring in the other voices as they are needed, or to force recording into a single voice.

Figure 2.26   The Voices area.

First, you can try recording with multiple voices selected and see how it compares to what you visualize your music should look like. Many professional users find that recording voice by voice is simply much more accurate. If that's the approach you'd like to follow, you'll need to make sure that you're in Overdub mode in the Existing Music area. Otherwise, you'll record over what you already did (which you don't want). Then, select the voice into which you're recording with the four choices.

Metronome Click. Flexi-time wouldn't be much use to you if you couldn't hear the click! Make sure the Click When Recording option is selected in the Metronome Click area (see Figure 2.27).

Figure 2.27 The Metronome Click area.

But this is only the beginning! There is a Click Settings button that you will want to check out; clicking on it results in the dialog box shown in Figure 2.28.

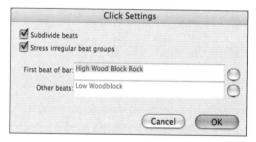

Figure 2.28 The Click Settings box.

In this dialog box, there are only two controls you need to worry about (for now, at least).

- **Subdivide Beats.** If you're recording into 6/8 or any other compound time signature, this will let Sibelius click on all of the beats (albeit lightly). You can also use this if you want to hear 4/4 broken into eighth notes.

- **Stress Irregular Beat Groups.** If you're working with an odd time signature, such as 7/8, with a particular beat grouping (such as 3+4), Sibelius will stress the first and fourth beats.

The last two controls let you set a different metronome click sound. Wait on that for now. The default click is fine for most purposes. When you get to the mixer and SoundWorld, it will be easier to explain what "unpitched.wood.high.woodblock" means to Sibelius. For now, just let it wash over you so you won't get bogged down with every single control. There's plenty of time to learn everything that Sibelius has to offer, but there's no need to make you learn it all on the *first day!*

That takes you through this window! To select and see the options for Notation, click on the Notation button at the top of the Flexi-Time Options window.

The Notation Window

The Notation window is very important to know. It sets up all the parameters for how Sibelius will interpret your live playing and translate it into notation. Like the Flexi-Time panel, this window is broken into four visual sections, discussed in the following subsections.

Note Values. Figure 2.29 shows how Sibelius will transcribe note values through Flexi-time.

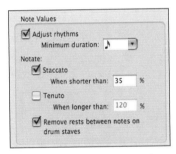

Figure 2.29   The Note Values options.

Here is an explanation of the controls in the Note Values section:

- **Adjust Rhythms.** You want this option selected! This is Sibelius's intelligent quantize feature. Without it, Sibelius relies on hardcore math to derive note values, and this never resembles music!

- **Minimum Duration.** This menu lets you select what you believe your minimum duration will be upon note entry. It's not a hard-and-fast rule, however. If you set it to quarter notes as a minimum and you play eighth notes, Sibelius has no choice but to squeeze in notes. However, setting this control correctly will greatly increase the accuracy of Flexi-time. Remember, you can always come back and change it later.

- **Staccato.** If you select this option, Sibelius will automatically add staccato markings to notes that meet the duration (in percent) set in the When Shorter Than field.

- **Tenuto.** If you select this option, Sibelius will automatically add tenuto markings to notes that meet the duration (in percent) set in the When Longer Than field.

- **Remove Rests between Notes on Drum Staves.** When you select this option, Sibelius will opt to notate notes of longer durations rather than rests in drum staves. This is because when percussive music is entered on a MIDI device, the durations are typically very short, and, if transcribed exactly, they would resemble shorter notes. Because this setting only affects drum staves, it can stay on all the time.

Keyboard Staves. When you record onto a grand staff for keyboard, Flexi-time will automatically distribute the notes to the correct staff. How it does this is defined by the "split point" between bass and treble staves. These settings are determined by the settings shown in Figure 2.30.

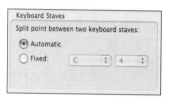

Figure 2.30 The Keyboard Staves options.

- **Automatic.** Sibelius will interpret the best spot to split the music based on the incoming MIDI data.

- **Fixed.** You can choose a specific key on the keyboard to force Sibelius to split the incoming music at that point.

Tuplets. The Tuplets section (see Figure 2.31) allows you to instruct Sibelius in how to deal with incoming tuplets and whether to notate them. You're basically telling Sibelius to allow tuplets and, if so, which kinds.

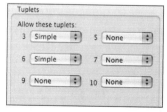

Figure 2.31 The Tuplets options.

Each type of tuplet (3, 5, 6, 7, 9, 10) has a menu with the following choices:

- **None.** Don't allow any tuplets based on this beat division.

- **Simple.** A simple tuplet is made up of all the same note values (for example, an eighth-note triplet with three eighth notes).

- **Moderate.** A moderate tuplet is made up of mixed rhythms (for example, an eighth-note triplet comprised of a quarter note and an eighth note).

- **Complex.** A complex tuplet may contain rests or dotted notes.

As always, the trick is knowing the passage in which you're going to play. If you're sure there aren't any tuplets, set them all to None; this will help Sibelius notate Flexi-time properly. If you're only playing certain tuplet divisions, turn only them on. The better you set up this window, the better Flexi-time does.

MIDI Messages. In addition to sending out note messages, most MIDI controllers send other data while you enter notes. These messages are called *MIDI messages*. Because Sibelius hides these messages in the score and they are of no consequence to 99.9 percent of the world, we'll leave the MIDI Messages section as is, with everything checked (see Figure 2.32).

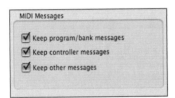

Figure 2.32 MIDI Messages options.

More? Nope, no more. That's all there is to setting up Flexi-time. You'll come back to this window often because Flexi-time settings will never have *one* setting that works for everything. On the contrary, the best "Flexi-timers" subtly tweak the settings often. Their reward is less tweaking of the final output in Sibelius. By all means, if Flexi-time isn't working well for you, tweak the settings.

Using Flexi-Time

This section contains several tips for using Flexi-time note entry that will help you on your way.

- To start a Flexi-time recording at a specific spot, you need to select the bar/beat on which you want to start.

- If you don't select any bars, Flex-time will assume that you're starting at Bar 1.

- If you're starting mid-measure, just let Flexi-time notate the rests for you.

- Remember to tweak your Flexi-time settings before you start!

- To stop your Flexi-time recording, press the spacebar.

- To record on more than one stave at the same time, the staves must be adjacent to each other. To record on two staves, Shift-click the bars of both staves to create a selection box around both, and enter Flexi-time.

- When recording onto a grand-staff piano stave, if the split point isn't right, remember to change its setting in the Flexi-Time Options.

- If your Flexi-time is a total mess, don't forget to look at the Renotate Performance plug-in.

That's a lot of information, but this is a critical step. Note entry in Sibelius may occupy at least 75 percent of your time, so the more you know about this and the more efficient you are, the better!

CD: Feel like a bit of sight reading? Example 2.14 has a line of music that you can enter in Flexi-time. (Yes, the original line will be muted!)

Last Thoughts and Tricks

There are a few last-minute things that apply loosely to note input that I should cover here as well. Elements such as playback (to verify how you did) and some basic editing, such as stem direction and accidental spelling, are part and parcel to the note entry process.

Playback

Assuming that you've got everything set up correctly on your Playback Devices page, Sibelius will play back everything you throw at it. When you're finished entering notes, you'll no doubt want to play them back. Playback is handled via key command or through the floating Playback window. Here are a few shortcuts to speed you along:

- Spacebar. This will start/stop Sibelius from the location of the playback line.

- P. This will start Sibelius from the currently selected note/rest.

-]. This will fast-forward Sibelius as you play back.

- [. This will rewind Sibelius as you play back.

- If you want to hear your Flex-time note velocities (dynamics) as you entered them, make sure you have Live Velocity engaged from your Playback window. Otherwise, Sibelius will play them back with default velocities as indicated in your score.

- If you make a selection (clicking on a bar and turning it blue with a selection box), Sibelius will only play back that bar when you press Play. To deselect all, press Escape until nothing is visually selected, and then press Play.

Playback during Entry

By default, Sibelius will play notes as you enter them. Some folks find this annoying. If that's you, you can stop this behavior a few ways. First, mute the output of your computer. If you're using Flexi-time, this will also mute the click, which won't do you much good. You have no choice but to take a sneak peak at the Mixer (see Figure 2.33). Open the Mixer by pressing the M key.

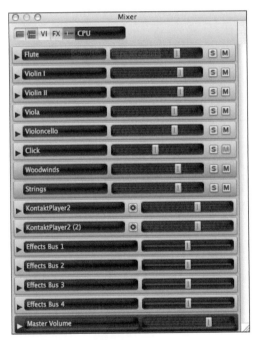

Figure 2.33 The Mixer!

The Mixer is honestly more than you need at this particular point in time, but you need it for a moment. The Mixer shows you each instrument active in the score. You can set levels, pan them from side to side, and do all sorts of neat things. To mute instruments, you'll see small M buttons, which stand for *Mute*. To completely mute an instrument, you need to click on the Mute button *twice* so that it glows red. Figure 2.34 shows all the tracks currently muted, although you can't see that they are red because this book is printed in black and white! (Sibelius has a

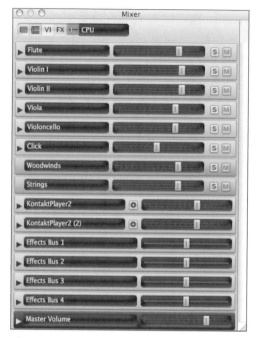

Figure 2.34   Muted tracks.

half–mute option, which reduces the volume by half. You get that effect by clicking on Mute once; to fully mute, you have to click Mute twice.)

When an instrument is muted like this, you can un-mute it by clicking on the Mute button one more time. You will learn all about the Mixer in a later chapter; it does some neat things. For the purposes of note entry, mute is all you want to mess with in the Mixer. However, if you're feeling adventurous, you can also adjust the level of playback by using the left-to-right volume sliders!

To hide the Mixer completely, press M again.

Golden Shortcuts   In this chapter, you've seen a few very easy shortcuts: N for note entry, P for Play, and M for Mixer. Sibelius has many more of these obvious shortcuts, based on single keys. Some have even called them "Painfully Obvious Shortcuts!" As you keep reading, you'll see more of them.

And one last note in this section: If you're listening through a MIDI keyboard that makes its own sounds (such as a Korg Triton) and you have it configured as a playback device (instead of Sibelius Sounds Essentials), then you'll have to refer to the documentation for the keyboard to learn how to mute and un-mute the keyboard (apart from using the volume knob).

Stem Flips

You haven't heard a peep about stem direction because, for the most part, Sibelius just gets it right by default. It knows which notes to stem in which direction. In the very unlikely event that Sibelius messes up or you would rather have total control over stem direction, a stem flip is only one key away. To flip a stem, simply highlight the note or notes you want to alter and press the X key.

Accidental Spelling

As you enter notes with a MIDI keyboard, Sibelius spells the accidentals according to built-in logic based on the key signature you are in. If you need to re-spell an accidental for any reason, all you have to do is select the note and press the Enter (Windows) or Return (Mac) key on your main keyboard to toggle the spelling of a note.

However, note that this will not take care of double flats/sharps, which are handled on the fifth keypad layout.

Watch the Selection When you go to flip stems, re-spell accidentals, or do any kind of editing in general (which is exactly what you're doing at this point), you want to keep an eye out for note selections. When you exit note entry mode by pressing the N key, the last note you entered will still be highlighted as the active note. Any edits you do will affect this note because it's currently selected. After you leave note entry mode, you should press the Escape key once to deselect everything. This is also very handy if you have a larger selection (such as a measure selection) and you want to start editing single notes. Pressing Escape is the easiest way to ensure that you're where you want to be, editing what you want to edit.

That's it! Now you can direct your attention in the next chapter to editing and adding/removing important elements of your score!

3 Creating Basic Score Elements

Essential Tips for Chapter 3

1. Sometimes it's really hard to select objects precisely with the mouse. When in doubt, zoom in!

2. Control-click on a Mac is the same as a right-click on a PC; it is indispensable for laptop users.

3. If you create an object with something selected in your score, the object is created *after* the object you selected.

4. If you create an object with nothing selected, Sibelius will "load up" your cursor, and you'll have to click where you want the object.

5. You can delete bars easily in Sibelius 5. Select the bar or bars and choose Edit > Delete Bars.

6. If you single-click a measure, you will select the measure.

7. If you double-click the measure, you will select all the measures in that system.

8. If you triple-click a measure, you will select the entire part.

9. Here are the essential shortcuts you'll learn in this chapter:
   - T: Add time signature
   - K: Add key signature
   - Q: Add clef
   - I: Add/remove instruments

Now that you have some music in your score, we need to talk about some basic elements of the final score. Believe it or not, once the score has notes correctly entered, you've conquered a ton of the work. What's left are creating and editing. As you enter notes, you start to realize that if the score isn't laid out correctly, you're going to work a lot harder than you should, especially when it comes to making changes later. It's best to get this right as you go along, and that means manipulating the score as you go.

Editing is a huge topic if you start including all the other possible elements that go into a score! It becomes unmanageable after a while, so I'm going to put it into digestible chunks over the next few chapters. This particular chapter is called "Elements" because, unlike other chapters, the focus is spread over a larger area. In the first chapter, you set up the score using the New Score wizard, which automated a great number of tasks for you (key signature, time signature, instruments). Chapter 1 also promised that you'd see how to change all these various "elements" yourself, and these next few chapters will take care of that!

Creating The title of this chapter has a hidden meaning. "Creating Basic Score Elements" happens from Sibelius's unified Create menu. You'll get used to answering your own questions as you go. "How do I do X?" you might ask. Get used to looking at the Create menu first when your answer can start with the phrase: "Creating a key signature (or other such creation)."

Creating Basic Elements

As you begin to shape your score, you'll most often need to access bar changes, key changes, and clef and time/meter changes. In this section, you'll learn how to make these changes easily in your score. More importantly, you'll learn about the power of selections, and how Sibelius deals with adding and removing score elements. Once you know the system, you'll fly!

Start with Create

As mentioned earlier, the Create menu is important in Sibelius. It houses many important functions within the Sibelius world. You can get to the Create menu in one of two ways. First, you can physically pull the Create menu down to access its parameters. Or, you can right-click on a blank part of your score. You don't want to touch your music; just right-click anywhere else on the paper to bring up the lovely menu shown in Figure 3.1.

Mac users may not have a right mouse button at all. This is easily solved: Holding down the Control key while you click will have the same effect as right-clicking on a two-button mouse. Alternatively, you can buy a very cheap two-button USB mouse—it will work without any drivers or intervention by you! Just plug and play. Sibelius likes the two-button mouse, so you'd be wise to look into one if you don't already have one.

Figure 3.1   The Create menu.

As you continue to learn about Sibelius, you'll be reminded about the importance of shortcuts (see Figure 3.2). More importantly, as you continue to use functions, you'll no doubt learn the shortcuts automatically. Just remember the power-user mantra: If you can avoid the mouse, you'll work faster!

Figure 3.2   Key commands/shortcuts.

Adding Measures

Sibelius starts each new score with a certain number of blank measures in it. You'll want to add more measures as you go along. Sibelius conveniently gives you three options for adding bars (which, as it happens, are the first entries in the Create > Bar menu).

- **At end.** Adds a single bar at the end of your current score.

- **Single.** Creates a single bar based on your current selection. (See the "Selections" section in a moment.)

- **Other.** Creates multiple bars with the option of creating "irregular" bars (bars that are not the same as the current time signature) in your score. This is handy for "pick-up" bars and other modern notation needs.

Adding a bar "at end" is pretty self-explanatory, but you should know the key command: Ctrl+B (Windows) or Command+B (Mac). What's cool is that if you hold down the key command for adding a single bar "at end," Sibelius will *accelerate* the bars as they are added, and you can add a whole mess of bars with a single shot.

For the remaining types of bar additions, I need to take a second and talk about selections.

Selections

Selections, or a lack of selections, affect Sibelius greatly. You need to understand how Sibelius thinks in this regard. Let's start by defining a *selection*. A selection can be a single note, object, staff, measure, system, or full score. When you select something, the selection becomes highlighted in some color. (The color is crucial—light blue for a passage selection or things in all voices, and purple for system objects and system selections; otherwise, voice colors.)

As you can see, what constitutes a selection can range widely. You'll know something is selected by its color—selected objects are always colored. The type of selection will vary the color, as detailed a moment ago.

Essential Tip: Bar Selections If you want to select a bar, you need to click on a portion of the bar that doesn't contain any music. If you click on a note, you will highlight that note, and Sibelius will think you want to edit it. You might find it necessary to zoom in to find a place to click a portion where no music exists.

If you have a measure selected in your score (or even just a note), and you go to the Create menu and add a single bar (Ctrl+Shift+B [Windows] or Command+Shift+B [Mac]), what you see in Figures 3.3 and 3.4 will appear on your score.

Figure 3.3 Single-measure selection.

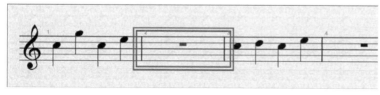

Figure 3.4 After adding a single bar.

As you can see, Sibelius created the single bar *after* the measure/note you originally selected. Follow this logic/conversation between you and your computer:

> You: I clicked a bar or a measure, and I told Sibelius to add a bar from the Create menu/ key command.

> Sibelius: Because you clicked on this bar, you must want that measure added right there. Sure, I'll add the measure directly after the measure/note you've selected.

The same logic holds true for adding other types of bars as well. If you select something and then invoke the command, Sibelius will add the item directly *after* your selection.

Remember, objects are always placed *after* the selection point.

So what happens when you don't select anything? To make this happen, press Escape until nothing glows with any colors. Then add a single bar from the Create menu. Notice how nothing happened? Follow this conversation:

> You: I told you to add a bar, and you didn't do anything. There must something wrong.

> Sibelius: You did indeed tell me to add a bar, but you didn't tell me where yet. I'll be happy to do so; just tell me where to do it.

All fun aside, Sibelius makes a good point: You haven't told it where to add the bar. But, do notice the color of your cursor. It's no longer black; it's now colored. (This is critical!)

A colored cursor (other than the default black) shows you that Sibelius is ready to do something. In this case, it's ready to do the last thing you told it—add a bar. Consider that glowing, colored cursor a loaded weapon; just point and shoot—or click, in this case.

Go ahead and click in your score now. Depending on where you click, a new bar will be added. You can use this same logic for multiple bars, and most importantly, this logic runs throughout Sibelius.

Sibelius is also sensitive to where in the score/measure you click. If you click the new bar at the beginning of a measure or at the start of your score, the new bar will be created *before* (to the left of) your first measure. If you click toward the end of a measure/score, the new measure will be created *after* (to the right of) your measure. Sibelius is sensitive not only to a selection, but also to the location of your mouse click. Like everything else, this will hold true throughout the software as you create elements.

CD: Example 3.1 will take you through placing new measures in a variety of ways (including mouse selection and pre-selection).

Essential Tip: Selection Recap If you select a bar and then create an object, Sibelius creates the object after the selection. If you have nothing selected, Sibelius loads the cursor with a color (which depends on the voice you're working on) and waits for you to tell it where to add the object. This holds true throughout the program.

Cursor Colors

There has been a lot of talk about the cursor glowing a "color" when you add objects or select notes/objects, and so far, you've only gotten a very general glimpse of what color the cursor will be. The color of the cursor *always* depends upon which voice you're in. If you're in Voice 1, then the cursor is blue. Each voice has a specific color.

- Voice 1: Blue

- Voice 2: Green

- Voice 3: Orange

- Voice 4: Purple

You'll want to keep an eye on what color your cursor is, especially when you're adding notes and objects to your score, because you'll want the additions to bind to the correct voice.

Removing Measures

If you use Flexi-time, you'll find that extra measures may be added to your score that you will need to delete. You might need to delete bars for other reasons as well. The first thing you need to do is understand the distinction between deleting bars and removing content. Removing a measure completely removes it from your score, and this is different than clearing preexisting measures.

To remove a single bar/measure in Sibelius 5, select the bar by clicking on it to bring up a light-blue selection box, as shown in Figure 3.5.

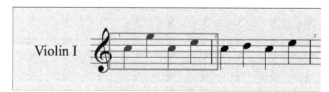

Figure 3.5 Single-measure selection.

Then, from the Edit menu, choose Delete Bar. Alternatively, you can press Ctrl+Delete (Windows) or Command+Delete (Mac). (You can also Command/Control-click, and then press Delete for the same effect.) As soon as you do so, the bar will change its color from blue (a bar selection) to a double-purple box (to denote a system selection), and the dialog box shown in Figure 3.6 will appear.

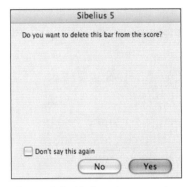

Figure 3.6 Delete bar warning.

Because deleting a bar is a fairly destructive action, you are warned about what you're going to do. There's a Don't Say This Again check box; selecting it will stop the message from coming up again.

If you want to delete multiple bars at once, you'll need to make a multiple selection. To make a multiple selection, click the first bar you want to delete (it will be highlighted in blue), hold down Shift, and click the last bar you'd like to delete. You'll get a very long blue bar (which looks like a box encompassing your selection) across your measures, as shown in Figure 3.7.

Figure 3.7 Multiple-bar selection.

Now that you have your bars selected, you can delete them by using the Edit menu or the keyboard shortcuts introduced a moment ago.

Bar Delete = System! Remember that if you delete a single bar, that bar is removed from all systems on your score (if you have multiple instruments).

Multiple Selection Clicks

You can use your mouse to make multiple selections easily. Here is the rundown:

- **Single-click a measure.** Only the measure you clicked on will be selected.

- **Double-click a measure.** All measures in the system will be selected, up to the system break. (See the upcoming "Double-Click!" note.)

- **Triple-click a measure.** All the measures in the score (for that part) will be selected.

Double-Click! Double-clicking on a measure will select that measure up to the system break. This only works when you're *not* in Panorama view. Panorama doesn't show system breaks, so a double-click in Panorama view will select all the measures in the piece.

Because all of the operations in the chapter work just fine when a single instrument is selected, I'll only briefly mention that if you hold down Ctrl (Windows) or Command (Mac) while you click (single, double, or triple), your selection will extend to all the instruments in your score. You'll learn more about this in the next chapter on editing, but for the moment you should be aware that it exists.

Adding/Changing Key Signatures

As you're starting to see, adding elements to your score depends a great deal on what you have selected in Sibelius, and changing key is no different. You can access key signatures from the Create menu or from the shortcut K, which is unforgettable.

If you invoke a key signature change with nothing selected (make sure to press Escape or click on a blank spot of manuscript paper), the Key Signature dialog box shown in Figure 3.8 will appear.

In this dialog box, you'll see several important controls.

- **Major/Minor Keys.** Yes, it does matter! When you're entering notes on a MIDI keyboard, Sibelius will favor the correct accidentals for a given key, so you should select the proper key.

- **Hide.** This suppresses Sibelius from creating a "cautionary" key signature at the system break. (You can always hide the cautionary key signature later if you forget this.)

- **One Staff Only.** In modern music, it's sometimes necessary to write instruments in different key signatures. If you select the One Staff Only option, the key signature change will only occur in the staff you choose. This is also helpful when you have instruments that prefer to read in sharps/flats, and you can make use of enharmonic this way.

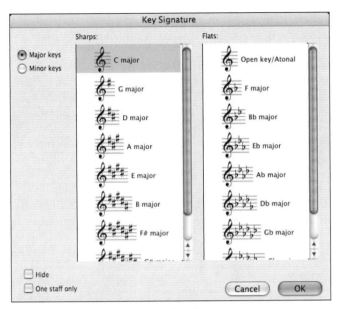

Figure 3.8 Key Signature dialog box.

When you click OK, you'll be in that all-too-familiar position of the *glowing colored cursor*. Because you invoked the key signature change with *nothing* selected, Sibelius waits to see where you want the key signature change to appear. Click the measure where you want the key signature to occur. Sibelius will create a new key signature, as shown in Figure 3.9.

Figure 3.9 New key signature.

Along with the new key signature, Sibelius creates a double barline preceding the change. This is important to note because in the future, as you deal with parts, double barlines will break multi-measure rests, so you probably want them. If not, you can change them. (See the barlines sections later in this chapter.)

Key Changes with Measure Selection(s)

If you have a bar or a range of bars selected when you change a key signature, the outcome is a bit different than if you have no selection.

If you have a single bar selected and you change the key signature, Sibelius will change the key from that bar and revert it back to the preceding key signature, as shown in Figure 3.10.

Figure 3.10   Changing to a major with a single-measure selection.

If you select a range of measures (Shift-click) a few bars, which is shown in Figure 3.11, you'll get the familiar blue box encompassing those measures—this shows you the multiple selection.

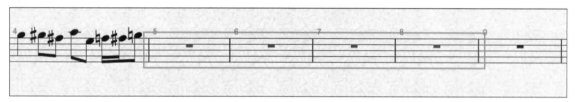

Figure 3.11   Multiple-bar selection.

Now, if you add a key signature change, look what happens in Figure 3.12.

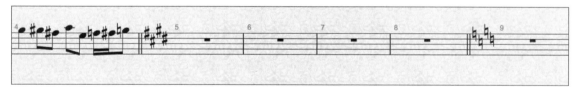

Figure 3.12   After adding a key signature change.

Sibelius did a very cool thing: It changed the key signatures in the measures you selected, and then returned the score to the previously used key signature. This is very handy for changing sections because it saves you the extra step of changing *back* to the old key signature. This won't do you any good if you want the newly created key signature to keep going for the rest of the piece, but in those instances when you have a set change for a set number of bars, don't forget the power of selecting before you go. Your selection can be as little as one bar or as many as you decide.

Key Changes with Note Selection

If you simply click on a single note and then add a key signature change, Sibelius will change the key signature directly after the note you've selected. This way, it's possible to have a key signature in the middle of the bar (which is not common, but possible). Select a note, as shown in Figure 3.13. (G is selected in blue, but will not show clearly in two-color printing in this book.)

Figure 3.13   A single-note selection.

Now, press K to bring up the new key signature. Sibelius automatically will place it after the note, as shown in Figure 3.14.

Figure 3.14   New key signature.

The difference between this method and selecting a bar is that when you select a note, the key signature goes on until it meets another key signature after it, at which point it stops. If there are no other key signatures present, it goes until the end of the piece.

CD: Example 3.2 gives you a plethora of key signature practice, going through every type of key signature addition you could possibly want.

Removing/Hiding Key Signatures

To remove a key signature, all you have to do is select it (it will turn purple) and press the Delete key on your keyboard. To hide a key signature, which typically happens with cautionary key signatures, select the key signature (again, you'll see a purple glow), go to the Edit menu, and select Hide or Show > Hide. This will hide the key signature, but it won't delete it forever. You can always redisplay the signature again by doing the opposite operation: Edit > Hide or Show > Show.

CD: Hide the key signature in Example 3.3 to make the scale examples look good.

Adding/Changing the Time Signature

Following suit with the Super Simple Shortcuts (SSS), to change the time signature, the likely choice would be the T key. Pressing it brings up the Time Signature dialog box shown in Figure 3.15.

Figure 3.15 The Time Signature dialog box.

This dialog boasts some important features that are worth illustrating in depth.

- **Default time signatures.** The preset time signatures you'll find most often in Sibelius have buttons you can select to choose the time signature.

- **Other.** If your time signature does not appear, you can make your own time signature by clicking on the Other button and selecting your top and bottom meter values. The top value can be up to 126 beats; the bottom value can be 1, 2, 4, 6, 8, 16, or 32.

- **Rewrite Bars up to Next Time Signature.** If there is preexisting music contained in the score, do you want it to rewrite the music that's already there into the new time signature? This is also called *rebarring* music.

- **Allow Cautionary.** Select this if you want a cautionary time signature to appear.

- **Start with Bar of Length.** This is for a pick-up bar; select it and choose the duration of the pick-up measure. When you click into the score, the first measure created in the new time signature will be the pick-up bar.

One last button exists in the dialog box: Beam and Rest Groups. Clicking this button results in the dialog box shown in Figure 3.16.

This dialog allows you to set how Sibelius will beam notes and rests together. You can manually define how each grouping works in each time signature. For example, in 4/4, the default beaming group is 4,4, as shown in Figure 3.17.

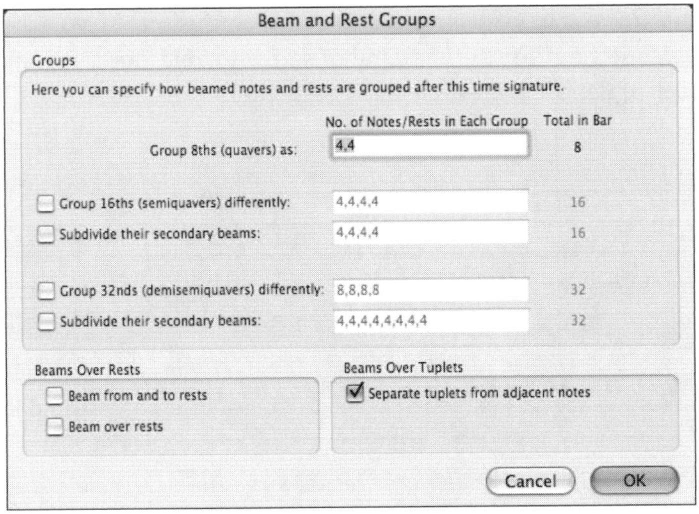

Beam and Rest Groups

Groups

Here you can specify how beamed notes and rests are grouped after this time signature.

	No. of Notes/Rests in Each Group	Total in Bar
Group 8ths (quavers) as:	4,4	8
☐ Group 16ths (semiquavers) differently:	4,4,4,4	16
☐ Subdivide their secondary beams:	4,4,4,4	16
☐ Group 32nds (demisemiquavers) differently:	8,8,8,8	32
☐ Subdivide their secondary beams:	4,4,4,4,4,4,4,4	32

Beams Over Rests
- ☐ Beam from and to rests
- ☐ Beam over rests

Beams Over Tuplets
- ☑ Separate tuplets from adjacent notes

Cancel   OK

Figure 3.16   Beam and Rest Groups dialog box.

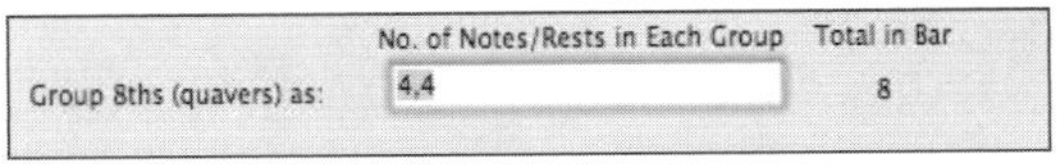

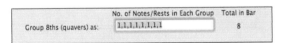

Figure 3.17   Beam eighths in fours.

By selecting 4,4, you are choosing how to group the eighth notes in the bar. A value of 4,4 means a group of four, followed by another group of four. The comma (,) separates the groupings of notes. If you want your eighth notes to beam in groups of ones (no beaming; used in Vocal literature), you'd change the Beam and Rest Groups dialog box to look like Figure 3.18.

	No. of Notes/Rests in Each Group	Total in Bar
Group 8ths (quavers) as:	1,1,1,1,1,1,1,1	8

Figure 3.18   Settings for beaming eighths singularly.

After you've done that, the result is automatic throughout your score, as shown in Figure 3.19.

Figure 3.19   Eighths beamed singularly.

Obviously, these settings are best done at the start of your piece to avoid confusion. As you can see in Figure 3.20, you can have separate settings for the beaming of sixteenth and thirty-second notes, beams over rests, and beams for tuplets.

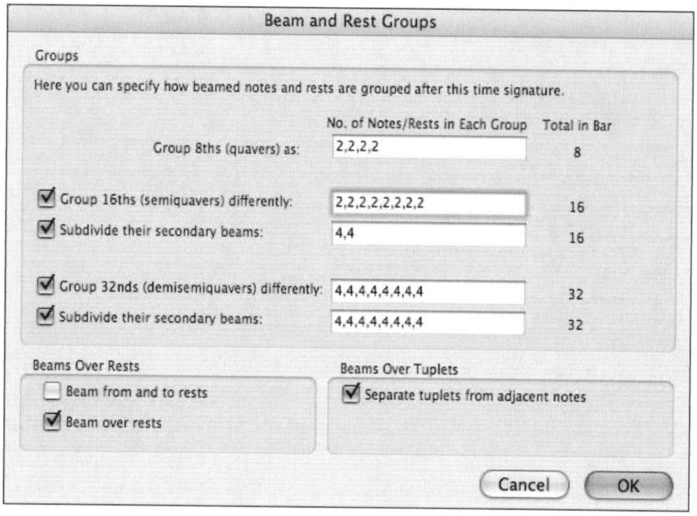

Figure 3.20   More beaming options.

There are many settings you can tweak here to globally change the look of your score.

Beaming Don't go crazy with the beam and rest groups unless they are completely consistent in your entire score. If you need to change the beaming of only a few groups of notes, you will learn in Chapter 7, "Properties, Editing, and Filtering," that this is done with the third keypad layout. Reserve using Reset Beam and Rest Groups for global changes only. You can take care of the odd change as you edit your score.

You Can Change This! You can change the beam and rest groups globally after you've written your piece by going to Notes > Reset Beam Groups, which will give you the same Beam and Rest Groups dialog box that you had in the Time Signature window—all without needing to change your time signature.

CD: Example 3.4 will let you practice adding several time signatures to a score.

Removing Time Signatures

To remove a time signature, all you have to do is click on the signature itself, and it will be selected in purple. Then, you can delete it using the Delete or Backspace key on your keyboard.

If you're removing a key signature, you'll be greeted with the question in the dialog box shown in Figure 3.21.

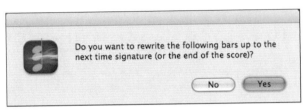

Figure 3.21   Rewriting time signatures.

The question is quite important! When you remove a time signature, the preexisting music will be affected. If you select Yes, then the music that's already there will revert to the last active time signature. (Sibelius will rewrite the bars to adhere to whatever time signature takes over at that point.)

If you select No, Sibelius will *not* rebar the music up to the next time signature, which will leave the music looking the same, even though you may have another time signature present! Figures 3.22 and 3.23 show the before and after.

Figure 3.22   4/4 and 3/4.

Figure 3.23   Remove the 3/4 and don't rewrite the measures.

For most situations, you'll want to avoid selecting No when you remove a time signature. Always remember that you can add a time signature back at any point to correct this. For example, if you say no by accident, and you're left with bars in 3/4, you can just reapply the initial 4/4 time signature. You'll want to make sure that the Rewrite Bars up to Next Time Signature option in the Time Signature dialog box is checked when you add your time signature.

Adding/Changing Clefs

It's no surprise that adding clefs works the same way that everything else does in Sibelius—the selection really matters! You can access clef changes from the Create menu or by right-clicking on a blank spot of manuscript paper. The shortcut for adding a clef is Q, which seems very illogical when you consider that time signature and key signatures are T and K, respectively. Unfortunately, C is reserved for the note C, and Q is as good a choice as any; it's also a slight play on "qlef."

Pressing Q with *nothing selected* brings up the Clef dialog box, shown in Figure 3.24.

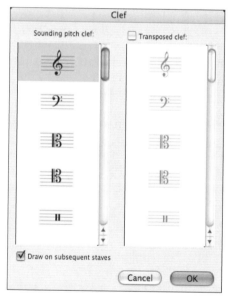

Figure 3.24 The Clef dialog box.

The list of clefs covers anything you'd need to add into your score. Select the clef you want and click OK.

Since nothing was selected at the time, your mouse pointer will glow a color (usually blue, because most folks are in Voice 1, but the color can vary) and will await direction from you on where to add the clef change. Here's a list of ways you can click in a clef change:

- Click at the very beginning of your score. Your entire score will change to the new clef (at least until the next clef change that appears).

- Click between two notes. The clef change will appear where you click.

- Click directly on a note. The clef will appear before (to the left of) the note you've clicked on.

As you've also seen, making selections usually speeds up creation in Sibelius, and clef changes are no different.

- If you pre-select a single note, the clef will be added before the selected note. This will affect music up until the next preexisting clef change or until the end of the score (if no other clef exists).

- If you pre-select a bar, the clef will change for the bar selected and then return to the original clef automatically.

- If you pre-select a range of music, the clef will change at the beginning of the selection and then return to the original clef automatically.

A very cool feature is that clefs can be dragged left and right! When you do this, the music will automatically change as you drag.

CD: Example 3.5 will let you practice adding and changing the location of some clefs.

Clef Options

In the Clef dialog box, you have two options called Transposed Clef and Draw on Subsequent Staves.

A transposed clef is an option if your instrument needs to show one clef in the non-transposing score view and another clef in the transposed score view. Many folks find this useful when working with the lower saxophones, for example. When you select the Transposed Clef option, you'll have two columns of clefs from which to choose. The left side always selects the sounding pitch clef, while the right selects the transposed clef.

Transposing View To see the effect of a transposing clef, make sure that you're in transposing view by selecting the Transposing Score button on the toolbar to change into this view (the small two-flat key signature) or by choosing the Transposing Score option from the Notes menu.

Draw on Subsequent Staves is the default option, and one that you'll likely want to keep on when you change clefs. Deselecting this option would draw the clef only on the current stave and leave the remaining ones empty. You will sometimes see this in jazz music/lead sheets and in some contemporary music. The other reason for not drawing on subsequent staves is for educational/worksheet types of sheets, where you leave blank lines of music for your students to draw in.

Cautionary Clefs

Figure 3.25 shows a cautionary clef. These are drawn automatically when your clef change is at the end of a system, a system break, or a page break. You can hide any cautionary clef by clicking on it and choosing the Edit > Hide or Show > Hide command, as shown in Figure 3.26.

Figure 3.25 A cautionary clef.

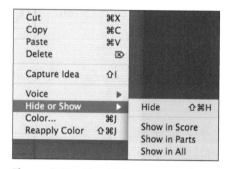

Figure 3.26 The Hide menu option.

Alternatively, you can right-click (Control-click on a Mac) on the clef and choose Hide from the resulting menu.

Hide The Hide option is very useful and will be dealt with a bit later in the book. For now, it's helpful for hiding cautionary clef changes as they come up, especially if you're doing tests and worksheets in which cautionary clef changes between examples in different clefs are necessary. You can also hide time signatures when you are preparing worksheets (such as a sheet of scales in a hidden 8/4 time signature to ensure proper spacing).

CD: In Example 3.6, learn how to hide the cautionary clefs.

Removing Clefs

To remove a clef, just click on the clef to highlight it and press Delete. The music will change to the clef that already existed in the score.

Note that you can't remove the initial clef. However, you can create a no-clef symbol by choosing Create > Clef and navigating down to the unpitched clef.

Changing Barlines

Managing the appearance of barlines on a case-by-case basis is done via the Create menu, as shown in Figure 3.27.

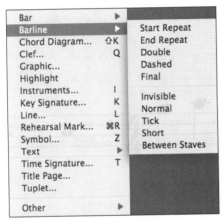

Figure 3.27   Barline choices.

Change all Barlines If you're looking to change the appearance of all barlines in your score, this is handled from the House Style menu, not from the Create menu. House Styles will be covered in detail in Chapter 8, "House Styles and Engraving Rules."

The following barlines are available to you:

- Normal

- Double

- Start Repeat

- End Repeat

- Final

- Dashed

- Invisible

- Between Staves

- Tick

- Short

To change a barline, simply select the barline you want to change (it will glow purple), choose Create > Barline, and select the barline to which you'd like to change. That's all there is to it!

Endings If you're looking for first and second (or third) ending barlines from the Create > Barline menu, you might have discovered that they aren't there! The barlines for these special endings are found in the Lines submenu of the Create menu and will be covered in Chapter 4, "Creating More Score Elements." The barlines will still change in the same spot: Create > Barline.

If you don't pre-select a barline, Sibelius will color the mouse pointer and wait for you to select the barline you want to change. It doesn't matter which way you choose to change a barline; both methods work the same. Either pre-select it or mouse-click it in.

Bar Selections If you try to select several bars and change the barline, this will *not* change every barline (unlike almost every other action in the Create menu). Instead, only the first barline will change.

Removing Barlines

If you add a barline to your score and you'd like to change it back to the default "normal" barline, there's no need to add the normal barline over the top of the existing barline. If you simply highlight the barline and press Delete, the barline will revert back to the original one, which is in fact the "normal" barline. Don't miss this tip—it will save you a great deal of time.

Special Barlines

"Special" barlines, especially those that occur in the middle of a measure, are created the same way as normal barlines with one notable exception: You can't pre-select a barline. You need to start with nothing selected and load up your mouse to click in a special barline mid-measure. The most obvious case is using a dotted barline to show the division in an asymmetric meter, although composers find other reasons to position barlines mid-measure. Figure 3.28 shows a measure of 5/4 broken into two asymmetric sections.

To create this, add a dashed barline from the Create menu and click it between the notes you want.

Figure 3.28 Mid-measure barline.

CD: Example 3.7 is all about adding special barlines to your score.

Repositioning Barlines (and Other Objects)

There is absolutely no way around this: If you want to move the barline in Figure 3.28, you need to access an advanced program feature. It's really a few chapters away from us at this point in the book, but you'll need it now.

Each element in Sibelius has properties that you can adjust. One such property concerns the X and Y axes where the element appears. This is useful for moving (in this case) barlines back and forth to the perfect spots, but it will also come in handy later, when you have to move other objects, such as notes, rests, and clefs to exact locations. To access the properties of an object, you have to access the Properties dialog box by choosing Windows > Properties (see Figure 3.29).

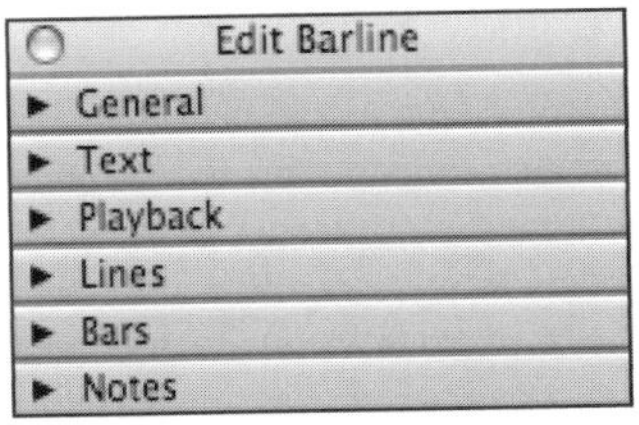

Edit Barline
▶ General
▶ Text
▶ Playback
▶ Lines
▶ Bars
▶ Notes

Figure 3.29 Properties.

The Properties dialog box is divided into six small tabs that can be extended to show additional features. You'll want to look at the General tab, which you can extend by clicking on the small arrow (see Figure 3.30).

The only thing to concern yourself with is the X property. There are many elements to tweak here, but for now the left-to-right adjustment is all you need, and that is done via the X property. Entering a positive value will move the selected object/note to the right, while a negative value will move the selected object/note to the left. To position the barline exactly between the notes, use a value of −1.5; the result is the barline moving to a nice visual spot, as shown in Figure 3.31.

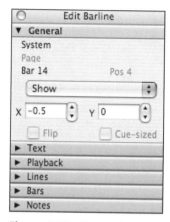

Figure 3.30 Open the General tab.

Figure 3.31 A perfectly positioned barline.

Power Tools The Properties dialog box bridges the gap between power and everyday use. Power users will come to it often, because it's an incredible way to change the onscreen properties in Sibelius. Not every user will need it the same way, but as you can see in the aforementioned example, you can't ignore this important window.

CD: Example 3.8 has a barline that needs to be moved; use the Properties dialog box to position the barline exactly.

Changing Instruments/Staves

When you start creating your score, you choose a manuscript paper that most closely reflects the type of score you're going to write. Each manuscript paper contains a preset list of instruments. Thankfully, you can change these instruments at any time. If you follow the steps in the new score setup, you'll have a chance to add or remove instruments from any manuscript paper. One of the goals of the early chapters (about creating) was to cover each of the steps in the new score setup individually, and this is one of the last major steps we need to cover.

Adding Instruments

To add an instrument to your score, you can navigate again to the Create menu and select Instruments, which has the wonderful shortcut of I. Figure 3.32 shows the Instruments dialog box.

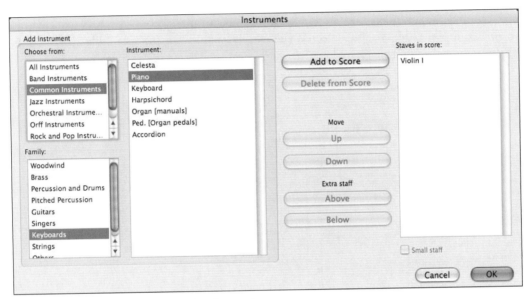

Figure 3.32   The Instruments dialog box.

What's an instrument? It is either a staff or a group of staves (for example, piano or harp). It's also a set of rules for the instrument's range, transposition, and playback sounds. Instruments are grouped according to the following large divisions:

- **All Instruments.** This includes every instrument that Sibelius uses.

- **Band Instruments.** These are typical instruments for bands of all types (wind, marching, military).

- **Common Instruments.** This category has fewer "historical" instruments and focuses on instruments that are used more often.

- **Jazz Instruments.** This contains instruments that swing.

- **Orchestral Instruments.** This consists of all the instruments that have ever appeared in an orchestra at one time or another.

- **Orff Instruments.** These instruments are used in the Orff Instrumentarium instrumental music pedagogy.

- **Rock and Pop Instruments.** This contains guitars, drums, bass guitar, and other rocking sounds.

- **World Instruments.** This consists of ethnic instruments from all over the world.

When you select any of the larger families of instruments just mentioned, the list directly below will separate out into the families of instruments. Families encompass groups such as woodwinds and brass, for example. Once you've selected the family, you'll see the available instruments directly to the right, as shown in Figure 3.33.

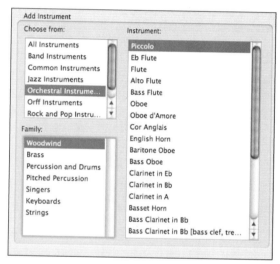

Figure 3.33 Individual instruments.

Now that you have instruments, you can add them to your score in a few ways:

- **Double-click on an instrument.** This adds the instrument to your score.

- **Click and drag.** This selects a range of contiguous instruments to add to your score. (You have to select Add to Score for the instruments to show up.)

- **Ctrl/Command-click.** This lets you select a range of noncontiguous instruments to add to your score. (You have to select Add to Score for the instruments to show up.)

When the instruments are added to your score, they show up in the right side of the Instruments dialog box, as shown in Figure 3.34.

Newly added instruments are shown with a plus sign (+) next to their names on the Staves in Score list. The instruments themselves will appear in proper score order. Instruments such as piano and harp (multi-staff instruments) will appear as Piano (a) and Piano (b), as shown in Figure 3.35.

Figure 3.34   Added instruments.

Figure 3.35   Pianos appear as Piano (a) and Piano (b).

When you've added instruments, you can use the Move Up or Move Down button to manually move an instrument in your score. This is helpful when you need to step outside the normal score order (when a solo instrument needs to appear at the top of your score).

You can also add a single staff above or below your currently selected staff by clicking the Extra Staff Above or Extra Staff Below button. This will create a multi-staff instrument in your score.

The Small Staff option will change any staff in the currently selected score to a small staff, which is useful when you are writing a piano accompaniment part in which the melodic line is typically written with a smaller staff, for example.

When you click OK, your score will contain the new instruments/parts, and the playback engine will add the new samples for playback.

Removing Instruments

To get rid of an instrument, you go right back to the Instruments dialog box by selecting Create > Instruments or by pressing I. Navigate to the instrument you want to remove in the left side list of Staves in Score, click to highlight the instrument, and click Delete from Score. Sibelius will respond with the warning shown in Figure 3.36.

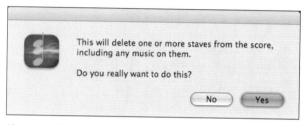

Figure 3.36 Are you sure?

Deleting an instrument permanently removes it from the score, so it's good that Sibelius gives you a warning about this. Although it's true that you can always undo this action immediately after you do it, just remember that deleting an instrument is a destructive process.

CD: Example 3.9 will have you add and remove some instruments from the score provided.

Dealing with Divisi Instruments

A simple divisi instrument is no problem for Sibelius; simply use two voices for the two parts on a single staff, as shown in Figure 3.37.

Figure 3.37 Simple divisi.

What gets tricky is when you start with two different instruments on two different staves, and then they jump onto a single divisi staff for a while, and then possibly jump back to a single staff. The only way jump from divisi and back is as follows (in the case of two flutes):

1. Create three flute staves: Flute I, Flute II, and Flute I II.

2. Write in the separate staves when needed.

3. Start divisi by writing in two voices on the Flute I II staff.

4. Write again on the separate staffs if necessary.

You'll end up with a score that looks like Figure 3.38.

Figure 3.38 Complex divisi.

Of course, this is not the way you want the final outcome to look. What you need to do is hide the unused staves when they aren't being used. You can do this by selecting Layout > Hide Empty Staves, as shown in Figure 3.39.

To hide empty staves, you need to select the passage on which you're working. In this case, select from the beginning of the piece to the end, using the shortcut for Select All: Ctrl+A (Windows) or Command+A (Mac).

After you've finished, your score should look like Figure 3.40.

The rule here is to create enough instruments to write the full-blown parts out and have an extra staff for the divisi parts; you can always hide the extra staffs when you need to.

Document Setup...	⌘D
Hide Empty Staves	⌥⇧⌘H
Show Empty Staves...	⌥⇧⌘S
Reset Space Above Staff	
Reset Space Below Staff	
Align Staves...	
Auto Layout...	
Break	▶
Format	▶
Align in a Row	⇧⌘R
Align in a Column	⇧⌘C
Reset Note Spacing	⇧⌘N
Reset Position	⇧⌘P
Reset Design	⇧⌘D
Reset to Score Position	⌥⇧⌘P
Reset to Score Design	⌥⇧⌘D

Figure 3.39 The Hide Empty Staves option.

Figure 3.40 Great-looking divisi.

Divisi Parts When you have divisi sections (as in Figure 3.40), note that when you look at the parts (in Chapter 10, "Dynamic Parts"), you'll end up with three separate parts, which you don't want. Look at Chapter 10 to learn how to add all three staves to a single part to make it look right.

Reduction If you have music on two staves and you decide that "imploding" them into a single stave and using a divisi is the way to go, there's no easier way than by using the new Reduce plug-in. Learn all about plug-ins in Chapter 16, "Using Plug-Ins."

Changing Instruments

An instrument change is a specific action, one that's new in Sibelius 5. Instrument changes are immensely useful when you have instrument doubles (for example, ♭ Clarinet changes to A Clarinet for a section, and then changes back) or in Broadway/show scores, where woodwind doubling is an extremely common occurrence. Because these involve changes of instrument, clef, and transposition, they used to require an involved process. In Sibelius 5, you now can change an instrument at any point by choosing Create > Other > Instrument Change, which brings up the Instrument Change dialog box shown in Figure 3.41.

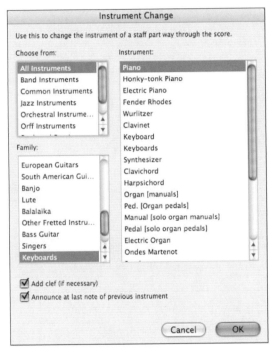

Figure 3.41   The Instrument Change dialog box.

The Instrument Change dialog box looks much like the normal Add Instrument section of the Instruments dialog box, with the large group, family, and individual instruments subgroups. Simply select the instrument you want to change to and keep track of the two check boxes at the bottom of the screen: Add Clef (If Necessary) and Announce at Last Note of Previous Instrument.

- **Add Clef (If Necessary).** If your new instrument is in a different clef, this adds the appropriate clef at the instrument change.

- **Announce at Last Note of Previous Instrument.** This adds the text "To (new instrument)" at the instrument change.

As always, the selection of notes makes a big difference to Sibelius. If you select a range of notes or measures and then apply an instrument change, Sibelius will change the instrument for the selected period and then return the staff back to the original instrument. If you only select a single note and apply an instrument change, the instrument will change *after* the selected note for the rest of the piece.

Figure 3.42 shows an instrument change in action: a change from Flute to E♭ alto saxophone.

Figure 3.42   Flute-to-sax instrument change.

When an instrument is changed, the following things happen:

- The new instrument plays back with the proper sound and soundID.

- The new instrument has the proper clef and transposition.

- If the staff type is different, it will change to the necessary staff.

- The name on new systems will reflect the new instrument.

Instrument changes were a real chore in earlier versions of Sibelius, and they are a piece of cake in Sibelius 5.

CD: Use Example 3.10 to place an instrument change within your score. Make sure to play it back and hear the result!

That's it for our "basic" creations. Now its time to explore more of the Create menu and add dynamics, symbols, slurs, hairpins, and many more useful symbols! On to Chapter 4!

Important Shortcut Review A few great single-key shortcuts came up in this chapter. They're easy to remember:

- K: Key signature

- T: Time signature

- Q: Clef

- I: Add/remove instruments

---

4 Creating More Score Elements

1. You can copy any selected element by holding down Alt/Option and clicking in the destination.

2. If you want to Alt/Option-click and ensure that your paste retains its proper "default position," hold down Shift while Alt/Option-clicking.

3. When you add any text-based markings, such as dynamics or expressions, don't forget about word menus. You can right-click (Windows) or Control-click (Mac) and see a list of default choices for the text with which you're working.

4. You can create slurs using a single shortcut key: S.

5. You can create a crescendo/hairpin using a single shortcut key: H.

6. In Sibelius, if you want something to do the reverse of the normal action, hold down Shift. Want a slur on the other side? Press Shift+S. Want a diminuendo (reverse hairpin)? Press Shift+H.

7. Slurs, hairpins, and other lines will draw themselves automatically for as long as you've selected. If you pre-select a range of notes before you add a line, Sibelius will make the line fit perfectly.

8. Symbols from the Symbols window (Z) don't ever play back.

9. You can extend slurs, hairpins, and lines by pressing the spacebar, which will extend the slur, hairpin, or line to the right. If you go too far and need to step back, use Shift+spacebar to retract the slur, hairpin, or line.

We're still in the Create section of this book, and it's going to take another chapter after this one to get through all the wonderful creations you can add to your scores. This chapter will add the next level of score elements for you: expression markings, slurs, hairpins, symbols, lines, and rehearsal markings. As always, anything you can create is found in the Create menu.

Creating Expression Markings

In Sibelius, *expression markings* are a text style that you can add from the Create menu. Expression markings instruct the player about dynamics and other performance-based instructions. These always have an *italicized* text style. Because expression markings are a text style, you need to select Create > Text > Expression, which has the shortcut Ctrl+E (Windows) or Command+E (Mac). You can add an expression marking in two ways, and this depends on the current selection.

If you have a note already selected when you create the expression text (either from the Create menu or from the key command), the expression text will attach to that note. If you haven't selected a note, when you add the expression text, your mouse pointer will glow a color (depending on what voice you're in), and you'll have to click on the note to which you want to attach the expression text.

After you've added the expression text, you might notice that nothing much happens! Adding expression text gives you a text box with a blinking black cursor. This text box has a great secret, called a *word menu*, which contains all the typical expression text that you'll need to attach to any score. To access the word menu, you have to right-click (Control-click on a Mac) inside the text box that you create. Doing so brings up what you see in Figure 4.1.

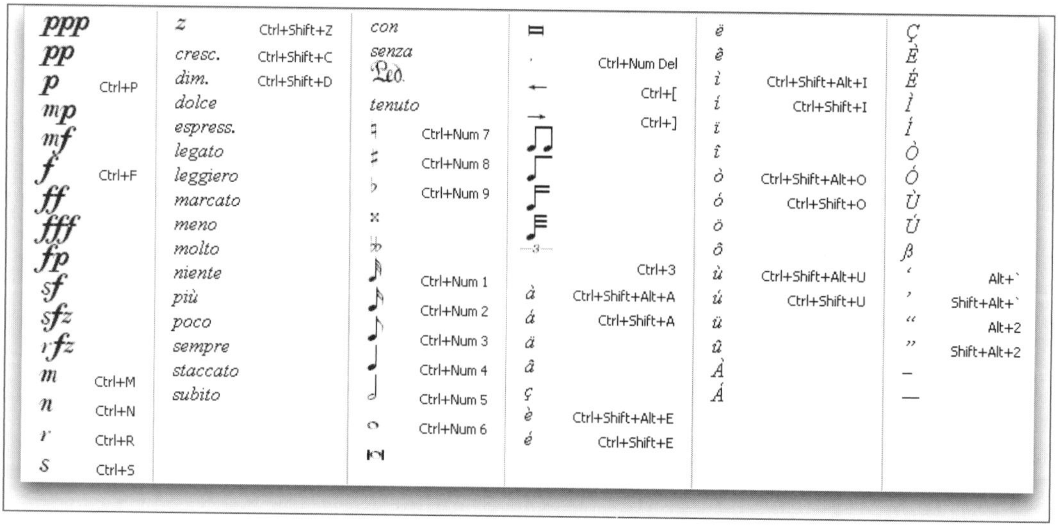

Figure 4.1 The Expression word menu.

As you can see, pretty much everything you'll ever need is in this word menu. Simply select the dynamic or expression marking (such as legato) from the list and press Escape to get back to your score. Figure 4.2 shows all the possible expression markings available to you in Sibelius.

Figure 4.2   Expression markings.

Because you can combine dynamics such as *sfz*, there are several dynamic markings you can make from the available dynamics. You can pull up the word menu at any time to add more dynamics. For example, if you wanted to build a mezzo piano dynamic, access the word menu and add a single mezzo marking, and before you leave the window, access the word menu again to add the piano.

Pasting Dynamics You can copy and paste any element in your score (in this case, a dynamic) by highlighting the dynamic and Alt/Option-clicking. Wherever you click, you'll get a copy of the original dynamic(s).

Essential Tip: Super-Click If you Alt/Option-click to copy, the dynamic may not go to the normal "default" position. Instead of just Alt/Option-clicking, hold down Shift while you Alt/Option-click, and the object will go right to its default position automatically. This is a *really* great tip that will make the art of copying anything in your score much faster because you won't have to align anything.

CD: Use Example 4.1 to copy some preexisting dynamics to a few spots in the example score.

Expression Placement

All expression marks automatically go to the right place. The right place is dictated, of course, by the instrument for which you're writing. Here's a quick rundown of the correct positions for expression text:

- **Instrumental staves (except piano).** Dynamics go below the staff.

- **Piano.** Dynamics go between the staves when the dynamics apply to both hands. They go under each individual staff when the dynamics differ from hand to hand.

- **Vocal staves.** Dynamics go above the staff to leave room for the lyrics below the staff.

It's very important to note that the correct position of the expression depends on the manuscript paper you choose. This has to do with a program setting called *Default Positions*. In vocal scores (with vocal manuscript paper), expressions are set to go above the staff automatically, so that they don't interfere with the lyrics. On instrumental-based manuscript papers, expressions go below the staff, because this is normal practice.

They Play Back! All of the standard dynamic markings will play back in Sibelius. The text-based expression markings for crescendo and diminuendo will not play back because Sibelius isn't sure how much louder or softer to get. You'd want to use a hairpin (which you can hide) if you needed the score to play back properly with just the expression text. Hairpins are detailed later in this chapter, in the "Creating Hairpins" section.

Creating New Expression Styles

As detailed in the previous section, Sibelius places its expression markings based on a program setting called Default Positions, which is saved in each and every manuscript paper. In vocal scores the default is set to above the staff, while in instrumental scores the default goes below the staff. Unfortunately, this doesn't guarantee that your expressions will go in the right place. Here is an example: Suppose you are scoring for vocals and a few solo instruments. You'd start out with a vocal-based manuscript paper and add additional instruments to the mix. Because you started with a vocal paper, the default position of expressions is above the staff, which is good for vocals but may not be good for instrumental parts. You might say, "Okay, I'll just drag those expression markings to the correct spot when I need to." That's fine, but when you get to the section of the book that deals with formatting, you might find yourself changing elements of the page to suit the overall layout. One side effect of this is that objects might need to "reset" themselves, and they will do this to their default positions, which will completely override the manual tweaking you just did. So, in short, you don't want to drag anything in Sibelius if you don't have to. There is a better way to do this.

We're going to create some new text styles—Expression Above and Expression Below. These text styles will deal with those times when you need to force the objects up or down. This is not documented explicitly in the Sibelius reference. (Creating text styles and positions is covered, but not the idea of this as a fix for default positions. Ideally, a future version of Sibelius will simply get the expression in the correct position based on the type of staff, not the type of score.)

This is not a difficult fix, and once you do these steps, you can save it as a House Style, which you can import into any score. We're getting into the deeper parts of the program for this, but have no fear—it's easy to follow!

1. Select House Style > Edit Text Styles. You will see the Edit Text Styles dialog box shown in Figure 4.3.

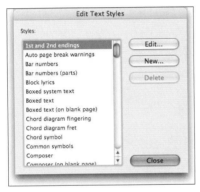

Figure 4.3   The Edit Text Styles dialog box.

2. Scroll down to Expression in the list of available text styles. Highlight this option and click the New button on the right side of the dialog box. Doing so will bring up the message box shown in Figure 4.4, asking whether you want to create a new text style based on the existing style. Click Yes.

3. With the newly created text style highlighted (which it is by default after creation), click the Edit button on the right side of the dialog box. This will bring up the Staff Text Style dialog box. There are many options here, but you only need to do one thing: Change the name of the style from Expressions (2) to Expression Above and click OK, as shown in Figure 4.5.

4. Now that you're back to the Edit Text Styles dialog box, complete Steps 2 and 3 again. This time, save the new text style as Expression Below.

    Now that you've created the new text styles, you need to edit the default positions and tell Sibelius where you want the dynamic markings to go every time you add them.

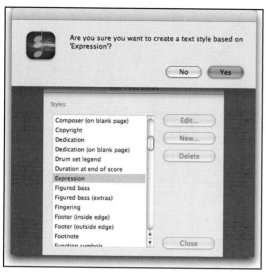

Figure 4.4   Create a new text style.

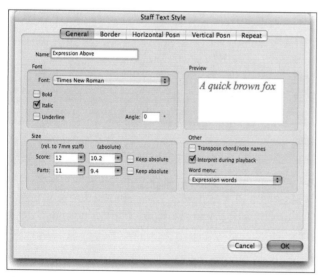

Figure 4.5   Renaming your text style.

5.   Select House Style > Default Positions, which will bring up the rather large Default Positions dialog box shown in Figure 4.6.

6.   In the list of text styles on the left side of the screen, navigate to Expression Above and highlight it. Select Above Top of Staff in the Creating Text section of the dialog box, as shown in Figure 4.7.

7.   Without leaving the dialog box, navigate to the Expression Below entry and change its location to Below Bottom of Staff. Click OK to leave the dialog box.

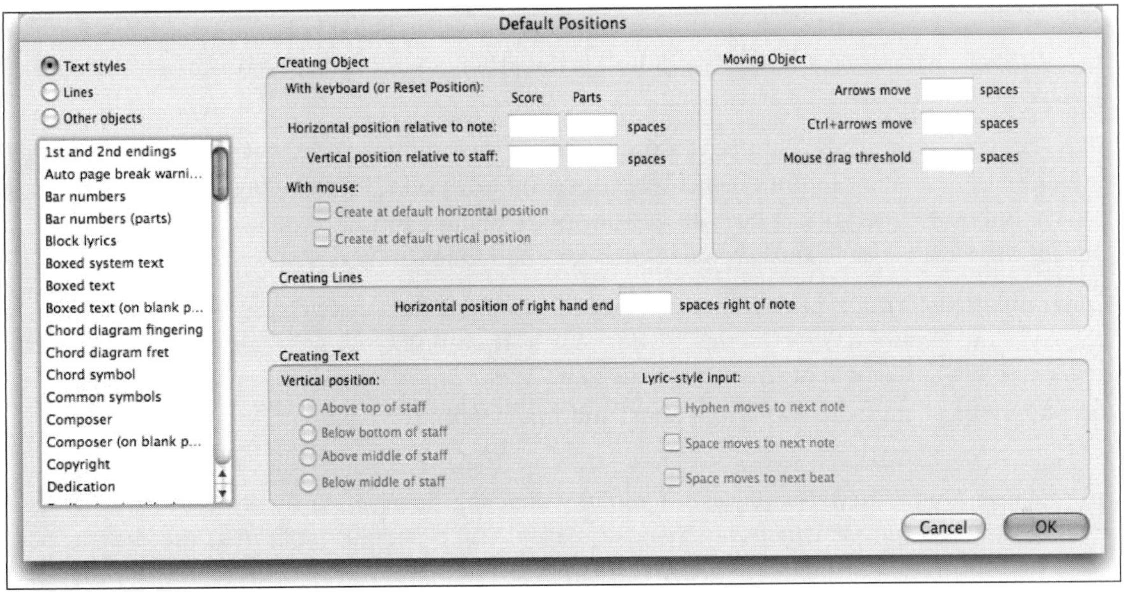

Figure 4.6 The Default Positions dialog box.

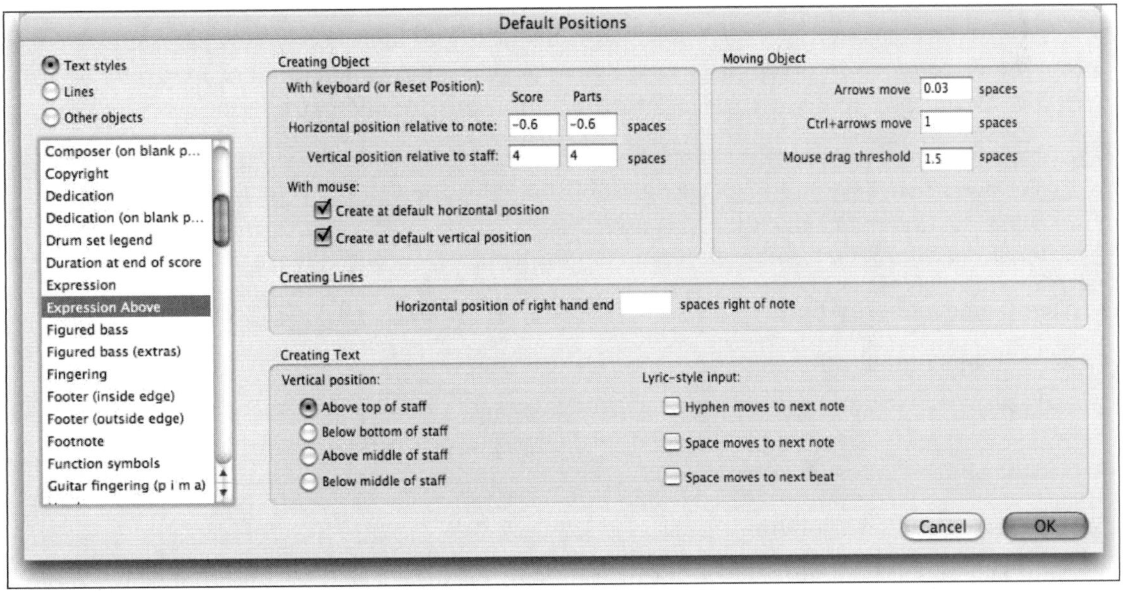

Figure 4.7 Moving the text above the staff.

8.   Select House Style > Export House Style. A Save As dialog box will appear, asking you to name your new House Style. Call it something akin to Expression Up and Down and click OK.

That's it—you're finished! You have now created a new House Style that gives you two additional text styles. You can import this House Style at any point, to any score, by selecting House Style > Import House Style. You will see your newly named House Style in the list for selection. During the New Score wizard, you can also use the House Style if you think you need it.

Congratulations! You've just custom-configured, renamed, and changed the default position of a text style and exported it for use in all your scores. It doesn't get any better than this—you can customize Sibelius as you need to. If the program is not doing what you want, there is always a mechanism to change the way it operates, and this is only the beginning!

Where Are the New Text Styles? If you're wondering how to use these neat new text styles, they appear when you choose Create > Text > Other Staff Text. By default they don't have keyboard shortcuts, but that's easy enough to do and is well-documented in the Sibelius reference (in your Help menu).

CD: Use Example 4.2 to create a new text style and place some dynamics below the instrumental stave.

Expression Shortcuts

Once you've brought up the expression word box with the blinking cursor, you don't have to access the word menu in order to place a dynamic. The following shortcuts are available from within the word box to greatly speed up the creation of dynamic markings.

Windows/Mac Keys In the following list of shortcuts, the Ctrl key is for Windows users, while the Command key is for Mac users.

- Ctrl/Command+F = Forte

- Ctrl/Command+P = Piano

- Ctrl/Command+M = Mezzo

- Ctrl/Command+N = Niente

- Ctrl/Command+S = Subito

- Shift+Ctrl+Z (Windows) or Shift+Command+Z (Mac) = The little z symbol whose name I can't quite figure out

- Shift+Ctrl+C (Windows) or Shift+Command+Z (Mac) = Crescendo
- Shift+Ctrl+D (Windows) or Shift+Command+Z (Mac) = Diminuendo

For example, to place the following forte in Figure 4.8, all you need to do is the following:

1. Select the C so that it's highlighted.

2. Press Ctrl/Command+E to enter an expression text. (You could also choose Create > Text > Expression.)

3. Immediately press Ctrl/Command+F.

Figure 4.8 Simple dynamic creation.

CD: Play with Example 4.3 to practice using the shortcuts for dynamic creation.

As you can see, using key commands greatly speeds up your efforts in Sibelius. Accessing the word menu to do the same thing would have taken more steps, a mouse click, plus sorting through a menu. This was very fast! Try to learn at least these shortcuts, because it's hard to find scores without dynamic markings!

Copying Dynamic Markings

Dynamic markings and expression text are good examples of a "staff text" style. This means that when the dynamics appear in your score, they attach to a single note on a single staff. It also means that if you have a marking that will affect multiple staves, you have to copy it to the other staves manually. There are two ways to do this.

This first method is used when all of your staves contain the same dynamic at the same rhythmic beat/time in your score. If this is the case, follow these steps for a multi-copy. Use Figure 4.9 as an example. You'll learn how to place a mezzo piano marking on all five staves at once.

1. Enter a single dynamic on a single stave. (It doesn't matter which one, but the bottom is usually a good one.)

2. Select the dynamic and copy it using Ctrl+C (Windows) or Command+C (Mac) or by choosing Edit > Copy.

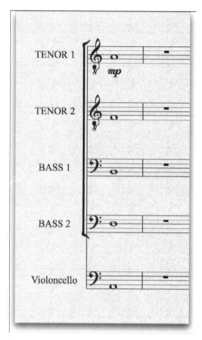

Figure 4.9 Before multi-copy.

3.   Drag a vertical selection box around the beat on which you want to place your dynamic. Make sure the selection box grabs all the staves at once. To make a vertical selection box, hold down Ctrl (Windows) or Command (Mac) while you click and drag your mouse. This will create a selection box that you can reposition as necessary. The visible blue selection box will show you what notes are being selected, and you can reposition this to make your selection more exact.

4.   Finally, paste using Ctrl+V (Windows) or Command+V (Mac) or by selecting Edit > Paste.

Selection Box By default, when you click and drag your mouse in a Sibelius score, you drag the paper (or whichever object you're touching at the moment). To create a selection box, you had to add the modifier key of Shift (Windows)/Command(Mac) to make a selection, instead of dragging the paper. You can change this so that the operations are reversed (in other words, click and drag makes a selection box, while Shift/Command drags the paper). To do so, go to Preferences > Mouse and change the Dragging the Paper option from Drag to Hold Command and Drag. This will let you click and drag to create selection boxes by default.

You should now have a successful multi-copy, with each of the staves containing the same dynamic. It should look something like Figure 4.10.

Figure 4.10   After multi-copy.

The other way to quickly copy dynamics (and, by extension, anything in a score) is to Alt-click (Windows) or Option-click (Mac).

Alt/Option-clicking automatically copies whatever is previously selected to the location that you click. It's really important that dynamic markings follow the correct default positions, and normal Alt/Option-clicking doesn't do that, so you'll want to super-click using Shift+Alt/Option-click to completely ensure that copied markings default to their correct positions. Follow the steps below to copy the dynamic marking already in your score to other locations.

1.   Select the dynamic you want to copy. Select *only* the dynamic, nothing more.

2.   Hold down the Shift+Alt/Option keys.

3.   With the keys still held down, click on the place in the score where you want to paste the expression marking.

4.   With the keys still held down, click on any other notes to which you want to apply the same dynamic.

5.   Press Escape to deselect the selection, and you're finished.

Power Copy The Alt/Option-click method to copy objects in Sibelius is a fast, powerful feature. You can use it to quickly copy large sections of music, text, and symbols. You can copy anything you can select using this method, including multi-measure selections. Just click and go.

Some of your dynamics might be a bit misaligned if you use this method. To alleviate this, read the next section on alignment.

CD: Use Example 4.4 for a multi-copy dynamic example. You'll get to try both the regular Alt/Option-click and the super Shift+Alt/Option-click!

Repositioning and Alignment

You can easily reposition expression markings by dragging them with your mouse. For finer movements, use the arrow keys on your keyboard. If you start to drag an expression marking too far, it might join to the next note because each expression text is joined to a particular note or a staff. How can you tell where the expression mark is joined? Make sure View Attachments is selected in the View menu. Once that's set, click on the expression in question, and you'll see a small dashed line pointing to the attached note, as shown in Figure 4.11.

Figure 4.11   Attachment line.

Zoom for Clarity You may want to zoom in a fair amount to see the attachment lines clearly.

If the dynamic is attached to the wrong note, it will play back at the wrong spot. So, if you find your score playing back oddly, this is something you might want to check.

If you used the Alt/Option-click method of copying expression markings, you might be left with a bunch of dynamics that aren't properly aligned. (You should have used Shift+Alt/Option-click instead, because it would have ensured proper positioning, but that's okay—maybe you didn't write the music.) This is easy to clean up because Sibelius gives you some great layout tools. Look at Figure 4.12 for an example of some badly positioned expression markings.

Figure 4.12   Misaligned expression markings (intentionally misaligned badly).

To fix this, use the following steps:

1.   Drag a selection box around all of the dynamics that are misaligned.

2.   With the dynamics selected and highlighted, choose Layout > Align in a Row.

You'll end up with what is shown in Figure 4.13.

Figure 4.13   Correctly aligned dynamics.

Your dynamics are now exactly aligned in a row. If you find that the dynamics are too close to or too far from the staff, use your arrow keys to move them where you want them. As long as you haven't pressed Escape or clicked something else, the dynamics will stay selected together, so any movements you make will happen together, and the dynamics will continue to be aligned. If you lost your selection somehow, just reselect the dynamics.

CD: Use Example 4.5 to align some badly misaligned dynamics.

Vertical Alignment

If you need to align dynamics vertically, such as dynamics in a larger score or between multiple staves, follow these simple steps to remedy a score that looks like Figure 4.14.

1.   Instead of making a vertical selection box, you need to make a *nonadjacent selection,* which is a fancy term for a simple thing—selecting only the objects you click on, and not the ones in between. A vertical selection box will grab the expressions, but also the notes, articulations, symbols, slurs, and so on. You only want to work with the dynamics, so hold down Ctrl (Windows) or Command (Mac) and individually click on each dynamic in the vertical row you want to align.

2.   Select Layout > Align in a Column.

Figure 4.14   Vertical misalignment.

The end result should look like Figure 4.15.

CD: Use Example 4.6 to practice not only making a noncontiguous (nonadjacent) selection, but also vertically aligning dynamics.

Essential Tip: Word Menus Don't forget that when you start any text style in Sibelius and you see a blinking cursor, you have a word menu available to you if you just right-click (Windows) or Control-click (Mac) on the blinking cursor.

Figure 4.15   Perfect alignment!

I should note that dynamics typically align themselves perfectly when they are entered. The only time they might get misaligned is when you move them by hand or you use the Alt/Option-click copy method. No matter how you slice it, it's very easy to fix.

Yet Another Way Another way to select only the dynamics/expression markings in your score is to use the Edit > Filter command. Make a selection (even a vertical selection) that contains more than just expression markings and select Edit > Filter > Expression Text or Edit > Filter > Dynamics (depending on what you want to filter), and only those objects will remain selected. The filter is very powerful! You'll learn more on that as we progress through the book, but don't be afraid to poke around the Edit > Filter menu.

Creating Technique Markings

Technique markings encompass the gamut of instrument-specific instructions you'd give to a player. The common technique markings are pizz. and arco., although there are many more. Technique text is always a plain text style that aligns itself above the staff. It's also another example of staff text, because it is attached to a specific note/staff. In addition, technique texts will play back thanks to Sibelius 5's excellent playback system that correctly reads technique markings.

To create technique text, navigate to Create > Text > Technique or use the shortcut Ctrl+T (Windows) or Command+T (Mac). You can add technique text in two ways, which of course depends on the current selection.

If you have a note already selected when you create the technique text (either from the Create menu or from the key command), the expression text will attach to that note. If you haven't selected a note when you add the technique text, your mouse will glow a color (depending on what voice you're in), and you'll have to click on the note to which you want to attach the expression text.

When you've clicked in to add technique text, you might notice that nothing much happens! Adding technique text gives you a text box with a blinking black cursor. Once again, you will see the word menu, which contains all the typical technique text you'll need to attach to any score. To access the word menu, right-click (Windows) or Control-click (Mac) inside the text box that you create. Doing so brings up the menu shown in Figure 4.16.

Figure 4.16   The technique text word menu.

CD: Use Example 4.7 to practice adding some technique text to a score.

One thing that's different about the technique text is this: Because technique text is always plain text, and none of the entries have shortcuts, you can just type the text in as you need it.

Reuse The previous section on expression text went into great detail about copying, pasting, and aligning expression text. For efficiency's sake, I'm not going to rehash the details here in the technique text section. Everything you read in the previous section applies not only to technique text, but also to Sibelius as a whole. Take a step back and realize that you can now copy, paste, select (including noncontiguous items), and align material in a row and a column!

Technique Playback

The items that you find in the technique word menu will play back in Sibelius automatically. Sibelius has gone to great lengths to make sure that the majority of technique text markings do, in fact, play back properly in the program. Sibelius can do this because it has a Playback Dictionary where it stores all the words and symbols it's going to read and how it will play them back. You can take a look at what Sibelius knows how to play back by selecting Play > Dictionary (see Figure 4.17).

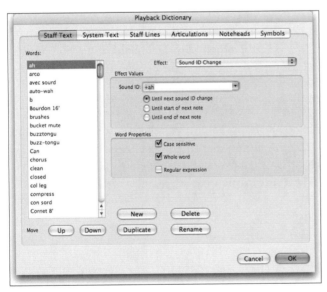

Figure 4.17   The Playback Dictionary.

We've dealt with staff text at this point, so make sure you select the Staff Text page from the Playback Dictionary window. Along the left side is the collection of words that Sibelius will recognize. It's possible to add words to this menu and teach Sibelius how to play them back. We will look at this in more detail later in this book, when we deal with the playback system as a whole.

The reason why you're even poking around in this menu is to show you what's going to play back automatically and what won't. The Playback Dictionary dictates this. So, if you're wondering why Slap Side of Guitar has no playback effect, you'll know why! Users who have experience in audio samples and MIDI can very easily create entries into the Dictionary that have an actual effect on Sibelius's playback. That being said, if you have no intention of using the playback engine or you don't care about accurate playback of every little element of your score, just add your technique text so that it looks right in your score, and don't worry about how it's going to play back.

Technique for Others In addition to using technique markings for traditional instructions, use technique text in your score for a wide variety of text. Too many users opt for Create > Text > Other Staff Text > Plain Text, which lacks a shortcut. Go ahead and use technique text because it has a shortcut key and thus is faster.

Creating Slurs

Slurs in Sibelius are one of the most intuitive aspects of the program. Technically, a *slur* is considered a *line* in Sibelius, but because slurs are common symbols, I'll cover them in this separate section. You won't find a clear entry in the Create menu called Slur. (As I said, it's a line, and it exists in the Line menu.) Thankfully, the key command is great. You want a slur? Just press S. Nothing else needed. S is for slur!

Slurs are created with the S key, but, as always, selections are very important. If you begin with a single note selected and press S, the slur will start at the note you've selected and extend to the next note to the right. To move the slur to the right, simply tap the spacebar. Each spacebar tap will advance the slur by one note to the right. Tap the spacebar as many times as you need to make the slur the proper duration. Figure 4.18 shows some nicely created slurs.

Figure 4.18   Magnetic slurs.

Retracing Slurs If you go one note too far, press Shift+spacebar, and the slur will back up one note to the left.

Here are a couple of things to note about slurs:

- Slurs automatically draw their arc based on the number of notes they span.
- Slurs always avoid stems and will automatically reposition themselves as your draw them.

■ Slurs can be flipped manually using the same technique as flipping a stem, using the X key once you've selected the slur.

If you have a range of notes selected, you can simply press S, and the slur will automatically draw itself over the selected notes. Slurs are very easy to deal with in Sibelius.

CD: Use Example 4.8 to practice adding some single slurs and extending them by hand, as well as some pre-selection–based slurs.

Slur, Phrase Marking, and Tie Although a player may interpret the terms "slur" and "phrase marking" differently, Sibelius does not. They are one and the same because they are the same symbol. However, a tie is a totally different thing (a tie connects notes of the same pitch to combine their rhythmic values), and Sibelius indeed considers them totally separate things. Please don't confuse them!

Other Ways to Select Notes

There's a few ways to select notes and selections in Sibelius. We've covered a few common techniques in this book, but here is a new one that is particularly useful when you are working with individual notes.

To start, select any single note (which will be colored depending on the voice it's in). Then, hold down the Shift key and click the right or left arrow key. This will extend a selection box one note at a time. When you create slurs and other objects that might only affect a minimal number of notes, you might like this selection method.

Another method is to use the Shift-click trick: Click the first note of a phrase (or selection), hold down Shift, and select the *last* note of the selection. Sibelius will automatically select all the notes in between.

Shift-Click for Measures The Shift-click trick for selecting a range of notes works perfectly for a range of measures. Click the first measure, hold down Shift, and click the last measure, and Sibelius will select all of the measures in between.

If you make your selection across a system of music, on multiple instruments, Sibelius will select all of the measures on all instruments!

Couple this with the measure and multiple-measure selection techniques you learned earlier, and you'll have a powerful system to deal with selections, no matter what their size.

Creating Hairpins

What's a hairpin? It is another term for a crescendo/diminuendo marking. It's more of a European term, and many Americans aren't aware of it. In any case, Figure 4.19 shows a hairpin.

Figure 4.19   A hairpin.

Drawing hairpins is very easy to do, just like drawing slurs. The key command to create a hairpin is H—another one of Sibelius's simple single-key shortcuts.

By default, the hairpin created with the H key is a crescendo marking. To add a diminuendo (see Figure 4.20), the key command is Shift+H.

Figure 4.20   A diminuendo.

As always, the way you select notes affects how your hairpins will appear. If you select a single note and then add the hairpin (either type), the hairpin will only last for the note you've selected. You can extend it to the right by pressing the spacebar to extend it a note at a time. If you go too far, hold down the Shift key while pressing the spacebar, and the hairpin will retract one note to the right.

If you pre-select a group of notes and then select a hairpin (either type), the hairpin will be drawn exactly the correct length for you. Remember that there are several ways to select ranges of notes—use the one that you like the best.

CD: Use Example 4.9 to create some crescendo and diminuendo lines in a score.

Position and Playback

Hairpins have their own default position below the staff. If you need to reposition them, you can drag them with your mouse or simply use the arrow keys for finer control. If you have a row of hairpins—especially hairpins with dynamic markings after them that collide with stems—you might need to align them in a row by selecting Format > Align in a Row, which will work wonders on something like what you see in Figure 4.21.

Creating Lines

In the previous section, I discussed slurs and hairpins as being part of a larger family of notations that Sibelius calls *lines*. Lines are accessible by choosing Create > Lines or by using the L key command. Either of these actions will bring up the Lines dialog box you see in Figure 4.22.

Figure 4.21 Misaligned hairpins.

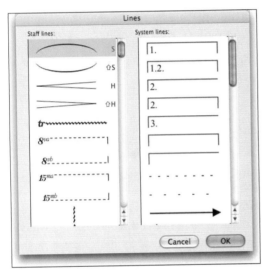

Figure 4.22 The Lines dialog box.

Lines fall into two categories—staff lines and system lines.

Essential Tip: Lines Pre-Selection Lines—which encompass slurs, hairpins, endings, and all sorts of things you can find by choosing Create > Lines—work great on pre-selected music. If you have a range of notes/measures selected and you go to add the line, Sibelius will draw the line to exactly the correct length!

Staff Lines

In the Lines dialog box, the lines are separated into two columns, with staff lines on the left and system lines on the right. Staff lines attach themselves to a single staff and encompass a pretty large category of lines, such as slurs, hairpins, trills, piano pedaling, octave markings (8va), and guitar-specific lines to specify techniques, as well as generic symbols, such as dashed lines and brackets found in modern notation.

Placing staff lines works the same way as placing most other objects in Sibelius.

- If you have nothing selected before you press L, Sibelius will load the cursor with the line, and you'll have to click the line in the score to place it. You can extend the line to the right by pressing the spacebar. If you go too far and you need to retract the line, use the Shift+spacebar key command. You can also use your mouse to reposition and extend lines.

- If you have a single note selected before you press L, once you select the line, Sibelius will start the line on the note you selected. You can extend it to the right by pressing the spacebar. If you go too far and you need to retract the line, use the Shift-spacebar key command. You can also use your mouse to reposition and extend lines.

- If you have a passage selected before you press L, Sibelius will place the line over the notes you've selected. You should not need to retract or extend the line using this method. You can also use your mouse to move lines around.

System Lines

The main difference between a staff line and a system line is how a system line appears on a page. A staff line attaches on a single staff. A system line attaches to the topmost staff in your score and automatically propagates itself to the other staves in your score—but it won't show you that it's doing this! The full score will always show the single line. However, when you access the Parts window and look at each part, you will see that many of the system lines have appeared there automatically. System lines encompass markings as diverse as first/second repeat lines, rit and accel lines, and any manner of dashed and solid lines.

Larger Scores In larger scores, such as orchestral scores, system lines show themselves more than once. This is common notational practice in a large score, and you will see staff lines repeat above the strings in much the same way that tempo text appears automatically, for example.

Placing System Lines

System lines place themselves in the score a bit differently than staff lines. The main difference is that you *can't* use the spacebar to extend system lines or the Shift+spacebar command to retract system lines. System lines still work with selections, just as staff lines do, but you have to reposition them with the mouse or by clicking on the small blue box at the end of the line, as shown in Figure 4.23. (The blue box is pretty small, even on the screen, because it won't show at higher zoom levels.)

Figure 4.23 Editing handle.

After you've selected the handle, you can drag it out with your mouse or use the arrow keys to extend or contract the selection. If you're using the arrow keys, you can hold down Ctrl (Windows) or Command (Mac) to make the line move farther for each keystroke.

Repeat Marking Playback

One of the nice parts about notation with Sibelius is how many markings will play back. Repeat markings/endings are a special case. As you can see in Figure 4.24, there are two different 2nd endings.

Figure 4.24   Different endings.

So, what's the difference? Sibelius has to distinguish between a 2nd ending in which you keep playing and a 2nd ending in which you repeat to 3rd ending, and so on. Because of this, you need to make sure you use the correct kind of rending line for your score. Ending lines that terminate with a "hook," as shown in Figure 4.25, will play back and repeat.

Figure 4.25   Hooked repeat.

Any ending line that is "open" and does not have a hook, such as the ending line shown in Figure 4.26, will not repeat—Sibelius will keep going!

Figure 4.26   Unhooked ending line.

As a side note: Not only will this make Sibelius play back properly, it's also common notation practice, so you should get it right anyway!

Power Tip When you are placing system lines, try this tip to paint them on: Do not select anything before you choose Create > Lines and select your favorite system line. Then, click and hold the mouse button and drag to the right in one action. Click and drag without letting go, and you'll paint the system line to the proper length in one fluid action.

CD: Use Example 4.10 to practice adding a bunch of different staff and system lines to a score, both with and without pre-selection.

Creating Symbols

The term *symbols* encompasses all the musical symbols you find in Sibelius, consolidated into one window. You can access the Symbol dialog box by choosing Create > Symbol or by using the key command Z. Using either method brings up the Symbol dialog box shown in Figure 4.27.

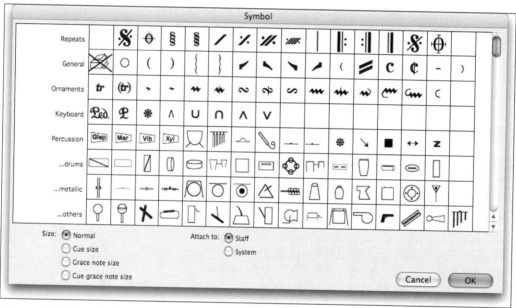

Figure 4.27   The Symbol dialog box.

In this massive dialog box, you see all the symbols subcategorized by type. There are hundreds of different symbols available, and you can even create your own. The Sibelius Reference (built into Sibelius through the Help menu) is really good about detailing exactly how to do this, so consult it for more information if you need to add a symbol not currently listed in Sibelius.

To create a symbol, you should first select the note to which the symbol will attach, and then choose Create > Symbol or press Z.

Each symbol has options for size and attachment:

- **Normal.** Normal size.

- **Cue size.** The size of a cue note—smaller than normal size.

- **Grace note size.** Smaller yet.

- **Cue grace note size.** The smallest available.

- **Attach to Staff.** The symbol will attach to only a single staff.

- **Attach to System.** The symbol will attach to the system and appear in the parts accordingly.

Symbols don't play back by default unless you get into the Playback Dictionary to define them, so in general, the Symbol dialog box is intended for non-playback graphical items.

The other great thing about symbols is that you have the option to attach them to a system. Fermatas are added on the F11/fourth keypad layout by default, and they only attach to a single staff. However, using the Symbol dialog box allows you to add a fermata to a system, disseminating to each and every stave in your score.

Symbols also give you access to graphical notation symbols not easily found in the program, including my personal favorite: the eyeglasses, or "Pay Attention," symbol shown in Figure 4.28. Where else are you going to find stuff like this?

Figure 4.28   Pay attention!

There's not much more to say about symbols!

CD: Use Example 4.11 to add some common symbols to a score.

Creating Rehearsal Markings

To round out this chapter, I'll conclude with rehearsal markings. You can create rehearsal markings by choosing Create > Rehearsal Mark or by pressing Ctrl+R (Windows) or Command+R (Mac).

This is *really* important: Choosing Create > Rehearsal Mark is different than using the key command associated with it. If you select Create > Rehearsal Mark, you will get the Rehearsal Mark dialog box of options, as shown in Figure 4.29.

Figure 4.29 The Rehearsal Mark dialog box.

This dialog box provides you with a great deal of flexibility in terms of how your rehearsal marks are created and placed onscreen. Let's go over the available options:

- **Consecutive.** This option will create a consecutive rehearsal marking. As you continue to add marks, they will automatically advance in number or letter (depending on how they are set up—more on this later in this chapter).

- **Start At.** This option is for creating a new sequence of rehearsal marks. For example, if you have preexisting markings in your score and you want to start the sequence over, you can specify to restart at A, and the subsequent marks will follow suit.

- **New Prefix/Suffix.** This option is for creating custom numbering/lettering schemes in your score, such as A1 or 1A.

If you use the Ctrl+R (Windows) or Command+R (Mac) shortcut, Sibelius will only provide a consecutive rehearsal mark for you. If you want other options, you need to use the Create menu for those. Because most composers commonly use the consecutive rehearsal markings, they are initiated by the key command to save time.

What happens when you add your rehearsal mark depends on whether you have something selected in your score, and it doesn't matter which method of invoking the rehearsal marks you choose.

- If you have a note selected in your score, the rehearsal mark will be created on the next barline (to the right).

- If nothing is selected, your mouse pointer will glow, and you can click the rehearsal mark directly onto the barline at which you want it to appear.

When you've added your first marking, it will look something like Figure 4.30.

Just like other special text (tempo and time), rehearsal markings will reappear above instrument sections on larger scores (such as above the strings) and will automatically populate to the individual parts.

Figure 4.30 Your first rehearsal mark.

Smart Markings and Moving

Rehearsal markings are very clever in Sibelius. As you add your markings, they will automatically appear in consecutive order. If you have a selection that contains a few rehearsal marks, like what you see in Figure 4.31, and you remove a rehearsal mark from the middle of the group, the rest will automatically renumber or re-letter as soon as you delete the mark, as shown in Figure 4.32.

Figure 4.31 Rehearsal marks.

Figure 4.32 Automatically renumbered/re-lettered rehearsal marks.

The same holds true when you add a rehearsal mark between two preexisting marks—the subsequent markings will always redraw themselves in the proper order.

You can drag a marking to the right or left, and it will snap automatically to the next barline. As for the vertical position, you can drag the rehearsal marking with your mouse or use the arrow keys to tweak the position up or down.

Default Positions If you find that all your rehearsal markings are coming in at the wrong vertical locations, don't change them all individually. You should visit the House Style > Default Position window to see how Sibelius is drawing the markings. Changing the position there will affect every mark in your score, which is much faster than dragging them individually!

Appearance

The appearance of your rehearsal markings is dictated by the Engraving Rules dialog box, accessed by choosing House Style > Engraving Rules (see Figure 4.33).

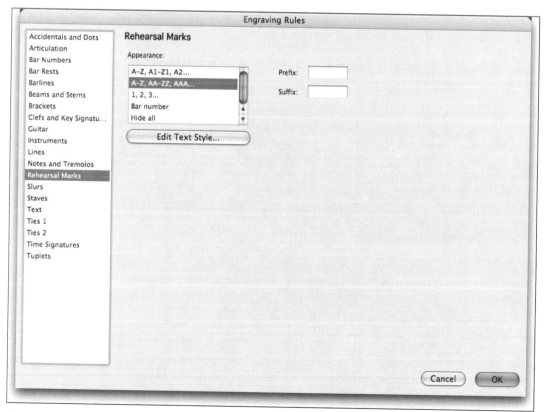

Figure 4.33 The Engraving Rules dialog box.

The Engraving Rules dialog box has multiple pages, accessible from a category list on the left side of the dialog. To access the Rehearsal Marks page, just click the Rehearsal Marks option to select it.

Depending on which manuscript paper you started with, the default appearance is usually A–Z, AA–ZZ, AAA, which is alphabetic. The Engraving Rules dialog box gives you the following options for the appearance of your rehearsal marks:

- **A–Z, A1–Z1, A2.** This pattern will progress through all 26 letters of the alphabet and then use A1 for the 27th, and so on.

- **A–Z, AA–ZZ, AAA.** This pattern will progress through all 26 letters of the alphabet and then use AA for the 27th, and so on.

- **1,2,3.** This pattern will sequentially number rehearsal markings.

- **Bar Number.** This style takes the bar number and places it in the rehearsal marking square.

- **Hide All.** This hides all the rehearsal markings in your score without deleting them.

Remember that engraving rules are global changes for your entire score. Changing a setting here will only affect the currently selected score. If you want to change this for other scores, you'll have to manually adjust the engraving rules or create a House Style based on these changes and either import it into your preexisting scores or save it in a blank score as part of a manuscript paper, so that it's available when you create new scores.

Custom Creating your own custom manuscript paper is detailed in Chapter 17, "Customizing Sibelius."

CD: Use Example 4.12 and follow the instructions for creating, deleting, and changing the appearance of rehearsal markings.

5 Creating Everything Else

Essential Tips for Chapter 5

There aren't too many Essential Tips for this chapter!

1. It's much quicker to use the Align Lyrics plug-in than to go to the trouble of aligning lyrics by hand.

2. When you're creating multiple lines of lyrics, make sure to use different lyric styles for each line (such as Lyrics Line 1, Lyrics Line 2, and so on).

3. When dealing with lyrics, you'll probably need more room between staves and systems. Don't ever drag staves! Go to House Style > Engraving Rules > Staves and increase the distance between staves and systems to make more room.

4. Never, ever drag a barline.

5. If you need to make a measure wider, you can nudge it by pressing Shift+Alt / Option while using the arrow keys.

By now, you can see why the Create menu is the central hub for adding musical material to your scores. It's taken about three chapters to detail all the important functions of the Create menu, and while my goal isn't to explain every single entry (the Sibelius reference does an amazing job of that), I want to go over the elements that most musicians employ on a daily basis. This chapter is largely based on adding text-based elements to your score, such as lyrics. We'll also deal with a few lesser-known elements of the Create menu, such as adding graphics and highlighting sections of music for reference.

Creating Lyrics

In the previous chapter, we dealt with some text, mostly in the form of expression, technique, and dynamic markings, but Sibelius provides you with the ability to create a great deal of other text for your score. The place to look is, of course, in the Create menu—choose Create > Text.

When most people think of text in a musical score, they think of lyrics. Sibelius provides you with a few different ways to enter lyrics. First, you can enter them word for word using some simple keystrokes for syllables and melismas; this makes text entry very fast. Sibelius will align the words to each note and keep the lyrics properly spaced. The second method is to take pre-existing text from a text file (such as a poem, sonnet, or other text) and have Sibelius paste it onto your music, automatically breaking the words into proper syllables as you go. (It does this automatically in five languages!) You can also paste blocks of text from a Word document (that is, *not* lyrics). There are many things you can do with Sibelius.

Let's start with some simple lyric entry.

Simple Lyric Entry

To get started, you'll want to have a score with your vocal melodies already entered. Lyrics attach to notes, so without notes, it's impossible to add lyrics. Ideally, you'll want to work with one of the pre-built vocal-based manuscript papers that you find in the New Score wizard. For this example, I have a single, solo voice (an alto) in a lead sheet–style, as shown in Figure 5.1.

Figure 5.1 Vocal melody (excerpt).

All the notes are entered already, so we need to add lyrics. First, select Create > Text > Lyrics to access the list of predefined lyric styles shown in Figure 5.2.

As you can see, there are a number of available styles. Most users choose Lyrics Line 1. Because this is a default choice for so many users, Sibelius has assigned the shortcut Ctrl+L (Windows) or Command+L (Mac).

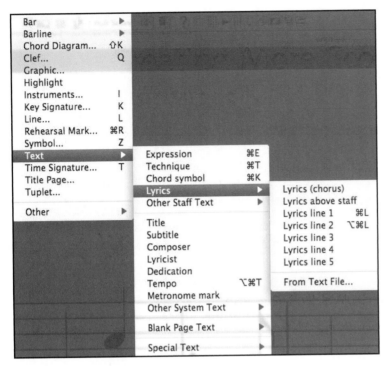

Figure 5.2   Lyric styles.

To start entering lyrics, select the note where your lyrics begin. (The note will glow in color depending on which voice it's entered in.) When the note is selected, call up the lyrics either from the key command or from the Create menu, as detailed a moment ago. Doing so will give you the text entry box with the blinking caret. You can start typing at this point, but here are some things you'll want to know before you get going:

- To hyphenate a word, press the - (dash) key, and Sibelius will insert the hyphen and automatically move you to the next pitch (to the right).

- At the end of a word, press the spacebar, and you will automatically jump to the next pitch in your melody.

- If a word or syllable lasts for multiple notes (called a *melisma*), you can press the hyphen or the spacebar as many times as you need to extend the word note by note.

- Because the spacebar moves the text box to the next note, you need to add punctuation to the word before hitting the spacebar.

Lyrics are fairly painless in this regard. Once you get the flow of entering words, you can just use the hyphen or the spacebar and enter large amounts of work at any given time.

Using this technique, it's easy to add lyrics to the example (see Figure 5.3).

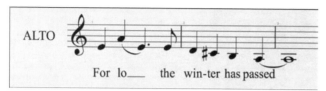

Figure 5.3 Simple lyric entry.

To leave lyric entry, press the Escape key once. This will take you back to "normal" Sibelius and will allow you to enter more music or edit the lyrics you just entered.

Here are a couple of things to keep in mind as you enter lyrics: First, make sure you look while you're entering your lyrics. If you forget a hyphen and your lyrics are misaligned, it's difficult (almost impossible) to fix this after the fact. If you make an error, stop and fix it. In Sibelius 5, there currently is no way to nudge the lyrics over a note, so if you forget a word or a hyphen, you're stuck with either deleting what you've done or copying the lyrics into a "dummy" stave and recopying them back at another location. (More on this in the section called "Copying Lyrics," later in this chapter.)

Second, you can always reenter lyric entry mode at any point, so don't feel as if you have to enter the whole lyric in one shot. One line at a time is fine—press Escape to leave lyric entry mode, and reenter by choosing the note and engaging the key command or selecting Create > Text > Lyrics Line 1.

CD: Use Example 5.1 to copy some lyrics into a simple melody.

Getting Back to a Hyphen If you stop entering notes mid-syllable, you can't just reenter lyrics on the next note—you won't get the appropriate dash. What you'll need to do is edit the last word you entered (the one where you ended mid-syllable), press the hyphen to take you to the next word, and keep going from there.

Additional Verses

If your lyric has a second verse, Sibelius provides you with a text style (Lyrics Line 2) that correctly positions the text below the first verse automatically. Because this is also a widely used text style, Sibelius provides the shortcut Ctrl+Alt+L (Windows) or Command+Option+L (Mac).

Sibelius provides up to five different Lyrics Line N options. You can always add more verses if you need to, by choosing House Style > Edit Text Styles. You'll also notice that the

Create > Text > Lyrics submenu has an entry for Lyrics Above Staff, which aptly places the lyrics above the staff. This style is traditionally used in hymns, in which more than one stave shares the same lyric content (see Figure 5.4), and it is also useful for sections of descant (as shown in the figure).

Figure 5.4   Lyrics above the staff.

In the submenu, you'll also see a Lyrics (Chorus) option, which varies the text style to use italics in the font. This is often used when your second line of music is a translation of the first line.

Custom The shortcuts that ship with Sibelius can be changed! If you make your living setting vocal music, you might want keyboard shortcuts to additional verses of music, for example. You can learn all about how to do this in Chapter 17, "Customizing Sibelius."

CD: Use Example 5.2 to add some different lyric styles (such as lyrics above and second-verse styles).

Lyric Editing

If you make a spelling mistake in your lyric entry, you can always go back and correct errors. To do so, double-click on the word in question; this will bring you back into the editing mode, where you can treat the lyric like any piece of text and backspace and/or replace words as necessary. When you're in the editing mode, you can use the arrow keys to move from word to word if there are other mistakes—this works in either direction.

Non-Breaking Spaces

When you hit the spacebar in Sibelius, it takes you to the next note. What happens when you need to enter a space into a word or a lyric and you *don't* want the word to break? There is a fix for this—non-breaking spaces! A non-breaking space designates that a line of lyrics belongs to a certain verse by placing a 1 (or the proper number) before the first word in the lyric. Here's how you create a non-breaking space (see Figure 5.5).

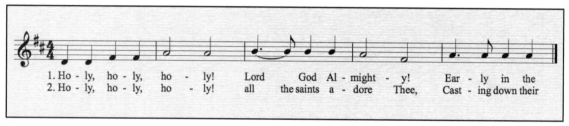

Figure 5.5   Non-breaking space.

Enter "1." and press Ctrl+spacebar (Windows) or Option+spacebar (Mac). This will create a single space so you can type in your first word. Then proceed as normal. If you want more space between the verse number and your first word (although one is typical), simply repeat the key command for a non-breaking space.

Another Use Another use for a non-breaking space is in opera or show music, when you have to identify which character is singing a particular line of music.

Another use for non-breaking spaces is found in vocal music that requires a single held note receive several syllables on the same pitch. This is commonplace in recitatives in opera and in operatic scores (as well as other vocal music on the whole). As you know, pressing the hyphen in this instance would force the caret to the next note, which isn't what you want. You can create a non-breaking hyphen in instances like Figure 5.6.

Figure 5.6   One pitch, many syllables!

To create a non-breaking hyphen, enter the first syllable. Instead of simply pressing the hyphen, press Ctrl+hyphen (Windows) or Option+hyphen (Mac) to create a non-breaking hyphen. Repeat this for as many syllables as your score requires. Note that Sibelius automatically re-spaces the measure to make room for all of the syllables to fit in the bar by creating space before or after the note as needed.

CD: Use Example 5.3 to create non-breaking spaces for scores with multiple verses that you have to number.

Helpful Plug-Ins

A few plug-ins in the Plug-Ins menu can help with vocal-based scores. The following list provides a very brief mention of these selected plug-ins:

- **Plug-Ins > Text > Add Verse Numbers.** This plug-in adds the appropriate verse number to each line of lyrics by placing the verse number before the first word or syllable in your score. This only works when you use a different text style for each line of lyrics. Make sure that you use Lyrics Line *N*, where *N* represents the proper verse number, through Create > Text > Lyrics.

- **Plug-Ins > Text > Align Lyrics.** This plug-in aligns lyrics that are in need of vertical alignment. This is handy if you dragged some lyrics to make room for other objects, and as a result, your score looks sloppy.

- **Plug-Ins > Text > Add Slurs to Lyrics.** When a word is sung over several notes, a slur is usually called for. If you have not added these to your score, this plug-in does it for you automatically.

- **Plug-Ins > Text > Export Lyrics.** This plug-in saves all your lyrics into a text file. It's very handy for program notes!

Plug-ins are very powerful tools and are covered in greater detail later in this book. Remember that if you don't like what a plug-in has done, you can always undo the action by choosing Edit > Undo or pressing Ctrl+Z (Windows) or Command+Z (Mac).

CD: Example 5.4 will let you practice using the helpful plug-ins detailed a moment ago to format your lyrics.

Copying Lyrics

Lyrics can be copied from stave to stave; the tricky part is selecting them! If you have a section of lyrics that you're going to reuse elsewhere in the song and you'd rather not re-type them, you can copy them instead. This is only possible, of course, when the rhythm of the words is the same from staff to staff; otherwise, the syllables and other text would be offset. Assuming that's all set, this is an easy process. You can proceed in one of two ways.

If your music only contains one line of lyrics and you've entered that consistently with Lyrics Line 1 or another consistent text style, follow these instructions:

1. Select the measure(s) that contain the lyrics you want to copy. Doing so will select the music and any attached lyrics, surrounding the measure in blue and the lyrics in whatever color voice they're attached to. If you are selecting the whole line, triple-click the measure; this will select all the measures.

2. Choose Edit > Filter and select Lyrics.

3. Now that only the lyrics are highlighted, copy them by choosing Edit > Copy or by pressing Ctrl+C (Windows) or Command+C (Mac).

4. Select the first note where you'd like to paste the lyrics.

5. Paste them by choosing Edit > Paste or pressing Ctrl+V (Windows) or Command+V (Mac). Another way of pasting is by holding down the Alt/Option key and clicking your mouse.

That's an easy way to go when you're dealing with a single line of lyrics. When you have more than one line of lyrics, you have to tell Sibelius a bit more specifically which line you'd like by using the Advanced Filter. If you followed the aforementioned steps for a score that has more than one line of music, you'd end up with all of the lyrics selected, not necessarily the verse you need. For more control, you need the Advanced Filter, as shown in Figure 5.7.

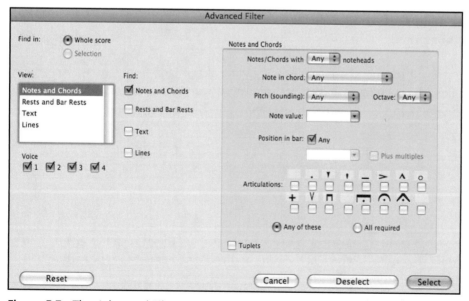

Figure 5.7 The Advanced Filter.

The Edit > Filter menu gives you many choices for filtering all sorts of things, but when it comes to lyrics, you have to take them all. To specify a certain verse or a specific text style, you'll need to use the Advanced Filter. Follow these steps with the example score for visual reference.

1. Select all the measures that contain your lyrics to copy (see Figure 5.8). They will glow with a measure selection. (Remember that you can select the first note, hold down Shift, and click on the last note to make a quick multiple selection.)

2. Navigate to Edit > Filter > Advanced Filter to bring up the Advanced Filter (see Figure 5.9).

3. Make sure that the Text box is selected under the Find section. Then, click the None button below the list of searchable text styles on the right side (see Figure 5.10). Navigate to Lyrics Line 2 or whichever lyric line you want to filter. Your screen should look like Figure 5.10.

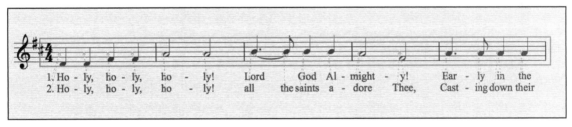

Figure 5.8 Selected measures.

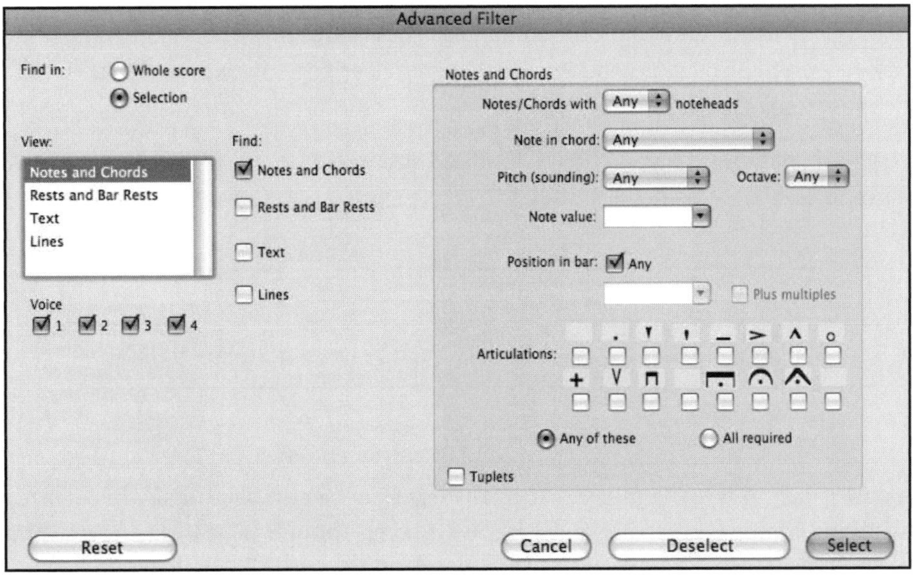

Figure 5.9 Advanced Filter.

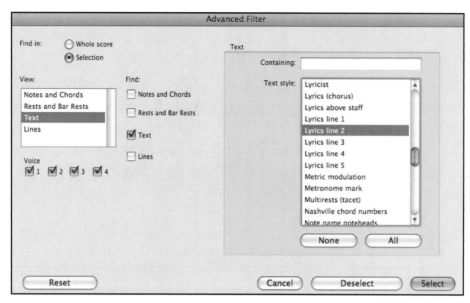

Figure 5.10 Filter configuration.

4.   When you click the Select button, your score will be returned to you with only the requested line of text highlighted. Copy and paste it using the same method referenced in the previous section (Edit > Copy, Edit > Paste.)

---

iForgot If you ever forget which lyric style you used for a particular section or verse, it's easy to figure out! Highlight the text in question and select Window > Properties. In the resulting window, open the Text sub-window. The screen that appears shows you the text style for any currently selected text.

Tip: Even though this window lets you change font and size, resist doing so! If you want to make changes to text, learn to do so through the House Style > Edit Text Style menu option.

CD: Example 5.5 will help you learn to use the filters to copy lyrics from line to line.

Lyrics Layout

Layout is always a tricky part of writing music, especially computer-engraved music. Lyrics are a great spot to start talking about formatting for a moment, even though layout and formatting won't be covered in full detail until Chapter 9, "Document Layout and Formatting."

Creating Space Globally

Here is a very important tip for you: Never drag a stave in Sibelius. You might be very temped to do so, especially when you need to work with multiple lines of lyrics and dynamics and you're simply out of room. Why shouldn't you ever drag a staff? Simply put, Sibelius is supposed to do this for you, and it does an impressive job of layout when it is working with the right parameters. Dragging with your mouse is a rather imprecise action. It's all too easy to end up with uneven spacing between staves, which makes your score look visually awkward. What you want to change is the spacing between staves to let your lyrics sit properly. This is done by choosing House Style > Engraving Rules, which brings up the Engraving Rules dialog box shown in Figure 5.11.

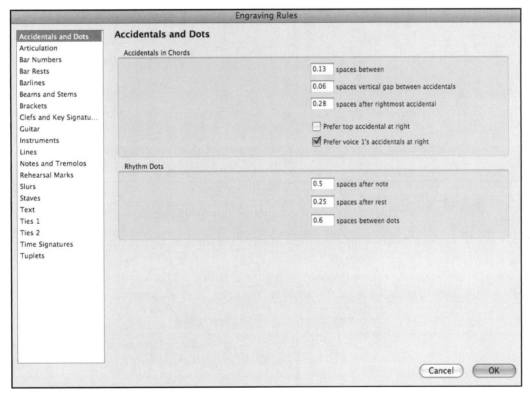

Figure 5.11 The Engraving Rules dialog box.

The Engraving Rules dialog box covers all the visual aspects of the current House Style. On the left-side list, select the Staves option, which will bring up settings and parameters that affect staves (see Figure 5.12).

You're interested in the Layout section, and more specifically the Spaces between Staves option. In the default SATB manuscript paper, Sibelius gives you eight spaces between each stave. This

Engraving Rules

Staves

Layout

5.5	spaces between staves
9.25	spaces between systems

Justification

Justify staves when page is at least [65] % full

System spacings may be contracted to [97] %

Staff Design

Staff line width: [0.1] spaces

Small staff size: [75] % of normal staff

Cancel   OK

Figure 5.12 Engraving rules for staves.

may or may not be enough room—but no bother, it's easy to fix. Just change the value from 8 to something higher, starting with moderate increases, such as 8 to 9 or 9.5, to enlarge the spacing between staves. The beauty of this dialog box is that you can come back whenever you need to and tweak the number. Take a look at the score in Figure 5.13, for example.

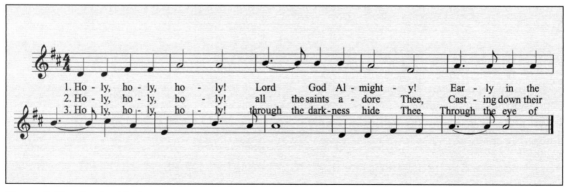

Figure 5.13 Crushed lyrics.

In this score, you can clearly see that there's not enough room for all three lines of lyrics. A quick look at the engraving rules shows that the default value of 9.25 spaces isn't enough room. If you increase the value to 12 in this case, the result is shown in Figure 5.14, which looks much nicer.

Figure 5.14   Perfect spaces.

Remember that engraving rules are global changes that affect the score on which you're currently working. This will make each and every stave farther apart, which might be what you want. There are, of course, times when only certain sections need more room, and we have a fix for that as well.

House Style Always remember that Sibelius is flexible! If you want to change the way Sibelius spaces staves in every score you open, you can export the House Style and import it into any score that needs it. Better yet, since every manuscript paper contains a House Style, just export new manuscript papers based on your own personal engraving and layout criteria. The House Style will always come up the way you want it.

CD: Use Example 5.6 to tweak the House Style to allow for more room between your staves.

Moving a Single Staff

What if you only need to adjust the spacing between staves in a small section? The engraving rules will only give you spacing between *all* staves! If you need to move just one stave or a small section, resist the urge to drag it with your mouse—there is a better way. Look at Figure 5.15, which shows a situation in which most of the staves are fine, but you need some extra space due to notes in the lower staff colliding with the lyrics and dynamics. (You see this a lot between tenor and bass clefs, for example.)

Figure 5.15 Small collision.

To increase the distance between these staves, first decide who has to move. In this case, it's clear that the bass needs to move down to create room. If you click once in the bass stave, you can use the key command Shift+Alt+down/up arrow (Windows) or Shift+Option+down/up arrow (Mac) to move it a space at a time.

This particular key command will move that staff *independently* of any other staves in your score. This means that as you create more room above the staff, you'll create less room below it. In small increments this is fine, but for larger things it looks odd. In such cases, you'll want Ctrl+Alt+down/up arrow (Windows) or Command+Option+down/up arrow (Mac) instead. This will move the selected staff and all the other staves below it.

Figure 5.16 shows how your score is easily fixed.

Just a few things to keep in mind when moving a stave using the key command detailed a moment ago. First, it only moves what you've selected. If you select a single bar, it only moves the *distance between staves in that system*. If you want it to increase the room between two staves in your score, you'll need to select all the measures in the score, which is done easily with a triple-click. With everything selected on a stave, now you're moving the distance between that stave throughout the entire score, something you can't do with engraving rules. It's up to you to figure out how much change you need, and whether it's a specific section or a global change.

It's important to use the right tool for the job. When you need to space music out, engraving rules will move it all, while these key commands will allow you to change the distance between one or more staves individually.

Figure 5.16   More room!

CD: Use Example 5.7 to change staff spacing without having to use the House Style.

Don't Drag Barlines!

Next up in our formatting tour: tight measures. Sibelius does a very good job of automatically spacing measures and lyrics so you don't get stuck with visual messes. Many users will try to grab a barline to create more room in a measure. This is a bad idea that you'll want to avoid.

Never, ever drag a barline!

Let Sibelius do its job—you just have to help it a bit. Following are things to think about when you lay out music:

1. Get the notes in.

2. Get the lyrics in.

3. How many measures do you need per line?

4. Where are the biggest visual issues happening, and can they be fixed by tweaking the answer to Step 3?

5. Fix small issues by nudging measures/notes wider.

Again, this may never happen to you, as Sibelius lays music out as you enter it. It will respace the music as you add lyrics, but nothing is perfect. If you have too many measures on a line, making your notes and lyrics crush together, the first thing to do is simply force a system break so that fewer measures appear on a line.

To force a page break, select the barline where you want the break to occur (the barline will glow purple when selected) and press the Enter or Return key. Figure 5.17 intentionally has too many measures per line, but it's a good illustration of this technique; you can really see how crushed everything is. By inserting a system break at the end of Measure 4, you're left with what's shown in Figure 5.18, which allows Sibelius to space out both the music and the lyrics much nicer.

Figure 5.17   There are too many measures on this system.

Figure 5.18   A system break makes all the difference.

When you have fewer measures on a line, Sibelius has more room and will evenly space out fewer measures. This is often the best fix: Go through a score and make sure you have your system breaks in the right spots.

CD: Use Example 5.8 to add more space in your scores/systems by adding some manual page and system breaks.

Nudging Measures/Notes

One last fix is to manually adjust the spacing in a measure or between notes by hand. This is referred to as *nudging*. To nudge a measure/note farther apart or closer, press Shift+Alt+right/left arrow (Windows) or Shift+Option+right/left arrow (Mac). These key commands can apply to either a measure or a single note.

If you apply the key command to a single measure, it will adjust the size of the selected measure. This of course will affect the size of the measures that come after it, and if you nudge it far enough to one side, Sibelius will force a system break. In that case, you should have just forced a system break! If you select multiple measures and use the nudge feature, all the measures will change together.

If you apply the key command to a single note, it will nudge the note over without changing the length of the measure.

Reset If you've mangled your score by accident by messing with spacing and so on, you can highlight a section and go to Layout > Reset Note Spacing, and Sibelius will revert back to its own note spacing.

As you can see, there is a lot to formatting, and the rest will come in Chapter 9. This should get you through the preliminary steps involved in adding lyrics and putting out fires as you add them.

Please remember that if you make major changes to engraving rules or any other part of the House Style, they won't spill over to other scores unless you go to House Style > Export House Style and import the House Style into other scores. There is no such thing as a global House Style in Sibelius (in other words, a change that will affect every score you've ever written). All you can do is create House Styles and export/import them as needed and create new manuscript paper as necessary for future scores.

Lyric Size The default size of Sibelius's lyrics is 10 points. For many engravers, reducing the size of the lyrics to 9 points can make the entire process of layout and spacing much easier. To change the size of a lyric, go to House Style > Edit Text Styles and edit any of the lyric styles you use in your score to adjust their size down a point. If you like the way this looks and you'd like to use this in all your other scores, export the House Style you've just created by choosing House Style > Export House Style. Export it with the name "Smaller

Lyrics," and re-import it into any score you want. To make this stick on all future scores, save an empty score as a manuscript paper and change the House Style there.

CD: Use Example 5.9 to manually nudge a measure or two wider than the normal Sibelius note spacing.

Importing Lyrics from a Text File

Here's a huge timesaver for you: Sibelius can import lyrics from a text file and automatically syllabify your text to the preexisting music! The software details other methods, including copying and pasting from Word and other programs, in Section 3.3 of the Sibelius 5 reference, so I won't reiterate that here. However, lyric input from a text file is new in Sibelius 5 and is worth showing—it's pretty amazing.

The premise is this: Sibelius can take any set of text from a standard text file and automatically add it to your score. The software figures out where the syllables should go and automatically adds them. It does this by essentially understand the incoming language. More amazingly, it does this in five languages (English, German, French, Spanish, and Italian). This is great for setting poetry and other texts (librettos) that already exist in a typed format. However, you'll need to make sure that the text is saved in a true text file—Sibelius doesn't read Word files. If the text is in a Word file, you'll have to save the file from Word as a text or a plain-text file.

To get this rolling, you'll need to have music entered into your vocal line because lyrics always attach to text! You need to select the measures/notes to which the lyrics will attach before you can invoke the command. If you select nothing, Sibelius will give you a warning: "You've selected nothing; should we select the entire score for you?" Most times this won't work, so please pre-select your measures.

Then, navigate to Create > Text > Lyrics > From Text File. Doing so will bring up the Create Lyrics from Text File dialog box shown in Figure 5.19.

Sibelius wants to know a few things:

- **Text File.** You'll need to specify the exact location of the text file on your computer.

- **Language.** Choose the language contained in the text file.

- **Automatically Syllabify Ambiguous Words.** This is selected by default to deal with words that have more than one way that they can be syllabified. When this option is selected, Sibelius will make its best guess based on the music and other lyrics as a whole. When this option is not selected, Sibelius will ask for your input on each ambiguous word. An example of an ambiguous word is "immediate," which can break into *im-me-di-ate* or *im-me-diate*.

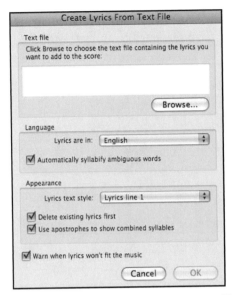

Figure 5.19   Create lyrics from a text file.

- **Lyrics Text Style.** Choose from the different lyric text styles (Lyrics Line 1, and so on) for the text to come in.

- **Delete Existing Lyrics First.** If lyrics are present in your score, selecting this option will delete them.

- **Use Apostrophes to Show Combined Syllables.** When Sibelius reduces the number of syllables in ambiguous words, it typically uses an apostrophe to show when the reduction has taken place [for example, Heav'n for Heaven (*Heav-en* or *Heav'n*)].

- **Warn When Lyrics Won't Fit the Music.** If your music is too long for the lyrics or vice versa, Sibelius will give you a warning.

Figure 5.20 shows a sample melody that's going to take the short lyric "Sibelius is the bee's knees," which is saved as a text file.

Figure 5.20   Melody ready for lyrics.

Select the notes and go to Create > Text > Lyrics > From Text File. All of the default settings in the window that come up are fine; all you have to do is point it to the text file on our computer. When this is done, click OK. The result is shown in Figure 5.21.

Figure 5.21 Automatic lyrics from text.

If you set lyrics often, this feature will save you hours. Remember that you can cut and paste from other applications as well, as detailed in the Sibelius reference.

CD: Check out Example 5.10 to use the Import Lyrics from Text File feature on a pre-made score.

Creating Text

Now that we're past lyrics, it's time to explore the other text-based objects that Sibelius allows you to place into your score. Sibelius breaks text like this into two forms: system text and staff text. System text applies to all staves in a score (even if they aren't seen in the full score, just the parts) and includes instructions to players, as well as specialized text, such as D.C. and D.S. markings. Staff text applies to only one staff and includes text styles such as fingerings, figured bass, percussion sticking, and much more!

In the following sections I'll detail the kinds of text styles available to you and remind you how to add text. Although we could spend a lot of time talking about each text style, we'll progress through this quickly because Sibelius treats text pretty uniformly.

Staff Text

Here are the most commonly used types of staff text in Sibelius. (Keep in mind that expression, technique, and lyric text have already been discussed.)

- **Chord symbol.** Am7 and all other text-based chords.

- **Plain text.** All-purpose text that's suitable for almost anything.

- **Roman numerals.** For harmonic analysis.

- **Figured bass.** For continuo instruments to realize chord symbols.

- **Fingering.** For any kind of fingering text.

- **Guitar fingering.** The right hand of the guitar uses PIMA to identify which finger to use when.

- **Boxed text.** Text in a box!

- **Small text.** Text with a smaller font than other standard text.

- **Nashville chord numbers.** A special way of writing chord symbols common in Nashville, Tennessee.

- **Footnote.** Text at the bottom of a single page. (This is different than a footer.)

To access these text styles (including styles other than those listed above), navigate to Create > Text > Other Staff Text, and you'll see a full listing of the text styles.

Because these are staff styles, you need to select the note to which you want to attach the text first, and then summon the text style. As always, the spacebar will advance the text to the next note, which allows for rapid movement from note to note—especially useful with fingerings.

Don't Forget the Word Menus!

When it comes to text, don't forget about the word menus! You'll remember that a word menu results when you right-click or Control-click in the blank text box you create when you summon a text style. Here are the types of things you'll find in the different word menus:

- For the chord symbols, you'll find all the extensions, such as 6/9 and proper diminished and half diminished symbols, all properly superscripted.

- In the figured bass, you'll find all of the common bass figurations already written out.

- All of the Roman numerals, plus their inversions (6, 6/4, 5/4/2) properly vertically aligned, in the correct text size.

Chord Styles Sibelius reference, Section 3.4, details many different ways that Sibelius can draw chord symbols. There are six different word menus that you can access, depending on the aesthetic look of your chords (which varies from publisher to publisher). Look at that section to see the different options for chord symbols, because the default may not provide you with the look you want.

Transpose When you add chord symbols and transpose the music to which they are attached, the chord symbols will transpose. This is very handy when you are copying music from instrument to instrument or simply making a change in the music.

In short, the word menus are there to save you time. There are three shortcuts about which you'll want to know. When you are adding a sharp, flat, or natural and you don't want to access the word menu for it, it's easier to just remember the shortcut:

- For a natural symbol, press Ctrl+7 (Windows) or Command+7 (Mac).

- For a sharp symbol, press Ctrl+8 (Windows) or Command+8 (Mac).

- For a flat symbol, press Ctrl+9 (Windows) or Command+9 (Mac).

Essential Tip: Keypad-Like The aforementioned shortcuts for sharp, flat, and natural are easy to remember because they follow the same keys from the first keypad layout! Just add Ctrl (Windows) or Command (Mac) to the number in your word menu, and you'll get the corresponding symbol!

System Text

There are fewer styles of system text in Sibelius due to the very nature of how system text works. System text is placed once in your score and automatically disseminates to all parts of the score. The Create > Text menu is broken into two smaller windows, divided by a vertical line, as shown in Figure 5.22.

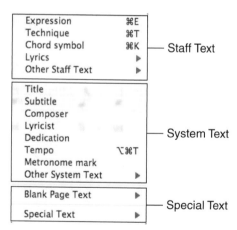

Figure 5.22 Menu divisions.

Here is a listing of the commonly used system text styles and their functions:

- **Title, Subtitle, Composer, Lyricist, Dedication.** These text styles are special in that they have strict default positions on each and every score. No matter where you click, the title will always be dead center!

- **Tempo.** This is for your Italian tempo markings, such as *adagio*, *lento*, and others. You can, of course, type in any information you want there, including such favorites as "As fast as you can!"

- **Metronome Mark.** This is for setting an exact tempo value. The word menu contains all of the note heads you'll need to add a proper metronome marking, and Sibelius will adjust its tempo to the setting you choose!

- **Metric Modulation.** This is similar to the metronome marking, but is specifically for metric modulation indications in your score.

- **Repeat (D.C./D.S./To Coda).** These repeat markings (found in Create > Text > Other System Text) are system text that plays back. The word menu contains the coda and segno symbols.

If you navigate to Create > Text > Other System Text, you'll see a listing of all of the available text styles you can use.

Blank Text There are additional text styles intended exclusively for blank pages, which is a whole lot easier in Sibelius 5! If you have additional blank pages, such as between movements, and you need to create blank-page text (objects that don't attach to a system or stave), select Create > Text > Blank Page Text to properly create these.

Special Text

One last submenu exists within the Create > Text menu: Create > Text > Special Text. This submenu sports text styles you might not use every day, but that are very handy to have. Figure 5.23 shows you all the menu choices within the Special Text submenu.

Many of the entries in this menu are text styles used elsewhere in the program, such as the Rehearsal Marks style.

Creating Chord Diagrams

Chord diagrams, or guitar frames, are the visual boxes that instruct guitar players about which chord to play and how to finger it on the neck. Figure 5.24 shows an example.

You typically see these sorts of frames in Guitar-Piano-Vocal arrangements of sheet and popular music. They are also very handy if you're creating music for guitarists and you're not comfortable arranging for guitar—Sibelius has an extensive library of built-in chords ranging from basic chords to quite extravagant jazz chords! You can summon chord diagrams by selecting Create > Chord Diagrams or via the shortcut Shift+K (both Windows and Mac). Doing so will bring up the Chord Diagram editor shown in Figure 5.25.

1st and 2nd endings
Auto page break warnings
Bar numbers
Bar numbers (parts)
Chord diagram fingering
Chord diagram fret
Common symbols
Duration at end of score
Figured bass (extras)
Hit points
Instrument name at top left
Instrument names
Multirests (numbers)
Multirests (tacet)
Note name noteheads
Note tails
Ornaments
Page numbers
Percussion instruments
Rehearsal marks
Special noteheads etc.
Special symbols
Special symbols (extra)
Time signatures
Time signatures (huge)
Time signatures (large)
Tablature letters
Tablature numbers
Timecode
Tuplets
Worksheet footer (first page, l)
Worksheet footer (first page, r)
Worksheet header (first page, l)
Worksheet header (first page, r)

Figure 5.23 Special Text choices.

Figure 5.24 Guitar frame.

Selecting from the pre-made library is a snap. Choose your root, extension, and bass note from the drop-down menus in the editor, and Sibelius will show you all the guitar voicings it knows for that particular chord. There are several options you'll want to explore in this editor:

- **Instrument.** If you're writing for an instrument other than guitar, choose the instrument here so that Sibelius can format the frets and strings properly for the chords. This is useful if you're writing for banjo, for example.

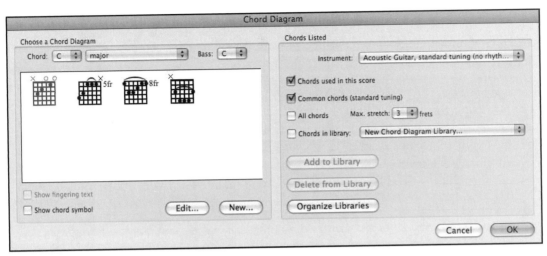

Figure 5.25 The Chord Diagram editor.

- **Chords Used in This Score.** This option lets you choose from chords already in your score that match up with the search criteria (root/extension/bass note).

- **Common Chords (Standard Tuning).** This chooses only "standard" guitar voicings for a standard tuned guitar. If you're using Sibelius to recommend voicings for you, and you're not a guitarist, these are the ones you'll want to choose because they are easy-to-play, safe bets.

- **All Chords.** When this option is selected, Sibelius shows you every chord, all across the neck, that matches the search criteria. This may display some chords that are awkward to play for an inexperienced guitarist, so you can set the Max Stretch value to a lesser number of frets (choices are 2, 3, or 4). Lower values will be easier to play, especially for younger students' hands.

- **Chords in Library.** If you decide to create your own chords, you'll save them to a chord library. To only use chords from a custom chord library, select this option and choose the appropriate library.

- **Show Fingering Text.** When a chord has saved fingerings, you can select whether you want this to show in your diagram.

- **Show Chord Symbol.** This option displays the name, kind, and bass note of your chord in text, above the chord diagram.

To place a chord, you can select the note to which you want the chord to attach, and then place the chord. Alternatively, after you've chosen the chord, you can click on the note with the glowing cursor.

No Space Many objects can be moved to the next note in Sibelius using the spacebar. Alas, chord symbols are not among these! If you want to add another chord diagram, you'll have to summon it manually each time.

If you're just using the pre-built library, you'll want to grab one of the first few chords that Sibelius recommends for you, because most guitar players prefer open position chords. Because Sibelius ships with thousands of chords, it's actually an incredible learning tool, even for an experienced guitarist. However, if you are a guitarist, you'll likely want to ascribe your own voicings and fingerings, so you'll want to learn how to make your own.

Transpose Guitar chord frames transpose automatically when you transpose music in Sibelius.

CD: Use Example 5.11 to add some guitar chord voicings to the score. Even if you aren't a guitarist, Sibelius will suggest voicings for you to use. (Text-based chord symbols are provided.)

Editing/Creating Your Own Frames

As detailed a moment ago, the built-in library of chords in Sibelius is very impressive, but if you're a guitarist, you'll likely have your own voicings. To build your own voicings, complete with fingerings, names, barrés, and such, you'll want to create your own frames. You can also edit preexisting frames as a starting point for your custom shapes.

To do so, bring up the Chord Diagram editor by selecting Create > Chord Diagram or by pressing Shift+K (both Windows and Mac). In this editor, choose the proper root and extension for your new chord (if you know it) and select New to design your new chord voicing. Doing so takes you to the Chord Diagram dialog box shown in Figure 5.26.

From this dialog box, you can design your own chord, complete with fingerings, and even a custom chord symbol (if you so choose). Here are a couple things to keep in mind when inputting your own chords:

- Barré indications are drawn automatically by dragging across any fret. Because this removes any existing fingers (dots), you'll want to draw in your barrés first.

- After the barré is drawn in, add your additional fingerings by clicking on the frets to add a dot.

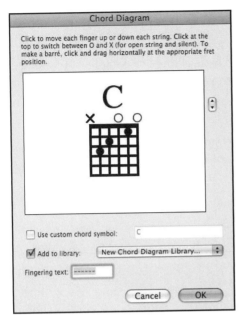

Figure 5.26   Creating a new chord.

- You can toggle a string from an open string (O) to a muted string (X) by clicking before the first fret shown in the Chord Diagram editor. Please note that opening or muting a string will remove the fingerings already on the string.

- If you have a custom chord symbol, you can add it by selecting the Use Custom Chord Symbol option and entering your symbol in the space provided.

- To change the library to which your chord is saved, use the Add to Library drop-down menu to direct the chord to a custom library or create a new one.

- To add fingerings below the diagram, fill in the Fingering Text field, where each dash (-) represents no fingering. (There are six "null" dashes.) To add a finger, substitute a dash for a number (1, 2, 3, or 4). The strings are written from left to right (low to high).

You can use the aforementioned steps to input brand-new chords or simply edit preexisting chords to your liking.

CD: Use Example 5.12 to create the custom chord diagram shown in the score.

Creating Bar Number Changes

In Sibelius, you can create bar number changes at any point in your music. Sibelius sets up bar numbers largely by default, and their appearance is governed by selecting House Style > Engraving Rules > Bar Numbers. With that said, there are times when you need to change the type of bar numbers in your score (or even just the format of them). You can do so by choosing Create > Other > Bar Number Change.

Just for clarity, here is a list of things you can do with the House Style options that don't require bar number changes:

- Change where in the bar the bar number occurs (top, bottom, centered)

- Change how frequently bar numbers occur

- Change whether the bar numbers are counted when a score contains repeats

- Hide bar numbers altogether

If none of the above applies to you, Create > Other > Bar Number Change is for you, as shown in Figure 5.27.

Here's what you can do with bar number changes:

- **New Bar Number.** Specify any bar number you want, and the bar numbers will change or start over from that point.

- **Follow Previous Bar Number Changes.** If you want to change the format of your bar numbers (from numbers to letters) and keep the original bar numbering intact, select this radio button. This is typically used with Change Format, which you'll learn about in a minute.

- **No Bar Number (and Don't Count the Bar).** Use this option to tell Sibelius to basically ignore a bar from counting. This is useful when you're doing special bar splits or when you're writing out cadenzas that shouldn't be counted.

- **Add Text.** You can specify a special prefix or suffix text that you will add to your bar numbers, such as Old 1 or 1, New. To access the controls for prefix or suffix, use the Before/ After drop-down menu.

- **Change Format.** Change the style of numbering from 1,2,3 to 1a, 1b, 1c; a, b, c; or A, B, C.

When you make changes to the format of the bar numbers, Sibelius will automatically show bar numbers on every bar, regardless of what the current engraving rule for the bar number currently says.

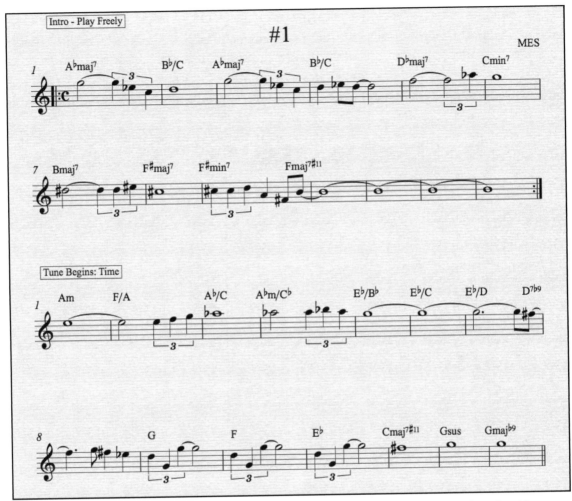

Figure 5.27 Bar number change. (This figure has a free introduction, which is numbered as Measures 1–13, and when the tune begins at "Tune Begins: Time," it's considered Bar 1 of the real "melody."

Also note that you can copy and paste bar number changes, reposition them manually, and delete them from within the score!

CD: Use Example 5.13 to create some bar number changes with a score.

Inserting Graphics

Sibelius lets you import and place graphics into your score. This is great for custom logos, instrument icons, and other educational aids that you might want to place into your score. Sibelius is particular about what kinds of graphics it lets you insert into your score. To insert a graphic into your score, the graphic must be saved in TIFF format.

If your graphic isn't a TIFF, you can change it easily enough. On a Mac, use Preview and choose TIFF in the File Type field of the Save As window. On a PC, you can use the built-in Image Viewer in the Windows Start menu and save as a TIFF.

Once your graphic is saved as a TIFF, navigate to Create > Graphic to bring up the Choose Graphic File dialog box shown in Figure 5.28.

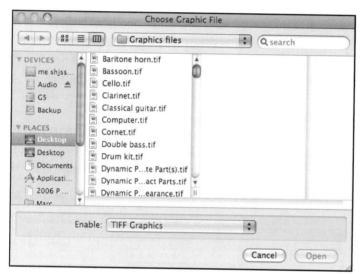

Figure 5.28 Importing graphics.

Sibelius needs you to locate the graphic on your hard disk or other media (CD, DVD, or network). Once selected, the graphic is placed into your score for repositioning.

What can you do to a graphic in Sibelius? You can move it, copy it, and delete it, just like you would any object. You can also scale it proportionally by dragging the handle on the bottom-right corner up and down to scale the image as needed, as shown in Figure 5.29.

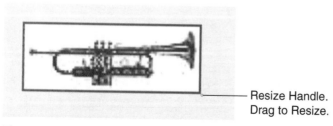

Figure 5.29 Graphic resize handle.

Creating Highlights

To round out our tour of the Create menu, let's visit the Highlight feature. This adds a colored (yellow) highlight into your score, just as if you had used a highlighter on a real score. This is very handy for music analysis projects and to point out very important pieces.

To create a highlight, all you have to do is select a range of notes or measures on a single staff (because Sibelius can only highlight a single staff at a time) and navigate to Create > Highlight. Sibelius will create a highlight for you (see Figure 5.30—the yellow highlight will appear as dark gray in this text).

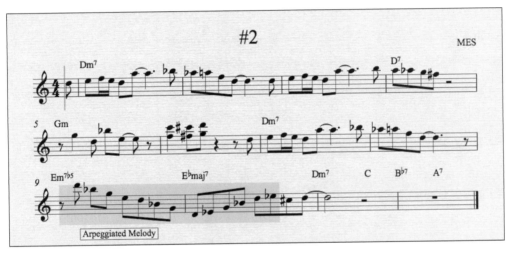

Figure 5.30 Highlight.

Once your highlight is created, you can edit or delete it. You can select the edge of your highlight—it will have a blue box around it when selected. Once selected, you can copy or delete it in the usual way.

You can also change the size of the highlight by dragging the edge of the currently selected highlight to extend or contract it. If you need to move a highlight, make sure it's selected and use the arrow keys to move it to and fro.

View and Printing Options

By default, you will see all highlights in your score, but they won't print unless you tell Sibelius to do so. Luckily, both of these aspects can be changed. If you want the highlights to remain in your score but not be shown onscreen, you can toggle this by choosing View > Highlights.

As for printing, Sibelius won't print elements such as highlights unless you tell it to do so. Highlights are part of a larger category of score elements called View Menu Options, which lets

Sibelius print elements from the View menu that would normally be excluded. When you go to print, make sure you have View Menu Options selected when you choose File > Print (see Figure 5.31).

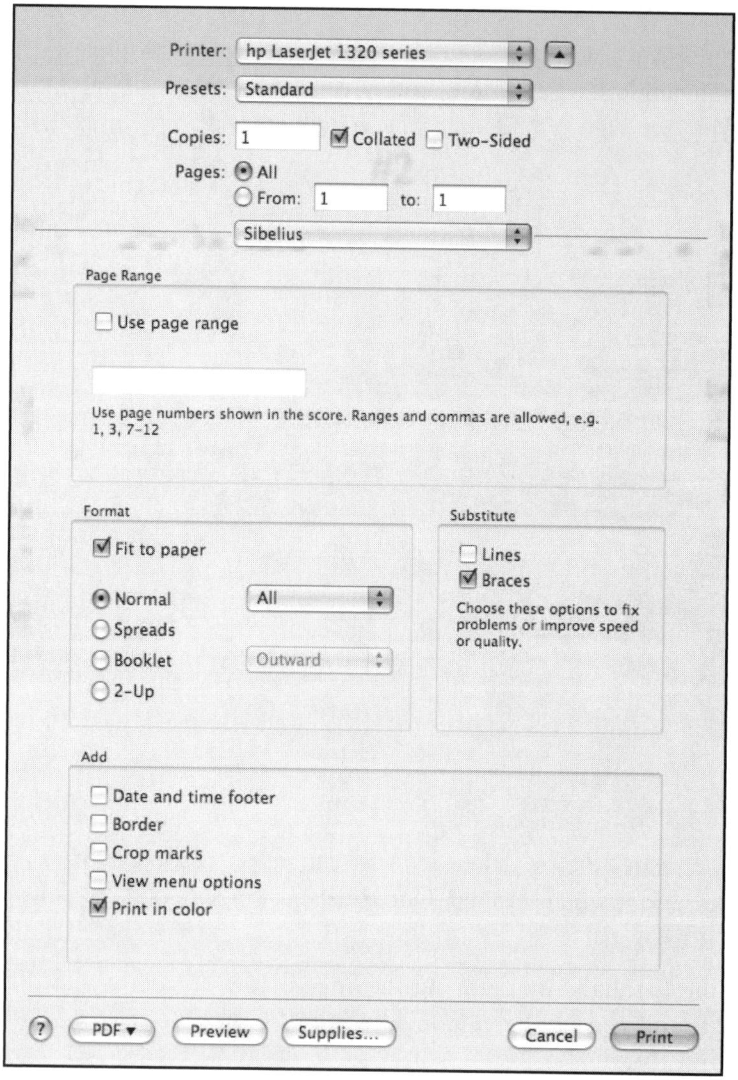

Figure 5.31 Print View Menu Options.

Please keep in mind that the View Menu Options category encompasses other elements than just highlighting! The View menu can show various rulers (when configured) in your score, and when you switch on View Menu Options in your print settings, rulers and other markings will print. To get around this, just toggle the entries in the View menu exactly how you want to see them in your final printed score, and all will be well.

6 Instrument-Specific Notation

Essential Tips for Chapter 6

1. You really want to know what's on the other keypads besides the first keypad layout.

2. Some of the instrument-specific notation, such as harmonics, doesn't play back by itself using Sibelius Sounds Essentials, but there is a plug-in that will help you fake it.

3. The majority of special symbols you need to create for instruments are found by choosing either Create > Line or Create > Symbol.

4. If you enter notes of a MIDI keyboard for percussion, Sibelius can automatically add the correct notehead for you, granted you set up the Preferences properly.

5. You can change noteheads by choosing Window > Properties or by pressing Shift+Alt/Option+notehead number.

6. If you want a notehead higher than 9 when you change noteheads using the key command, you have to type the double-digit number in fairly quickly.

Thus far in this book, we've worked very hard on understanding the basic underpinnings of Sibelius's Create menu. Now it's time to look at some more project/task-oriented information. This chapter is devoted to the specific notation used for particular instruments, as well as general topics that can apply to other instruments, too (changing noteheads and so on). We'll tackle this by family of instrument (not all are necessary here) and talk about the specific needs you'll encounter as you work with Sibelius. Think of this as the "How do I do this?" chapter.

You Forgot You might look at this chapter and say, "You forgot a bunch of important indications and markings." This chapter is devoted to the common non-text indications you find in a score. I covered most text in preceding chapters, so in this chapter I won't cover any marking that is indicated in text. I've done my best to cover all I can, but there's no way to cover every single score marking that ever existed, especially in modern music.

On a final note, this chapter will look at the "how" part of Sibelius notation, not the "why." There is no substitute for a good book on notation and orchestration, especially when dealing with instruments that are unfamiliar to you, but in the case of technical requirements for instruments (such as the forthcoming section on string harmonics), this book will not deal with the musical aspects—instead, it will focus on how to achieve the proper notational results. I could do a whole book on this topic, so in this chapter I'll only discuss the most common examples. However, this chapter should give you enough insight into the process for you to take the information and apply it to other situations in Sibelius. I'm also not going to give you many CD examples for this chapter, unless there's something special to do (such as hiding playback parts or changing noteheads, which you haven't done yet).

Instruments For those of you who want to learn more about the instruments, their ranges, and special techniques, Sibelius makes *Instruments*, a software title designed to show you just that. Complete with audio and musical excerpts, it's a great place to get started learning about orchestration.

String Notation

I'm going to divide this chapter between orchestral strings and guitar, both of which have some interesting notational practices.

Bowing

Bowing indications are a typical part of string writing. In Sibelius, you add bowings through the fourth (or F11) keypad, as shown in Figure 6.1.

Figure 6.1   Fourth keypad—bowings.

The up-bow and down-bow use the 5 and 6 keys, respectively, on this keypad layout. Bowings are added after note entry has concluded. Thankfully, that's all there is to adding specific bowings.

Of course, in traditional notation practice, slurs in string writing indicate that a passage should be taken in a single bowing, as shown in Figure 6.2. It's understood that all notes under the slur, or phrase marking, are taken in a single bow if possible.

Figure 6.2   Slur/phrase marking.

Guitar Bowings Guitars use the same symbols as traditional string instruments with respect to bowing. Because the guitar is not bowed (with the notable exception of some adventurous sorts), the up-bow and down-bow are read as an up-pick and down-pick when applied to plectrum (or pick-based) guitar writing.

Harmonics

Harmonics come in a few flavors for stringed instruments, and they have spawned a few different types of notation practices to deal with them. I want to start with the standard string harmonic, as shown in Figure 6.3.

Figure 6.3   Standard string harmonic.

The symbol for a natural harmonic is found in the fourth (F11) keypad layout and uses the . (period) key.

As a practice, the natural harmonic indicates to the player only which note should be lightly stopped and does not indicate the sounding pitch of the resulting harmonic. The sounding pitch can be shown with another note head above the harmonic, as shown in Figure 6.4.

Figure 6.4 Natural harmonic with sounding note.

Here's how to make this happen in Sibelius:

1. Begin by entering the single quarter note E in Voice 1.

2. Open the Properties window by choosing Window > Properties or by pressing its button on the toolbar, and expand the Notes sub-window.

3. Toggle the note from Notehead 0 to Notehead 2 using the drop-down menu. The second notehead is the open diamond you'll need for the harmonic. (Alternatively, you'll soon learn about a shortcut for noteheads: Pressing Shift+Alt/Option+2 will bring up the diamond notehead.) Once that's done, you'll see the result in Figure 6.5.

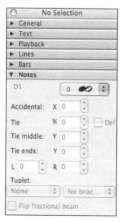

Figure 6.5 Changing noteheads.

4.   To add the cue-sized note in parentheses, bring up the second keypad layout (by pressing F9), select the bracketed cue note, and add it above the diamond note. (The interval will depend on which harmonic is used.)

5.   The cue note may not be positioned correctly, so use your mouse to drag it from side to side. Alternatively, use the X parameter in the Properties > General submenu or the floating Properties menu you used to change noteheads, and change the X value to move it from side to side.

Oh, Mahler Although it's true that most of the time, when a harmonic is used, it's display-ing where the string player should stop the string, occasionally you will see harmonics that only indicate the sounding pitch! Mahler uses this in his orchestral writing. In Sibelius, there's no difference in how you'd engrave this—only a slight bit of thought for the poor string player who has to read it.

CD: Use Example 6.1 to practice writing a few string harmonics and using the Properties window to manually adjust the notes to perfect alignment.

Artificial Harmonics

An artificial harmonic is notated by a dyad—the lower note shows which note is stopped with the first finger, while the diamond-shaped note shows which note the player lightly stops with his pinky to produce the harmonic (see Figure 6.6).

Figure 6.6   Artificial harmonic.

You can make dyads easily; just follow these steps:

1.   Enter both the B and the E as a dyad in a single voice.

2.   Select the higher note (E) and, from the Properties > Notes sub-window, change the notehead from type 0 to type 2 as detailed a moment ago.

In some cases, you'll find the sounding pitch written above, as shown in Figure 6.7.

Figure 6.7   Artificial harmonic with sounding pitch.

CD: Use Example 6.2 to make some artificial harmonics.

To make this, start by following the aforementioned instructions and add the cue note in parentheses from the second (F9) keypad layout.

Harmonic Playback Harmonics won't play back in Sibelius by default, but the Harmonic Playback plug-in from the Plug-Ins > Playback menu will sort you out.

Different Pizzicatos

While the traditional pizzicato is indicated by technique text, you'll find two notable styles of pizzicato in string writing: left-hand pizzicato and Bartok pizzicato.

Figure 6.8 shows left-hand pizzicato, with a + symbol attached to a standard notehead.

Figure 6.8   Left-hand pizzicato.

You'll find the symbol for left-hand pizzicato in the fourth keypad layout (F11), using the 4 key.

Not Just Pizz The symbol for pizzicato is the +, but other instruments use this same symbol for other tasks: guitar tapping, hi-hat closure, or brass mutes.

A "snap" pizzicato, or Bartok (as Bartok made great use of it), is when the sting is pulled so hard that it snaps against the fingerboard, making a distinctive sound. Sibelius provides the symbol, but not in any keypad layout (because the keypad is for common symbols, and snap pizzicato is hardly common). Rather, you can find the symbol by choosing Create > Symbol or by using the shortcut Z. When you are in the Symbol window, scroll to the collection of Articulations to find your pizzicatos. Figure 6.9 shows the snap pizz symbol.

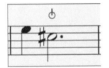

Figure 6.9   Snap/Bartok pizz.

CD: Practice making pizzicato symbols in Example 6.3.

Tremolos

While other instruments use tremolo techniques, it's extremely common in string writing to see a measured tremolo in action. Creating these tremolos in Sibelius is very simple. Figure 6.10 shows the third keypad layout (F10), which takes care of all of your tremolo notations.

Figure 6.10   Third keypad.

Changing the look of a stem is something you do after you've entered in a note value and a pitch. For example, to enter Figure 6.11, follow these steps:

1.   Enter the quarter notes C, D, E, F in the first measure.

2.   Select the C and the D so they are highlighted.

3.   Go to the third keypad layout and select the eighth-note tremolo (single stroke).

4.   Select the E and F so they are highlighted.

5.   Go to the third keypad layout and select the sixteenth-note tremolo (double stroke).

Figure 6.11 Tremolo example.

This procedure will take care of any measured tremolos on a single note. The other sort of tremolo you often see is a tremolo between two notes, or an interval tremolo, as shown in Figure 6.12.

Figure 6.12 Interval tremolo.

Interval tremolos are notated a bit differently in that the full value of the tremolo is always written. (A quarter-note tremolo between two notes takes up two beats, not one, so Sibelius will double the values for you automatically.) To recreate Figure 6.12, follow these steps:

1. Enter in quarter notes for C and D.

2. On the third keypad layout (F10), click the two-note tremolo button (shortcut: Enter), and Sibelius will automatically turn the quarter notes into half notes and mark them as a single stroke.

3. Change the stroke to two strokes using the same third keypad layout.

4. Enter the final half note as normal.

Tremolos will appear in other instruments as well, so you can use this knowledge to help you in various places in Sibelius.

CD: Use Example 6.4 to practice writing some measured tremolos and intervalic tremolos.

Guitar Arpeggio Indications

On the guitar, when a chord is to be played as rolled, or *arpeggiated*, the rolled chord line is used. You can find the rolled chord by choosing Create > Line (shortcut: L); it is applied after you enter the notes. Because there are a few variations, Figure 6.13 shows several different arpeggio lines, all found by choosing Create > Line.

Figure 6.13   Arpeggio lines.

Spread The same wavy vertical line is used on harpsichord and is referred to as a *spread* indication.

When you add any of these lines, you'll need to extend the line for the length of the chord. When you click on any of the arpeggio lines, a small blue box will appear (typically at the bottom of the line), in which you can click and drag the line to the appropriate length. Please note that the normal arpeggio line (no arrow) and the reverse roll (arrow down) only overextend downward. In order to make them work, place them at the top of the arpeggio and drag the line down. The last arpeggio line has an up-facing arrow, and that line has its blue handle on the top (which is reversed from the previous two locations on the arpeggio lines).

Can't Find the Blue Box The small handle that lets you extend a line out might be difficult to see if you're zoomed out too far. Try zooming in more to see the box more clearly and make accurate mouse-grabbing easier!

Please note that arpeggio lines can be used for any polyphonic instrument (pitched percussion, guitar, piano, or harp, just to name a few).

CD: Use Example 6.5 to add a few rolled chord indications to a classical guitar piece.

Guitar Barré Chord/Position Indications

When writing for the classical guitar, it's common to use indications to specify when a guitarist is supposed to take a passage in a particular position—or, in the case of barré chords, to identify when a barré chord is used. This makes life much easier for the player. If you're an engraver, you'll probably see the markings and need to know how to make them. Figure 6.14 shows both a position indication and a barré chord indication.

Figure 6.14   Classical guitar markings.

The good news about the markings is that they're very easy to make:

- The fret indication is plain text, which you'll create by choosing Create > Text > Other Staff Text.

- The line is taken from the Create > Line menu (shortcut: L). You'll need the line that has a hook on the right side.

- You manually position the line and text together by eye.

The trick to this one is that there isn't a predefined, single element in Sibelius that accomplishes this task, so you have to use your ingenuity and combine two smaller elements. Although Sibelius supports many custom lines, and you can easily define your own, it's much easier to do it in two steps, rather than creating a line style for each possible fret (because you can't edit the text once it's on) and exporting/importing the House Style each time.

CD: Use Example 6.6 to copy a preexisting guitar score and add the proper lines using Create > Line.

Guitar Tablature

Although guitar tablature isn't a new way of writing music (tablature goes back to the 1300s), it's not common for all instruments; guitar is the most common focus of tablature (or tab). Guitar tablature is a special six-line staff (one line for each string) on which numbers represent the correct fret for a given note. The numbers are placed on any of the lines to signify which string is used. Sibelius supports tab for a whole variety of common and world stringed instruments, but guitar is clearly the most common.

Because tablature represents exactly where to play music on the guitar, you should take care when writing in guitar tab. If you create a tab instrument along with another line of music, you can copy the standard notation to the tab staff, and Sibelius will automatically convert the music to tablature, as shown in Figure 6.15.

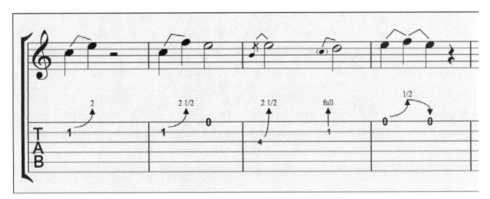

Figure 6.15   Automatic tab conversion.

Figure 6.15 was generated with a simple copy and paste from one staff to another. Now, for a guitar player, is this the best place to play this particular passage? No, it's impossible (well, nearly impossible) to bend open strings. In this case, we need to tweak the tab a bit. You can do it by hand, or you can educate Sibelius about your preferences so it does a better job by itself.

If you need to tweak the output of any tablature staff, Sibelius gives you a simple way to re-spell notes. For any note, you can use the mouse to drag a note from one string to another. (You can also use Ctrl/Command+up/down arrow.) This is due to the guitar's unique tuning, where a single note can be played at more than one place on the fretboard at the exact same pitch. If you shift a note to a string where it can't be played, Sibelius will give you a question mark, and you'll have to find a better place for the note.

Using this system, you can pull any of the odd notes to better string positions. But better yet, let's teach Sibelius that we'd rather not use open strings (and other options that pertain to guitar tab).

Changing How Sibelius Spells Tab
You also have control over how Sibelius converts music to tab (which strings are used, what the lowest frets are, and what the highest frets are) by choosing Preferences > Note Input to view the Note Input screen of the Preferences dialog box, as shown in Figure 6.16.

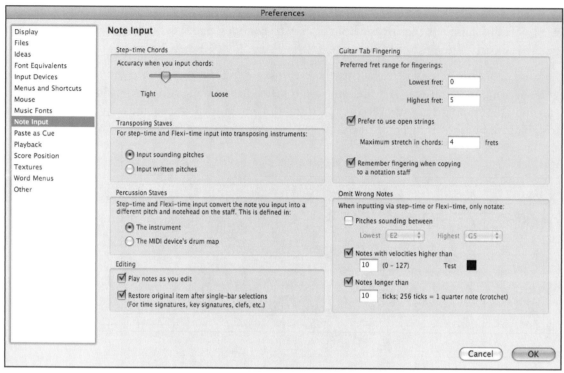

Figure 6.16 Note input/tab preferences.

Most notably on this page, you see options for the following:

- **Preferred Fret Range for Fingerings.** The values for lowest and highest fret govern how Sibelius converts notation to tab. The default settings will force tablature to use open and first-position fingerings on the guitar, which is great for education but not always suitable for professional musicians.

- **Prefer to Use Open Strings.** This refers to the way that many notes on the guitar can be spelled as a fretted note or an open string (refer to Figure 6.15). Selecting this option forces Sibelius to use open strings over fretted-note equivalents.

- **Maximum Stretch in Chords.** This is a value you set when copying chords into tablature. Sibelius will try to position the chord in the tab so that your default value is respected. Note that guitar is a quirky instrument, and not everything is playable without some fiddling.

These options deal with music input into tab during a copy or paste. If you change these values, they will only affect future music you input. To influence and change music you already copied in, select Notes > Reset Guitar Tab Fingering, and the result will adhere to your settings in Preferences > Note Input.

CD: Use Example 6.7 to copy some pitched music into a tab stave, and use the Preferences dialog box to adjust how Sibelius draws tab for you.

Writing Only Tablature–Writing Tablature First

Copying music from a tab staff is only one way to generate tab in Sibelius. You can, of course, start with a tab staff. For many guitarists and other copyists who need to get the tab exact, this is the best way to go. To start, add a tab staff and start entering notes the following way:

1. Click in the tab staff and press N to enter note entry mode, and you'll see the familiar note input caret.

2. Choose your pitch value from the numeric keypad, as you always have.

3. The up and down arrow keys let you select the string on which you want to write, while the number keys (at the top of the keyboard) let you write in the frets.

4. The left and right arrow keys take you to and fro in the bar.

Once you've entered notes into the tab staff, you can copy the music to a regular notation staff using a simple copy and paste operation. Guitar notation is a slightly larger topic, because some of the performance techniques involved are specialized and require special symbols. The next section will give you an overview of what Sibelius can do and where you'll find these functions.

Tab Styles

There are many different types of stringed-instrument tablature, ranging from lute tab to banjo tab, but six-string acoustic and electric tab remains the most common. In Sibelius, there are two styles used most often: tab with and without rhythms.

By default, if you start a new score using the New Score wizard, you'll get a tab staff that has rhythm stems attached to the tab notes in order to show the duration of the tab. In most press and music books, tab is shown along with a line of traditional notation, and the rhythms are learned from there. Consequently, the tab has no rhythms attached to the fret numbers. In Sibelius, you can choose between the different types of tablature staves when you select Create > Instruments (shortcut: I) to access the Instruments dialog box, as shown in Figure 6.17.

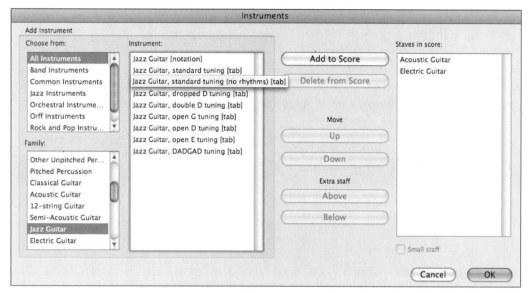

Figure 6.17   Adding new tab instruments.

In this dialog box, you see choices for instruments with tab and instruments with tab and no rhythm. This is all well and good when you're adding to a score, but what if you create a score and you need to change the type of tab staff? You could add a new instrument and cut/copy and paste the music to the other staff, but Sibelius 5 gives you a much easier way to deal with this: instrument changes.

Instrument changes, as you recall from the last chapter, allow you to change an existing staff to any other type of staff at any point. For a guitar tab change, this is the best way to go. Start the instrument change by choosing Create > Other > Instrument Change and selecting the instrument you want (which will be the same staff you already have, just with tab rhythms on or off). When that's finished, you'll have to click the instrument change before the first bar to make the instrument change take place for the entire instrument. Figure 6.18 shows you where to click.

That's all there is to it!

I Can Do This Already? If you've used Sibelius 4, you might recall that you could change a staff type at any point from the Properties window, and in the case of guitar tab, you could change from rhythms to no rhythms there. Sibelius 5 has added instrument changes, a far more robust way to deal with this, and removed the Staves page of the Properties window.

You need to
click right here!

Figure 6.18   Starting an instrument change at the beginning of the score.

CD: Use Example 6.8 to add an instrument change to make the score change from a tab without rhythms to tab with rhythms.

Guitar: Bending Strings

On electric guitar music, bending, or stretching strings, is a common notational challenge. It's used quite often by players, and when transcribing guitar solos, it's absolutely essential.

There are a few different types of bends: standard bends, pre-bends, bend and release, and unison bends. The following sections provide a rundown of how to make each happen in Sibelius. Before you go any further, you need to know the shortcut J, which places a bend between two notes. You can find the same option in the Create > Line menu, but J is an easy shortcut to memorize.

Standard Bend

A standard bend is simply a bend between two notes. On your notation staff, always notate the notes as they sound, not as they are played, and add the bend (J) between the notes. When you convert to tab, Sibelius will calculate how far the bend is and add the appropriate arrow and number of frets you need to bend (see Figure 6.19).

Bend and Release

A bend and release is when you start from a normal note, bend up, and bend back down, all in the same pick stroke. On your notation staff, write all three notes in as normal, and place a separate bend symbol between the bend up and a separate bend between the bend down (both using the J key). When you copy to tab, Sibelius will draw the bend and release symbol for you (see Figure 6.20).

Figure 6.19 Standard bend.

Figure 6.20 Bend and release.

As a slight precaution: When Sibelius creates the tab, it notates the bend down, and in typical guitar tab, the final note would have parentheses around it because it's not struck with your pick again. You can add parentheses to the tab note by selecting it and going to the second (F9) keypad layout and choosing the open parenthesis.

Pre-Bend

A *pre-bend* is one that is started silently—in other words, you bend the note before you audibly strike it. On your notation staff, you enter the original pitch as a pre-bend notehead [second keypad layout (F9)], then enter the note to which you'll bend and create a bend between the two notes. When you copy to tab, Sibelius shows a pre-bend as a straight vertical bend (see Figure 6.21).

Unison Bend

The unison bend, made famous by Jimi Hendrix, is a truly unique sound that only the guitar can make. You bend a note of a lower pitch up to match the pitch of a second note that you fret, and you play both the notes at the same time; the result is quite something.

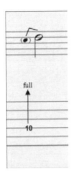

Figure 6.21   Pre-bend.

To create a unison bend (one of the few tab functions that's not automatic):

1. Make a note with a unison notehead. [Add the first note, then type 1 from your number row (not the keypad) to add the unison.]

2. Add a grace note for the bent note (second keypad).

3. Now, connect the grace note and the unison notes with a bend symbol (J).

4. Finally, copy and paste to the tab staff.

You'll need to add the second note manually because Sibelius doesn't do this fully right now. Go to Create > Text > Special Text > Tablature Numbers to place your extra tab number by hand. Figure 6.22 shows a unison bend in action.

Figure 6.22   Unison bend.

More Techniques If you're into writing a lot of guitar music, section 2.13 in the Sibelius reference covers all the different ways of writing whammy bar dives, rakes, and other extended techniques. Check it out.

Here are some other things to think about:

- You can select House Style > Engraving Rules > Guitar to change whether you want Sibelius to write words, such as Full, or intervals, such as 2, when you bend. Using Full on tab bends will toggle this from words to numbers.

- Vibrato, trills, bar dives, and other lines are aptly found by choosing Create > Line.

- You can create slides from the second keypad layout (F9).

- For tremolo picking, the third keypad (F10) provides you with all the tremolos you could ever need.

Although this is just the tip of the string world's notational iceberg, it's more than enough to get you started!

Mid-Chapter Break We're mid-chapter, and it's time for a quick reminder about the simplicity of Sibelius. When in doubt, check your keypad layouts (all five of them)—the basic symbols are found within them. Still can't find the symbol you need? Go to the Create > Symbol and look there. Still stumped? The last option is to choose Create > Line. If you can't find what you're looking for, check the index of this book and your Sibelius reference, but in all likelihood, you'll find what you need in a keypad, symbol, or line menu.

Percussion Notation

Percussion instruments are complex to write for, so there are many different techniques, noteheads, and other symbols to help you along. When it comes to noteheads, no other instrument relies on changes to noteheads like a percussion instrument does. Noteheads are covered later in this chapter, so this section is a detour to that later topic. Although percussion may have many more notehead choices than other instruments, the act of changing a notehead in Sibelius is exactly the same whether you're going for a rim shot or writing rhythmic notation for guitar or piano. Please visit the "Changing Noteheads" section later in this chapter for the full scoop.

Reusing Symbols The + and o symbols you learned about for strings are also used in percussion notation (choking symbols, closed and open hi-hats). The symbols are found on the fourth keypad layout (F11).

Rolls

All of the rolls in percussion writing are handled by the third keypad layout (F10), which deals with stems, and rolls are notated with special stems. Take a look at Figure 6.23, which shows the third keypad layout.

Figure 6.23 Third keypad layout.

In Sibelius, rolls are notated by changing the stem type to a rolled/tremolo stem. When you input your notes, you enter the pitches and durations normally through the first and second keypads. When you notate the rolls, the rhythm of the notehead governs how long the player is to roll, while the type of stem (and the number of subdivisions) sets the speed of the roll. Take a look at Figure 6.24, which has a bunch of timpani rolls entered without the rolls (so far).

Figure 6.24 Measured, without rolls.

To complete this, go to the third keypad layout (F10) and choose the speed of your rolls. If they are all the same, you can select a range of notes and change them all at the same time by clicking on the correct roll in your keypad. In Figure 6.25, different roll subdivisions are used to illustrate what you can do with a few simple key presses.

Figure 6.25 Rolls!

Buzz Rolls

The buzz, or *multi-stroke*, roll is added much the same way that traditional rolls are: You add the note value in first, and then add the appropriate symbol. You'll find the symbol on the same third keypad layout (F10) as the other rolls, with the buzz roll appearing on the 6 key. Figure 6.26 shows a few buzz rolls in a score.

Figure 6.26 Buzz rolls.

Roll Wrap-Up Just to summarize, your rolls are entered as follows: Enter your notehead and note duration first, then navigate to the third keypad (F10) and add the speed of your roll through a tremolo of the correct subdivision.

CD: Use Example 6.9 to practice creating some measured rolls and buzz rolls for percussion instruments.

Timpani Notes

There are a few ways that composers indicate how to tune timpani in a score. The most common method nowadays is to indicate in plain text at the beginning of the piece the tuning of the individual tympanum used in the piece, as shown in Figure 6.27. You do this by adding plain text to the first measure of your piece.

Figure 6.27 Text timpani tunings.

Another way that composers notate the timpani tuning is by specifying it in the instrument name. If there are three timpani used, you'd see this name: Timp. in G, C, F. To edit the instrument's name, follow these steps:

1. Go to the beginning of the piece.

2. Double-click on the name of the timpani staff.

3. Change it to the proper name, including the tuning.

4. Press Escape to return to your piece.

5. Because instruments have different names when abbreviated on subsequent pages, scroll to the second (and subsequent) page and verify that the names are correct there as well. If they are not, change them the same way as mentioned earlier.

CD: Use Example 6.10 to add text-based markings to indicate the tuning of your timpani.

Both of these methods are pretty easy to achieve in Sibelius. There is one last method of showing timpani tunings—showing a short first bar that contains the tuning notes. This is a bit trickier to notate, but not difficult overall. You need to add an extra bar to the timpani, and not add the extra bar to the other instruments. When you add a bar, you typically add it to all instruments, but you're going to learn about a powerful feature: hidden instrument changes. To create the notation in Figure 6.28, you need to change every staff (except timpani) to hidden instruments for the first bar (and a few other things you already know about).

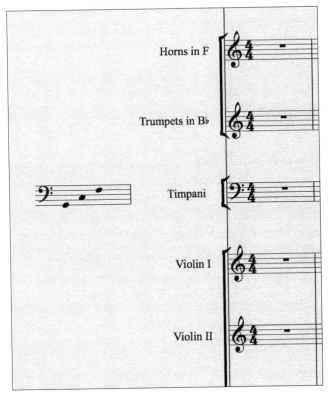

Figure 6.28 Timpani tunings—hidden instruments.

Here's how you do it:

1. Select the first bar of each staff (except the timpani) and choose Create > Other > Instrument Change.

2. In the Instrument Change window, select No instrument (hidden) from the All Instruments/ Other category.

3. To create space between the timpani tuning bar and the score, select the first bar (that is, the first visible bar), go to Window > Properties, and access the Bar panel. From there, change the gap before the bar from 0 to 10 (tweak it to your taste).

4. On each staff, reposition the name of the instrument from the top of Bar 2 to the middle of the first stave (as you'd normally see it).

5. On each staff, reposition the hidden bar (the small blue box) slightly to the right so the instrument change happens on a clean barline.

6. Create a bar number change in Bar 2 and restart the bar numbers there.

7. Chose noteheads without a stem (Notehead 8) for the timpani tuning. And that's it!

CD: Use Example 6.11 to recreate Figure 6.28, starting with a full score, adding the hidden bar, and putting in the tuning notes.

Although it's true that this style of timpani notation isn't useful for everyone, it does illustrate a salient point: You can get Sibelius to do pretty much anything you need it to do. All of the aforementioned steps are useful in their own right when used separately. When used together, they can help produce specific notation that reaches farther than your single timpani solution!

Percussion Symbols There is a bevy of percussion symbols available if you select Create > Symbol. Many of the symbols came in response to a conference on music notation held in Ghent, Belgium, in 1974. The symbols include graphical icons for percussion instruments and a full set of mallet/beater choices.

Percussion Staves and MIDI

Without a MIDI keyboard, it can be a real pain to enter music into a percussion stave—especially a drum-set stave (in which there are many changes in noteheads). Sibelius is set up to convert your MIDI keyboard input into the correct notation/noteheads, granted you set it up to do so.

The first place you have to look is the Note Input page of the Preferences dialog box (Sibelius > Preference > Note Input), as shown in Figure 6.29.

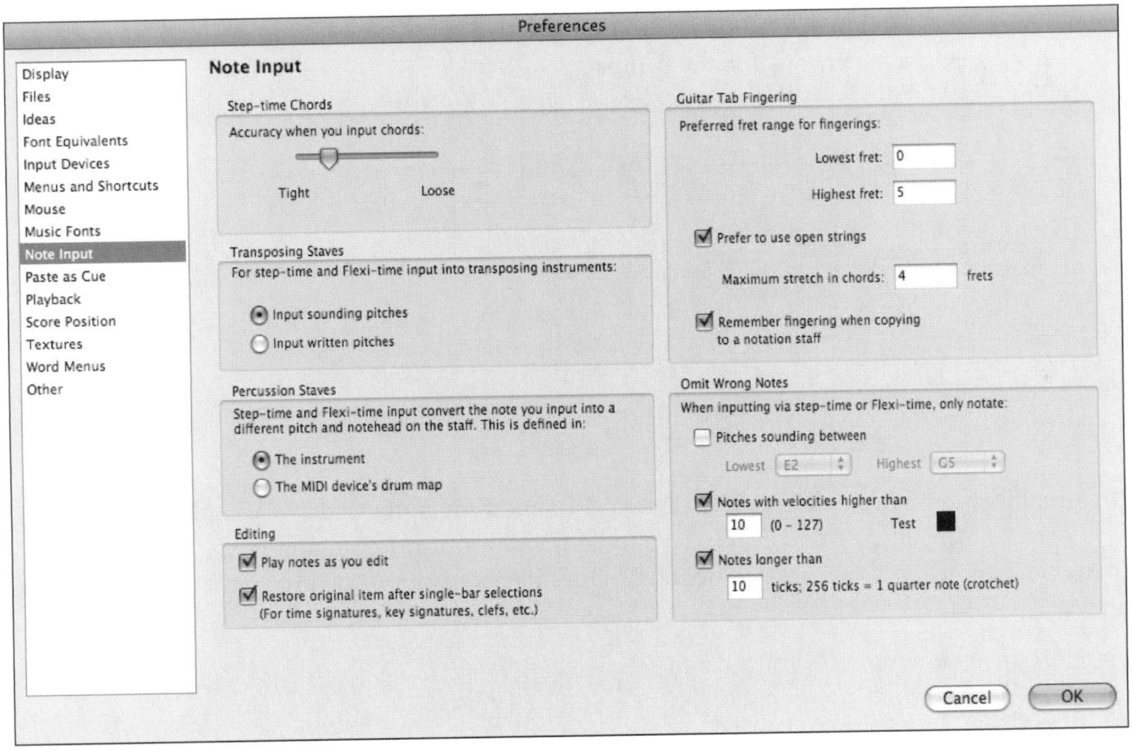

Figure 6.29 Note Input options.

We want to focus on the Percussion Staves section, which reads, "Step-time and Flexi-time input convert the note you input into a different pitch and notehead on the staff." There are two options for this, and I should clearly define what they mean:

- **The Instrument.** The drum instrument you select from Add Instruments has a defined drum map, and Sibelius expects that your MIDI input matches what's in the staff. This is expected for most users with controller keyboards.

- **The MIDI Device's Drum Map.** If your keyboard has its own MIDI map (General MIDI, for example)—so that when you play notes on your keyboard, you get drum sounds that don't match up with the conventional bass drum on F—then Sibelius will convert the MIDI input from your keyboard and make it look right on the page. Only use this option if your keyboard has General MIDI or other special drum mapping.

Let's use a drum set as an example, because it's pretty well standardized these days. If you create a score with just a drum set and you want to enter the following pattern (see Figure 6.30) without a MIDI keyboard, you need to do the following steps:

1. Enter the notes one by one.

2. Change the noteheads for the cymbals.

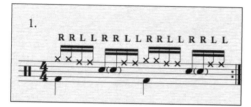

Figure 6.30 Simple drum example.

Because Sibelius lets you use a MIDI keyboard to enter the notes and replaces those notes with the correct noteheads, automatically, let's look at a chart of the common notes and how to use them in a percussion score. (Note: Sibelius defines its percussion staves from the Percussive Arts Society.)

Here are the common notes for a drum set:

- **Bass drum.** Input using pitch F4.

- **Floor tom.** Input using pitch A4.

- **Snare drum.** Input using pitch C5.

- **Snare drum (sidestick).** Input using pitch C#5.

- **Mid tom.** Input using pitch D5.

- **High tom.** Input using pitch E5.

- **Bell of ride cymbal.** Input using pitch F5.

- **Ride cymbal.** Input using pitch F#5.

- **Hi-hat "closed."** Input using pitch G5.

- **Hi-hat "open."** Input using pitch G#5.

Keep in Mind The mappings we used for the standard drum set input work with the Use Instrument preference is in Sibelius's Preferences for note input. If you use the MIDI device's drum map, than you'll be hitting the keys on your General MIDI–based keyboard that "sound" right, and Sibelius will take care of the rest.

When you use a MIDI keyboard this way, Sibelius will place the correct notehead/symbol on the staff for you, saving you a ton of time. If you work with drum/percussion parts, you'll definitely want to know about this and use it frequently. You can now notate Figure 6.30 much more efficiently using a MIDI keyboard.

Each Drum Instrument Each and every percussion instrument in Sibelius (all 150) has special mappings for MIDI entry and playback. If you'd like to access more information about your percussion map, click on the stave; go to House Style > Edit Instrument; in the resulting window click Edit Instrument; then answer yes when Sibelius asks you whether you want to edit the instrument. In the next window, click on Edit Staff Type, which will bring you to a window that defines the pitches and noteheads. If you click on any notehead, you can see the sound that's associated with it and which MIDI keystroke Sibelius is looking for to produce the right notehead. You can, of course, change this around and save the instrument if you'd rather define your own mappings. Just remember that you'll have to export a new House Style if you'd like these settings to stick in a new score.

Hiding Playback Parts

As is common with percussion parts, many times you'll see nothing but "time" or slash marks for the drummer to invent his own part. The side effect of this is that when you play back your score at home, you can't hear anything. Possibly worse, you hear nothing but the sound associated with middle space V! It's useful to learn how to create a drum part that plays back, hide it so no one sees it, and add the slash marks to keep the score looking as it should (and make the slash marks silent).

Okay, let's dig in. First things first, notate your drum part just as you normally would (see Figure 6.31).

With the drum time entered, select all those bars and go to Edit > Hide or Show > Hide. This will hide the notes, yet they'll still play back (see Figure 6.32).

Now you need to enter the slash marks in an unused voice. Let's go for Voice 4 because it's probably not being used in your hidden drum part. Switch to Voice 4 from the keypad or by using the key command Alt/Option+4 and start entering quarter notes on the middle line B. Do this to fill up your score (see Figure 6.33).

Figure 6.31   Drum time.

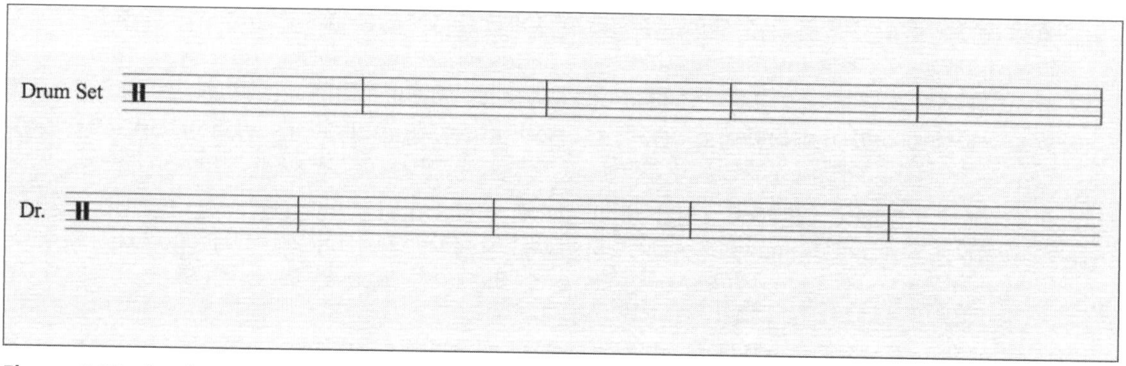

Figure 6.32   Look Mom, no music.

Figure 6.33   Time markings.

With that set, you'll need to change the noteheads. Select all your bars and go to Edit > Filter > Voice 4 so that only your time markings are highlighted. With them highlighted, press Shift+Alt/ Option+3 (which changes your time markings to slash noteheads).

One last thing: Go to Window > Properties and open the Playback panel. Deselect (uncheck) all of the Play on Pass boxes, which will stop those notes from playing back.

Now you can sit back and hear the proper drum part while you work, but your score will still look as you'd like it to (see Figure 6.34).

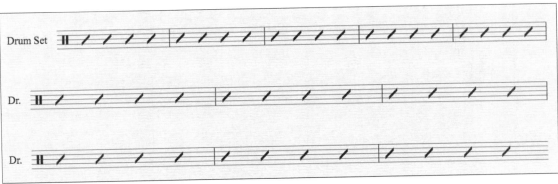

Figure 6.34 Looks good, and plays back even better!

CD: Use Example 6.12 to hide a written drum part and replace it with slash/time markings.

Piano/Organ Notation

As this chapter rolls on, you've picked up a bunch of tips that apply to all instruments. Piano notation has a few techniques that you don't find other places. In this section, we'll deal with the various ways of pedaling and cross-staff beams.

Arpeggio Piano uses the same notation for arpeggio/rolled chords as specified for guitar earlier in this chapter. Please refer to that section for guidance with these markings.

Piano Pedal Indications

It's too bad that no one can agree on anything when it comes to notation! There is not one single way to notate pedal changes on piano—rather, there is an old style and a modern style.

You'll find all of the lines by choosing Create > Line (shortcut: L), and you'll find the symbols by choosing Create > Symbol (shortcut: Z). Because a picture is worth a thousand words, look at Figure 6.35 to see some common pedal markings.

Figure 6.35 Piano pedaling example.

Figure 6.35 is an example of some of the pedaling lines—there are more, depending on the style and effect you're going for.

> **Quick Recall** If you write for piano often and you need to quickly recall your pedal lines, you can assign a shortcut to each line, rather than going to Create > Line each time. Go to Preferences > Menus and Shortcuts, select Line Styles, and scroll down. You'll see all the piano pedal lines, which you can then assign to shortcut keys for super-quick access.

> **Align** Pedal markings should be aligned on the page. To ensure that everything is perfectly lined up, select a line of markings and navigate to Layout > Align in a Row.

Organ Pedals

It has been said that organ is all about the feet, and anyone who has ever played the organ might agree. There are two easy markings to denote heel or toe pedal markings in organ music. You'll find both by choosing Create > Symbol to access the Symbol dialog box; look in the Keyboard row, as shown in Figure 6.36.

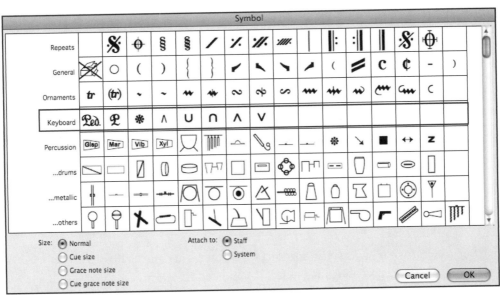

Figure 6.36 Symbols for pedaling.

Cross-Staff Beams

In piano music (and any music that writes on grand staff—organ, harp, some mallet percussion), it's sometimes necessary to have a beam cross from one staff to the other as the hands cross each other. Take a look at Figure 6.37.

Figure 6.37 Cross-staff example (J.S. Bach).

Let's talk about how we achieved this result:

1. Enter the notes, keeping any beams that start in the treble staff on the treble staff, and do the same for the bass clef.

2. Select the first note that you need to send to the lower staff and choose Notes > Cross-Staff Notes > Move Down a Staff.

3. Repeat Step 2 for the remaining notes.

There are shortcuts for moving a note cross-staff. To move a note up a staff, press Ctrl+Shift+up arrow (Windows) or Command+Shift+up arrow (Mac). To move a note down a staff, press Ctrl+Shift+down arrow (Windows) or Command+Shift+down arrow (Mac).

CD: Use Example 6.13 to set a few notes in a piano score to cross-staff notes.

Here's one final tip: If you're moving several notes cross-staff at once, you can select the notes you want to move and send them up or down a staff with one action.

Selecting Nonadjacent Notes If you want to select several notes at once, Shift-clicking only works when you're selecting contiguous notes. If you need to select notes that are not adjacent, you need to hold down Ctrl/Command while you click to select the notes properly.

Harp Notation

I'm going to keep this section brief because many of the notational issues for harp were already covered in the sections on guitar and piano. With that said, harp has a few specialized issues that we should talk about—namely, when *not* to play arpeggios and pedal markings.

Non-Arpeggio Bracket

In harp music, chords are typically rolled slightly by default, with arpeggio lines denoting more dramatic rolls. Sometimes it needs to be stressed to the player *not* to roll a particular chord. To do this, you use a vertical bracket (see Figure 6.38). You'll find this bracket by choosing Create > Line.

To draw the line the correct size, you need to drag it to fit your chord. Zoom in a bit (so you can see better) and click on the lower part of the bracket, which will expose a small drag handle. You can resize the bracket as large or as small as you need.

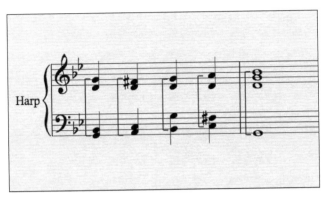

Figure 6.38   Non-arpeggio bracket.

Pedal Indications

For those of you who are unfamiliar with the harp's inner workings, the harp is tuned to all flats (Cb, Db, Eb, Fb, Gb, Ab, Bb), and a series of pedals is used to change the strings from their natural state of a flat to a natural or a sharp, depending on the musical passage at hand. Pedal indications are specified in the music itself in two main ways—either with text or with a graphical symbol to denote which pedal is in which position.

If text is used, you'll see the following text in your harp scores (see Figure 6.39), and you'll use Create > Text to add the pedal markings as needed. Alternatively, you can have Sibelius create the text automatically via a plug-in (details on that process in a moment).

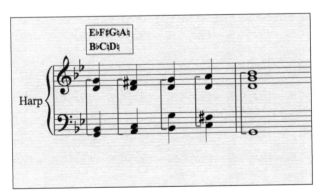

Figure 6.39   Pedal changes: text.

The pedals are organized around the base of the harp, and they correspond to the following notes: DCB|EFGA. When writing out pedal indications, make sure to spell them in the correct order.

The other way that harpists read is through a pedal diagram (a kind of tablature), as shown in Figure 6.40.

Figure 6.40   Pedal diagram.

What you're seeing is a visual depiction of the seven pedals (DCB|EFGA). A block under the mainline is down (flat), through the mainline is in the middle (natural), and above the mainline is up (sharp). To help facilitate this custom notation, Sibelius provides a plug-in to draw the diagram for you automatically. Navigate to Plug-in > Other > Add Harp Pedaling, and Sibelius will greet you with the Add Harp Pedaling dialog box shown in Figure 6.41.

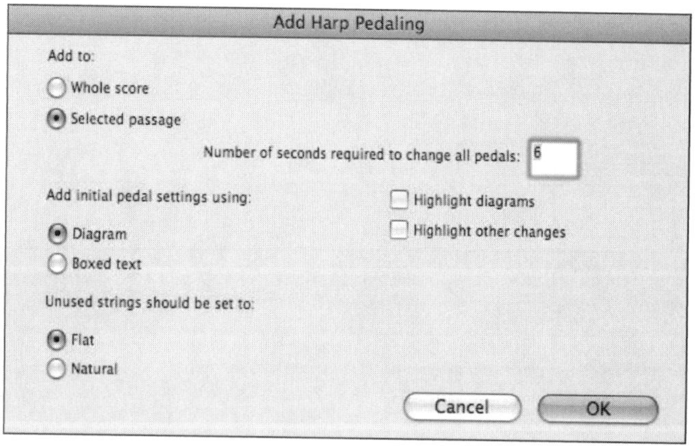

Figure 6.41   The Add Harp Pedaling dialog box.

In this dialog box, make your selections based on these basic criteria:

- In the Add To section, choose Selected Passage if you want the plug-in to affect only the selected passage (if you made a selection previously); otherwise, choose Whole Score.

- Choose the final display of the diagram: text or diagrams.

- Change the Number of Seconds Required setting to an appropriate amount of time to make Sibelius wait until there is enough time for a pedal change. You don't want the harp player changing more often than is comfortable/physically possible.

- Change the pedaling to a highlighted object to make finding, filtering, and changing the placement of the inserted diagrams easier.

When you click OK, Sibelius will adds the diagrams (or text) automatically. It's really pretty amazing!

CD: Use Example 6.14 to see how well the Add Harp Pedaling plug-in works!

Changing Noteheads

I saved the best for last: noteheads. Changing noteheads can apply to almost every instrument, and in each case it can have a different effect. Percussion noteheads give instructions on how to play and which techniques to use; slashes help guitar, piano, and bass keep time and play together; and diamonds show harmonics. The list is endless. You'll find that notehead changes are necessary in the oldest of scores (plainchant) and in the most modern of scores.

To start, I want to talk about where you find notehead changes in Sibelius. Open your Properties window by selecting Window > Properties. The resulting window shows a great number of sub-panels: General, Text, Playback, Lines, Bars, and Notes. You can open any panel by clicking once on the name. To start, make sure you have at least a single note selected in your score. To change noteheads, you'll want to look at the Notes panel, shown in Figure 6.42.

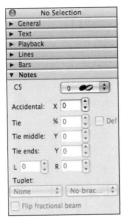

Figure 6.42   Notes panel.

As you can see from the Notes panel of Properties in Figure 6.42, you can control many aspects of notes in this panel, the first of which is noteheads. In Figure 6.42 and in your Properties window, you'll see that the first drop-down menu is for noteheads. By default this will read 0, which is the default notehead. A quick click of the drop-down menu shows you all 31 possible noteheads!

By changing the value in the Notehead menu, you can grab any notehead you'd ever need. The noteheads can be changed for a single note or a full score. This works by selection—just select the note(s) and change the notehead via the Properties window. There are more than 30 noteheads predefined in Sibelius, and you can even create your own if you're feeling brave enough (or if you need them for special notation). Figure 6.43 shows all of the noteheads in Sibelius.

Here's where you might use some of the common noteheads:

- **Notehead 0: Normal.** Traditional noteheads.

- **Notehead 1: Cross.** For unpitched percussion or other unpitched sounds.

- **Notehead 2: Diamond.** For harmonics.

- **Notehead 3: Beat without Stem.** Great for guitar, piano and walking bass, and other situations where time is kept, but the player decides what to play in those measures.

- **Notehead 4: Beat with Stem.** Used for providing a rhythmic notation for chord symbols; used in jazz and show writing.

- **Notehead 5: Cross or Diamond.** Seen in drum-set notation, crosses for closed noteheads and diamonds for open noteheads.

- **Notehead 8: Stemless.** Used in plainchant and educational scores and worksheets.

Plug-In Help When working with Notehead 3 and 4 (rhythmic slash notation), the piano or guitar often is mimicking a rhythm already in the score. If that's the case, there's a great plug-in that can help: Make Pitches Constant. You'll find it by choosing Plug-Ins > Notes and Rests > Make Pitches Constant. With the plug-in, you can take a preexisting excerpt, transpose it (say to middle line B, where rhythmic notation falls), and change the notehead to type 3 or 4 all in one shot. What a timesaver!

Silence Not all noteheads play back in a score, which can be great for worksheets and other educational examples.

Built-in Notehead Styles Sibelius 5

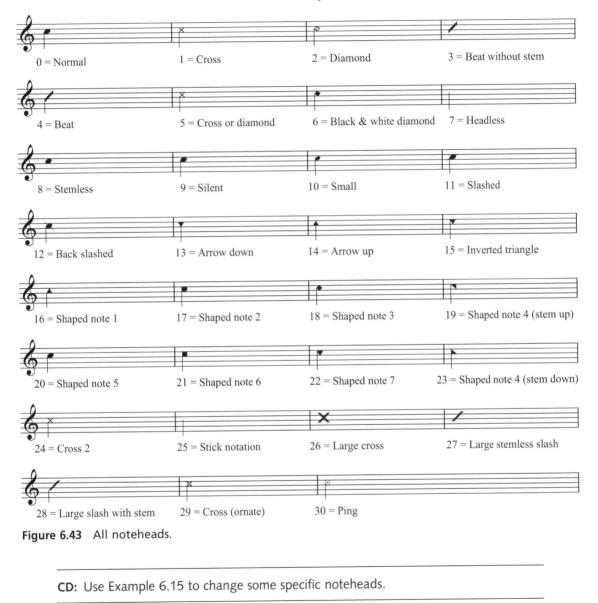

Figure 6.43 All noteheads.

CD: Use Example 6.15 to change some specific noteheads.

Notehead Shortcuts

Instead of using the Properties window to change the notehead, you can also use a key combination, granted you know which kind of notehead (by number) you need to use. The key combination is Shift+Alt+notehead number (Windows) or Shift+Option+notehead number (Mac).

If you know what number of notehead you need (which you'll learn if you change noteheads often), just select the note(s) first, and then use the key combination to change noteheads without ever viewing the Properties window.

A Reason to View Although the key combination/shortcut is useful and can potentially save you a great deal of time, if you're unsure of which notehead goes with which number (or if you just want a preview), the Properties window will give you a visual preview.

Essential Tip: Act Fast When typing in a notehead shortcut that's greater than 9—for example, notehead 25—you'll need to enter the 25 quickly for it to register in Sibelius. Keep that in mind when using the Shift+Alt/Option+notehead number shortcut.

---

7 Properties, Editing, and Filtering

1. Don't forget that you can copy music by selecting it first, and then Alt/Option-clicking on the destination measure.

2. Make sure you remember that you can always toggle the score from concert pitch to transposing score view from the Transposing Score button or by choosing Notes > Transposing Score.

3. You can use the arrow keys to move music up and down diatonically. If you hold the Ctrl/Command key and use the arrow keys, the music will move in octaves.

4. The second keypad has longer note values, faster note values, grace notes, and double and triple dots. It's also the only spot to find a whole rest.

5. The third keypad deals with stem and beam groups, as well as rolls and buzz rolls.

6. The fourth keypad deals with articulations, harmonics, and fermati.

7. The fifth keypad deals with special accidentals and microtones.

8. When you're using the Properties window, it will only show you information if music or text is selected.

9. You can cycle through the four default bar rests by clicking on a bar rest and using Shift+− (dash). Using this method, you can access a repeat barline and a hidden rest as well.

10. You can't hide a barline from the Edit > Hide or Show menu option. However, you can add an invisible barline by choosing Create > Barline.

11.   For selecting text-based elements, try Edit > Select More (Ctrl/ Command+Shift+A). Just select the first appearance of the text, and Select More! Use this option to select lyrics instead of using a filter. (It's faster.)

12.   There's probably a filter to help you select what you're after. Don't forget to check Edit > Filter.

Now it's time to focus your efforts on dealing with music that has already been created and learning about the tools within Sibelius to help you edit your music. We'll look at transposing music, both diatonically and by interval/key; learning about the other three keypads in Sibelius and their functions; using the powerful Properties window; and finally, understanding the extensive filtering within the Edit menu, which is one of Sibelius's most powerful features.

Essential Tip: Alt/Option-Click Although this chapter doesn't deal with cutting or copying, please remember that you can copy any selected music by simply holding down the Alt/ Option key and clicking with your mouse where you want the selected music to appear! This will save you time.

Transposing

Although this chapter is largely about editing music in Sibelius, you can think of transposing music as a sort of edit; you're changing music that's already there. In Sibelius, the Transpose feature is found in the Notes > Transpose menu, not in the Edit menu. Regardless of its location, the Transpose feature is central to working with music in Sibelius.

There are two ways to transpose music in Sibelius—one is by diatonic steps or octaves, and the other is through transposition by key or interval. Let's start with diatonic transpositions, which you shouldn't confuse with viewing a transposing pitch score! This is about taking sections of music and changing their key/transposition.

Transposing Diatonically

If you are transposing music diatonically, you can use the arrow keys to step music up and down the current key signature. This is very helpful when you are creating a harmony part (usually at a 3rd of 6th intervals) and you need to copy, cut, and paste music from one staff to another and transpose the melody.

Essential Tip: Transposing Score In this section, we're dealing with transposing music, not toggling between concert pitch and transposing score views for instruments that transpose.

To toggle between concert pitch and transposing views, go to Notes > Transposing Score or click the Transposing Score button on the toolbar to toggle back and forth.

Let's run through the steps to copy a single-line melody from one staff to another and create a diatonic transposition:

1. Select the range of music you want to copy by Shift-clicking the first and last notes you want to select.

2. Copy the music using the Edit > Copy command or the appropriate key command (Ctrl/Command+C).

3. Select the location to where you want to copy the music by clicking in the measure and pasting it using Edit > Paste or the shortcut Ctrl/Command+V.

4. Step the music (already pre-selected) up a third interval by pressing the up arrow key three times.

If you start with Figure 7.1 and follow the aforementioned steps, you can achieve the results shown in Figure 7.2 in about 30 seconds (or maybe faster).

Figure 7.1 Single-note melody.

Figure 7.2 After a quick diatonic transposition.

CD: Use Example 7.1 to practice a few diatonic and octave-based transpositions. You'll also get a chance to copy music from instrument to instrument and fix the octave disparity quickly.

You can modify the arrow keys with the Ctrl or Command keys to shift music up or down an octave, which is useful if you're pasting into a staff that has a lower pitch and the default paste is out of range for your new instrument. Once the music is in the proper range, you can use the single arrow keys to move it diatonically.

Because the arrow keys only move diatonically, you'll need to look at other options for transposing music by interval or by key.

Essential Tip: Diatonic Steps If you're transposing by larger diatonic steps, you should know that the full Transpose function (as detailed in the following section) has a function for transposing by diatonic interval, which could speed up larger interval movements. However, you can achieve a diatonic seventh up by shifting the music up using Ctrl/Command+up arrow followed by a single down arrow, rather than using any menus. Whichever way you go, Sibelius gives you some flexibility in your working style.

Transposing by Interval or Key

As promised, let's look at how to transpose music by interval or key. This is done by selecting Notes > Transpose or by using the key command Shift+T. When you call up this command, you'll get a warning if you have not selected anything to transpose. If you have, you'll be greeted with the Transpose dialog box shown in Figure 7.3.

The Transpose dialog box allows you to transpose selected music by interval (ascending or descending) or to a particular key. Let's go through the options in the window:

- Choose whether you'll transpose by key or interval. Clicking on an option will enable the lower sections (either Key or Interval).

- If you choose the Key option, you can select the destination key and either the closest, up, or down transposition. Transposing by key is new in Sibelius 5, and it calculates how far you need to transpose to get your source (regardless of the key) into the new key of your choice.

- If you choose the Interval option, you can select the direction (up or down), the quality of interval (Major/Perfect, Minor/Diminished, Augmented, or Diatonic), and finally the size of the interval.

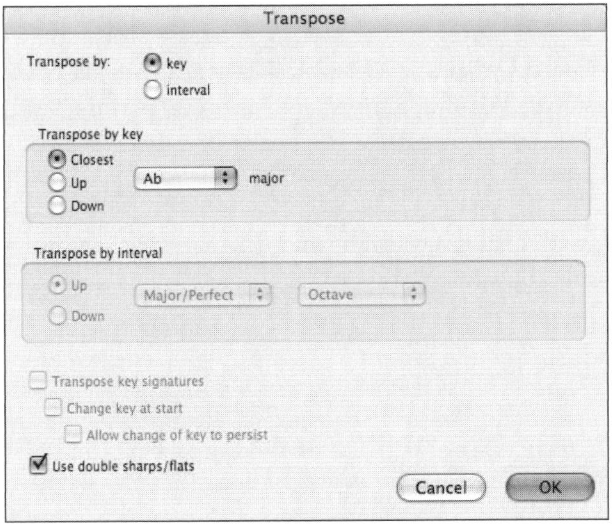

Figure 7.3 The Transpose dialog box.

- If you have selected a full system or the entire score, the lower section will become active. From there you can choose whether to transpose the key signature, change the key at the start of your score, or allow a persistent key change. These options are all selectable check boxes.

- You can also force Sibelius to spell notes with or without double sharps and flats.

That takes care of transpositions! Just remember that you don't need to transpose when you copy and paste between instruments; Sibelius takes care of that for you. If it looks like Sibelius isn't transposing properly for you, make sure your score is set to view transposing and not concert pitch. You can toggle this with the Ctrl/Command+Shift+T key command, which is also good for instruments that transpose their clefs, such as saxophone, which displays in bass clef in concert pitch scores and in treble clef in the transposing score.

Don't Use a Key Signature! Adding a key signature change will not have the effect of transposing your music; you'll be left with a mess of accidentals in your score. If you need to transpose, do it through the Notes menu.

CD: Use Example 7.2 to transpose the selections by interval and by key.

Rest of the Keypads

Let's take a brief look at the remaining three keypads that Sibelius uses. These last three keypads fit well with the "editing" scope of this chapter because many of the symbols help you change existing notes into something else.

F10: Stems

The third keypad (F10) deals almost entirely with changes to stems and, by extension, tremolos and rolls (see Figure 7.4). Here is a list of each key's function:

- 1: Single-stroke roll/tremolo.

- 2: Double-stroke roll/tremolo.

- 3: Triple-stroke roll/tremolo.

- Enter: Convert to interval tremolo.

- 4: Quadruple-stroke roll/tremolo.

- 5: Quintuple-stroke roll/tremolo.

- 6: Buzz or Z roll.

- +: Next keypad layout.

- 7: Break the beam (from the previous note).

- 8: Join the beam to the previous and subsequent notes (beam).

- 9: Break the beam (to the next note).

- - : Return to first keypad layout.

- / : Don't connect the beam on either side of the selected note.

- = : Join with a single beam.

Figure 7.4 The third (F10) keypad: stems.

CD: Use Example 7.3 to utilize the third keypad on several examples for beaming and rolls.

F11: Articulations and Fermati

The fourth keypad (F11) contains fermati and articulations commonly found in scores (see Figure 7.5).

- 0: No pause.

- .: Harmonic/open hi-hat.

- 1: Fermata—indeterminate pause.

- 2: Take a medium pause.

- 3: Take a short pause.

- 4: Left-hand pizzicato/brass stop/guitar tap/closed hi-hat.

- 5: Up-bow/up-pick.

- 6: Down-bow/down-pick.

- +: Next keypad layout.

- 7: Wedge, a baroque staccatissimo.

- 8: Marcato.

- 9: Staccatissimo.

- -: Return to first keypad layout.

Figure 7.5 The fourth (F11) keypad: articulations and fermati.

CD: Use Example 7.4 to use the fourth keypad layout on a wide variety of musical examples.

F12: Other Accidentals

The last keypad layout (F12) takes care of accidentals that range from common to less commonly used symbols for microtonal pitch (see Figure 7.6).

- 0: Remove all accidentals.

- 1: Natural flat (go from a double flat to a single flat).

- 2: ¾ sharp.

- 3: ¾ flat.

- Enter: Place accidental in bracket (cautionary accidental).

- 4: Natural sharp (go from a double sharp to a single sharp).

- 5: Quarter sharp.

- 6: Quarter flat.

- +: Next keypad layout

- 7: Natural.

- 8 : Sharp.

- 9: Flat.

- -: Return to first keypad layout.

Figure 7.6 The fifth keypad: accidentals.

- =: Double sharp.

- /: Double flat.

CD: Use Example 7.5 for some practice adding some unusual accidentals to a variety of musical examples.

Keep in mind that the microtonal accidentals will not play back by themselves. They are for graphical purposes. If you need them to play back, check out the Quarter-Tone Playback plug-in, which will add the proper hidden pitch change indications to enable this.

The Properties Window

In Sibelius you have two ways of affecting the appearance of music onscreen: House Styles and properties. House Styles effect global changes; if you muck with the House Style, it changes that parameter in your entire score. If you want to make changes on a smaller scale, you'll want to know all about the Properties window. The Properties window is one of the main floating windows that Sibelius makes available through the Window menu. The Properties window is a collection of six panels (General, Text, Playback, Lines, Bars, and Notes) that detail some important properties and functions that you can change as you create your score.

Rather than drilling down through what each menu contains and detailing each and every function, we'll look at each of the Properties panels from the perspective of what it can help you do and what most users typically use it for. We'll also look at situations in which you are better served by changing properties through a House Style or some other means.

Call up the Properties window by choosing Window > Properties, by clicking the icon on the toolbar, or by pressing Ctrl+Alt+W (Windows) or Command+Option+W (Mac). You'll see that the Properties window contains six small sub-panels, as shown in Figure 7.7.

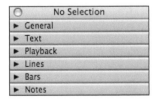

Figure 7.7 The Properties window.

To expand the window to view any of the sub-panels, simply click on the small black arrow on the left side to expand that panel to show its properties.

Essential Tip: Select! Each of the Properties panels is based on selections, so make sure that you have an object selected if you want to see what the Properties window will allow you to control.

General

The first panel is the General panel, shown in Figure 7.8.

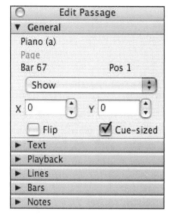

Figure 7.8   General properties.

The General properties show you a few controls to tweak. The first ones are information about what is selected: instrument name, page number, bar number, and position in bar. This information is very helpful if you're trying to figure out which instrument a dynamic is attached to, for instance.

Next up, you'll see a drop-down control for Show or Hide, which lets you show or hide the selected element(s).

The X control sets the left-to-right placement of your selected object, while the Y control sets the up-and-down placement. This is great for precise positioning of notes and objects, including stem length.

In this panel you can also flip any object (stems, objects, slurs) and make any number of notes/ objects cue-sized.

Here are a few situations where you'd use the General panel of the Properties window:

- You have an object, such as a time signature that you want to hide. Select the object and set the Show or Hide option to Hide, and the object will be hidden. Another typical use for hidden objects is anything you want to play back but not see in your score, such as a drum part hidden behind rhythmic slash notation.

- If you're trying line up noteheads in several voices, and Sibelius isn't doing what you like by default, select a notehead and use the X parameter to move it left and right. (Positive integers move to the right, while negative integers move to the left.) This is great for precise positioning of objects.

- If you find that the mouse makes exact positioning difficult, use the X and Y offsets, and you'll know exactly how much you moved every object.

- If you're coming to this panel to flip objects, you're wasting time! The key command to flip is X, and it works on single and multiple objects at once.

- If you're making a note cue-sized, it's best to do it through the Properties window. However, if you're making a cue and you're pasting from another instrument, you should be using the Paste as Cue option (see the "Paste as Cue" section later in this chapter) instead. It's also possible to make a note into a cue-sized note from the second keypad layout (F9).

CD: Use Example 7.6 to learn to use the General panel of the Properties window to change various aspects of your score.

Text

The Text panel is one of the simplest panels in the Properties window. It has only a few options: Text Style, Font, Size, Bold, Italics, or Underline. When you select any text-based object, this panel will show you the properties for the selected style (see Figure 7.9).

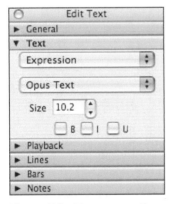

Figure 7.9 Text properties.

To change the details about the text style, just change any of the properties onscreen.

Here's a list of things you can, or possibly shouldn't, do with the Text panel:

- You can change the style of text if you've chosen the wrong one. Suppose you've chosen a technique and you really wanted something more like plain text—you can flip it from here.

- You can make any text bold, underlined, italic, or a different size once in a while. However, if you feel like your text needs to be bigger every time you insert it, you'll want to change this globally, which is accomplished via the House Style menu—don't change it all from Properties.

- You can only change the text style in Properties if the text is in the same family. For example, you cannot change system text into staff text, no matter how nicely you ask.

- If you decide to add a new line of lyrics and you need to move your other lyric entries up a lyric style (for example, Lyrics Line 1 to Lyrics Line 2), you can easily do that here. You'll need to read a little bit further in this chapter to see how to filter just a single line of lyrics, but it's easy!

CD: Use Example 7.7 to change some of the text using the Text panel of the Properties window. You'll learn to change type, size, and bold/italics/underline.

Playback

The Playback panel is slightly more involved than the previous Properties panels. This panel covers elements relating to playback—what will or won't playback and how it will sound upon playback (see Figure 7.10).

Because this window is a bit more involved, let's look at each function. You'll need to know what each does, even if it's just a short description.

- **Play on Pass.** This bunch of check boxes tells Sibelius to play the selected object (or not to play it) based on numbered repeat structures.

- **Last Time Ending.** This sets a repeat ending line as the last one and lets Sibelius keep going.

- **Jump at Bar End.** This is used in the special occasion when a numbered repeat takes place mid-bar.

- **Live Velocity, Live Start Position, and Live Duration.** These options all deal with live playback features, which you'll know a lot more about when you read up on playback as a whole in Chapter 12, "Playback and Virtual Instruments."

- **Gliss/Rit/Accel.** This tells Sibelius how to play back written glissandi, ritardando, and accelerando in your score if you need to change them from the default.

- **Hairpin.** If you need to change how much a hairpin affects playback dynamics, you can do it here.

- **Trill.** You can set the type of trill, its speed, and the starting note (upper or lower) using check boxes.

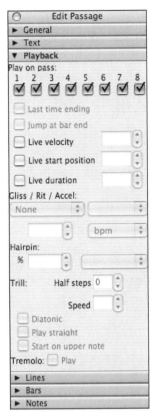

Figure 7.10 Playback properties.

- **Tremolo.** This tells Sibelius whether to play single-stroke tremolos. Normally, you wouldn't turn this off unless the sample from which you're playing is a sampled tremolo (in other words, a single note, not repeated notes sent from Sibelius).

It should be said that this entire panel is for controlling how Sibelius deals with specific playback issues, and the types of folks who tweak these settings are using Sibelius to produce mock-up audio realizations. If that's what you need to do, you'll find that this panel provides plenty of options to tweak. Here are some real-world situations you might find yourself in:

- You have some music marked "Second time only" and you really want it to play only the second time. Highlight the music and deselect 1 from the Play on Pass section.

- You have a dynamic marking you only want to play at a specific time. Highlight it and check (or uncheck) the appropriate Play on Pass option.

- You have cue notes that you need to play back (by default they do not). Select them and switch on the Play on Pass boxes.

- You want your rit line to slow down more. Select it and change its percentage from the stock 75% to a lower number, or set it from % to BPM and set a metronome marking for the rit. You can do the same for other lines, such as gliss and accel. Note: The BPM will specify the ending BPM of any ritardando, rallentando, or accelerando marking.

By default, Sibelius does a very good job playing back scores. The Playback panel is for times when you need to change the default playback behavior.

CD: Use Example 7.8 to not only silence certain notes, but also to control aspects of hairpin playback and rit/accel markings!

Lines

The Lines panel deals with slurs and hairpins (see Figure 7.11). These controls will not be used by every Sibelius user, but the controls for making a single hairpin open on both sides aren't found anywhere else!

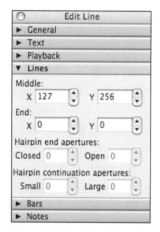

Figure 7.11 The Lines panel.

The controls for slurs have the following properties:

- **Middle X and Y.** This controls the horizontal and vertical positions that affect the curve of a slur. The Y parameter has the most dramatic effect—0 produces a flat slur, and higher integers produce more curve.

- **End X and Y.** This controls the end of the slur and sets its vertical and horizontal positions.

So who's going to tweak slurs? By default, Sibelius does a fairly good job with slurs—they are magnetic and are set to avoid objects in your score. If you're engraving music and you need to have the utmost control over shape, especially when copying a preexisting part, these properties are for you. While you're able to click and drag the arc of a slur manually, some folks will want more control.

If you choose House Style > Engraving Rules > Slurs, you will access global settings that affect how Sibelius draws scores score-wide. Properties are good for changing a few slurs, but anything else should be done from the House Style menu.

As for hairpins, those, too, are controlled by the Properties window with the following controls:

- **Hairpin and Apertures.** The closed value sets the closed size of your hairpin. The default is 0 and will show a closed end; if you need an open hairpin, use a higher value. The Open parameter controls how wide open the mouth of the hairpin is.

- **Hairpin Continuation Apertures.** These control hairpins that exist over system and page breaks. The Small and Large parameters deal with the start and end of hairpins spread across system and page breaks.

The default hairpins are drawn by Sibelius based on the settings in House Style > Engraving Rules > Lines. You should only tweak the properties of a few hairpins using the Properties window (such as one or more hairpins that are open on both sides). Any large-scale changes should be handled through the House Style menu.

Bars

The Bars panel of the Properties window is probably one of the most useful ones in all of the Properties panels. Shown in Figure 7.12, the Bars panel covers a wide range of parameters related to how bars are drawn and formatted.

Figure 7.12 Bars properties.

The first things you see are check boxes for the following items:

- **Brackets.** This sets whether Sibelius should draw brackets at the start of a bar, at a section break brought on by a forced system break, or at a manual "gap before bar." (This option will be discussed in a moment.)

- **Initial Barline.** This sets whether Sibelius should draw an initial barline at the start of a bar, at a section break brought on by a forced system break, or at a manual gap before bar.

- **Clefs.** This options sets whether Sibelius should draw a clef at the start of a bar, at a section break brought on by a forced system break, or at a manual gap before bar.

- **Key Signature.** This options sets whether Sibelius should draw a key signature at the start of a bar, at a section break brought on by a forced system break, or at a manual gap before bar.

- **Split Multirest.** If you'd like to set a barline to force a multirest break, you can select this, and Sibelius will break the multirest at this point.

- **Section End.** If you mark a bar as a section end, Sibelius will add an instrument name at the next bar (as long as it's set up to do so in House Style > Engraving Rules > Instrument > At New Section).

Many of these options deal with the drawing of initial bars and bars after system breaks or other breaks in your score. Just like every other object in Properties, you first have to select the bar on which you want to work.

There are three more options in this panel that read as follows:

- **Breaks.** This drop-down menu lets you set whether there will be a break at this barline. Many folks will set up breaks by choosing Layout > Break, and this menu lets you set or override measure or system breaks.

- **Bar Rest.** This drop-down menu lets you set how bar rests are drawn. There are four to choose from: Blank, Repeat Previous Bar, Normal, and Vertical. By default, the normal bar rest is drawn (Type 2). Note: The repeat previous bar rest does not play back a repeated bar. (It's only visual.)

- **Gap before Bar.** This is very useful! You can force a split by adding a gap before any bar. You can use this for codas, starting new sections, and much more. If you're doing educational tests, the Gap before Bar option will give you bars with gaps on both sides, which are great for laying out worksheets and other educational materials.

For many users, this panel is a powerful find. Knowing about the Gap before Bar option helps most users in the difficult task of score layout, especially codas and more advanced notation.

Essential Tip: Cycling Through Rests If you're changing the appearance of bar rests, you can go to the Properties window and change the bar rests, or you can just click on the bar rest in question and press Shift++ or Shift+− to cycle through the four types of bar rests available in Sibelius.

CD: Use Example 7.9 to see how useful the Bars panel of the Properties window is! You'll find loads of examples to help you understand when to use the Bars panel.

Notes

The Notes panel sets the appearance of notes, noteheads, accidentals, ties, and tuplets, as shown in Figure 7.13.

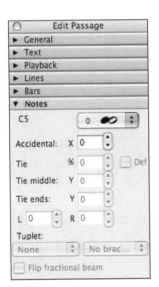

Figure 7.13 Notes panel.

Let's break this panel down and see what's going on:

- **Notehead.** This menu lets you set the appearance of any notehead(s) in your score. There are 31 noteheads from which to choose. Refer to Chapter 6 for more information on noteheads.

- **Accidental.** This control lets you move the accidental closer to or farther from the notehead. Although Sibelius will position noteheads in the proper spot, you might feel the need to move them around, and this is how you do it!

- **Tie.** This option sets how "curvy" your ties are. Lower numbers have more arc, while higher numbers provide a flatter tie.

- **Tie Middle.** This option sets the vertical height of the middle of the tie.

- **Tie Ends.** This option sets how high (vertically) the end of your tie will be.

- **Tuplet.** These two drop-down menus set the appearance of the selected tuplet. The first drop-down menu lets you choose from the following choices: None, Number, Ratio, Ratio & Note. The second drop-down menu sets the appearance (or lack thereof) of brackets. The choices are No Bracket, Bracket, and Auto. No Bracket and Bracket are pretty self-explanatory, but Auto needs some explanation. When Auto is set, the bracket hides itself if the number of tuplets matches the number of notes in the beam (for example, a triplet eighth-note pattern would have no bracket).

- **Flip Fractional Beam.** If you have a fractional secondary beam in your score, you can flip it by selecting this check box.

For most users, changing noteheads and tuplet appearance are the most common uses for the Notes panel. The Notes panel is also the only way to move an accidental by itself, so it's a very useful panel to know.

That concludes our look at the Properties window. The next step in our editing adventure is to look at the Edit menu. (Go figure.)

CD: See Example 7.10 to use the Notes panel of the Properties window! You'll learn how to change the appearance of tuplets and much more.

The Edit Menu

The Edit menu is a consolidation of typical editing features in Sibelius. Although we won't look at each and every item in the menu, we will look at the important and powerful menus. I'll also highlight some of the new features in Sibelius 5, along with some features that will save you hundreds of hours—features that you didn't even know about!

Paste as Cue

A new feature in Sibelius 5 is the ability to paste as a cue. This is a major timesaver for anyone who creates parts with cue notes. Figure 7.14 shows a cue in action.

Because cues are commonly preexisting parts from other instruments, most folks will copy and paste them in. In the days before Sibelius 5, after you pasted the music in, you then had to change the selected passage to cue-sized using the General panel of the Properties window. In Sibelius 5, you can select a range of music using Edit > Copy or the shortcut Ctrl/Command+C.

Figure 7.14 Cue.

To paste as a cue, instead of using a normal paste, use Edit > Paste as Cue—which has a fairly immense shortcut of Ctrl+Alt+Shift+V (Windows) or Command+Option+Shift+V (Mac)—and you'll automatically have your music pasted in cue size.

Paste as Cue has its own page in Sibelius's preferences. Figure 7.15 shows the available options.

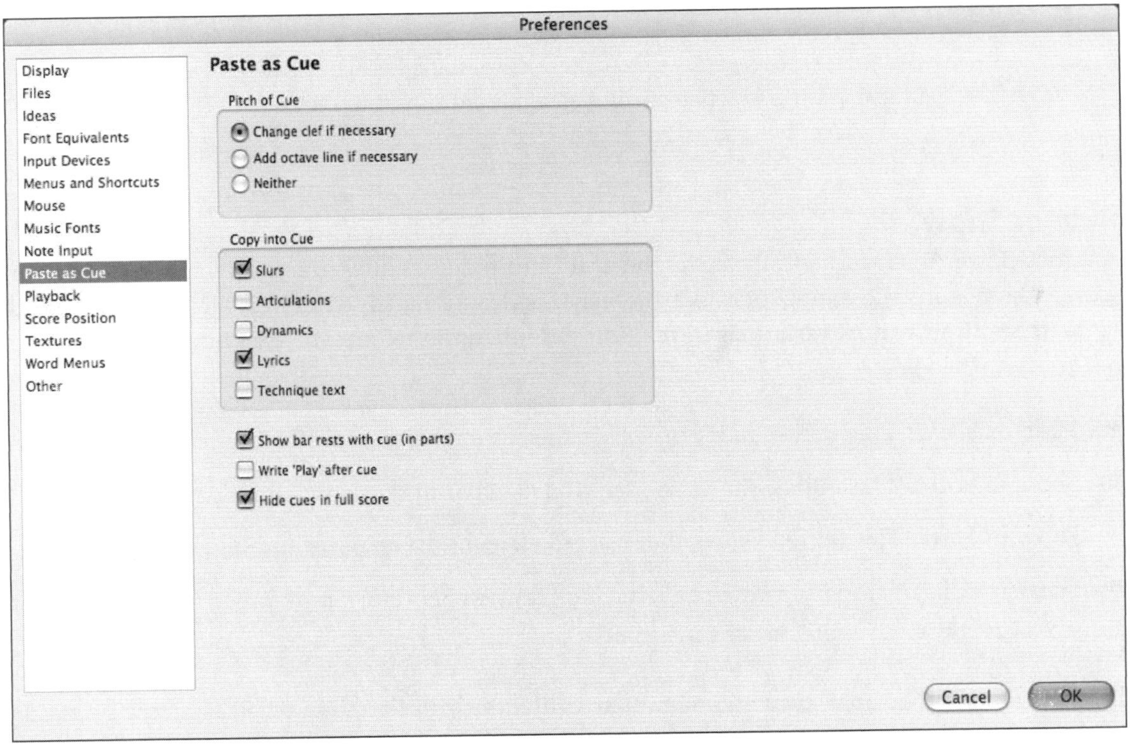

Figure 7.15 Paste as Cue preferences.

The choices are fairly self-explanatory, but they greatly increase the power of the feature. It's not just pasting as a cue; it does a great deal more if you configure it for your own needs.

Here are a few important things to know about the Paste as Cue function:

- By default, notes that you paste as a cue do not play back. This is because their Play on Pass check boxes in Properties > Playback are disabled by default. You can make them play by selecting the notes and rechecking the Play on Pass option.

- You can have Sibelius suggest some proper cue locations using a plug-in. Navigate to Plug-Ins > Other > Suggest Cue Locations and run it on your score, and Sibelius will suggest the best spots for cues.

- You can also have Sibelius check your cues for you. Cue checking is important if you've added cues and then changed the source music that originated the cue. Run the Check Cues plug-in from Plug-Ins > Proof-reading > Check Cues for a little extra peace of mind that nothing has changed.

- You can create notes in cue size by flipping their size either from the second keypad layout (on the Enter key) or from the Properties > General panel if pasting as a cue isn't what you need.

CD: Use Example 7.11 to practice pasting as a cue from part to part.

Hide or Show

Another powerful feature of Sibelius is the ability to hide or show practically anything in your score. The feature is a simple one, but the benefits are extremely wide-reaching. You can find Hide or Show and all its variations in the Edit > Hide or Show menu. The Hide or Show menu has four variations:

- **Hide or Show.** This option hides or shows the selected element.

- **Show in Score.** This option shows the selected element in the score and hides it in the parts.

- **Show in Parts.** This option shows the selected element in the parts and hides it in the score.

- **Show in All.** This option is used to override Show in Score or Show in Parts or to force an object to show in both the score and parts.

Now, you can bring up a great submenu that contains all of the Hide or Show items by right-clicking on an object or selection. If you right-click (or Control-click for Mac users), you will see the menu shown in Figure 7.16.

You can use this for easy access to Hide or Show commands and, as you can see from Figure 7.16, you can access more functions with this!

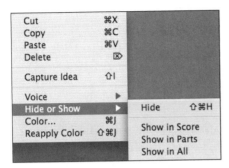

Figure 7.16 Right-click submenu.

Hide Anything You can hide any object in your score! Yup, pretty much everything!

Here is a list of things you can do with Hide or Show that you might not have thought of:

- You want to create a measure for a cadenza or another "free-time" musical movement. Create a measure with the proper time signature to allow all the notes you need, click on the time signature, and hide it. Note: Time signatures can be deleted, and they still have the same effect! When you hide a time signature, you get the gap in the measure where the signature should be, and this might not be what you want. Instead, you may want to add the signature and delete it, which has the same effect as hiding it, but without the gap.

- You want to create an ear-training test for students. Create the music and hide the notes—this will play back but won't be visible normally.

- You have a drum-set part that contains only slash notation (simple quarter-note rhythmic notation). In the real performance, this will be improvised by the musician, but for the purposes of the playback, you want something to play but not be seen. Create a drum part and hide it. Then add the slash notation in another voice. You'll get the playback you want without seeing the notation you don't.

- You are creating a score for playback purposes and you want to add any lines, dynamics, and hairpins that you don't want in the final score, but they need to play back. Create them and hide them!

- You want to add text for the composer, but you don't want it to show in any of the parts. Use Show in Score, and it will appear only in the score.

- You want cues to show in the parts, but not in the score. Use Show in Parts on the selected music, and it won't appear in the score.

Essential Tip: Hidden Barlines You can't hide a barline using the Hide or Show command. Instead, create a hidden barline from the Create > Barline menu. Keep in mind that musically, Sibelius knows that the barline is there and treats it accordingly with regard to note spacing and other factors.

Once you've hidden objects, they aren't gone forever; they're just hidden for now. Hidden objects appear as a pale color when you select them. When you deselect them, they do in fact disappear.

One last thing you'll want to know about is the View menu control. You can choose to view hidden objects in your score (they won't print unless you tell them to do so), which can help you keep track of all of the hidden items in your score. Navigate to View > Hidden Objects, and you'll see all of your hidden objects in your score at all times (just slightly paler).

CD: Use Example 7.12 to practice hiding elements in a preformatted score.

Select More

One of the most unsung, yet powerful, commands in Sibelius is Select More. It definitely needs its own section. Select More allows you to select a single text object (such as a lyric) and choose Edit > Select > Select More to select all other text objects in the same style (such as the rest of your lyrics). Once the text object is selected, you can move it all at once, resize it all at once (using Properties), or even delete it all at once. Any way you slice it, this feature is a huge timesaver.

Select More is perfect for quickly selecting multiple lyrics, expressions, and techniques. But remember that Select More only works on text-based objects.

Essential Tip: Select More The key command for Select More is Ctrl+Shift+A (Windows) or Command+Shift+A. You must select one object first in order for Select More to function.

If you want the functionality of Select More on other objects than text, you'll want to learn more about how Sibelius lets you filter pretty much anything!

Example Here's a great example of when Select More really saves your life. You import a MIDI file from the Internet, and when it imports, you have tons of off MIDI messages in your score and you need to get rid of possibly hundreds of messages at ones. Click on the first one, choose Select More, and press Delete—they'll all go away with a single delete.

CD: Use Example 7.13 to see the power of Select More for text selections.

Simple (Quick) Filters

Sibelius starts with Select More as its first way of selecting multiple objects easily in one swoop, but it's limited to text objects. To select multiple objects like this, you'll want to look at Sibelius's simple filters.

Before we go any further, it's worth explaining how filters work. Filters work by taking a selection of many objects and reducing them to fewer objects based on criteria you choose. Remember that filters only work when you select music beforehand.

Let's look at the simple filters. Figure 7.17 shows the Edit > Filter menu.

As you can see in Figure 7.17, there are many things you can filter. Let's talk about some common uses of these simple filters:

- Moving or aligning of any text, dynamics, chord symbols, or any object you can select.

- Mass deletion of particular objects.

- Changing properties. (For example, changing slur properties all at once—select all the slurs and use the Properties > Lines panel to affect all slurs at once.)

- Selecting notes in a particular voice for coloring.

- Copying music or score elements quickly.

I want to use an example to illustrate the power of simple filters.

In Figure 7.18, all of the lyrics are too close to the notes. Rather than do a House Style change for the text style, I just want to move this down.

1.   Select all of the measures in which the lyrics are too close. If this pertains to all of your measures, do a triple-click to quickly select all.

2.   Go to Edit > Filter > Lyrics.

3.   Use your arrow keys to move the lyrics down by hand, or use the mouse.

This is just one of the uses of filters—the simple filters will surely save you a great deal of time when editing or copying music. The simple filters are limited to the preset categories that Sibelius provides you with. If you want to make filter selections in a more advanced way, you'll want to look at the Advanced Filter, which lets you filter in some amazing ways.

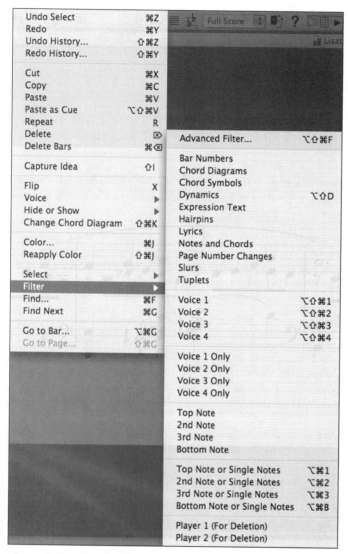

Figure 7.17 Simple filters.

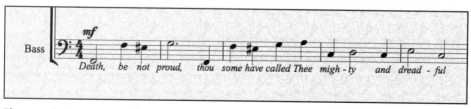

Figure 7.18 Lyrics too close.

CD: Use Example 7.14 to quickly filter and delete some lyrics.

Advanced Filter

What if the quick filters don't have what you need? The next place you want to look is the Advanced Filter dialog box (see Figure 7.19), which you access by choosing Edit > Filter > Advanced Filter.

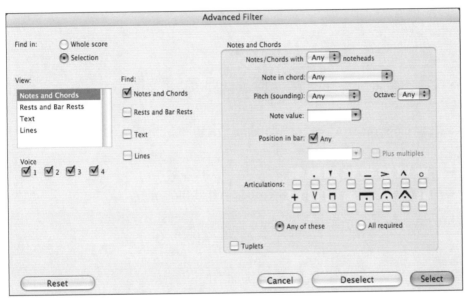

Figure 7.19   The Advanced Filter.

As you can see from Figure 7.18, it's pretty advanced! There are literally thousands of different combinations you can set. However, please don't let that scare you! This filter is as advanced as you need it to be. Rather than run down an explanation of every control (which you have in your Sibelius Reference Help > Sibelius Reference), I want to look at a few typical scenarios in which the Advanced Filter is an exceptional tool, and I'll provide screenshots!

I want to start with a rough look at the interface. On the left side you'll see a panel called View. By selecting Notes and Chords, Rests and Bar Rests, Text, or Lines, you'll change the display on the right side of the interface; the right side shows you deeper controls for the view you've selected. Above the View panel, you can choose whether you want the filter to work on just your current selection or the entire score.

Below the View panel, you'll find check boxes for all four voices—these let you choose which voice you want the filter to work on. Finally, there is a set of check boxes marked Notes and Chords, Rests and Bar Rests, Text, and Lines, in which you can have Sibelius filter in multiple categories at once.

Drum Set Filters

Let's start with a drum example. You want to change all of the ride cymbal notes from their default notehead (Notehead 0) to the proper notehead (Notehead 1). You could go note by note and change the noteheads, but that would take a very long time! Let's set up an Advanced Filter to do this for us.

Follow these steps (after you select the drum notation you've already entered):

1. Set the view to Notes and Chords.

2. Leave all voices selected.

3. Leave the Find In option set to Selection.

4. Change the Pitch (Sounding) option to F (because Sibelius still refers to notes in drum staves as if they were in treble clef).

5. Change the Octave option to 5 (because Sibelius treats middle C as C5).

6. Click Select.

See Figure 7.20 to view the correct settings for the ride cymbal filtering.

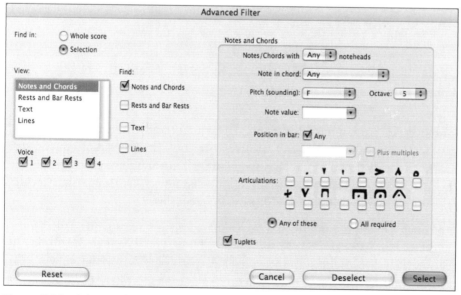

Figure 7.20 Advanced Filter: ride.

Now all of your ride cymbal notes are selected in your score, and you can change them all at once using Properties > Notes. You could change the note and octaves to help you pick other notes in the drum set as well.

Here's a recap of why the Advanced Filter is set the way it is. We wanted to select notes based on their pitch (to find a particular note we needed to edit). So, we found the note name and octave and told the filter to find it. That's all we had to do!

Which Octave? If you're not used to selecting an octave by number (F5, for example), you can select a single note and go to the Properties > Notes panel, and it will show you the pitch name and octave to the left of the notehead.

Accent New Notes

Suppose you're an educator, working on worksheets for some beginning music lessons. In your lesson, you want to highlight a new note in some way, to help accent it in the learning process. Many methods will have an accent or fermata placed on new notes to help students. You can set up a simple filter to do this.

In the filter, we'll ask the filter to find all of the As above the staff (a common new pitch for first-year flute students). We'll set up this filter in much the same way as we did our drum filter, as shown in Figure 7.21.

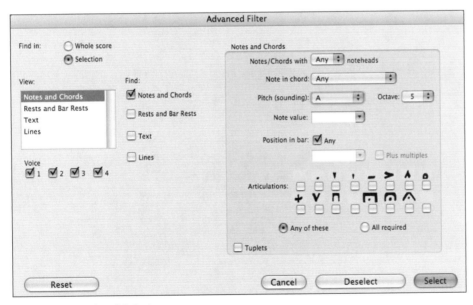

Figure 7.21 Filter high A.

Select the music that contains the high A (or any other pitch you want to highlight).

1. Set the view to Notes and Chords.

2. Leave all voices selected.

3. Leave the Find In option set to Selection.

4. Change the Pitch (Sounding) option to A.

5. Change the Octave option to 5.

6. Click Select.

Now navigate to the keypad and add either an accent or a fermata (whichever you choose). Alternatively, you could simply color the notes to highlight them as new and important notes. Choose Edit > Color (shortcut: Ctrl/Command+J) and recolor those pitches.

Particular Rhythm

The next example involves placing an accent on the first beat of each bar. Because the pitches are changing, cut and paste won't work; you need to select the first beat of each bar regardless of which pitch is present. To do so, we'll use the Position in Bar function for the first time, as seen in Figure 7.22.

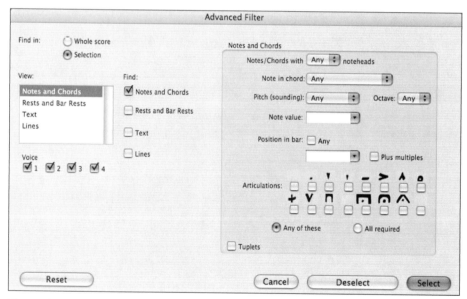

Figure 7.22 Position in Bar filter.

Follow these steps to select the first beat in each bar:

1. Set the view to Notes and Chords.

2. Leave all voices selected.

3.   Leave the Find In option set to Selection.

4.   Deselect the Any option from Position in Bar.

5.   Leave the Position in Bar empty. (More on this in a moment.)

6.   Click Select.

The only tricky part of this filter is the Position in Bar option. It's not totally clear from the Advanced Filter dialog box that leaving the option blank will select the first beat. Here's how it works: The Position in Bar option lets you choose how far into the bar to look. You set this with a rhythmic value. For example, if you entered an eighth note, it would select any notes that were an eighth note into the bar (on the "and" of Beat 1). So, if you wanted to select a note on Beat 2, you'd need to enter a quarter note in the Position in Bar field. Once you get this, it's not difficult at all.

One more note: In the Position in Bar section, there is a check box for Plus Multiples. If you select this option, it will select all notes that take place in whatever rhythmic value you choose. So, if you set Position in Bar for a quarter note and select Plus Multiples, it will select all notes that fall on quarter notes (including those on the first beat)!

Re-Beam Help Another great use for filters is to re-beam large amounts of music to a special beaming convention by using Position in Bar to select the proper note and using the third keypad (F10) to change the beaming.

CD: Example 7.15 shows several ways to use Advanced Filters to help control and speed up your workflow in Sibelius.

Deselect Filters

One last choice in the Advanced Filter is the possibility to deselect, instead of selecting based on matching note events. This is essentially a reverse filter. Suppose you wanted to select everything except a certain pitch or rhythm and add an action to that note. You could use the Deselect function to help you set this up.

Let me provide a clear example. In this example, Beats 2, 3, and 4 are staccato, while Beat 1 is unaccented. We can set up a reverse filter to grab all the notes except Beat 1 and accent them with a single press. You'll enter the music without any accents/articulations and let the filter do the work for you.

Figure 7.23 shows what we need our final version to look like.

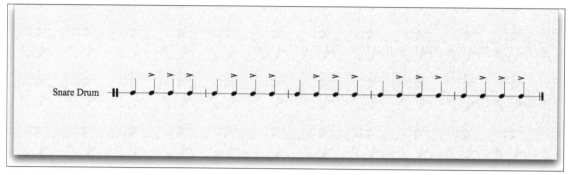

Figure 7.23 Deselect example.

Here's how to set this up with the Advanced Filter (see Figure 7.24):

1. Set the view to Notes and Chords.

2. Leave all voices selected.

3. Leave the Find In setting on Selection.

4. Deselect the Any option from Position in Bar.

5. Leave the Position in Bar option empty.

6. Click Deselect.

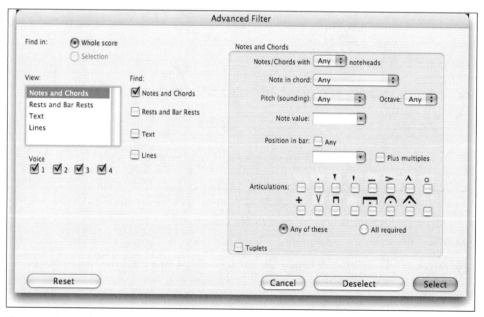

Figure 7.24 Advanced Filter settings for the deselect example.

This looks at the first beat in every bar and deselects it, leaving Beats 2–4 selected. You can now apply whatever articulation you want with a single key press.

Other Uses: Advanced Filter

The aforementioned examples should give you some insight into how the Advanced Filter is a powerful tool to help you. Here are a few final ways that you can use the Advanced Filter:

- Select all lines (any type of lines that you want) in your score or selection and align them using Layout > Align in a Row. (Use the Lines option.)

- Change all visible bar rests in your score in one shot. (Use the Rests and Bar Rests option.)

- Change notes in a particular notehead to another notehead. (Use Notes and Chords > Notes/Chords with X Noteheads.)

- Hide a certain pitch/rest/line throughout the score. (This is useful for playback purposes.)

- Select notes that have a certain articulation. (Use Notes and Chords > Articulation.)

- Many, many more ways!

As stated before: The Advanced Filter is as advanced as you want to make it. The best way to find out whether you should use it is to ask yourself, "Do these have anything in common?" the next time you find yourself spending a long time adding or editing large amounts of music. If the answer is yes, you can configure the Advanced Filter to do pretty much anything you could ever need.

Find

Take a look at Figure 7.25. It looks just like the Advanced Filter, right? Actually, it's the Find dialog box, which you can access by choosing Edit > Find or by pressing Ctrl/Command+F.

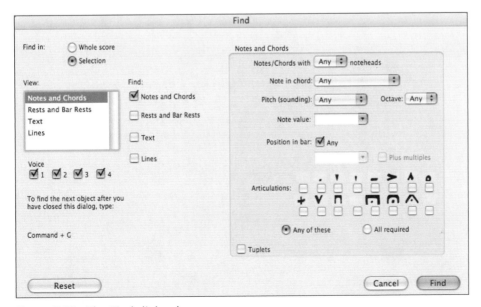

Figure 7.25 The Find dialog box.

The Find dialog box lets you select and find the exact same variables as the Advanced Filter does. What's the difference? The Find dialog box lets you select objects one at a time, whereas the Advanced Filter selects a larger range of objects at one time. Use the Find dialog box when you want to step through events that match your criteria.

After you find the first event, use the key command Ctrl/Command+G to find the next matching event. For example, suppose you're looking at an arrangement, copying part to part, and you want to see how many notes fall into a particular octave (one that you might think is problematic for the player). Set the Find dialog box to look at all notes in a particular octave (maybe Octave 5 or 6) and step through each matching pitch to see whether there are spots you should change by octave.

8 House Styles and Engraving Rules

Essential Tips for Chapter 8 (and the Things for Which You'll Want to Use Engraving Rules)

1. A House Style only affects the score on which you're working. If you want to use your House Style settings in other scores, you have to export the House Style and import it into a new score. House Styles are not preferences.

2. You'll head to House Style > Engraving Rules to change the appearance of your score.

3. If you want to change how Sibelius handles bar numbers, you'll do so by choosing House Style > Engraving Rules > Barlines.

4. If you want to change how Sibelius draws its bar rests by default, you'll do so by choosing House Style > Engraving Rules > Bar Rests. You can hide them and also change how the multi-rests are drawn.

5. The default barline choice is set in House Style > Engraving Rules > Barlines. Although you can make a single change using the Create menu, the Engraving Rules menu is where you can change all of the barlines!

6. If you want to change how and when Sibelius shows instrument names in your score, go to House Style > Engraving Rules > Instruments.

7. To access the most important window for many users, choose House Style > Engraving Rules > Staves. Here you can set the distance between staves and the distance between systems, as well as control how Sibelius will justify (spread out) your music across a page. There's no way you can lay out a score and *not* visit this window.

8. How Sibelius draws the time signature is determined by the Time Signatures window you access when you choose House Style > Engraving Rules > Time Signatures. You can make time signatures larger or even have them displayed between staves (*à la* Stravinsky).

In the previous chapter, you dealt with the Properties window, which enabled you to make temporary changes to the visual behavior in Sibelius. Keeping with that theme, we'll look at the proper way to change how Sibelius draws music and formats text, instruments, and everything else related to music engraving: House Styles. Sibelius defines a House Style as "exactly how a score looks," which is a perfect description.

House? By "House," Sibelius is referring to a publishing house. Each major music publishing house has different engraving standards for how they format their scores. House Styles enable a composer or engraver to save specific settings and differentiate them for each situation he or she encounters.

Where Do House Styles Live?

The easiest way to explain what a House Style does is to look at some manuscript paper in Sibelius. At its simplest, manuscript paper is a combination of a House Style and a grouping of instruments. Each saved manuscript paper contains a House Style. Go to File > New and start a new score based on Orchestra, Film. As you can see from Figure 8.1, this score has a different style of bar numbers (among other changes from the standard House Style).

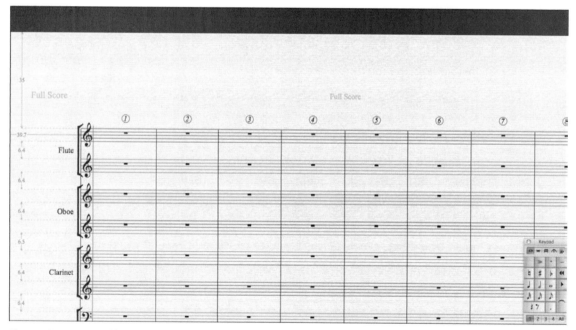

Figure 8.1 Special bar numbers.

This score is a combination of a pre-built set of instruments and the influence of a House Style. The bar numbers are shown as centered numbers in circles. You can tweak these kinds of visual changes in the House Style. What other kinds of things can you tweak in a House Style? I thought you'd never ask!

- The type of musical font used (handwritten versus plate-engraved)
- The appearance of text styles and the ability to create new ones
- The ranges of instruments, their names, and their playback sounds
- The ability to create custom instruments and staves
- The spacing between staves and systems
- The appearance and frequency of bar numbers
- The appearance of multi-measure rests
- The appearance of rehearsal markings
- The ability to create your own symbols

Basically, you can tweak anything that Sibelius does. This list is just a glimpse of what's possible in a House Style. Now, House Styles were part of the Quick Start detailed in Chapter 1 of this book, and at that time we didn't have much reason to change the default House Style. However, as you go along and work, some of the questions you'll ask will be answered with, "Fix that in the House Style."

House Styles is a fairly large topic, with literally thousands of entries. Rather than detail every one of them, I'll hit upon the common ones that most Sibelius users need to know, and I'll leave the Sibelius reference to the job of detailing every window and its uses.

Mantra and Scope

Here's a little mantra for you to keep in mind when dealing with House Styles: House Styles are used when you want to change how Sibelius draws or engraves something every single time you ask it to do so.

Simply, these are global changes and should only be utilized when you know you need to make completely global changes.

If you have to change the visual nature of Sibelius one factor at a time, you'll probably need to tweak the Window > Properties menu.

With that behind us, let's talk about the scope of a House Style. A House Style is contained within the score to which it's attached. Every score has a House Style saved within it. If you make changes within one score, they will not change how your next score is drawn unless you export the House Style, and then re-import it. The logic is simple: What works for one score may not work for another. Thankfully, you can export any House Style you create and import it later. Or, better yet, create a manuscript paper based on your needs and have it load each time Sibelius starts. (This will be detailed in Chapter 17, "Customizing Sibelius.")

Let's start by looking at some of the included House Styles.

The Included House Styles

Sibelius ships with a number of predefined House Styles that you can apply to any manuscript paper. When you start the New Score dialog box, after you've chosen your instrument list/manuscript paper, the second window shows the list of built-in House Styles available to you (see Figure 8.2).

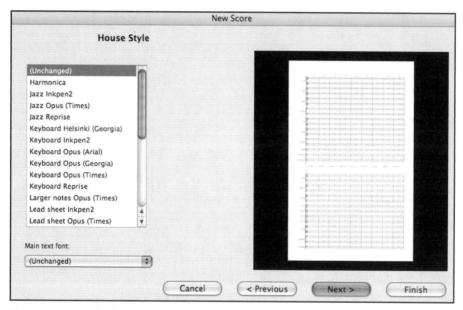

Figure 8.2 Pre-built House Styles.

The House Styles are organized by style, music font used, and text font. Take a look at the music font choices:

- **Unchanged.** This is the current House Style embedded within your chosen manuscript paper. Big Band would use Reprise, for example. Select this option if you don't want to override the default setting.

- **Inkpen2.** This font mimics the handwritten appearance of jazz and Broadway show music.

- **Reprise.** This option is for the West Coast–style of handwritten scores. The text has a rubberstamp appearance.

- **Helsinki.** This is a traditional plate-engraved font that many traditional engravers favor.

The style refers to particular engraving styles used in genre- or instrument-specific notation (for example, dynamics above a vocal staff and between the grand staff of instrumental staves).

The text refers to the main text font used in your score (Times, Georgia, or Arial).

In addition to these choices, Sibelius has two more types of House Styles available:

- **Lead Sheets.** Available in all music fonts, this House Style draws the first (initial) barline on all single-instrument systems (as found on standard lead sheets).

- **Larger Notes.** Great for education, this House Style produces music with a slightly different notehead that displays in a larger size, making it easier to read.

No matter what initial manuscript paper you choose, you can apply any of these House Styles to your score. Better yet, you can always import a House Style later if you decide to change the look of your score after it has been composed. Now that you've seen a bit of the available House Styles, let's get practical and explore the most-used aspect of House Styles: engraving rules.

Engraving Rules

For most folks, the first stop is the Engraving Rules dialog box, found by selecting House Style > Engraving Rules or by using the shortcut Ctrl+Shift+E (Windows) or Command+Shift+E (Mac), as shown in Figure 8.3.

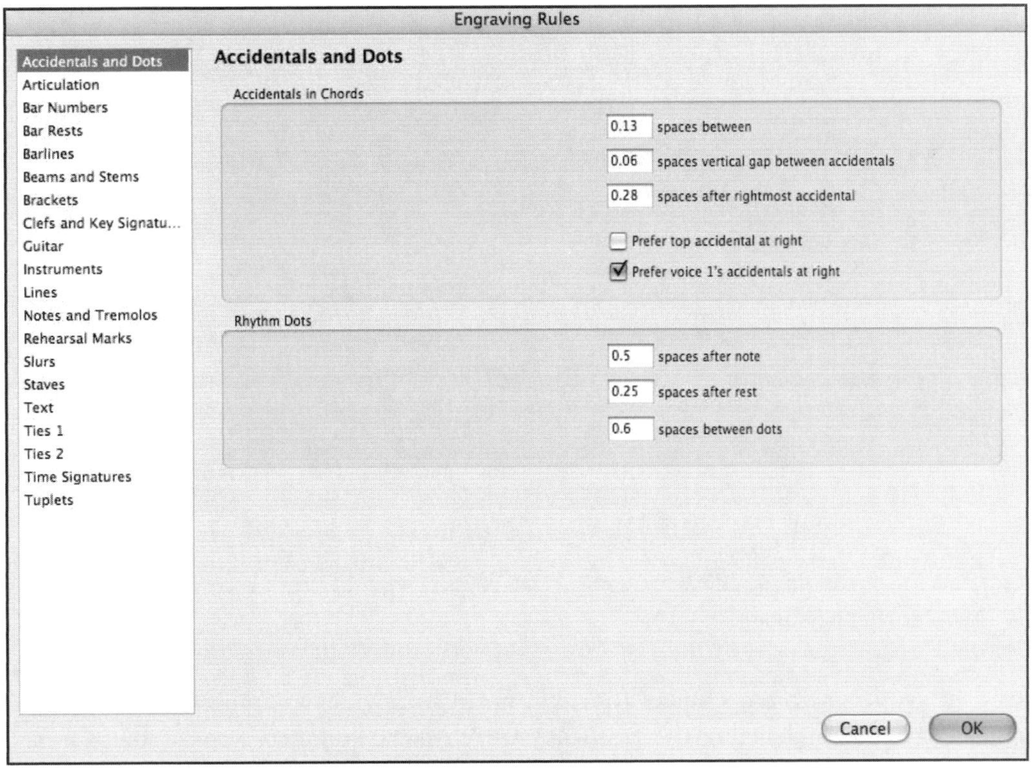

Figure 8.3   The Engraving Rules dialog box.

What are the engraving rules? They're a set of rules that dictate how the music is drawn or engraved. There are some *very* tweaky parts of engraving rules that most folks don't need to set, such as the distance of an augmentation dot from the notehead. However, there are many more practical aspects to engraving rules, and those will be our focus for this section—the most-used ones and what you can do with them.

The Engraving Rules dialog box is split into two parts—the left side, where you select the type of function you want to edit, and the right side, which shows you further options based on your present selection.

Bar Numbers

The Bar Numbers page (shown in Figure 8.4) shows you myriad choices for how Sibelius shows (or doesn't show) bar numbers.

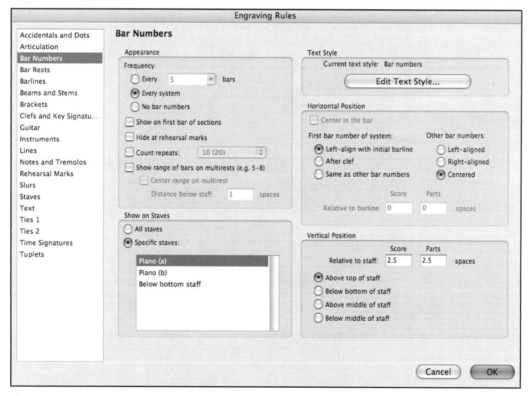

Figure 8.4 The Bar Numbers page.

From this page, you have many choices for how Sibelius draws bar numbers in the score. A common change includes changing the frequency of when bar numbers appear, but you can do more than that. In fact, look at what you can do, all from one window:

- You can change the position of the bar numbers (above or below the staff).

- You can have bar numbers hide at rehearsal marks.

- You can have Sibelius count the bars of a repeat structure automatically.

- You can show bar ranges during multi-rests.

- You can have the bar numbers only show on particular staves.

- You can change the text style (change the font or have the bar numbers in a circle or a box).

- You can change the vertical or horizontal default position of the bar numbers.

All of this is done from the same Engraving Rules > Bar Numbers page. Because these changes are made score by score, if you want these changes to affect other scores, you'll need to export the House Style and re-import it later. More on that in the final section of this chapter.

CD: Use Example 8.1 and follow the instructions provided (in the example) to change the bar numbers though the House Style menu.

Bar Rests

The Bar Rests page of the Engraving Rules dialog box is pretty simple—it has a limited number of uses (see Figure 8.5).

Most people only go to this page if they are going to create blank manuscript paper and they want to hide all of the bar rests that Sibelius creates automatically. To do so, just deselect the Show Bar Rests box, and they will go away magically.

Worksheets Blank manuscript paper is available though the Worksheets feature in Sibelius as well. In any case, it's nice to know you can make your own.

Of course, there are other settings on this page too, and they pertain to the appearance of multi-measure rests and the way in which Sibelius draws them. You can change the default appearance of multi-measure rests on the same page.

CD: Use Example 8.2 to learn how to change the appearance of the multi-rests.

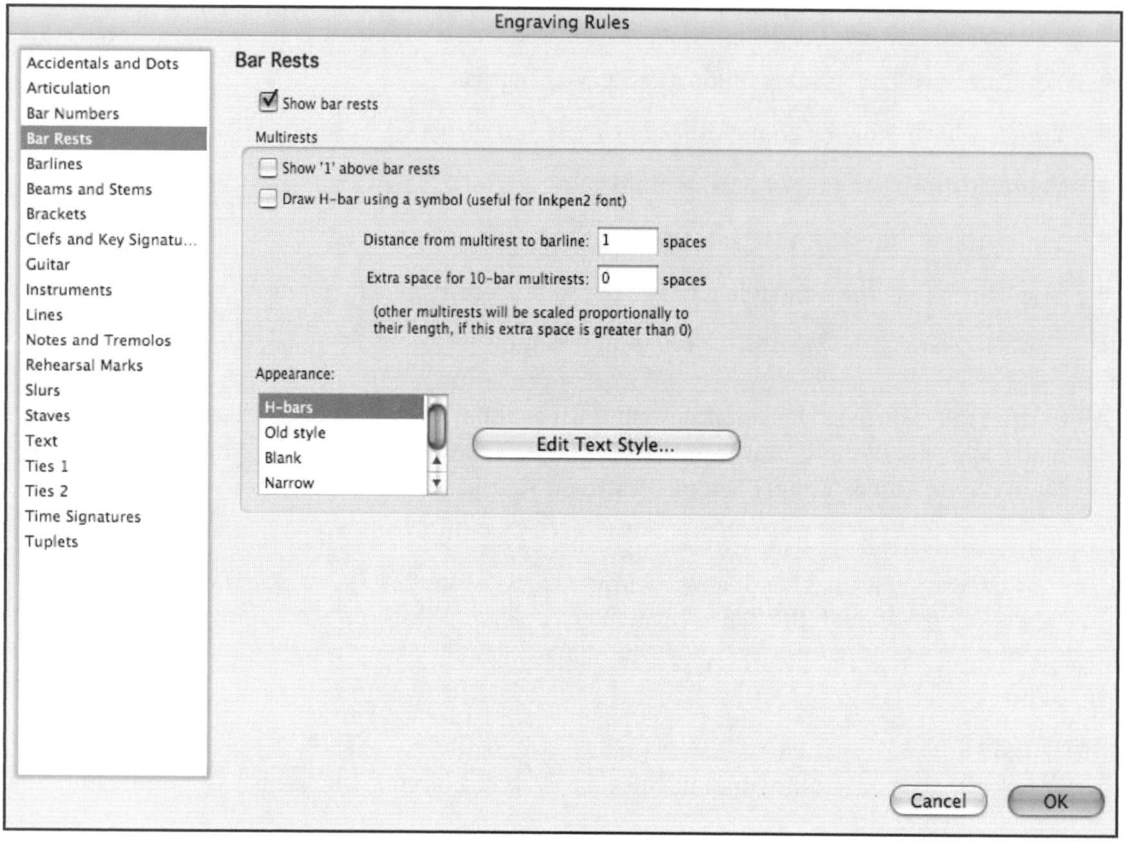

Figure 8.5 The Bar Rests page.

Barlines

The Barlines page of the Engraving Rules dialog box details the default appearance of barlines throughout your score (as shown in Figure 8.6).

Remember that the Barlines page deals with the default barline that Sibelius draws on each and every bar, so you'd only want to change this if the whole score needs to change. You can still make your changes to individual barlines by choosing Create > Barline.

An obvious use of this feature is creating tests or example worksheets in which barlines aren't necessary, or when creating blank sheet music in Sibelius. Just select Invisible as your default barline type. You can choose from seven different barline options.

A few other gems: You can change your repeat barlines to have "wings" and employ a barline at the beginning of single staves, which is useful on lead sheets.

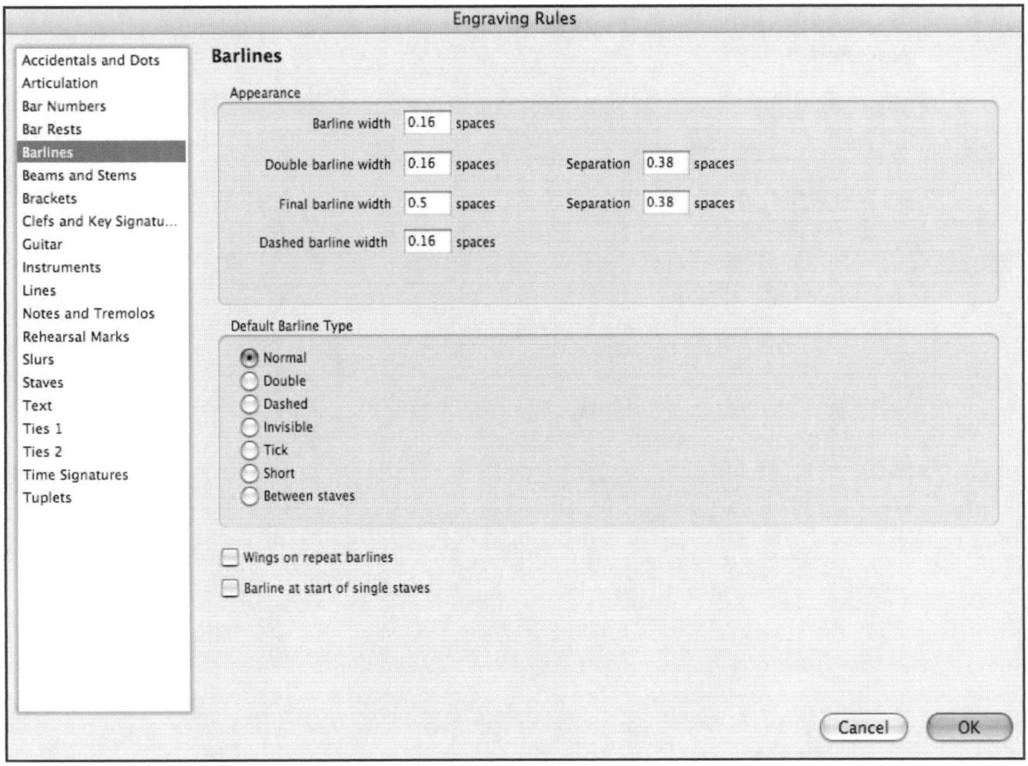

Figure 8.6   The Barlines page.

CD: Use Example 8.3 to combine changing barlines and bar rests to make custom manuscript paper. Use Example 8.4 to learn how to make bars between systems.

Instruments

The Instruments page lets you set how Sibelius draws instrument names in your score (see Figure 8.7).

Each instrument has a predefined full name and abbreviated name, which you can set by choosing House Style > Edit Instruments. In the Engraving Rules, you set how Sibelius shows the instruments names at the start of the score, at subsequent pages, and at new sections. Your choices for all three aspects are always the same: You can show the full instrument name, the short or abbreviated name, or nothing at all.

CD: Use Example 8.5 to learn how to add or remove instrument names from your score.

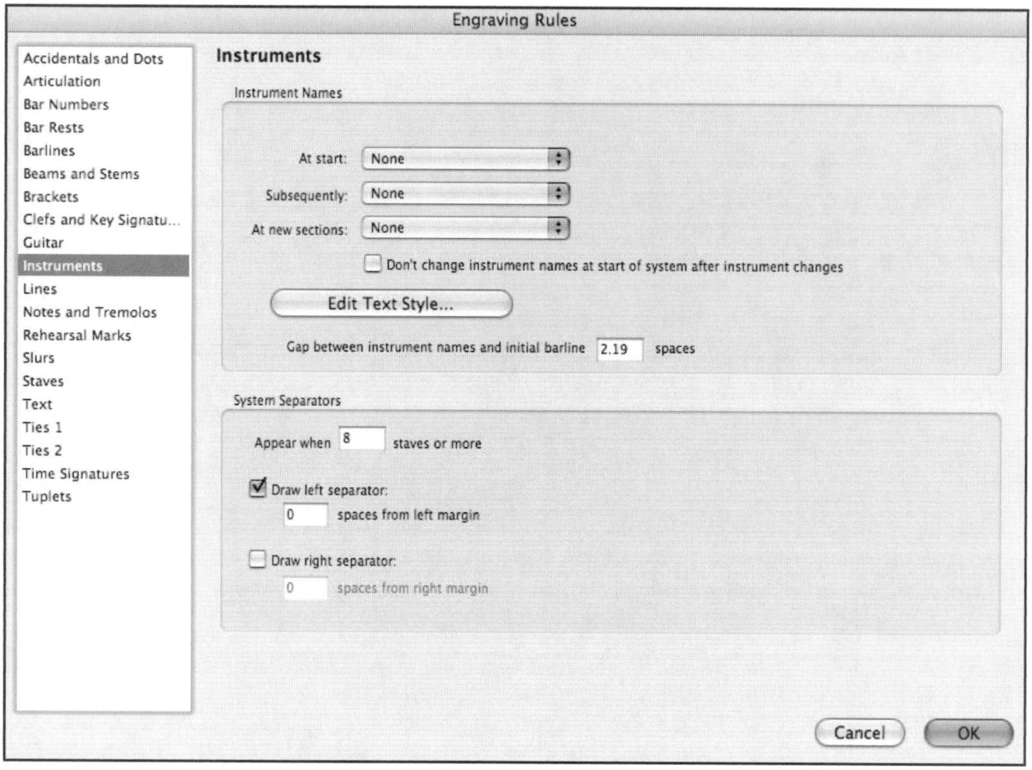

Figure 8.7 The Instruments page.

Staves

The Staves page of the Engraving Rules dialog box is one of the most important aspects of Sibelius and is crucial to getting your scores to look right. Everyone should look at this window when laying out their final score (see Figure 8.8).

The first controls set the distance between each stave/system. If you have a lot of dynamics, ledger lines, and other markings between scores, you'll likely need some extra room. Before you go dragging staves around (a big no-no in my book), you'll want to start by increasing the default distance from 5.5 to a higher value. The same holds true for the default distance between systems. If you have a lot of markings, and your systems feel a bit crunched, just increase this value.

The Justification section might be one of most misunderstood parts of the Sibelius layout/engraving engine. Have you ever dragged a staff and suddenly had it jump to a really far distance? This is justification at work.

Justification is trying to spread out music so that it fits a full page. The percentage that you set under the Justify Staves When Page Is At Least X% Full option sets the point at which Sibelius will try to spread the music across the page. Take a look at Figure 8.9 for an example from a lead sheet–style tune.

Engraving Rules

Staves

| Accidentals and Dots |
| Articulation |
| Bar Numbers |
| Bar Rests |
| Barlines |
| Beams and Stems |
| Brackets |
| Clefs and Key Signatu… |
| Guitar |
| Instruments |
| Lines |
| Notes and Tremolos |
| Rehearsal Marks |
| Slurs |
| Staves |
| Text |
| Ties 1 |
| Ties 2 |
| Time Signatures |
| Tuplets |

Layout

5.5 spaces between staves

9.25 spaces between systems

Justification

Justify staves when page is at least 100 % full

System spacings may be contracted to 97 %

Staff Design

Staff line width: 0.1 spaces

Small staff size: 75 % of normal staff

Cancel OK

Figure 8.8 The Staves page.

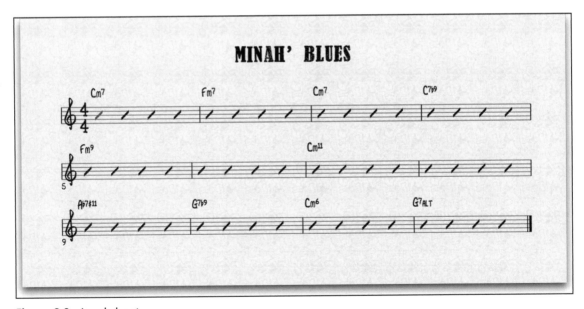

Figure 8.9 Lead sheet.

This lead sheet looks pretty good, but let's look behind the scenes at the justification value. This score was set to justify at 99%. Why does this make sense? It means that Sibelius would have to have a page 99% full before it started to justify. In essence, 99% or 100% means, "Don't move my staves." Because this short lead sheet only has a few lines on it, to get Sibelius to justify you'd have to grab a much smaller value. Choosing 30% makes Sibelius's justification engine kick in and gives you the unsatisfactory result shown in Figure 8.10.

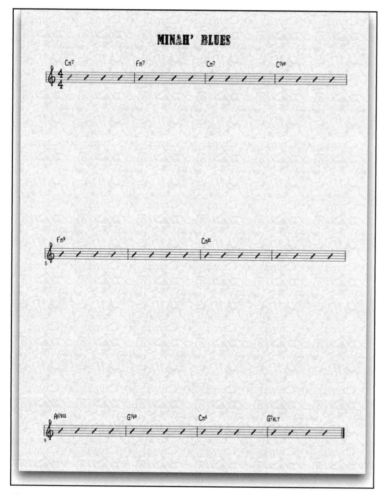

Figure 8.10   Over-justified.

CD: Example 8.6 is an important exercise in how to use the Staves page to leave room for text and dynamics.

So when is justification a good thing? When your music takes up most of a page and you have a blank spot at the bottom of the music. At that point, set the justification to 65% to 70%, and Sibelius will distribute your staves across the page equally to fill it. Just know that you can come back to the engraving rules at any time and change this!

As one last bit of warning: *Never, ever* drag the final stave of a page. Don't drag anything. Let the engraving rules do it for you. Stave draggers are typically unhappy with the look of their scores, and with good reason—they're overruling Sibelius's sophisticated layout engine.

Justify Next The next chapter deals with the intricacies of laying out your score, and you can be sure that the Justify Staves option is a major component of getting a nicely laid-out score and parts. More in the next chapter!

CD: Use Example 8.7 to see what playing with the justification value does to a score and how powerful a feature it is in final layout.

Time Signatures

The last thing we'll look at in the Engraving Rules dialog box is the Time Signatures page (shown in Figure 8.11).

This simple page allows you to set how time signatures are displayed throughout your score. The Time Signatures (Large) and Time Signatures (Huge) options are useful in modern music engraving and film scoring when you see examples like the one in Figure 8.12, in which the time signatures are between the staves and shown in very large text.

In the Engraving Rules dialog, you have the Edit Text Style button, which will take you to a window where you can edit the size and placement of text and even create your own if you so choose. You can also change the default gap before the time signature is drawn in your score if you find it's too close to the clef and key signature.

CD: Use Example 8.8 to change your time signature from the default size to a huge time signature (appropriate for a film-scoring session).

Edit All Fonts

What if you want to change the fonts used in your score after the fact? This is easy to do and can be done simply through the Edit All Fonts dialog box (see Figure 8.13), which you can access by choosing House Style > Edit All Fonts.

Engraving Rules

Accidentals and Dots
Articulation
Bar Numbers
Bar Rests
Barlines
Beams and Stems
Brackets
Clefs and Key Signatu...
Guitar
Instruments
Lines
Notes and Tremolos
Rehearsal Marks
Slurs
Staves
Text
Ties 1
Ties 2
Time Signatures
Tuplets

Time Signatures

Text style:

| Time signatures |
| Time signatures (huge) |
| Time signatures (large) |

Edit Text Style...

Gap before time signatures:

0.25   spaces

(To apply this to existing time signatures, use Reset Note Spacing on the Layout menu)

Cancel   OK

Figure 8.11   The Time Signatures page.

Figure 8.12   Time signature change.

This simple dialog box allows you to do just what you'd expect. Through the three sections (Main Text Font, Main Music Font, and Music Text Font) and their accompanying drop-down menus, you can change the fonts used in your score. Note that the main music font will change the music text font automatically. This makes sense because it would look quite

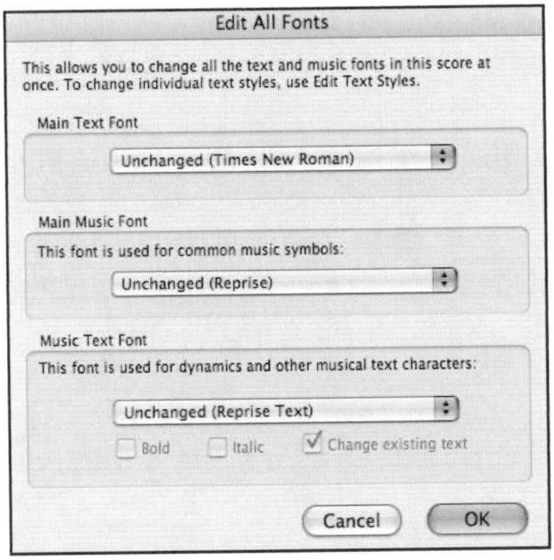

Figure 8.13 The Edit All Fonts dialog box.

odd to have your score in Reprise, while the music text was in another font. You can also change the music text independently, as long as you change it after you change the main music font.

> **Essential Tip: Edit All Fonts** What about a House Style import as a way to change the music font used in a score? Sure, this is one way, but House Styles take more than just fonts into consideration; they actually look at all the different positions, spacing, and instrument definitions in your score and change them all at once. If you're just taking a look at what your score might look like in Helsinki as opposed to Reprise, the Edit All Fonts option is a much simpler way to go. Rest assured that importing a House Style will definitely change the fonts, but it will change other things as well.

There are times when the Edit All Fonts dialog box can produce some odd results. For example, when you change the main music font, there might be some spacing irregularities in time signatures (Reprise), and when you switch the music font this way, it might not look that great. In those occurrences, it might be preferable to do a House Style import to change your music font. Here's some general advice: It might be easier to change your text fonts using Edit All Fonts, and when music fonts are in question, import a House Style.

Edit Text Styles

What is a text style? Have you ever noticed that lyrics know enough to snap into place below a score, while a text style, such as Fingering, knows to attach right next to a note? The text styles know where to go due to settings in the Edit Text Styles dialog box, which allows you to set the size, appearance, and position of any text.

So who will use this? Anyone who finds the included text styles in Sibelius lacking something he needs in a score. If you're happy with the included text styles in Sibelius, then you'd never have to look at this window.

I want to provide a clear example. Suppose you like the Fingering text in Sibelius, but you find it's a bit too small next to the notes, and you'd like to change that. As you've learned up to this point, you can select the text in question, go to Window > Properties > Text, and change the size of the text, but that is a bit arduous to do on each and every fingering in a score. If you want them simply to come in larger, you can edit the text style once and for all, and have that size change impact each and every score that uses the House Style.

To change the size of the Fingering text style, start by navigating to House Style > Edit Text Style to access the Edit Text Styles dialog box, and then scroll down and select Fingering. Then, click Edit (see Figure 8.14).

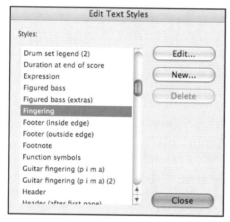

Figure 8.14   The Edit Text Styles dialog box.

Once you've clicked Edit, you'll be taken deeper into the Edit Text Styles dialog box to show you a screen with five pages for precisely controlling every possible aspect of the text. Because you're looking to change the size, you'll stay on the first page, which is the General page. In the General page, you have controls for size (both for the score and for the parts). Right now, your dialog box is set to show Fingering text at a 7-point size. Just change that to 10 in both the score and parts (as shown in Figure 8.15).

Now you can click OK and return to your score, and your fingerings will all be larger!

Making a New Text Style

Rather than editing over the top of a preexisting text style, you can create your own text style, which would be useful if you needed to have two very similar text styles (such as small chord

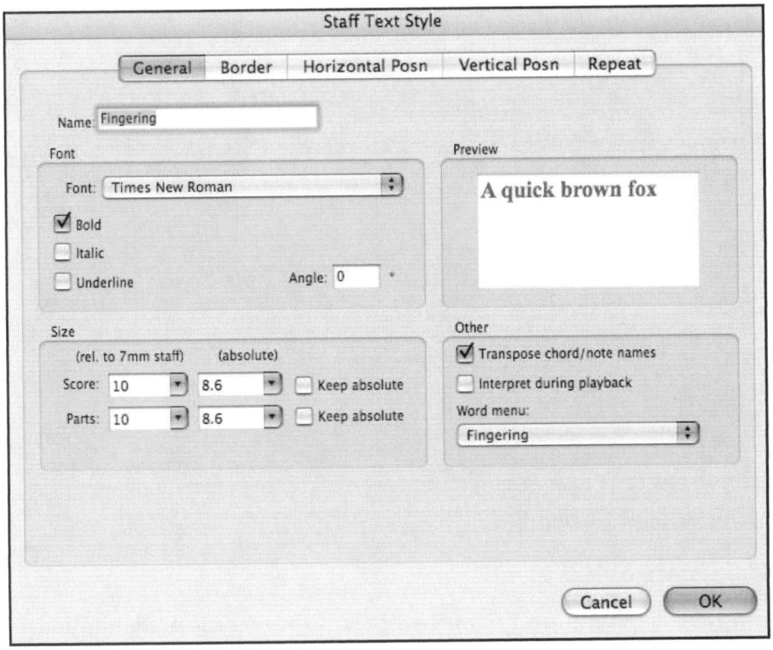

Figure 8.15   Changing text size.

symbols and large chord symbols) that are clearly based on the same style. To make this happen, you still call up the Edit Text Styles dialog box from the House Style menu. However, you scroll down to Chord Symbols, and instead of clicking Edit, you'll click New to create a new text style based on your selection.

Sibelius will ask you whether you want to make a new text style based on Chord Symbols; say yes. You'll then be taken to the Text Style editor, where you can make your changes and then click OK to return to the score. Make sure to rename the text style something easy to find (such as Chord Symbols Larger); the default name is Chord Symbols(2).

You'll now see your new text style if you select Create > Text > Other Staff Text. You can use this technique to create a new text style based on any preexisting style and edit its appearance and position to taste. As always, any changes you make to text styles are contained within the House Style, so these changes won't be seen in other scores until you export the House Style out of your score and import it into other scores.

System Object Positions

Another aspect of the House Style menu is the System Object Positions dialog box (as shown in Figure 8.16).

System objects refer to metronome/tempo markings, rehearsal marks, and other symbols that are drawn in a few spots in a larger score. For example, it's customary to have these markings

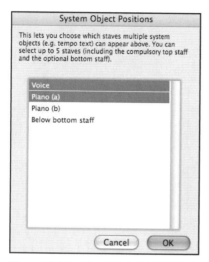

Figure 8.16   The System Object Positions dialog box.

appear above the strings in symphonic music. If you want to control the way in which Sibelius draws these system objects, you choose House Style > System Object Positions to pull up the System Object Positions dialog box and highlight the staves in your score above which you want the markings to appear.

Bar Numbers System object positions do not deal with bar numbers, which have their own controls in the Engraving Rules dialog box.

CD: Use Example 8.9 to control how the rehearsal and tempo markings are displayed throughout the example score.

Text Styles Vertical Positions

Once you choose a text style to edit in the Edit Text Styles dialog box, you are presented with five windows. In the previous section on editing text styles, we only dealt with the General page. Another screen that deals with system object positions is the Vertical Posn page (inside the System Text Style dialog box), which covers the vertical position (see Figure 8.17).

This page shows you how Sibelius deals with system text and how it will draw staves using system object positions. For example, the composer system text would only draw above the first stave in any score, so you'd select Top Staff only to make that text show up above your top staff. For something like a rehearsal mark, you'd select Top Staff, 2nd Position, 3rd Position,

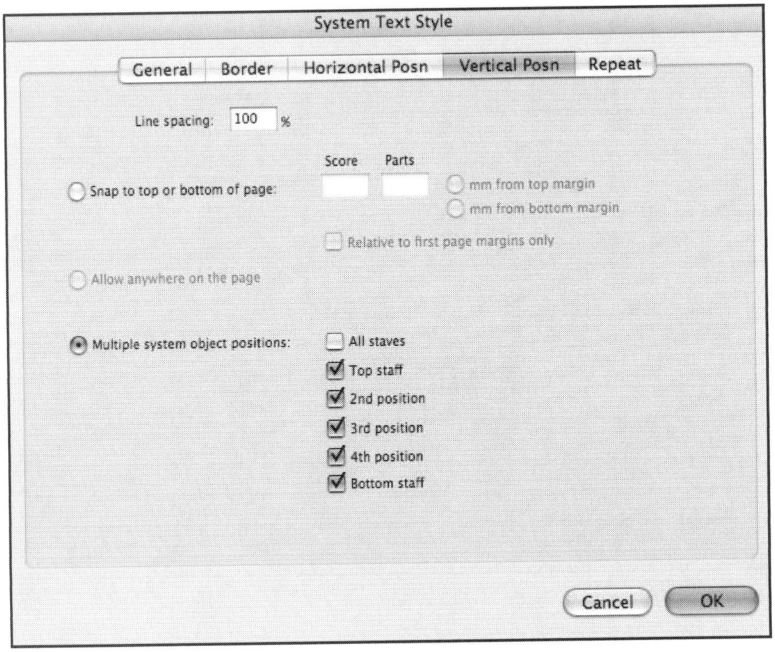

Figure 8.17   The Vertical Positions page.

4th Position, and Bottom Staff because rehearsal markings typically repeat above many staves in your score (and you control how they appear on a score-to-score basis by choosing House Style > System Object Positions). If you're defining new system text styles, you'll want to look at this page and select how you want the Multiple System Object Positions settings to look.

Not Lines   System lines don't have any control over system object positions like text does. (They always show up at all positions.) If you want to get rid of them on a case-by-case basis in your score, you'll have to do it by deleting instances as you go.

Default Positions

The Default Positions dialog box, which you access by choosing House Style > Default Positions, lets you control the default positions for text, lines, and pretty much everything else you create within Sibelius (in other words, where on the score these items position themselves). The screen shown in Figure 8.18 details all of the controls you'll need to change the default positions of any object in Sibelius.

A good example of default positions at work is adding a title using Create > Title Page. Notice how the title is at the top of the score, perfectly centered? This is because the default position of

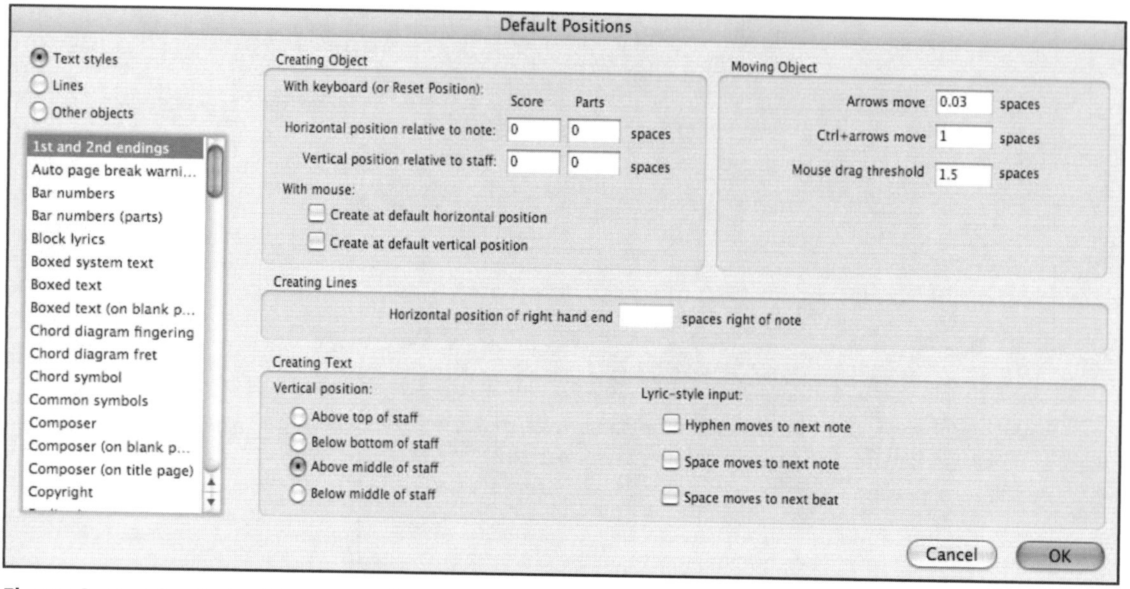

Figure 8.18   The Default Positions dialog box.

that text style has been set a certain way. Let's look at the details of the title text to see what settings make it work (see Figure 8.19).

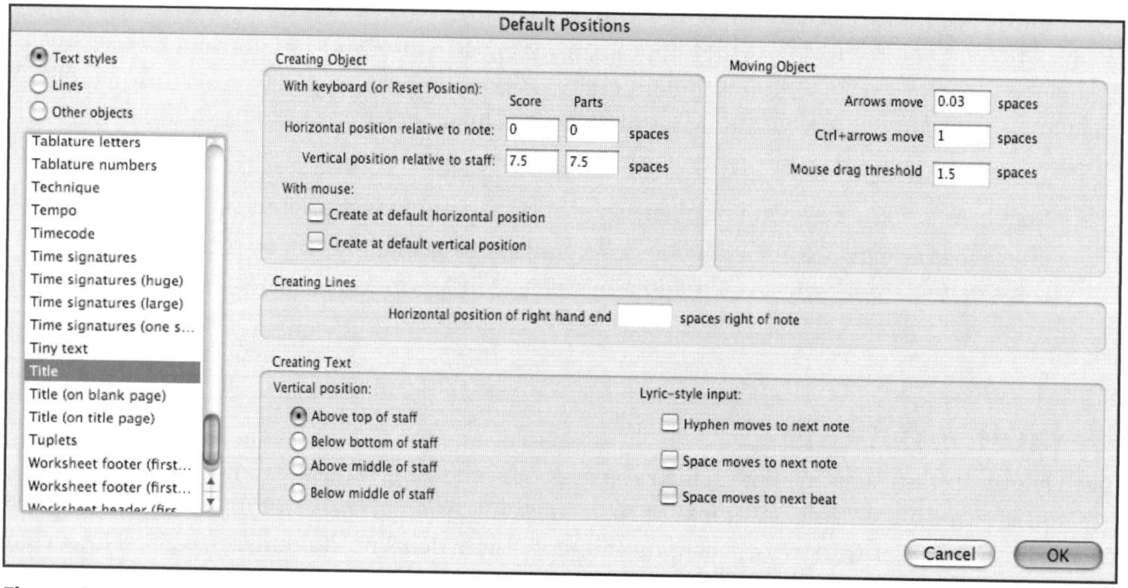

Figure 8.19   Title text positions.

To show this, make sure that the Text Styles option is chosen, and in the listing directly below, scroll down to Title to expose its settings. Currently, the title is set to appear 7.5 spaces above the top staff, and the text is set to appear above the top staff, as you'd expect for title text. You can see from these settings that it's not difficult to define a new text style and then come to the Default Positions dialog box to force your text to appear in the correct spot.

There's much more you can do with this dialog box! But here's a slight annoyance you may have noticed: When you create an object (such as a guitar chord symbol) with the mouse, sometimes it is placed at an odd spot in relation to your music. Counter that with pre-selecting a note, when things are always engraved perfectly. Look at Figure 8.20 to see what I mean.

Figure 8.20   Chord symbols—alignment issues.

The first two chords were entered while the notes they attached to were highlighted, and thus they went in perfectly. The last chord had no note pre-selected; it was clicked in with a mouse. Because a mouse is far from being an accurate positioning tool, the chord symbol is now out of line.

You can change this for the better. Go back to the Default Positions dialog box, choose the Other Objects option, and call up Chord Diagrams. In the window to the right, there is a section for With Mouse; you'll want to select both settings here. This tells Sibelius that chords entered with a mouse should snap to the default position no matter what (which is what you want). Click OK and return to your score. Now, when you delete the chord symbol in question and reapply it with the mouse, it should snap perfectly into position because you tweaked the default positions to do so (see Figure 8.21).

Figure 8.21   Aligned chord symbols.

It's pretty easy to see what you can do here. In general, if things are not going where you want them to by default—and this applies to text, lines, symbols, and other graphics in Sibelius—you need to look no further than the Default Positions dialog box to adjust the score to taste.

Essential Tip: Default Position You can always revert any object back to its default position by clicking on it and selecting Layout > Reset Position.

Importing and Exporting House Styles

As I've stated many times in this chapter, when you change an aspect of a House Style, it won't affect other scores unless you export the House Style and import it to other scores.

To learn how to do that, let's start by exporting a House Style we're working on. In any score in which you've adjusted the House Style, go to House Style > Export House Style to bring up the Export House Style dialog box shown in Figure 8.22.

Figure 8.22 The Export House Style dialog box.

All you have to do in the dialog box is name your House Style. When that's done, your House Style will appear in the New Score dialog box under the available House Styles. In addition, you can take any existing score and import the newly created House Style into it by choosing House Style > Import House Style to access the Import House Style dialog box shown in Figure 8.23.

The dialog box has two sides. The left side shows you all of the available House Styles (both factory and user-created). You can scroll down to the appropriate House Style you've just created (in this case Reprise, Larger Chords) and select it. The right side lists all the different aspects of a House Style. You can mix and match certain parts of a House Style. (You don't have to take everything.) It's worth talking about what each checkmark entails:

- **Instrument Definitions.** This covers changes you've made to instruments, their range, playback sounds, and associated staff types.

- **Lines.** This covers any user-created or modified lines as found when selecting Create > Line.

- **Noteheads.** This covers any user-created or modified noteheads as found when selecting Window > Properties > Notes.

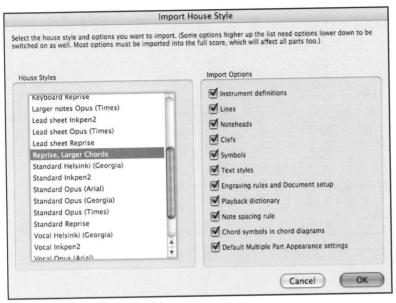

Figure 8.23 Importing a House Style.

- **Clefs.** This covers any change to the default clefs.

- **Symbols.** This covers any additions or alterations to the symbols in Create > Symbol.

- **Text Styles.** This covers newly created or edited text styles.

- **Engraving Rules and Document Setup.** This covers any changes made to the House Style > Engraving Rules or the Document Setup (which specifies margins, paper size, and orientation).

- **Playback Dictionary.** This covers any changes to words in the Playback Dictionary.

- **Note Spacing Rule.** This covers any changes you might have made to how Sibelius spaces notes by default.

- **Chord Symbols in Chord Diagrams.** This covers any additions to the Chord Diagrams library.

- **Default Multiple Part Appearance Settings.** In the Parts window, you can change how parts are engraved.

> **Importing House Style Links** It's worth noting that the options in the Import House Style dialog box are dependant on each other, so you may not be able to deselect certain items unless other dependant items are also deselected.

Not all of these options have been covered thus far. Some of them belong in Chapter 9, "Document Layout and Formatting," and others are out of the scope of this part of the book. For more information on how to define your own instruments or notes, please see Help > Reference in Sibelius for all the information.

Plug-In to the Rescue

Plug-ins are total timesavers! A great plug-in worth mentioning is the Plug-ins > Batch Processing > Import House Style to Folder of Scores plug-in, which lets you import any House Style of your choice into a folder of scores. So, if you wanted to change the appearance of a great many preexisting scores at once, collect them in a single folder on your desktop (or anyplace you want) and launch the plug-in, which gives you the options shown in Figure 8.24.

Figure 8.24   House Style plug-in.

Choose the House Style, then choose the folder you want to process, and boom! Instant House Style updating.

9 Document Layout and Formatting

1. Please don't ever drag a stave! You'll thank me later. (This might be the most important rule in the whole book.)

2. Please don't ever drag a barline. You'll also thank me later. (This might be the second most important rule in this book.)

3. If you've dragged a stave, select all, and go to Layout > Reset Space Above Staff, and then Layout > Reset Space Below Staff. This will reset back to Sibelius defaults.

4. If you've dragged barlines, select all, and go to Layout > Reset Note Spacing to get back to normal.

5. If you need more room between staves or systems, choose House Style > Engraving Rules > Staves.

6. Staff justification is your friend; it works for you, not against you.

7. If you have to make a measure wider, do so by selecting it and using Shift+Alt/Option+arrow key.

8. If you have to manually move a stave, select the stave in question and use Shift+Alt/Option+arrow key.

9. Layout is tough! Don't get down if it's not looking like Hal Leonard on your first time; you will get it.

The terms *layout* and *formatting* refer to the final look of the score when it's printed. This is usually the last step in score preparation, after all of the musical decisions have been made. Sibelius makes decisions along the way about how it will format your score based on engraving rules and myriad other features. But, as clever as Sibelius may be, some folks want it to look the way they envision, and Sibelius gives these folks a bevy of powerful tools to help their music lay out on a page just the way they want.

This chapter will conclude with a look at a score, which was sent in just for use in this book. The score has some large formatting issues, and you'll see the step-by-step process needed to make this score look amazing. The first stop is definitely the Document Setup dialog box.

Document Setup

The first step in laying out a score is going to the Document Setup dialog box, which you can find by choosing Layout > Document Setup (see Figure 9.1).

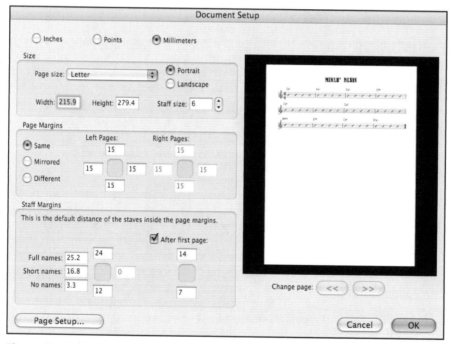

Figure 9.1   The Document Setup dialog box.

In the U.S.   Users in the U.S. might want to change the display from the default millimeters to inches in the Document Setup dialog box.

This fairly straightforward dialog box contains a collection of controls for specifying the size of your workspace. The first group of controls deals with the size of the staves, the size of paper you'll be printing to, and its orientation (either portrait or landscape). What's nice about the document setup is that it's a nondestructive way to work, so you can change these settings over and over again until you feel you've nailed them. Also, your changes are "undoable," so if you change something and shudder at what you've done, just go to Edit > Undo, and you'll revert back to the score's layout before you changed anything.

When you initially set up a score, you have controls for the size of paper (letter, tabloid, and others) and its orientation. The Document Setup dialog box lets you change the paper size and orientation at any point, but it also takes you a step further—it allows you to set up a custom height and width for your paper. This is very useful if you're publishing examples for a textbook or another printed medium that doesn't fall into the normal canon of paper sizes.

You should treat staff size with care. If you make the staves too large, you'll create frequent page turns because you cannot fit as much music on a page with larger staves. Conversely, if you make the music too small, it can be difficult to read, which might result in a greater number of errors from your players. The staff size controls are very handy for education, in which larger staff sizes are a welcome addition, and in special cases, such as EZ-Play piano editions, where the staffs and notes are quite a bit larger for younger readers.

CD: On your CD, open up Example 9.1 to experiment with changing staff sizes for children.

Staff Size The staff size settings affect everything in Sibelius, not just staff size! They make all elements in the score larger, so size is entirely relative in Sibelius.

The next stop in the Document Setup dialog box is the margins, which set the amount of white space at the top, bottom, right, and left edges of the paper. By reducing the margins you can have your music take up more of the page, but be aware that you'll have less room for additional markings, such as text, if your margins are too small.

The staff margins control the distance between the top stave and the top of the paper (and also the bottom, left, and right). You might need to adjust these parameters if you have a great deal of text at the top of your initial page, such as long, multi-line titles. Because the first page might take up more room than any other page in the score, you can set up different values for the initial page and subsequent pages through the Document Setup dialog box. Also, notice that Sibelius is clever enough to have different settings for the right-side staff margins depending on the display of your instrument names—there is a different margin when the full name is shown versus a short name or no name.

Printers That Steal Occasionally, printers won't follow your margins exactly, and you might lose some text at the bottom of your page. Because each printer driver is different, make sure to check your printouts. If you're losing some text, add some more bottom margin to adjust for this. Again, not all printers do this, and most are fine, but if it does happen to you, now you'll know what to do.

Here's a list of reasons why you'd want to visit the Document Setup dialog box:

- You're printing to different paper than the standard 8.5 × 11-inch paper.

- You want to change the orientation of your music (portrait or landscape).

- Your default stave size is incorrect, and you'd like to make it smaller or larger.

- Due to a publisher's requirement, you need to change the page margins to fit their standard engraving style.

- There's not enough room at the top of your first page for the text and title information you need in this score.

If any of those reasons applies to you, you now know where to go in Sibelius to change these important aspects.

Remember that you can come back to the Document Setup dialog box at any time and change values to suit!

In the House Document setup is part of the larger House Style, so if you make changes to the document setup to suit a particular style of engraving, you can import that House Style into other scores with ease.

The Layout Menu

Sibelius is really well designed. You never need to search for things in the program. The Layout menu is an excellent example—it encompasses practically every command you could ever need to assist you in score layout. Figure 9.2 shows the contents of the Layout menu.

In the next few sections, I'll go through this very important menu and show you examples of the sorts of problems you can solve using various features in the Layout menu. I won't cover these in order of the menu, but rather in their order of usefulness.

Breaks

Adding breaks to your music is the first step in getting a good final format. The following types of breaks are available to you in Sibelius, as shown in Figure 9.3.

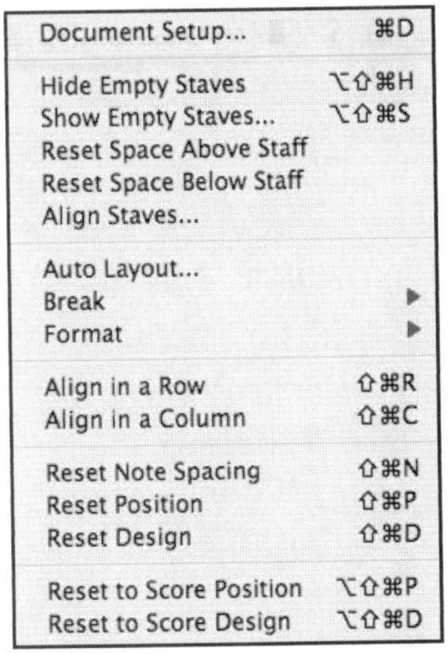

Figure 9.2 The Layout menu.

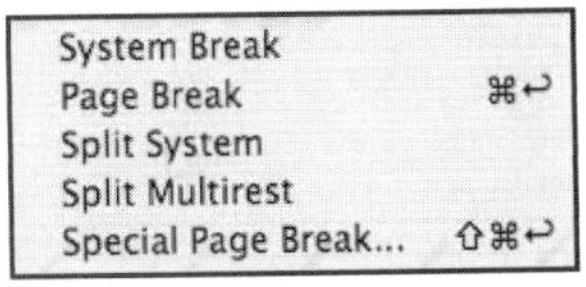

Figure 9.3 The Layout > Break submenu.

The first break you'll encounter is a system break, which forces Sibelius to start a new system any time you tell it to. If you choose a single barline by selecting it and then press the Enter or Return key on your keyboard, you'll insert a manual system break. You can also choose Layout > Breaks to invoke the same action, but pressing Enter/Return is much faster and is an easy shortcut to learn.

The rest of the breaks function as follows:

- **Page Break.** Sibelius will force all music after the selected barline onto a new page.

- **Split System.** Sibelius will insert a system break, adding space after the selected barline and restoring the clef and key signature. This is useful for codas and other special gaps in your music. It only works when you choose a barline in the middle of your score—choosing the last barline in a system won't do much. (You can achieve a similar effect by choosing Window > Properties > Bars > Gap before Bar.)

- **Split Multirest.** When your score isn't showing multi-rests (see the "Auto Layout" section later in this chapter for information on how to show or hide multi-rests), you can select a barline to split your multi-rest. Then, when you switch on multi-rests again, you'll have a split at the point you specified.

- **Special Page Break.** This allows you to insert multiple/special blank pages one at a time or change the margins of your music from a certain point forward. This is very useful when you need to insert enough blank pages to make your next bar start on a right- or a left-facing page (which are both options in this window). Blank pages are also great for adding large amounts of text, useful for additional pages of lyrics or instructions in a worksheet. You can also insert a change to your score's margins midway through the score using the Special Page Break feature.

Careful with Those Page Breaks Be careful using page breaks. You only want to use them at the very end of a piece/movement. Because Sibelius will dynamically lay out your score, if you add a page break on an earlier page and add more music, you'll be left with some odd, short pages due to your page break. In general, you should only use page breaks at the end of your piece—Sibelius will take care of everything else.

This is very important: All of these breaks always work the same way! You have to select a single barline in order to break music; otherwise, you'll get a warning telling you to do so.

Undoing a Break Forced breaks show up in your score with special page layout markings. You can undo a break by clicking on the layout marking and pressing Delete or Backspace. If the break was your last action, you can also choose Edit > Undo.

CD: On your CD, go to Example 9.2, where you'll be instructed to add a bunch of breaks to (or remove them from) a score.

Formatting the Page

The next stop is the Layout > Format submenu, as shown in Figure 9.4.

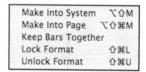

Figure 9.4 The Layout > Format submenu.

The Layout > Format submenu provides you with powerful formatting features that will allow you to do the following things:

- **Make into System.** This option groups the selected measure(s) into a single system.
- **Make into Page.** This option groups the selected measure(s) into a single page.

- **Keep Bars Together.** This option groups the selected measure(s) together so that no matter what formatting changes ensue, those measures will stay on the same line.

- **Lock Format.** Once you've gotten things the way you want them to look, lock the format so nothing can alter your layout.

- **Unlock Format.** This option allows you to unlock a previously locked format so you can alter the format of your score.

All of these commands deal with making changes to how Sibelius lays out your music by default. As we lay out the piece of music later in this chapter, we'll make frequent use of these commands. However, even without an example, it's pretty easy to see what you can do with these and when you'd use them.

Glossary of Layout Markings

When you lay out your score, you'll notice that Sibelius inserts special layout marks that are visible when editing a score, but that do not print. Sibelius shows these markings by default, but you can toggle their view at any time by choosing View > Layout Marks. Figure 9.5 shows a glossary of the layout markings used in Sibelius 5.2.

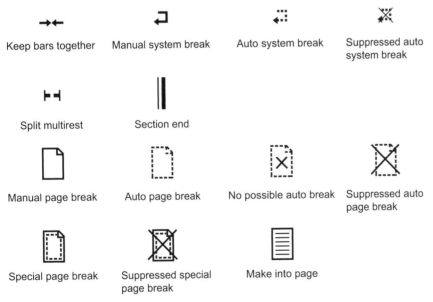

| Keep bars together | Manual system break | Auto system break | Suppressed auto system break |

| Split multirest | Section end |

| Manual page break | Auto page break | No possible auto break | Suppressed auto page break |

| Special page break | Suppressed special page break | Make into page |

Figure 9.5 Layout markings.

Remember that by selecting a break or another symbol, you can delete it, thus undoing the formatting.

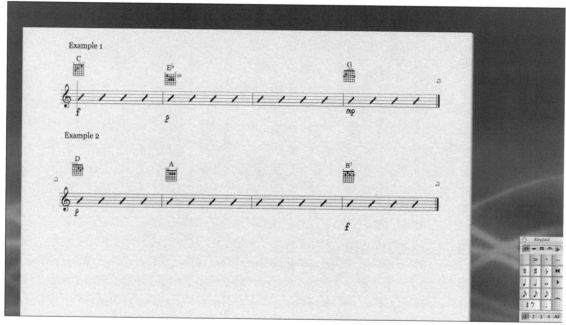

Figure 9.6 Alignments needed.

Aligning Objects

Getting objects to align onscreen is essential to creating professional-looking scores. Figure 9.6 provides a good example of several elements that need aligning.

The following items are not aligned properly:

- Dynamics
- Guitar chord frames
- Text

> **CD:** Go to Example 9.3 on your CD and try your hand at aligning these elements for yourself.

Sibelius gives you two powerful tools in the Layout menu: Align in a Row and Align in a Column. These two tools will help you align the items in Figure 9.6.

Let's start with the dynamics, which are not in horizontal alignment. Align in a Row/Column works by taking the currently selected objects and aligning them in a vertical (when using a column) or a horizontal line (when using a row). What you need to do is select all the dynamics in the first line of music. To do so, select the first dynamic and go to Edit > Select > Select More, which will select similar objects (in this case, dynamic markings).

Now you only have the dynamics highlighted. With the dynamics selected, go to Layout > Align in a Row (shortcut: Ctrl/Command+Shift+R), and, magically, all of your dynamics will be horizontally aligned. Because they're now aligned and still highlighted, if you find that they're not in the correct vertical position, you can always use your arrow keys to nudge the dynamics up or down. You'll need to repeat this step on each staff where the dynamics are misaligned, but because Select More and Align in a Row both have keyboard shortcuts, you'll make fast work of this.

Essential Tip: Super Secret Don't forget that when copying objects, Shift+Alt/Option-clicking makes the objects snap to their default position, but you shouldn't need to align them at all (unless they are colliding with a note).

The guitar chord frames will align the same way as the dynamics. What's different is how you have to select them, because Edit > Select > Select More only works for text-based styles. (It would have worked perfectly with chord symbols, but not with guitar frames.) To select all the guitar frames, double-click the staff, which will select everything, and go to Edit > Filter > Chord Diagrams, and then Layout > Align in a Row. Your guitar frames for that system will be aligned perfectly now.

Click-Happy Sometimes it's faster to just Ctrl/Command-click on a few chord diagrams than to filter them out. It really depends how many you need to select.

Now onto the text. The text you're aligning is across systems (Example 1, Example 2), so Edit > Select > Select More won't help you grab those. You'll need to learn a new trick for selecting these objects! If you were to Shift-click the text (which is the standard way to select multiple items), you'd end up grabbing all the music in the middle. You don't want that! To get around this, use Ctrl/Command-click, which allows you to select noncontiguous items, such as text. Click the first bit of text and then Ctrl/Command-click the second bit of text; both bits will be highlighted together. Because these words need to align vertically, you'll need to use Layout > Align in a Column, which lines them up perfectly. Take a look at the finished product, shown in Figure 9.7.

You can see how powerful these commands are and how you'll use them often as you lay out music. Align commands work for all objects in your score: text, lyrics, dynamics, chords, symbols, and anything else you can think of. You'll make use of these commands in the upcoming example.

Align Lyrics Although there's nothing to stop you from using Layout > Align in a Row to align lyrics, Sibelius ships with a great plug-in to automate the task across your entire score—just go to Plug-Ins > Text Align Lyrics.

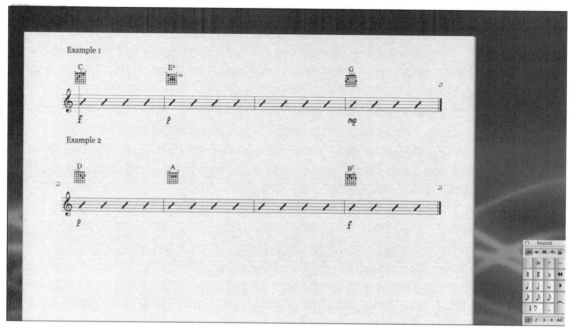

Figure 9.7 After alignment.

Hiding Empty Staves

In a musical score, you often see scores in which instruments have long sections of rests. Rather than showing blank measures, the score simply hides that instrument on the page or system when it's not in use. If you want to achieve this result, it's very easy to do in Sibelius 5. The Layout menu has two commands for this: Hide Empty Staves and Show Empty Staves. As always, the staves you hide are completely dependent on what you select, so if you only want a certain section hidden, you should only select that section. (In other words, don't just use Select > All.)

Hiding of staves happens the instant you choose Layout > Hide Empty Staves. When you want to see your staves again, go to Layout > Show Empty Staves, which brings up the Show Empty Staves dialog box shown in Figure 9.8.

Another Way to Hide If you double-click in any empty staff and press Delete, it hides that staff!

Because hidden staves are impossible to select, when you invoke the Show Empty Staves function, you'll always get this dialog box, showing you all the staves in your score. You can then select which of the hidden staves you want to see again.

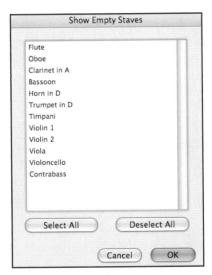

Figure 9.8   The Show Empty Staves dialog box.

Just a final note: When showing or hiding staves, you must have something selected in the score; otherwise, both commands will present you with errors.

Gotta Have One You can't hide all staves in a score—at least one needs to be displayed.

CD: Example 9.4 contains a score that needs some hidden staves. Practice with that score.

Reset Position

You've started to make some changes to your score, you've moved some things around, and you've decided, "You know what? I've made things worse." Have no fear! You can always have Sibelius go back to the default position for every object in your score that has one. (Remember that from the last chapter.) Simply select any of the objects (or ranges of measures) that you want to revert back to its default and choose Layout > Reset Position. The selected object will snap back to its default position.

Not Just for Errors If you change the default position of anything in Sibelius using the House Style menu, you'll notice that the objects don't automatically move—you need to reset their positions first. You do that by selecting Layout > Reset Position.

CD: Example 9.5 on your CD has many objects that need repositioning. Practice resetting positions in this example.

Reset to Score Position

The Reset to Score Position function of the Layout menu takes elements in your parts and reverts them back to the default position of the main score. You can run this in any part you need to clean up, or if you run it in the full score, it will clean up all of the parts.

Reset Design

The design of your score encompasses changing the appearance of objects such as slurs, ties, hidden text, hidden beams on notes, and the scale factor of imported graphics. When you select Layout > Reset Design, all of these elements revert back to their original appearance. Also, just as Reset to Score Position allows you to reset elements in parts, you'll find a Layout > Reset to Score Design command that resets the design of parts when run from an individual part, or resets the design of all parts when run from the full score.

Align Staves

Sibelius gives you a great tool to polish your final score output: Align Staves. You can format your score carefully, get the correct number of measures on a line, and so on, but this won't guarantee that your staves are aligned from page to page like they are on professional scores. Figure 9.9 shows an example; there are three systems per page on this piece, but notice how they aren't aligned properly.

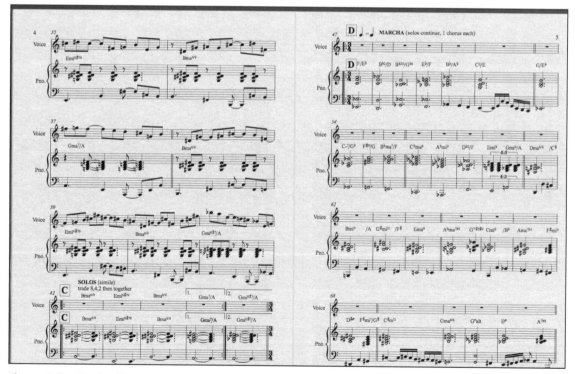

Figure 9.9 Needs alignment.

There are other pages in the score, but you can see how the systems don't line up on these two pages. We'll select the two pages (by clicking the first measure and Shift-clicking the last) and choose Layout > Align Staves, which brings up the Align Staves dialog box shown in Figure 9.10.

Align Staves

This operation affects all pages in the current selection, not individual staves or systems. It is advisable to lock the format so that the changes don't affect other pages.

☑ Align staves on selected pages

☑ Lock format before making changes

◉ With first selected page
○ With last selected page
○ Right pages with facing left pages
○ Left pages with facing right pages

Reset position of staves:

☐ At top of page
☐ At bottom of page

[Cancel]   [OK]

Figure 9.10   The Align Staves dialog box.

There are a few options in this dialog box, but in our case, the default settings will work just fine. When we click OK, our staves are magically aligned (see Figure 9.11).

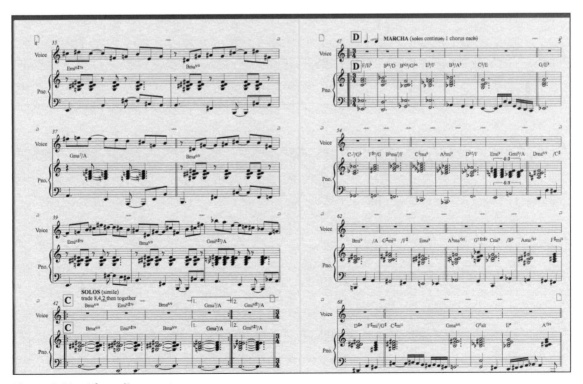

Figure 9.11   After alignment.

Of course, you won't need to do this to every score—there are times when staves won't line up because you've added extra space to make room for staff markings and high notes. However, when possible, run Align Staves, which you can always undo; it really does make most scores look better when everything is visually aligned.

CD: Example 9.6 on your CD provides the same example for you to practice aligning staves. Follow the instructions just given on the file and make it look great.

Locking the Format

After you've made all these wonderful changes to your music, you'll probably want some way to ensure that nothing can mess up your precious format. In the Layout > Format menu, you'll find the Lock Format option, which does exactly that—it locks your format and stops inadvertent changes from taking place. You can always come back and unlock the format whenever you need to do so by choosing Layout > Format > Unlock Format.

Rulers to the Rescue

Even with all the nifty alignment tools Sibelius gives you, there's no way to ensure that each chord symbol (for example) is exactly the same height if you've moved and realigned them. In cases like this, you'll want to turn on the different rulers by choosing View > Rulers. The following rulers are available to you:

- **Selection rulers.** These rulers show you how far an object is from the staff or system to which it's attached.

- **Object rulers.** These rulers are always on; they show you the distance of all objects attached to their staves.

- **Staff rulers.** These rulers tell you how far each staff is from another and how far the start and end are from the page margins.

Figure 9.12 shows rulers in action.

There are many rulers in this shot; I want to go through them so you can see what they are showing you.

- The chord symbol Gma^7/A is 4.38 mm from the staff to which it's attached.

- The space between the Piano staves is 11 mm.

- The space between the Voice staff and the top Piano staff is 10.9 mm.

- The Voice staff is indented 28.3 mm from the margin.

- The 22.9 mm value shows how far the system is from the systems directly above it.

Figure 9.12   Rulers.

When it comes to publishing music, you want this kind of control over your final output, and it's also really handy when you have to move objects and you want to ensure that they are exactly the same distance away.

Default Positions The default positions specify how far objects are from their attachments (the staves). But as soon as you move one object and realign, you're not following default positions anymore. You can always regain default positions by selecting the object(s) and choosing Layout > Reset Position.

Staff Rules You can change the unit of measure for the staff rulers by choosing Preferences > Other.

Auto Layout

For a more hands-off approach, you can try the Layout > Auto Layout command, which will automatically lay out the score for you, based on some criteria you can select. Selecting Layout > Auto Layout brings up the Auto Layout dialog box shown in Figure 9.13.

Essential Tip: Multi-Rests Even if you have no interest in having Sibelius format your score (you'd like to do it yourself), one aspect of the Auto Layout dialog box is the ability to turn multi-measure rests on and off. It's the only obvious place in the program where you can do this, so you'll want to know about it! Or you can try the key command Ctrl/Command+Shift+M.

As you can see from Figure 9.13, you can set up a great deal from this dialog box. The dialog is divided into three areas: System Breaks, Page Breaks, and Multirests.

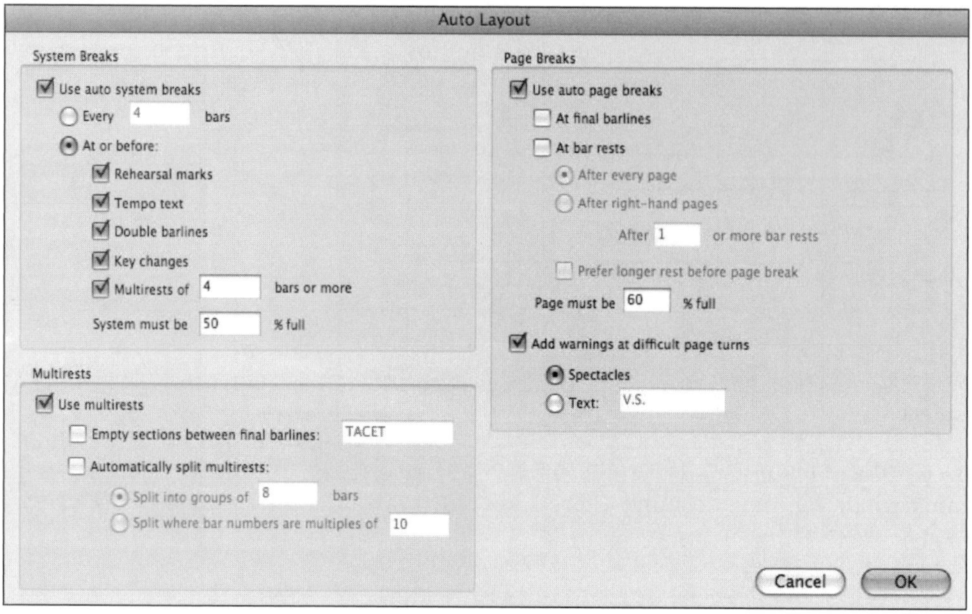

Figure 9.13 The Auto Layout dialog box.

I want to start with the System Breaks section (see Figure 9.14). To enable the system breaks, you'll need to deselect the Use Auto System Breaks option in the top-left corner.

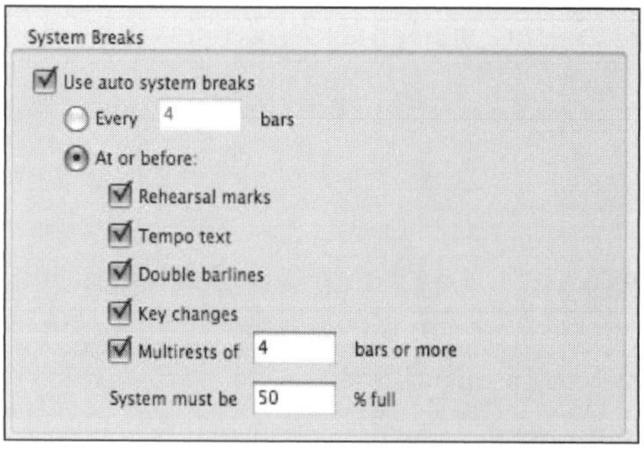

Figure 9.14 The System Breaks section.

■ **Every *x* Bars.** Using this option, you can set the number of bars before Sibelius will automatically enter a system break for you.

■ **At or Before.** If you select this option, Sibelius will enter a system break at or before the following score elements (when selected):

  ■ Rehearsal marks

  ■ Tempo text

- Double barlines
- Key changes
- Multi-rests of x bars or more
- When the system is more than x% full

Most people find that starting with the default four bars per system works out nicely. You can add in breaks at additional elements, such as double barlines or rehearsal markings. The beauty of Auto Layout is that everything is undoable by choosing Edit > Undo or pressing Ctrl/Command+Z.

Now I want to look at the Page Breaks section (see Figure 9.15), which becomes active when you select the Use Auto Page Breaks check box at the top-right corner of the screen. In the Page Breaks section, you have the following choices:

- **At Final Barlines.** After a final barline, Sibelius will add a page break, which is great for multi-movement work, but not so great if you have a D.C. al Fine and a double bar midway through a piece.

- **At Bar Rests.** If this option is selected, Sibelius will do the page break after a bar rest to reduce the difficulty when making a page turn.

- **After Every Page or After Right-Hand Pages.** Use these options to let Sibelius know whether you want to an auto page break after a rest only at right-hand pages or whether it can do it on each page.

- **Prefer Longer Rest before Page Break.** Because adding a page break after each and every empty bar rest isn't practical, you can ask Sibelius to look for longer rests before it inserts a page break.

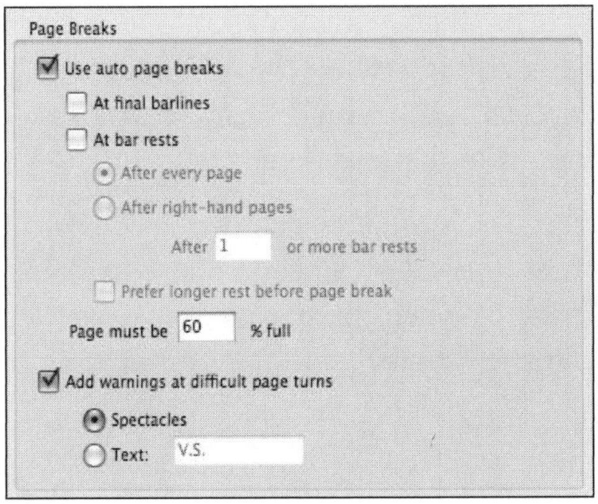

Figure 9.15 The Page Breaks section.

- **Page Must Be *x*% Full.** Along the same lines, Sibelius won't add a page break unless the music is the specified percentage full. This keeps it from adding page breaks after only a few bars. You can add any value to the percentage field.

- **Add Warnings at Difficult Page Turns.** Have Sibelius add either eyeglasses or the V.S. symbol automatically when page breaks occur at odd spots, making it hard for the player to manage.

Lastly, we come to the Multirests section (see Figure 9.16). To use multi-rests, you need to select the Use Multirests option.

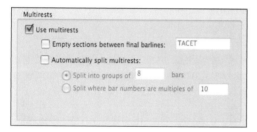

Figure 9.16 The Multirests section.

Multi-Rest Key Combination If the only reason you need to go to the Auto Layout dialog box is to toggle multi-rests on and off, you can just use the key command Ctrl/ Command+Shift+M to turn multi-rests on and off as you go!

Here are the options for how Sibelius will automatically draw multi-rests:

- **Empty Sections between Final Barlines.** If you have a section between the initial and final barlines that has no music, Sibelius can add the customary term "Tacet" above the multi-rests for you. You can also specify your own word in the text field.

- **Automatically Split Multirests.** Multi-rests are split by system objects and certain types of barlines, but if you want to split multi-rests at other intervals, you can choose to split them either after a specified number of concurrent rests or when the bar numbers are multiples of 10 (or any value you wish to add in). This will make counting of longer multi-rest sections easier for your players.

Based on the criteria you set in the three sections of the Auto Layout dialog box, Sibelius will take a crack at laying out your score. In general, I think it's a good idea to use this feature when possible—you can always come back and undo your changes or manually control the layout through the other features of the Layout menu you've already learned about in this chapter.

Parts! One size does not fit all, and in the case of score versus parts, it's pretty common for a full score to lay out one way and for your parts to follow a different set of formatting and engraving rules. Chapter 10, "Dynamic Parts," will deal with the Multiple Part Appearance function, which governs the look of the parts you create within Sibelius.

CD: In Example 9.7, you can use elements of the Auto Layout dialog box to help make the example look professional. Instructions are provided within the Sibelius file itself.

Super-Secret Layout Tips

Really, these are hardly secrets, but here are a few excellent professional tips to help you lay out your music!

- Don't forget to select Engraving Rules > Staves to set spacing between staves/systems and to set how Sibelius automatically justifies staves. More often than not, this is the place to start when laying out a score.

- Graph paper is your friend! You can change the background paper texture on which Sibelius writes by selecting Preferences > Textures. One cool texture is the Graph Paper, which (as you'd expect) gives you blue and white squares. This is an amazing tool for lining up music and objects when the align commands don't work (such as when you are aligning system and staff text in a column). The visual grid makes life really easy.

- When in doubt, use your staff rulers by selecting View > Staff Rulers. If you like the way a score is laid out, see how far apart things really are and try to use that in your own scores.

- Never, ever drag a stave with your mouse! It's imprecise and really hard to work with. More often than not, you'll end up worse than you started.

- If you want to move a stave up or down, you have a couple options:
  - To move a stave (and everything else after it), click on the stave and press Alt/Option+up/down arrow.
  - To move the selected stave independently of the other staves in your score, select the stave you want to move and press Alt/Option+Shift+up/down arrow.

- Remember that these choices are sensitive to selections. You can move a single stave, a stave throughout a page, or a stave throughout an entire piece, depending on how you've selected the music (single-, double-, or triple-click).

- You can reset anything you change; nothing is ever destructive. The Layout menu gives you the ability to reset note spacing, reset the design, reset the space above the staff, and reset the space below the staff.

- Never, ever drag a barline. If there's not enough room in a measure, there are much better ways to make a measure wider.

- You can make a measure wider (or smaller) by clicking on the measure and pressing Alt/Option+Shift+arrow.

- You can select a single note and add space after it (or contract it) by pressing Alt/Option+Shift+arrow.

- If all hope is lost, and you've mucked up your score, you can always create a new score and copy and paste just the music from the broken score to a fresh score. Then, try your hand at laying out the score again.

Now that we've gone over all of the elements of House Styles and the Layout menu in the last two chapters, let's actually try our hand at going through a score and finding out how to make it look great.

When Bad Layouts Happen to Good Music

Brazilian guitarist Richard Boukas sent me a score to look at some time ago, and it dawned on me that it was a perfect example for this book: It was raw, freshly input, and suffered from some typical problems that you may face in your work. To his credit, Boukas never tried to lay out this score before he sent it, and he is clearly capable, but it's a good example of how things can sometime get really messy without you even trying too hard. (He may have broken the Essential Tip of "never drag a staff," but he's such a good guitarist that we can forgive him.) The work is called "Sambacatu," and it's a samba written for voice and piano. It's written as a lead sheet; Figure 9.17 shows the first page of the multi-page work for us to fix.

CD: Example 9.8 is the first page of this score, which is available on the book's accompanying CD-ROM. Open it up to follow along with the forthcoming steps to clarify the entire process of layout.

I want to identify the issues and then work on the best way to fix them using what we already know about Sibelius's layout tools. Here are the issues present on Page 1:

- Rehearsal marks are crashing into other symbols.

- Rehearsal markings are not needed above the piano part.

- Chord symbols are not aligned.

Figure 9.17 Page 1.

- There is not enough room between staves.

- The note spacing isn't right.

- There are too many measures on each system.

Let's tackle these issues one at a time.

Issue: Rehearsal Marks Are Crashing into Other Symbols

At letter A, you can see that the segno is colliding with the markings. The larger issue is that there isn't enough room at the top of the score. We need to adjust the spacing a touch. Remember how I said, "Never, ever drag a stave?" Dragging the top system to make room for a title is the *only* time when you can. Drag the stave down a bit to make some room. Figure 9.18 shows the result.

Margin Instead of dragging the first stave, you can go to Layout > Document Setup and set your staff margin larger than 14 on the initial page to create more space in your top margin.

As you can see, we have one fewer system on the first page, which is fine! Things were too cramped anyway. As for the rehearsal marking crashing, move it up by selecting it and pressing the up arrow key a few times until it's clear of the segno marking. Don't worry about the lower rehearsal marking getting in the way—we'll take care of that in a second. While we're here, move the title of the piece up because it's too low now; use your arrow keys for precise positioning.

You'll notice that letter B is also too low—select it and press the up arrow key until it's no longer in the way.

Issue: Rehearsal Markings Are Not Needed above the Piano Part

This one is easy. If you remember from the House Style menu, elements such as rehearsal markings and other system objects appear at different parts of your score based on the settings when you select House Style > System Object Positions. In this case, because we're seeing a lead sheet, there's no reason for system objects to appear on the piano part. To fix this, go to House Style > System Object Positions to open the System Object Positions dialog box (shown in Figure 9.19) and select the option for system objects to only show above the voice staff. Click OK, and the colliding extra markings will be gone (see Figure 9.20).

System Objects What sorts of things are system objects? Rehearsal marks, tempo text, and first and second endings.

It's starting to look better already!

Figure 9.18   Adjusted top height.

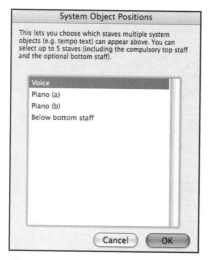

Figure 9.19   The System Object Positions dialog box.

Issue: Chord Symbols Are Not Aligned

To solve this one, we'll make use of filters and Sibelius's alignment tools. To select all the chord symbols in one fell swoop, select all (press Ctrl/Command+A) and then choose Edit > Filter > Chord Symbols, which will select all of your chord symbols and leave them highlighted. To align them, go to Layout > Align in a Row, and all of the chords will magically align! Chords align to the average height, not the default position. If the average is satisfactory, then keep them as is. Because they're all highlighted together, you can use the up/down arrow keys to nudge the chords into position. See Figure 9.21 for the end result.

Not bad, huh?

Issue: Not Enough Room between Staves

Because this score has chord symbols and other markings, we'll need some extra room between the staves. Sibelius controls this through the Engraving Rules dialog box, which you can access by selecting House Style > Engraving Rules (see Figure 9.22).

Changing the space between staves from 5.5 to 8 and the space between systems from 9.25 to 11 should give more room and make the score look much cleaner. Figure 9.23 shows the fruits of our spacing labor.

Things look much better now—the spacing is better overall, and there is room for the chords and other markings.

Figure 9.20 Repaired positions.

Figure 9.21 Aligned chords.

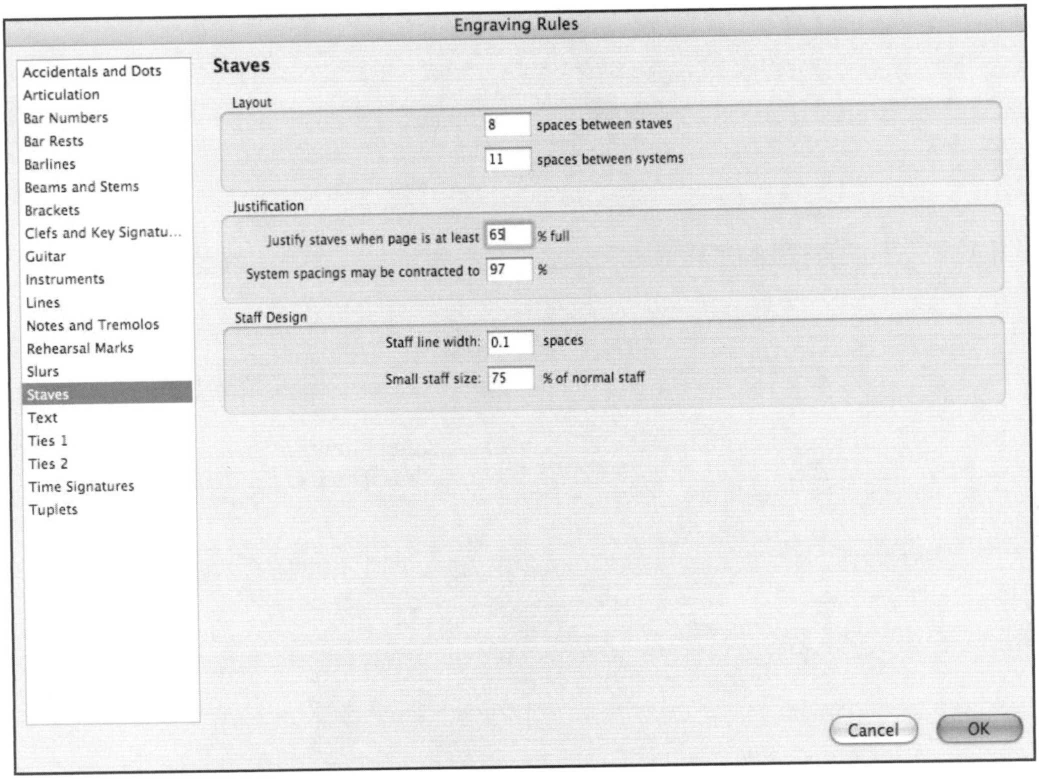

Figure 9.22   The Engraving Rules dialog box.

Issue: Note Spacing Isn't Right

Note spacing is definitely off in this piece. This is easily fixed. Select all the measures and go to Layout > Reset Note Spacing. Sibelius will fix this up for you instantly, yielding Figure 9.24, which looks much better for note spacing. However, we still have one last problem—way too many measures per system!

Issue: Too Many Measures on Each System

Resetting the note spacing actually changed some of our formatting because Sibelius automatically lays out the score dynamically. What has become clear is that after the note spacing was reset, there are just too many bars on each line. We can manually add some breaks, but Sibelius has an Auto Layout feature that we should check out and see how it works for us. We can always fix things manually later.

If we select all of our measures and go to Layout > Auto Layout, we can set up some parameters. This score isn't the "four bars per system" sort of piece; we'll have to let Sibelius make some decisions for us. We should select Use Auto System Breaks and stay with the default settings that Sibelius provides (see Figure 9.25).

When we come back to the score (see Figure 9.26), Sibelius has made some good decisions for us—it has added a break so that rehearsal mark B starts its own line. We now have four systems,

Figure 9.23 Better spacing.

Figure 9.24   Reset note spacing.

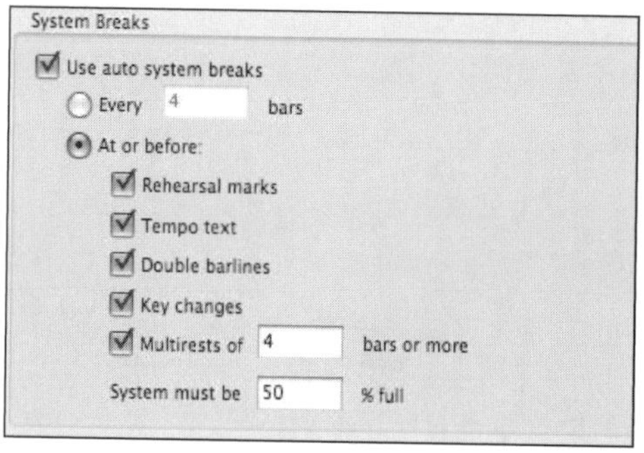

Figure 9.25 Auto layout.

good note spacing, and good overall design. Things look pretty good. But as always, when you lay out a score, the process is dynamic, and you make changes as you go along.

Issue: Bar Numbers Are Present with Rehearsal Markings

If you look at letter B after our auto layout, you can see that the bar number for Measure 19 is also present. What's worse is that it's colliding. When you have a rehearsal mark, it's not necessary to also have a bar number, as you'll refer to it as "letter B." To fix this, Sibelius lets you automatically hide bar numbers when rehearsal marks are present. To activate this feature, go to House Style > Engraving Rules > Bar Numbers and select the Hide at Rehearsal Marks option (see Figure 9.27). No need to show a full-score screenshot; it does what it says and cleans up our problem pretty easily.

Last Details

As a result of our changes, a few things look a bit wrong now. Some of the text around rehearsal mark A is scrunched, and a few other ancillary bits of text markings are a little low. Now's the time to make some adjustments by hand.

Letter A, the segno, "Vocal," and the 8vb are all too close together. Let's put the segno to the right of the rehearsal mark and the Vocal 8vb under both markings. Let's also move the "gtr loco" at mm. 18 up a bit. Also, the Gma9 at mm. 7 is off, so we'll move it to the right as well. Finally, there are a few rests floating above the left hand of the piano—probably due to the way that the chords originally entered and converted to rhythmic notation. Select all the rests that are out of place and choose Layout > Reset Position to get them back to where they should be.

Finally, to be really picky, there are a few rests out of position. We'll select them and move them (by choosing Window > Properties > General).

Figure 9.28 shows the results of all our work!

Figure 9.26   After auto layout.

Figure 9.27 With hidden bar numbers.

Figure 9.28   Layout!

Figure 9.29   Now we're finished!

One Last Thing

Something's still not right, and a careful look at our staff rulers shows a problem with staff spacing. Even though we went into the engraving rules and chose definite values for spaces between staves and systems, our score isn't following those. At some point, the composer must have inadvertently dragged a stave up or down, creating more space, which is why the score looks off. This step is pretty important to explain because you might also have this issue and need a reset. Select all your measures and go to Layout > Reset Space above Staff. This will make the score stick to the positions in the engraving rules and will generally make things look tidy. Never underestimate the effect of symmetry on the eyes. Our score was only a few spaces off, but look at the result of even spacing shown in Figure 9.29.

This is just one example of many possible scenarios, but as you can see, layout is a mixture of House Style > Engraving Rules and Layout menu items. Sibelius does a really good job of making this task easy for you so you can spend your time being creative.

Clarity Proper layout and formatting can affect the performance of a piece—yes, they're *that* important. Players make mistakes if the score is hard to read and isn't well designed. The absolute final rule is that clarity wins. Keep this in mind as you learn to lay out your scores and keep notes when you look at well-laid-out scores.

10 Dynamic Parts

Essential Tips for Chapter 10

1. You can switch between the score and the part by clicking on a stave and hitting the W key. Hit W again, and you'll return to the full score.

2. Once you're in a Parts window, you can switch from part to part using the key command Ctrl+Alt+Tab (Windows) or Opt+Command+~ (Mac).

3. Parts have their own House Style that is different from the score's own House Style.

4. You manage the look of the parts by clicking on the Multiple Part Appearance button after you select Window > Parts.

5. You can make a custom part that contains any staves you like—just click the New Part button in the Parts window.

6. You can make the layout exactly the same on all your parts using the Copy Part Layout feature in the Parts window.

7. Extracting parts isn't dead; if you're sharing with a user who has Sibelius 3 or earlier or Sibelius Student, you'll need to extract parts to share parts with them.

Dynamic parts are an innovation that was introduced in Sibelius 4 and that changed the way musicians work with parts. Parts, whether hand-copied or computer-generated, are a pain to work with! Scores begin with all instrument parts in one main score, and at the end of the creation process, the parts must be "extracted" into individual parts and checked for their individual legibility.

In the past, part extraction on a computer entailed the software "extracting" each instrument into its own Sibelius file for later editing and printing. Once each instrument was extracted, you had to go through each file and make sure it looked as you expected it to. Because each was a separate file, changes you made in the score after the fact had no effect on the part. Sibelius has changed the game with Dynamic Parts, a system in which you never have to extract a part; they are made automatically, and the score is constantly updating the part as you compose (hence the term "dynamic"). Even better, Sibelius stores all the parts in a single file, so you never have to keep track of multiple copies of parts and scores. This has saved hours and prevented much frustration for Sibelius users.

Because Dynamic Parts are created automatically, this will be a nice, light chapter! Of course, there are some options that you'll want to know about, but in general, Sibelius has made the process of parts as simple as humanly possible.

Accessing Parts

When you create a score, the parts are created automatically for you. On the main toolbar of your Sibelius 5 window, you'll notice a menu button that reads Full Score (see Figure 10.1); this is your gateway into your Dynamic Parts.

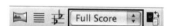

Figure 10.1 The Parts drop-down menu.

When you click on the term Full Score, you will be shown all of the Dynamic Parts that Sibelius has created for you (see Figure 10.2).

Figure 10.2 Parts listing.

You can release your mouse on the part you want to see, and you'll be automatically taken from the full-score view to the individual part you've selected (see Figure 10.3).

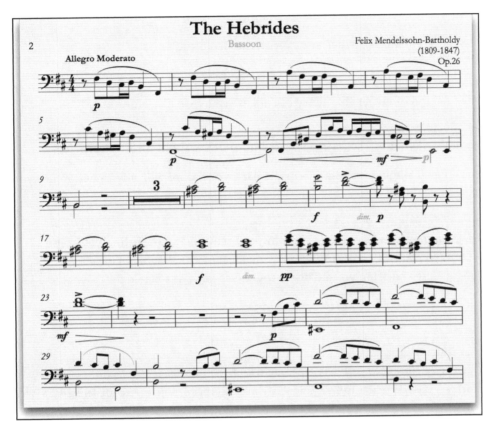

Figure 10.3 The Bassoon part.

When you're in the part, the score changes to a yellowish texture so you know that you're in a Dynamic Part and not an old-style Extracted Part, which Sibelius can still do on request from the Parts window, which you'll learn about in "The Parts Window" section. Using the same method, you can flip to any of the other parts in the score.

Essential Tip: Access Your Parts Quickly To switch back and forth between the score and the parts without having to go to the menu bar, click on the stave you want to see as a part and press the W key. Hitting W in the score with a stave selected will take you to that part, and pressing W again will take you back to the full score.

What's even cooler is that you can scroll through all the parts one by one (once you're already in a part) by pressing Ctrl+Alt+Tab (Windows) or Command+Option+Tab (Mac).

What a Part Is and What It Isn't

It's very important to understand how the score and Dynamic Parts interact in Sibelius. To start, any changes that you make in the score are immediately reflected in the parts—that much is always true. However, if you switch to the part and start making changes, the score isn't necessarily changed. Here's a listing of what you can expect from the parts:

- If you change the note in a part, it will change in the full score.

- Changes to the position of objects in the part (slurs, hairpins, text, dynamics) will not change in the full score.

- You can change the layout of the parts (breaks and such) without affecting the score.

To sum it up, other than changing note names in the part, your score will stay intact even if you fiddle with the parts quite a bit.

Not Focused Even though we haven't gotten to the Focus on Staves feature yet, some readers will know what it is. It's worth mentioning that Focus on Staves might look like you can segregate out just a part, but you are not in any way looking at a part in the "Dynamic Parts" sense of the word.

Differences in Parts

A useful feature is the Differences in Parts option, which you can select by choosing View > Differences in Parts. When this option is selected, any changes you make in the parts will be highlighted in orange so you can clearly see what is different (position of objects, for example) between the score and its parts. In addition to moved objects, notes that are cue-sized in the parts and any hidden text in the part will also appear in orange. This feature is only visible when you're looking at the part, of course. If the orange display of the objects bothers you, you can turn off that feature by going back to View > Difference in Parts and toggling it off.

Parts in the Full Score View > Difference in Parts also shows you changes from your parts in the main score. It does so by highlighting changes in orange, just like in the parts. This makes it easy keep track of what has moved from the score to the parts.

The Parts Window

To help you control your parts, Sibelius has a consolidated Parts window, which you can access by choosing Window > Parts (see Figure 10.4).

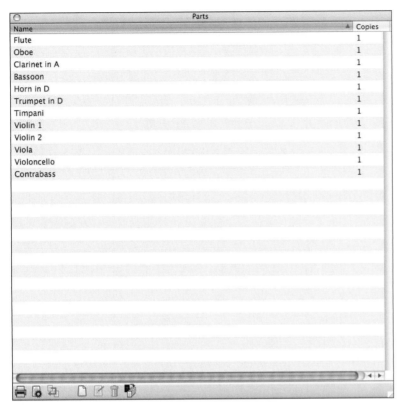

Figure 10.4   The Parts window.

The Parts window has a number of buttons across the bottom, which are shown in Figure 10.5. Here is some more detail about the icons at the bottom of the Parts window:

- **Print Part(s).** Prints the selected parts. The number of copies is dictated by the number you select in the Copies column of the Parts window.

- **Multiple Part Appearance.** Changes the House Style, engraving rules, or other visual elements of multiple parts at once, independent of the score.

- **Copy Part Layout.** Takes the layout you've made in one part and applies it to the selected part in the Parts window.

- **New Part.** Makes a new part from a selection of staves from the score. For example, you might want to have a part that contains all the woodwinds from your score—great for sectional rehearsals.

- **Staves in Part.** Edits a part and changes which staves are contained within the part.

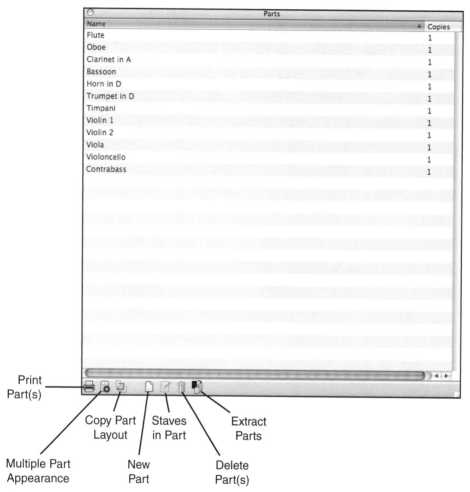

Print Part(s)

Copy Part Layout   Staves in Part   Extract Parts

Multiple Part Appearance   New Part   Delete Part(s)

Figure 10.5 The Parts window explained.

- **Delete Part(s).** As you'd expect, deletes the selected part(s). This, however, doesn't delete the music from the main score!

- **Extract Parts.** Go old school: This takes the parts from being dynamic and saves them to individual files.

Power Selections Because many of the operations in the Parts window can apply to several parts at once, you should remember how to make a multiple selection! Hold down the Ctrl/Command key while you click within the Parts window to select multiple parts at once. (This is the only way to select noncontiguous parts.)

At first glance, the Parts window shows you the active parts in your score and how many copies will be printed for each part. You can change the name of the part or the number of copies by clicking once on the Parts window and changing the text field for Name or Copies.

Next, I want to go through two of the most frequent uses for the Parts window—creating and changing parts.

Creating Parts

To create a new part (one that wasn't automatically made, or a custom part you'd like to make for rehearsal purposes), click on the New Part button at the bottom of the Parts window to bring up the New Part dialog box shown in Figure 10.6.

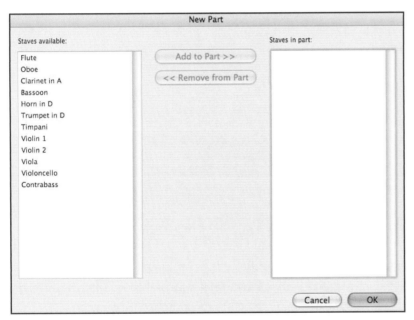

Figure 10.6   The New Part dialog box.

The dialog box is simple—all of the staves in your score are displayed on the left side. Highlight the stave you want to add and click the Add to Part button to add that stave to a new part. Add as many staves as you need to create your part and click OK. A new part will be made for you, as shown in the Parts window.

CD: Open Example 10.1 and follow the instructions in the Sibelius file to create some new parts from the provided score.

Changing Parts

To change the appearance of an already-made part, click on the part in the Parts window and click on the Staves in Part button at the bottom of the window. Doing so will bring you to the Staves in Part dialog box, shown in Figure 10.7.

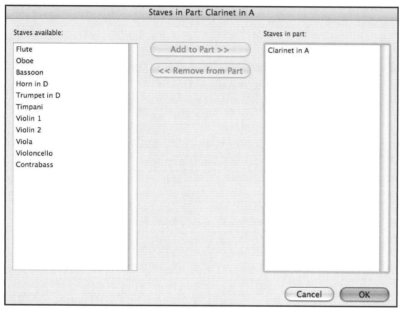

Figure 10.7   The Staves in Part dialog box.

This dialog box, which looks remarkably like the New Part dialog box shown in Figure 10.6, works in reverse: It shows you the staves in the selected part, and you can remove or change staves from the same window. The Add to Part and Remove from Part buttons allow you to add or remove staves.

This is useful, for example, if you're doing a score for choir and orchestra and you need to combine the SATB parts into one single part, as is the common practice for singers.

CD: In Example 10.2, follow the instructions to change the instruments assigned to the parts.

Part Appearance

The work of a copyist has only just begun once the notes of the full score have been entered! Preparing legible parts is just one of the challenges for any engraver. Because the score and the parts will almost always require different visual layouts, Sibelius gives you two powerful tools for working with your parts: The Multiple Part Appearance and Copy Part Layout features help you control the look of your parts before you start tweaking the parts individually.

Multiple Part Appearance

Yet another useful icon along the bottom of the Parts window is the Multiple Part Appearance button, which is only present when you select either a single part or multiple parts, hence the name. Selecting a single part and pressing the magic button will yield the message box shown in Figure 10.8.

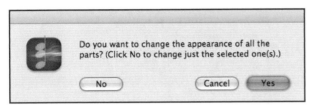

Do you want to change the appearance of all the parts? (Click No to change just the selected one(s).)

No   Cancel   Yes

Figure 10.8   How many parts should be changed?

When you invoke Multiple Part Appearance without all of the parts selected, Sibelius asks you whether you want to edit them all, because it's customary to change the appearance all at once. If you need to work on the appearance of a single part, you can click No in the message box and work on a single part.

Either way you slice it, you'll be taken to the Multiple Part Appearance dialog box shown in Figure 10.9.

As is the case with many Sibelius dialog boxes, this dialog has three pages embedded in it, the first of which is the Document Setup page. I want to look at each page separately.

Document Setup

The Document Setup page does the same as choosing Layout > Document did for your full score, but this page does so for your parts. You can specify margins, page size, and staff size, all independent of your setting for the full score. If you've only selected some of your parts, you can specify different settings for different parts—just revisit this window for the other parts you want to change.

Layout

The Layout page of the Multiple Part Appearance dialog box deals with various aspects of the overall layout of your parts (see Figure 10.10).

Many of the entries on these pages are analogous to the options for your full score, but these options only change the parts.

- **Auto Layout.** These are the same Auto Layout options found in the Layout menu, but with settings suitable for parts.

- **Breaks.** This section is devoted to which breaks in the main score should propagate to the parts. Because not every break in a score should be observed, Sibelius gives you the control.

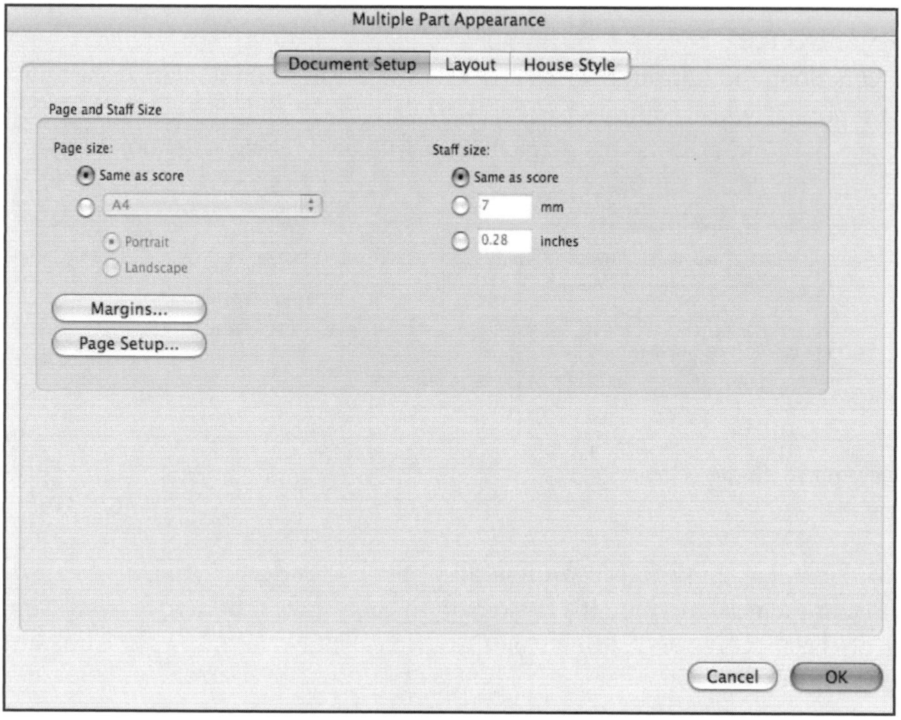

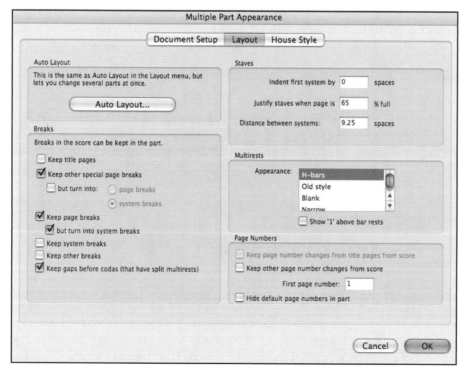

Figure 10.9   The Multiple Part Appearance dialog box.

Figure 10.10   The Layout page of the Multiple Part Appearance dialog box.

- **Staves.** In this section, the most frequently used items in the Engraving Rules dialog box (such as staff indentation, justification, and distance between systems) are included for your parts.

- **Multirests.** You can change the appearance and style of multi-rests drawn in your score (which are on by default in the parts).

- **Page Numbers.** You can opt to keep the page-number scheme used in the score or hide page numbers in the part completely.

House Style

The House Style page of the Multiple Part Appearance dialog box takes you through the rest of the visual setup and engraving rules for your parts, including the ability to import a House Style for your parts, independent of the House Style used in your full score (see Figure 10.11).

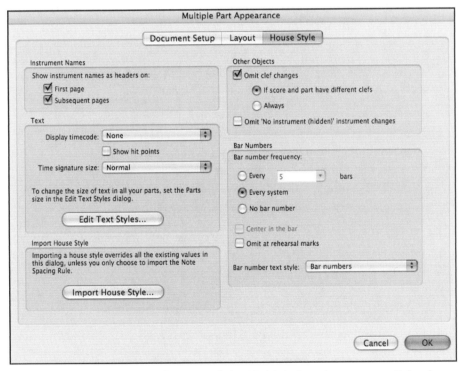

Figure 10.11 The House Style page of the Multiple Part Appearance dialog box.

Here is a rundown of the settings you can change through the House Style page of the Multiple Part Appearance dialog box.

- **Instrument Names.** In this section, you can control whether you want to use the instrument name as a header on parts and on which pages it should appear.

- **Text.** Here, you can show or hide timecode/hit points (video) text in your score and change the appearance of the time signature to normal, large, or huge.

- **Edit Text Styles.** Here, you can change any of the formatting, fonts, size, and other aspects related to text styles in your score.

- **Import House Style.** As you'd expect, you can import a House Style to only the selected parts.

- **Other Objects.** Here, you can control whether clef changes are omitted from the score or parts, including the special "no instruments (hidden)" instrument changes.

- **Bar Numbers.** Here you have complete control over the appearance and frequency of bar numbers in the selected parts.

As you can surmise from the sections, the Multiple Part Appearance dialog box is all about giving you the same control you had over the layout of your full score using the Layout and House Style menus, but providing independent access to changes in your parts. If you can get good results using the features described in the full score, you'll have no trouble getting your parts in order using the Multiple Part Appearance dialog box.

CD: In Example 10.3, you'll be asked to use the Multiple Part Appearance dialog box to change various aspects of a score. The directions are in the Sibelius file.

Copy Part Layout

There are many times when you'll want the layout of all your parts to look identical. This can include page and system breaks, the number of measures per system, and so on. This is prevalent in film and TV part creation. To accomplish this, format a part that you'd like to copy as your "model" part.

1. Make sure that the model part is currently in view. (It must be in a part window, not the full score.)

2. Choose Window > Parts.

3. Highlight all the parts to where you want to copy the current format.

4. Click the Copy Part Layout button in the Parts window.

5. Sibelius will ask you whether you want to copy the format of the current part to the selected parts. You'd be wise to say yes....

And in one simple mouse click, all of your parts will look the same. Don't worry, you can always undo this!

CD: Example 10.4 will teach you to make all of your parts look identical (in other words, have the same layout).

Hide/Show in Parts

Another useful feature when dealing with scores and parts in Sibelius is the ability to hide or show objects in either the score or the parts. Suppose you want to add some instructions to your conductor's score that should not be seen by the players. Conversely, you want to add some markings or objects to a part that should remain only in the part. Because this is likely to happen to you, Sibelius gives you the ability to do so.

The Edit > Hide or Show menu has options for:

- Hide/Show in Score

- Hide/Show in Parts

- Hide/Show in All

A faster way to accomplish this is to right-click (Control-click on Mac) when pointing to an object, which brings up the menu shown in Figure 10.12. This menu has the full Hide or Show submenu contained within it. You'll find some other useful commands in this menu as well!

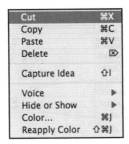

Figure 10.12   Right-click/Control-click menu.

Great Use of Hide A great use of the Hide/Show in Score/Parts feature is when you are preparing parts for transposing instruments in a jazz context. To add rhythm slashes for chord improvisation, you'd normally add middle-line Bs to the score and then change the noteheads. Unfortunately, the parts will have the transposed notehead on the wrong line. You can have the sections of middle-line B show in the score, and then create similar markings in the parts using the Show in Parts command. If you're doing a lot of this, Sibelius has a great plug-in: Add Slash Noteheads for Parts.

CD: In Example 10.5, you'll learn how to add some markings to the score and parts and control how they are shown and hidden.

Extracting Parts

Finally, you can still extract parts into individual files by going to the Parts window and clicking the Extract Parts button at the bottom-right of the window. Doing so will bring up the warning message box shown in Figure 10.13.

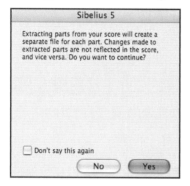

Figure 10.13   Warnings about extracting parts.

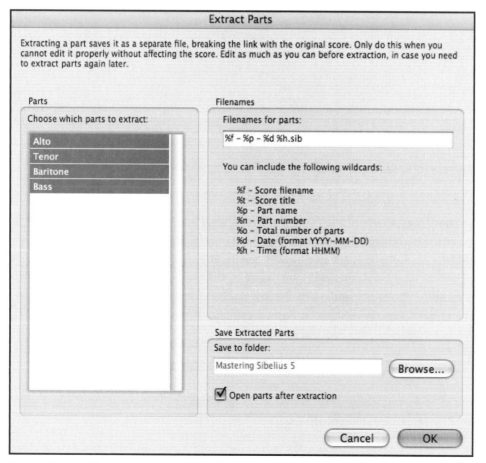

Figure 10.14   The Extract Parts dialog box.

When you click Yes, you'll be taken to the actual Extract Parts dialog box, as shown in Figure 10.14.

In this dialog box, you can select which parts in the score to extract (from the left side), how the filenames are automatically drawn (using wildcards), and where to extract the parts to on your computer or connected media drive.

Why Extract? If Dynamic Parts are so great, then why even have the choice to extract parts in the old way? In truth, you won't have to do this often, but in a few isolated cases you might want to. For example, if you want to publish parts online using Scorch, you need to have the parts as separate files. Also, if you need to share with a person who has an earlier version of Sibelius [Sibelius Student (Old or New), 2, 3, or 4], you need to extract and export the parts for those versions of Sibelius.

Printing Parts

Printing parts is done from one of two places. The first is from the familiar Parts window, where the Print Part(s) button will invoke your operating system's normal Print feature (see Figure 10.15).

Figure 10.15   Printing from the Parts window.

You can also print your parts by choosing File > Print All Parts. Both commands accomplish the same action.

And that's about all there is to do with parts!

11 Ideas

Essential Tips for Chapter 11

1. If you have no interest in the built-in Ideas library, you can tell Sibelius not to load it, and you can build your own Ideas library.

2. You can export your Ideas library and share it with your colleagues or students.

3. You can tag your Ideas with as many keywords as you want to make searching faster.

4. The Detailed view is the only place where you can access the importing and exporting of Ideas.

5. You can't drag and drop Ideas from the Ideas window to your score. You must copy and paste.

6. Even if you think you'll have no use for Ideas, they will grow on you once you start using them.

7. Ideas are not loops.

8. You can audition an Idea by clicking and holding on the selected Idea.

In this chapter, you'll learn about the Ideas feature. The Ideas feature is new in Sibelius 5 and can be thought of as "Post-it notes" for musical Ideas. You can capture any piece of music, small or large, and store it for later use. You can tag the Ideas with keywords and search for the Ideas at a later date. Better yet, you can browse the library of pre-built Ideas and use them as snippets to help you compose, which is a great way for students to get involved with composition. You can even share them!

No matter how you use them, the Ideas feature is a revolutionary one that I think you'll really like. If you're an educator, there are some really obvious benefits to teaching composition this way. It's also great for those times when you have a great Idea, but you can't utilize it in your current work; capture it for later use.

What Are Ideas?

The Ideas feature was created to be a sort of "musical notepad" where you could keep a record of any musical material in your score and recall it later. It could be the main motive for your new symphony or just a chord progression you composed but couldn't fit into your current score. The heart of Ideas is the Ideas window, which you can access in a few ways. You can hit the Light-Bulb icon in the main toolbar, or you can select Ideas from the Window menu. Either way, the Ideas window will appear, as shown in Figure 11.1.

The Ideas window is a floating window, so you can keep it open as you work on your score. What you're seeing now are the Ideas (which are color-coded by style) in the main window. Along the bottom of the Ideas window, you'll see various buttons that control aspects of the Ideas window. Figure 11.2 details each of these buttons.

The functions of these buttons are as follows:

- **Capture Idea.** This captures the selected music in Sibelius into the Ideas library.

- **Copy.** This allows you to copy the selected Idea so you can paste it into your score.

- **Paste.** This allows you to paste the selected Idea or the Idea that was copied into the Clipboard using the Copy function. Remember that the Paste function is always sensitive to selections. If you invoke Paste with music selected, it will paste at that spot. If you have nothing selected, you will get a blue cursor, and you can choose where you want the material to be pasted.

- **Edit.** This brings the selected Idea into a new window, where you can edit its contents.

- **Edit Idea Info.** Here you can edit the keywords, color, and description of your Ideas to help organize them.

- **Delete Idea.** This allows you to delete the currently selected Idea.

Figure 11.1 The Ideas window.

- **Add to Score.** This will add the currently selected Idea or music to the Ideas library for this score only.

- **Add to Library.** This will add the currently selected Idea or music to the main library, accessible from any score.

- **Detailed View.** You can switch to a Detailed view that lists more information about the Ideas and shows the music in a larger, easier-to-read format.

Figure 11.2 The Ideas buttons.

Essential Tip: Audition If you click and hold your mouse on any selected Idea, it will play back with the correct sound. Use this to audition Ideas at any point.

There are a few other aspects of the interface, but you'll learn about those as you learn more about Ideas on the whole.

Capturing Ideas

Capturing an Idea is a simple affair. All you have to do is select some music in Sibelius and capture the Idea. So how do you do that? In one of a few ways. The first method is to use the Capture Idea button in the Ideas window. (It shows a net around a light bulb.) The other way to capture an Idea is by pressing Shift+I.

Once you've captured the Idea, it will show up at the top of your Ideas window, as shown in Figure 11.3.

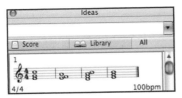

Figure 11.3   A newly captured Idea.

Naming The name of your captured Idea will get its information from the file name of the piece. So if you have not saved the piece's file, the Idea will lack a title and will have a number rather than a name. However, you can edit the Idea info to add a proper name at any time.

When you capture the Idea, several things happen. In the Idea preview, you will see that the Idea has been captured along with its tempo and time signature. You'll also notice that your new Idea is white. (This is done by default, and you can color-code it later.)

Mouse Over If you hover your mouse over the Ideas library, you'll get a pop-up window showing you some additional information about the Idea.

Here are some important things you'll want to know about Ideas:

■   Ideas are captured with the correct sounds. When you capture an Idea from a trumpet stave and audition it, it will play back with a trumpet sound.

■   Ideas can be as many measures, instruments, or staves as you choose. There is no limit.

- By default, when you capture an Idea, it goes into the Score library. If you want the Idea to go to the library so it can be accessed by any score, you can change this through Sibelius's Preferences. If I were you, I'd select Preferences > Ideas and change captured Ideas to the main library, so you can use your Ideas in any score.

- You can add any Idea to the main library from an individual score using the Add to Library button.

- Notes are not the only things added to an Idea. Text, expressions, articulations, chords, and other markings are copied as well.

- You might want to choose Edit > Filter if you only want *music* captured as an Idea, and not the extra score markings.

- You can back up and transfer your Ideas to other computers or colleagues.

Now that you know how to capture Ideas, you'll want to know what else you can do to them.

CD: Use Example 11.1 to practice capturing some Ideas into the Ideas library.

Editing Ideas

Whether you're working on preexisting Ideas or individual Ideas that you've created yourself, you'll probably want to edit an Idea at some point. Let's start by looking at the content of any Idea as a score, so you can use Sibelius's familiar tools to edit your Idea. If you double-click on any Idea in the Ideas window, you'll be taken to a new window in Panorama view that contains the contents of the Idea (as shown in Figure 11.4).

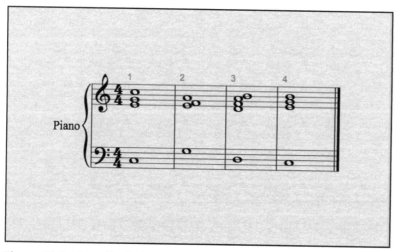

Figure 11.4 An edited Idea.

Once you're in this window, you can feel free to change any aspects of the Idea you want. When you're finished editing, you'll want to save the Idea by choosing File > Save. Alternatively, if you simply close the window, you'll be asked to save the Idea. Your changes will be reflected immediately in the Ideas library.

Edit, Please If you're planning to use the Ideas feature with composition students, editing Ideas periodically is a great way to keep the new compositions fresh and original.

There are other things to edit besides just the notes. You might want to edit other information about the Idea. You can do this in the Edit Idea Info dialog box.

CD: In Example 11.2, edit the Idea as instructed in the example.

Editing Idea Info

To access the Edit Idea Info dialog box, you should have your Idea highlighted. Then you can click on the Edit Idea Info button at the bottom of the Ideas window. Or you can right-click (Control-click on Mac) to access a context menu that contains an option for Edit Idea Info. Regardless of the method you use, the Edit Idea Info dialog box shown in Figure 11.5 will appear.

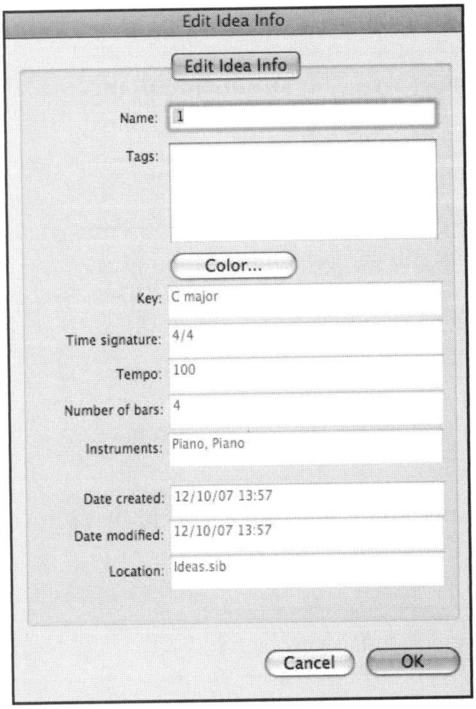

Figure 11.5 The Edit Idea Info dialog box.

In this dialog box, you can see details of your Idea. It's important to note what you can and can't change. You can only change the name of the Idea, the tags (more on that in a second), and the color. The other elements of the Idea are hard-coded and can't be changed—unless you edit the actual musical information in the Idea (such as key) in the Edit Idea Info dialog box.

You can add any name you want to the Name field—realize that the names are only for your organization. When you search for Ideas, the names will be searched for, so the name should be something memorable (although tags will help you in this regard as well).

CD: In Example 11.3, rename the Idea that you'll capture within the example.

Tags

You can set tags for your Ideas. A *tag* is a keyword or a group of keywords that helps you search for your Idea. Search engines and websites have long used *metatags* to make your Google searches more exact, and Sibelius uses them to help you find your Ideas more quickly. For example, if your Idea is a jazz riff based on a C Mixolydian scale, you could add the keywords *jazz* and *Mixolydian*.

When you search for jazz- or Mixolydian-based Ideas later, you can simply search for either of those keywords, and the Ideas search will only show you matching entries. We'll cover searching Ideas in the "Searching Ideas" section, coming up.

Search Clear When you clear out the search box, you have to press Enter/Return to truly "clear" all the results and see all of your Ideas again.

Auto Tags The tags you create aren't the only elements you can search for within Ideas. The non-editable portions of the Edit Idea Info dialog box, such as time signature, tempo, key signature, and instrument, can also be searched, even though you can't edit them!

When you create tags, it's very important that you don't separate them with commas or any other punctuation! Just create a list like the one in Figure 11.6.

You can come back to this dialog and add more tags at any point, and there's no limit to how many tags you can have!

CD: Example 11.4 will help you practice tagging an Idea with custom search words.

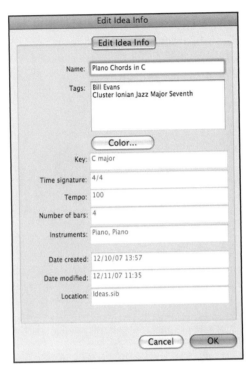

Figure 11.6   Idea tags.

Color-Coding Ideas

As you might have noticed in the built-in Ideas library, the Ideas are color-coded! For example, all of the classical Ideas are lime green, and the jazz Ideas are light pink. When you create an Idea yourself, it won't contain a color automatically, but you can add one later, especially if it will help you organize your Ideas. You set the color in the Edit Idea Info dialog box (the same place you added the name and set your search tags). Directly below the field for adding tags is a Color button—clicking on it brings you to the Colors dialog box shown in Figure 11.7, where you can select your color of choice.

Note that Figure 11.7 shows the standard Mac OS X color selector. If you're on a Windows system, your color selector will look a bit different, but it will have the same functionality.

Color-coding is a simple and effective way to organize your Ideas.

Progression Here's a creative use of Ideas in a composition class: Create a set of Ideas for your students and color-code each Idea based on the harmony. All the I chord Ideas are green, IV chord Ideas are red, and so on. Then, when the students compose, they can pick Ideas based on harmonic relationships that are clear and easy to see.

Figure 11.7 Setting Idea color.

Now that you've done some editing and you've color-coded your Ideas, you'll want to make use of the Ideas search feature.

CD: Example 11.5 will teach you to color-code a few captured Ideas.

Searching Ideas

The top of your Ideas window contains a search box, as shown in Figure 11.8.

You can search for your Ideas by using a variety of search terms here. If you've added tags yourself, you can search by tags. Or, you can search the automatically created tags (time, tempo, key signature). It's important to note that you can search in a few different ways. Directly below the search field, you'll see three tabs: Score, Library, and All. By clicking on any of the tabs, you'll be able to search within that category only.

- **Score.** This tab will allow you to search for Ideas that are contained in the score only.

- **Library.** This tab will allow you to search for Ideas that are in the main library (and available to all scores).

- **All.** This tab will allow you to search for Ideas in both the score and the main library.

Figure 11.8 Ideas search.

It's important to note that the Ideas search is dynamic. This means that the second you start typing in the search field, Sibelius begins searching. So if you're looking for a jazz Idea, the moment you type in J, Sibelius will start looking for all Ideas that contain the letter J. It's not until you've fully typed in "jazz" that Sibelius will start to show you all of your Ideas that match the word jazz.

CD: In Example 11.6, use the search box to find an Idea that you'll newly capture and tag.

The Detailed View

So far, you've been looking at the Compact view for the Ideas, but Sibelius gives you a Detailed view as an option. To extend your Ideas into the Detailed view, hit the Detailed

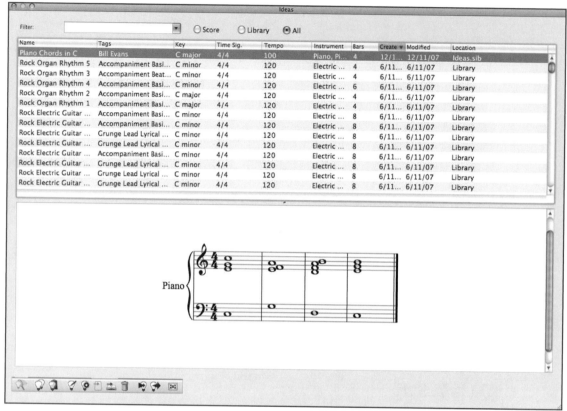

Figure 11.9   Ideas Detailed view.

View button at the lower-right corner of the Ideas window. Figure 11.9 shows an example of the Detailed view.

As you'd imagine, you get a lot more details in this view. Although the majority of this window is self-explanatory, there are some things worth discussing.

- You can extend the size of each column; just click and drag each one to make it longer.

- The order of the columns is not fixed. Just drag the columns around to suit yourself.

- You can sort the order of the Ideas by clicking on the column names (Name, Tags, Key, Time Signature, Tempo, Instrument, Bars, Created, Modified, and Location). When you click on Created, for example, it sorts the list by oldest first and newest last. Click again on Created to flip the display order.

- The Detailed view is the only place where you can access the importing and exporting of Ideas.

- The Detailed view does not show Idea colors.

- You can make the notation preview larger; just drag the divider between the Ideas and the notation to make more space.

At any point, you can switch back to the Compact view by clicking the View button, which is the last button at the bottom of the Ideas window.

Auditioning Ideas

Here's a simple one! You can listen to any Idea by clicking (and holding) your mouse on it. As long as you click and hold your mouse, the Idea will play back. You can stop this behavior through the Ideas window by choosing Sibelius > Preference.

Multiple Audition If your Idea contains multiple staves, the Ideas list will only show the top stave. When you audition the Idea, Sibelius will have to load up the sounds for *all* of the staves!

Getting Ideas into Your Score

You'll want to know a few important things about Ideas and how they interact with your score. Here is a list of things you'll want to know about pasting Ideas into your score:

- Ideas are not loops; they won't drag and drop. You must select the Idea, then copy, then paste.

- If you have music pre-selected before you paste your Idea, the Idea will appear after your selection (just like everything else in Sibelius).

- If you don't have anything selected when you go to paste your Idea, you'll get a blue cursor, and you'll need to click the location in your score where you want the Idea to go.

- Sibelius will automatically transpose the key of the Idea to match the key signature of your score when you paste.

- Sibelius will automatically transpose the range of the Idea to best suit the instrument to which you're pasting.

- If you capture an Idea for multiple instruments, you can't paste that Idea onto a score that has fewer staves (for example, string quartet to piano).

Transposing Ideas By default, Sibelius will transpose the Ideas by both key (to match the key of the piece) and octave (to match the range of the instrument) when you paste. However, you have control over this by choosing Sibelius > Preference > Ideas.

CD: In Example 11.7, paste a few Ideas into the provided score as instructed.

Sharing Ideas

You can share your Ideas with colleagues and students. If you want to export your Ideas, you'll need to switch over to the Detailed view and start selecting the Ideas you'd like to export. To select the Ideas, you'll need to use one of the following selection methods:

- If your Ideas are all in a row together, you can Shift-click to select all of your Ideas. Click the first Idea in the list, and then Shift-click the last Idea, and Sibelius will select all the Ideas in the middle.

- If your Ideas are not in a continuous list, you can use the Ctrl or Command key while you click to select individual Ideas, one at a time.

Regardless of how you select your Ideas, you can now export them. In the Detailed view, you'll find two buttons that were not present in the Compact view—the Import Ideas and Export Ideas buttons (see Figure 11.10).

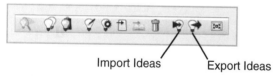

Import Ideas   Export Ideas

Figure 11.10 Import Ideas and Export Ideas buttons.

Naturally, you'll click Export Ideas. You'll be asked to name your Idea and pick a suitable save location in the Export Ideas dialog box, as shown in Figure 11.11.

Now you can take the file (which will end with the extension .ideas) and email it to anyone who wants it.

To import an Idea, click on the Import Ideas button. You will be asked to find an .ideas file on your disk to import. When you've done that, you'll be greeted with the Set Idea Destination dialog box shown in Figure 11.12.

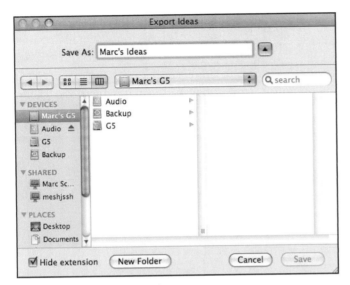

Figure 11.11   Save your Ideas.

Figure 11.12   Importing Ideas.

Sibelius simply wants to know whether you want these Ideas to be available to all scores (Add to Library) or to just the score in which you're working in (Add to Score).

Sharing a Single File

When you share a file that contains Ideas, you can control how the file transmits to other people. If you choose File > Score Info, there is a preference that pertains to Ideas. Figure 11.13 shows the Score Info window.

Within this window, you can set the Show Ideas from This Score Only check box. This is very useful if you're distributing a song as a composition assignment or as template for students to compose. You prepare the file, add the appropriate Ideas, then go to File > Score Info, and select

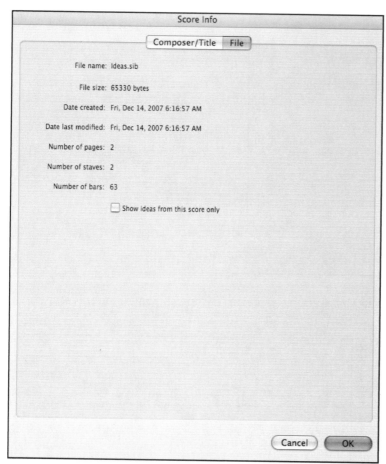

Figure 11.13   The Score Info window.

the Show Ideas from This Score Only option. Your students or colleagues will only see the Ideas that you choose.

Please note that if your Ideas are loaded into the main library and not the Score library, you won't see anything when you choose Show Ideas from This Score Only. You will have to manually transfer the Ideas to the Score library. Or, if you use this feature often, go to the Preferences > Ideas and choose the option for all Ideas to go to the Score library by default.

Ideas Preferences

To round up our look at Ideas, you'll want to see the available preferences you can set within Sibelius's Preferences. These are accessed (as always) through the File menu in Windows or the Sibelius menu on a Mac. The Ideas page in the Preferences dialog box is shown in Figure 11.14.

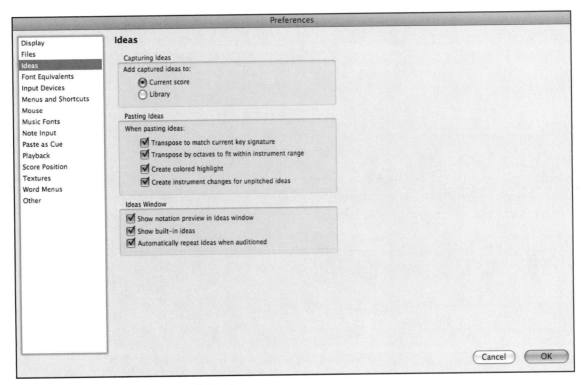

Figure 11.14   Ideas Preferences dialog box.

Because this window is also pretty straightforward and there are many other things I want to show you in Sibelius, we'll call it a day for Ideas. I've referenced many things about Ideas, such as their tendency to transpose by key and octave when you paste, as well as the default destination for captured Ideas; all of these can be changed through the Ideas page of the Preferences dialog box.

Highlights If you select the Create Colored Highlight option in the Ideas page of the Preferences dialog box, make sure you have View > Highlights turned on as well; otherwise, you won't see them!

12 Playback and Virtual Instruments

1. You need to install Sibelius Sounds Essentials separately from Sibelius (it's not included in the default installation) if you want to hear the better playback sounds in Sibelius.

2. Make sure that you've updated to Sibelius 5.2 or later by going to Help > Check for Updates. Sibelius 5.2 introduces a number of really nice additions that make playback easier, such as automatically letting you know whether you need more instances of KONTAKT PLAYER 2 to handle all of the sounds required by your score.

3. Playback doesn't have to be complicated: Just use Essentials, let Sibelius make all the decisions for you, and press Play.

4. You can load VST or AU virtual instruments and effects in Sibelius for playback, but don't expect them to work without telling Sibelius where the sounds are loaded (either by using a sound set file or by telling Sibelius about each sound individually in a manual sound set).

5. In addition to virtual instruments, you can load audio effects into Sibelius, such as reverb and equalization, for a high degree of control over your sounds.

6. Sibelius is *not* a sequencer. If you're used to other sequencers and how they interact with virtual instrument plug-ins, you will find Sibelius very different.

7. You will have to get used to some audio-related terms to fully understand the Mixer and virtual instruments in Sibelius 5.

8. There's no great reason to expose the KONTAKT PLAYER 2 plug-in interface. Sibelius takes care of configuring that automatically for you. In fact, you may end up tying yourself in knots if you spend too much time tweaking parameters in the KONTAKT PLAYER 2 window, so try not to go there.

9. Do not save your Playback Configuration when using Sibelius Sounds Essentials if your score has already played back. Once the sounds are loaded into KONTAKT PLAYER 2, Sibelius cannot automatically unload them, and they will load up every single time you switch to that configuration, which is annoying! If you need to save a new Playback Configuration, do it when no samples have loaded —for example, just after you start Sibelius and before you open a score.

10. The Playback Dictionary defines what Sibelius does when technique text and other symbols are placed into the score.

11. If you're using words from the Playback Dictionary in your score and they don't have an effect on playback, make sure you're using the correct kind of text styles (technique text for playing techniques, tempo text for tempo changes, and so on).

12. No matter how densely packed your score is with instruments and regardless of whether the computer can play them back in real time, Sibelius will always export to audio cleanly. (It just might take a bit of extra time.)

13. If your score has too many instruments, it might stutter on playback. Go to Play > Playback Devices, then click Audio Engine Options and increase the buffer size to a higher value—this usually stops it.

The Three Levels of Playback

For this chapter, which is probably the most in-depth chapter in the book, I've decided to break up playback in Sibelius into three levels. The levels are as follows:

- **Level one.** You want to play your scores using the built-in sounds. You'll use the Mixer to adjust sounds, but you likely won't add additional plug-ins or other elements to Sibelius. You're largely going to let Sibelius do the work for you.

- **Level two.** In addition to basic playback, you'll use some additional libraries and plug-ins to make your sounds more realistic. You'll make use of the Mixer, including changing sounds from the Mixer. You'll make use of Preferred Sounds to manage which device plays back which sound, and you'll start making better use of the Playback Dictionary.

- **Level three.** You'll be using the playback system to its fullest in Sibelius. You'll want to use plug-ins of all types (audio and virtual), explore and add to the Playback Dictionary, check out manual sound sets and Preferred Sounds, and you'll even look into adding MIDI messages to your score.

Even if you're an advanced MIDI expert, you'll probably still want to read this entire chapter to ensure that you fully understand how playback works in Sibelius.

Level One

As a level-one user, you'll want to start by installing Sibelius Sounds Essentials, which is the sample library supplied with Sibelius 5; learning about which elements contribute to good playback performance on your computer; learning to adjust sounds and balance in the Mixer; learning about which elements will play back in your score; and adjusting the Performance settings so that Sibelius plays back as realistically as possible. You may or may not have much experience with audio (either in a studio or on a computer), and you may or may not have used a sequencing program in the past. In short, you want things to work without a lot of fuss!

Sibelius Sounds Essentials

Sibelius Sounds Essentials is a set of sounds that ships for free with Sibelius 5. To install this set, follow the instructions in your Sibelius 5 handbook or in the "Upgrading to Sibelius" booklet that you received with your copy of Sibelius. The samples in Essentials are large, and it might take quite a while to install them, so be patient! When they are installed, you need to launch Sibelius and navigate to Play > Playback Devices, as shown in Figure 12.1.

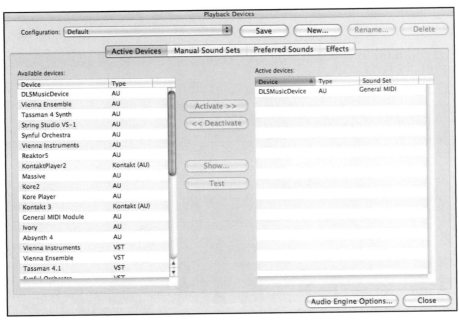

Figure 12.1 Playback Devices.

This window is pretty important, and we'll come back to it often. For now, focus your attention on the Configuration drop-down menu, as shown in Figure 12.2.

Sibelius stores Playback Configurations, which we'll learn about later in this chapter. For now, simply select Sibelius Essentials (32 Sounds). This will activate the proper plug-ins needed for

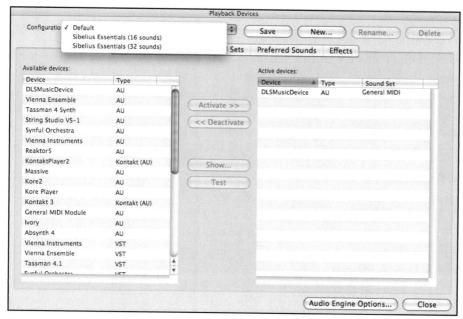

Figure 12.2 Configurations.

Sibelius to utilize the new Sibelius Sounds Essentials. When you're finished there, click Close, which will close the Playback Devices window.

Simple Playback

The transport control (called the *Playback window*) is the best way to control playback in Sibelius. The transport (shown in Figure 12.3) should look familiar to anyone who has used a VCR/DVD/DVR player.

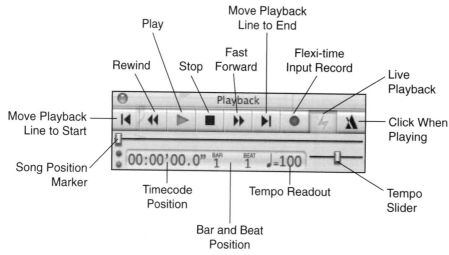

Figure 12.3 Transport.

To start playback of your score, simply press the Rewind to Start button (the one second farthest to the left) and then press Play (or press the spacebar). Sibelius will load up the required sounds into KONTAKT PLAYER 2 (the plug-in that hosts the sounds for Sibelius Sounds Essentials), and in a jiffy, you'll hear your score. You can click the Stop button to stop playback or simply press the spacebar again. (The spacebar toggles playback on and off.) You'll notice that a playback line (in light green) will step in sync with your score, showing you where you are.

If you'd like to play back from a specific part in the score, highlight a single note in the score and press the P key, which will start playback from that note. You can stop playback by pressing the spacebar.

Playback Selections Be careful of selections when you are playing back scores. If you select a whole measure or a group of measures, Sibelius will only play back the staves you've selected. It's okay to select a single note, but anything larger will act as a solo for that instrument.

Once you've started to play back, you will want to know how to best manage your computer's resources, because getting the best performance out of your computer is very important!

Tempo While you can adjust the tempo of your score from the tempo slider in the Playback window, it's probably best to create metronome markings in your score by choosing Create > Text > Metronome Mark. Sibelius will play them back for you.

Playback Performance

A number of factors will influence how well your computer can play back your scores using Sibelius Sounds Essentials. The first thing you need to get right is the basic minimum requirements for using Essentials in the first place. The following list will help you:

- Requirements for Windows: Pentium or Athlon 1.4 GHz (or faster), 1 GB RAM, 3.5 GB available hard disk space, ASIO-compatible soundcard

- Requirements for Mac: G4 1.4 GHz or Intel Core Duo 1.66 GHz (or faster), 1 GB RAM, 3.5 GB available hard disk space

Those aren't the minimum specs; they are just Sibelius's posted recommendations, and if you exceed them, you'll clearly have an easier time. You just have to sit back in amazement sometimes at what your computer can do—it's playing back a full orchestra's worth of sound, all by thinking, so you'll want to give it as much power as possible. In computer terms, power equates to CPU speed and the amount of RAM you have installed. Now, as your scores play back, you have a very delicate balance to maintain. The balance is between *latency* and *buffer size*. Let's get into more detail.

Latency and Buffer

This next part has some highly technical roots, but you do not have to get mired down in it at all. I'm going to explain what latency and buffer size are so you know, and then I'll give you a much simpler way to deal with them.

Latency is the amount of lag from the time you ask Sibelius to play back a sound until it actually processes it. (We dealt with latency a bit when talking about playing in real time with Flexi-time.) In a digital system, there is always some degree of latency. Latency is directly controlled by something called the *buffer size*. A buffer controls how much data is sent in each burst to the computer. When the bursts are small, it takes less time to get there. When you play back a score, if the buffer is set too small and your computer is trying to play back a ton of instruments, you're going to hear choppy audio—it simply won't sound good. You can easily configure Sibelius to let you play into Flexi-time with minimal latency and still have enough juice for playback. This is done by setting the buffer size. If you go to Play > Playback Devices and click Audio Engine Options (as shown in Figure 12.4), you'll see a control for the buffer size.

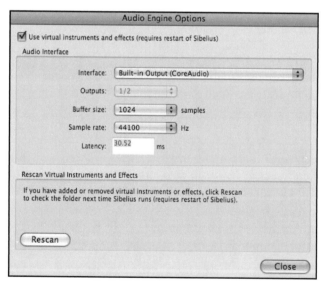

Figure 12.4 Audio Engine Options.

All you have to do is change the number of samples in the Buffer Size field. Try 512 as a good middle-of-the-road setting. If your computer isn't happy, you can always raise the buffer size by visiting the same window. The readout of latency is automatically computed for you, and there's no reason to worry about it.

Clean Exports No matter what you do or how slow your computer is, you'll be able to have a clean, glitch-free audio file exported from Sibelius 5 because Sibelius takes as much time as it needs to ensure a perfect mixdown. If you're on a slow computer, expect that it will take longer to export than the total duration of your score. However, if your computer is fast enough, it will often take less time to export than it takes to play from beginning to end.

Using Built-In Sounds (My Computer Isn't Fast Enough)

Sadly, not everyone has a fast enough computer for Sibelius Sounds Essentials, and if your primary goal is to write music, and if playback is secondary, you might want to use the built-in synthesizer in your computer for playback. The upside to this is that the built-in synthesizer is very light on your CPU, and you'll be able to run it without issue on an older computer. The downside is that it's just not going to sound anywhere near as good as Sibelius Sounds Essentials or another playback device. In any case, Mac and Windows have their own built-in synthesizers, and I'll show you how to make a Playback Configuration that uses them.

Using DLS on a Mac

To use the built-in synth on a Mac, which plays through Apple's own QuickTime synth, you'll have to do a quick visit to the Play > Playback Devices menu. We previously looked at the Playback Devices window to instantiate Sibelius Sounds Essentials through the Configurations drop-down box. Figure 12.5 shows the Playback Devices window. The default configuration on

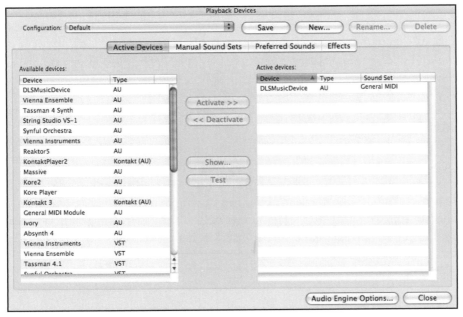

Figure 12.5 Playback Configuration > DLS.

a Mac comes preconfigured by Sibelius to include the DLS built-in synth. All you have to do is select this Playback Configuration, and you'll be using the efficient DLS synth for playback.

Multiple DLSMusicDevices If you're playing back a big score, you might have to add more than one DLSMusicDevice to your score to cover all the sounds needed. You can load as many DLSs as you feel like without compromising your CPU, so you might want to make a large configuration and keep it saved with four DLSs to handle large playback on a slower computer.

Use Sounds on Startup If you navigate to Sibelius > Preferences > Playback, select When Starting Sibelius, Load This Playback Configuration, and choose Default from the drop-down box, you'll automatically load the DLS synth when you boot up. Alternatively, you can load any configuration upon startup by choosing a different configuration.

Simply close the window and play back with your built-in soundcard. If at any time you move that score to a stronger computer with Sibelius Sounds Essentials, revisit that window and change the configuration to one of the Sibelius Sounds Essentials configurations (either 16 or 32 sounds).

Using Microsoft GS Wavetable Synth

To use the built-in synth on Windows, just choose the default configuration, which includes the Microsoft GS Wavetable Synth, which is the built-in synthesizer for Windows.

High Latency Just as a word of warning, if you're using the MS Wavetable as your play-back device, you will notice very large latency when you play into Sibelius using Flexi-time. You'll want to switch to Sibelius Sounds Essentials during note entry.

What Will Sibelius Play Back?

What sorts of things will play back in your score? Besides the obvious elements like notes, here is a list of important elements in your score that will play back when they're correctly placed in your score. Also, make sure they're in the right text family—if you're effecting just one instrument (such as a playing technique like pizzicato or other instrument performance markings), make sure to use the appropriate staff text style. Conversely, if you're making tempo-based changes (which would affect all staves), make sure to use a system text style.

- Notes (all types)
- Clefs, time and key signatures
- The correct instrument sound for the staff you're writing on

- Instrument performance indications, such as pizz. and mute

- Text-based dynamic markings (f, p, and so on)

- Articulations from the keypad

- Special stems (tremolos and rolls)

- Tempo text, metric modulations

- Repeat endings from Create > Line

- Special lines from Create > Line (slurs, trills, octave markings, and piano pedaling)

- Guitar tablature

- MIDI messages written in text

- Sibelius will continue to play back objects that are hidden using Edit > Hide or Show

Sibelius is set up to play back almost anything that you place in your score, but you might run into a few notable exceptions. The biggest is that symbols from Create > Symbol do not play back, with the notable exception of scoops and falls, which do have a playback effect, but by and large, symbols do not play back. The Playback Dictionary contains entries for all of the symbols, but they are not defined to do anything. The truly adventurous can define those elements in the Playback Dictionary, which is covered in the "Level Three" section later in this chapter. Other score elements, such as harmonics, have plug-ins in the Plug-Ins > Playback menu to have Sibelius play back elements such as harmonics, ornaments, and even quarter-tone playback!

Playback Dictionary For a complete listing of the words that Sibelius will read and that will affect playback, take a look at Play > Playback Dictionary.

Repeats Sibelius will play back all written repeats by default in your score. If you don't want repeats when you play back your score, go to Play > Performance and uncheck Play Repeats.

Play on Pass If you have a score element, which could be a note, or text that you only want to play back on a certain pass on repeating playback (or for that matter, that you don't want to play back ever), show the Properties window, open the Playback panel, and uncheck the relevant Play on Pass check boxes. For example, to have something play back the first time only, uncheck all the boxes but 1. To have it silent at all times, uncheck all the boxes.

The Mixer

If you'd like to control the balance of your instruments when played back, you'll want to check out the Mixer, which you can access by pressing M or by going to Window > Mixer. Figure 12.6 shows the Mixer.

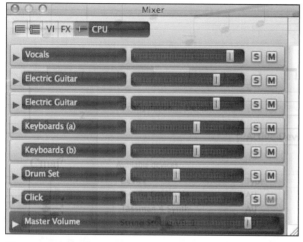

Figure 12.6   The Mixer.

If you've ever used a mixing board or another audio workstation program such as Pro Tools, you'll notice the Sibelius Mixer is sideways! Each instrument is listed on the left side of the Mixer, and each instrument has the following controls (going from left to right):

- **Volume slider and meter.** The volume slider adjusts the loudness of the selected stave. Pull to the right for louder sounds and to the left for lower sounds. The slider is sitting on a meter, which shows the strength of the track while playing back.

- **Solo.** When engaged (and glowing green), this button will mute all other tracks, effectively soloing the selected track.

- **Mute.** This button silences the selected track. The Mute button does not work like a traditional Mute button. The first time you click Mute, it will reduce that track's volume by half (called a *half mute*). The icon will glow half red as a result. To fully mute and silence a track, make sure to click Mute twice.

The last element of the Mixer is the master volume, which is the black slider on the bottom of the Mixer. This controls all of the sound coming out of Sibelius.

When you adjust any of the controls on the Mixer, those changes will be saved in your score. In terms of making basic changes to the Mixer, that's it! However, there are a few other things that you might find useful when using the Mixer.

Mixer Groups

Along the top of the Mixer, you might have noticed a row of small buttons. These buttons are detailed in Figure 12.7.

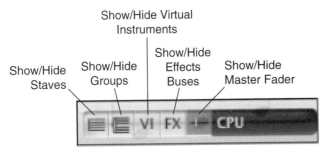

Figure 12.7   Mixer controls.

The button you'll want to expose is labeled Show/Hide Groups, and it changes your Mixer to look like Figure 12.8.

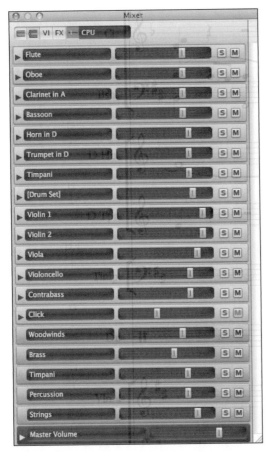

Figure 12.8   Exposed Mixer groups.

Mixer groups allow you to adjust groups of staves at once, and they are divided into families. When you expose the groups, you'll be able to solo, mute, and adjust the balance of the strings, brass, or percussion with a single Mixer element. This functionality is standard in audio editing programs and is a lovely addition to Sibelius. When you move the single group fader, all of the associated strips move together.

Live Playback

The last element of "level one" playback understanding in Sibelius is the idea of Live Playback. When you play into Sibelius using Flexi-time, Sibelius records your exact timings and MIDI veloc-ities and stores them. To make the score look more presentable, Sibelius performs input quantizing, moving your notes to a grid to make them print out a bit cleaner. When Sibelius plays your score back, although it may look quantized, it is playing back with the Live Velocities that you played in with. Live Velocity is a feature that is on by default; you can turn it off by choosing Play > Live Playback or by clicking the icon in the Playback window (the Live Playback icon is a small thunderbolt). You can even edit the velocity if you've played some of the velocities unevenly.

No Velocity? You'll only see Live Playback velocities when you've entered music from a MIDI file or when you've used Flexi-time. Step entry, mouse, and alphabetic entry will not have any associated playback velocities.

Live Playback Velocity

If you want you view and edit the velocities of your notes when using Live Playback, go to View > Live Playback Velocities, which will show velocity as a small vertical fader in blue, as shown in Figure 12.9.

Figure 12.9   Live Playback.

If you simply click on any of the vertical velocities, you can drag the slider up and down to change/edit the velocity of any of the notes. You wouldn't want to edit every single note, but it's great for fixing a thump here and there. You can click and drag across a bunch of these Live

Playback velocity bars to "draw" a change of velocities across a whole run of notes. Remember that you can always turn off Live Velocity at any time.

Just a Note of Caution When Live Playback is engaged, certain score elements do not play back. Since Live Playback takes care of dynamics and note timings, typical expressions, such as piano and forte, crescendos and diminuendos, and other tempo-based markings, do not play back. To have them play back, turn off Live Playback.

Play Performance

One of the last elements you want to look at is the Play > Performance window, as shown in Figure 12.10.

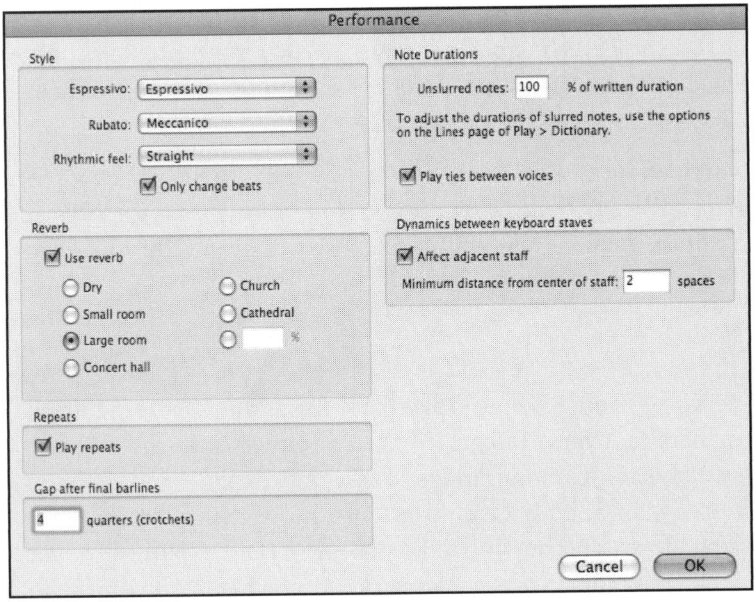

Figure 12.10 Play > Performance window.

There are a bunch of neat things to look at in the Play > Performance window. Let's start with the Style section. When Sibelius plays back your score, it adds a human element to break up the mechanical nature of how scores play back. The way in which it does this is handled in the Style section of Play > Performance, which I'll detail here.

■ **Espressivo.** Espressivo is Sibelius's way of changing the subtle dynamics to simulate a live performance. By default, your score will be set to Espressivo, but you can toggle the drop-down menu to defeat this entirely by choosing Meccanico, which will play the score back to the utmost mathematical degree. You'll also see settings for varying degrees of expressiveness, which will alter the dynamic content on playback to varying degrees.

- **Rubato.** Rubato is Sibelius's way of altering the timing between notes to stop the computer from sounding quite so mechanical. The default is Meccanico, which plays back rhythms exactly as they are written, which is the normal way of playing back. If you want to add some more human-like rubato to the performance, the drop-down box will provide you with other choices that affect the rhythmic playback in Sibelius. Beware that setting rubato to a high setting in a score with many instruments can produce rather peculiar results.

- **Rhythmic Feel.** This tells Sibelius whether to play with straight eighths or from a variety of other eighth-note styles, ranging from swing to funk.

The last section you'll want to know about here is Reverb. Reverb is short for *reverberation*, which simulates space, as in rooms and halls. All rooms have their own sound based on the size of the room and the materials used—great concert halls are often modeled for their acoustical properties with regard to natural reverb. Reverb is an essential part of a performance, and by default Sibelius has reverb turned on. There are some different selections that will influence whether it sounds like you're in a small room or the largest of stone churches.

That's about all you'll want to worry about at this level. You're now able to play back a score with both Sibelius Sounds Essentials and your built-in synth, you understand what symbols and elements play back, and you can adjust them. When you're ready to get deeper into playback, read on.

Level Two

As a level-two user, you're going to expand Sibelius's playback by adding some additional sounds from Sibelius or other partners that have integrated their products into the Sibelius 5 playback system, understand how Playback Configurations work, and explore and add some new words to the Playback Dictionary. In addition, you'll go into more detail on the Mixer, including changing sounds and using effects and bussing in the Mixer. You'll explore Live Playback a bit and even use some of the plug-ins to affect playback in Sibelius. You've probably dabbled a bit in audio and sequencing on other programs, and you have a decent understanding of MIDI. The first thing you need to do is gain a more thorough understanding of what virtual instruments are.

Understanding Virtual Instruments

What is a virtual instrument? Let's just go back in time a bit. When MIDI was first gaining ground, keyboards ruled the roost; if you had a sound-generating device, chances are it was some sort of keyboard. Since these keyboards, and by extension samplers and sound modules, were real (in other words, you could pick them up and feel them), we still refer to those devices as *hardware* or *real instruments*—even though the sound they made was typically computer-generated. Fast-forward to the present day, and instead of keyboards and other physical devices, we now have sound-generating devices that live completely inside your computer. Because you can't touch these devices (called *plug-ins*), we refer to them as *virtual instruments*. To put it simply, a virtual instrument is a piece of software. In this case, it's a piece of software that makes sound, and it does so by responding to MIDI input. Sibelius is able to host these virtual instruments and play back with them.

Plug-In Formats

Plug-ins come in a few varieties, called *plug-in formats*. Simply put, virtual instruments were born into DAW (*Digital Audio Workstation*) programs such as Pro Tools and Cubase well before they ever came into Sibelius. Each DAW manufacturer has its own plug-in format that software developers must code in. Because of this, we find ourselves with a bunch of different file types to support the common programs. Pro Tools uses a format called RTAS, while Cubase uses VST, and Logic uses Audio Units, or AU. Should you care? Yes! Most plug-ins these days support the majority of plug-in types anyway, but not all of them. You'll want to know what Sibelius can work with before you add any third-party optional plug-ins into your system.

- On Windows, Sibelius uses the VST plug-in format for all of its virtual instruments.

- On Mac, Sibelius uses the VST and Audio Unit (AU) plug-in formats.

In any case, when you shop for plug-ins, you'll need to look at the supported plug-in formats and make sure they will work with Sibelius. Thankfully, most plug-ins ship supporting multiple plug-in types, so you'll likely be fine. The first virtual instrument that you'll encounter in Sibelius is KONTAKT PLAYER 2, a virtual instrument plug-in that is the cornerstone of Sibelius Sounds Essentials.

KONTAKT PLAYER 2

When you load Sibelius Sounds Essentials, Sibelius loads all of the sounds into a plug-in virtual instrument called KONTAKT PLAYER 2, which is a simpler version of Native Instruments' KONTAKT sampler. All of the sounds you hear in Sibelius Sounds Essentials are actually samples—audio recordings of the instruments note by note to re-create as faithfully as possible the true sounds of the instruments. Since you're a level-two user, let's take a look at the interface of KONTAKT PLAYER 2. To do so, make sure you're using a Playback Configuration that makes use of Sibelius Sounds Essentials and open the Mixer. Once the Mixer is open, expand any of the instrument strips by clicking on the small triangle on the right side of the Mixer; this will expand the instrument's strip to show more detail. What you'll see is a listing of which virtual instrument is playing back the sound (in this case, KONTAKT PLAYER 2), which MIDI channel it's playing back on, its pan from right to left, and finally, the name of the sample being used (see Figure 12.11).

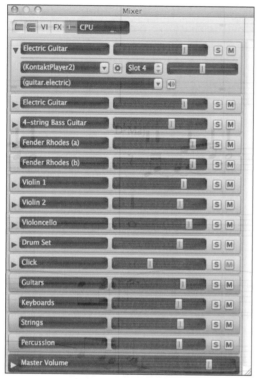

Figure 12.11 Expanded virtual instrument strip.

As we get deeper into the Mixer, we'll look at some cool things we can do, but for now there is a small gear that shows the plug-in interface. Click it to show the KONTAKT PLAYER 2 interface, as shown in Figure 12.12.

This is a great example of a piece of software that responds to MIDI input and produces sound. We'll get into virtual instruments much more as this chapter goes along, but for right now, you can close the KONTAKT PLAYER 2 window.

Kontakt Player Is Automatic Sibelius takes care of controlling the KONTAKT PLAYER 2 window for you. It loads all the sounds automatically and takes care of the details. While you can show the window and make changes, in the case of KONTAKT PLAYER 2, there's no reason to do anything, and in many cases you may muck things up, so just leave it be. If you use optional third-party plug-ins with Sibelius, you'll have plenty of chances to play with plug-in interfaces.

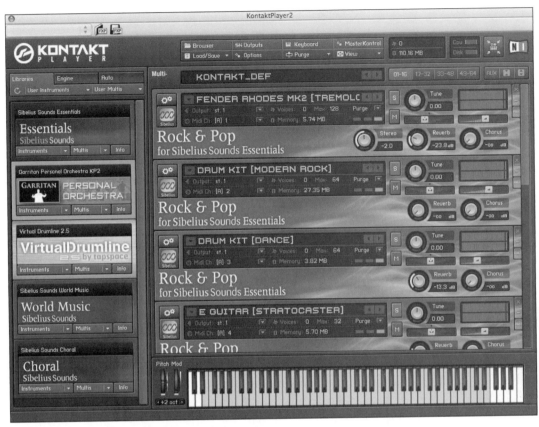

Figure 12.12 The KONTAKT PLAYER 2 interface.

Now that you've gotten a crash course on virtual instruments, you'll want to know as much as you can about Playback Configurations, because this is where you add virtual instruments and control how they work in Sibelius.

Playback Configurations

What is a Playback Configuration? In Sibelius, you can think of a Playback Configuration as your ensemble—on a computer, that ensemble is populated by either plug-ins/virtual instruments or assignments to external MIDI-capable synthesizers and sound modules. Playback Configurations contain the information that Sibelius will use to play back the sounds in your score. To access Playback Configurations, go to the Play > Playback Devices window, as shown in Figure 12.13.

On the left side of the screen you'll see the available sound-generating devices attached to or installed on your computer. This list can contain virtual instrument plug-ins and MIDI devices. Think of these as musicians that you can hire for your gig. On the right side, you'll see the active devices, which are the musicians that you've actually hired! The devices will only be able to play back in your score if they are added to the Active Devices list. You do this by highlighting a

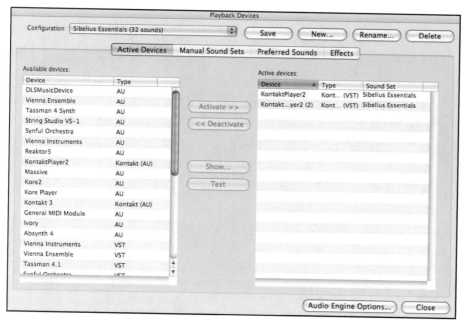

Figure 12.13 Playback Devices window.

device on the Available Devices list and clicking the Activate button. Once you have a device activated, it is available for use in your score. Once it's been added, you can either show the interface of the plug-in or test it to make sure your device is playing back properly.

Now, think of the listing you just made as an ensemble—you'll want to be able to recall this ensemble again. You can save a configuration at any point in Sibelius by clicking the Save button at the top of the Playback Devices window. You'll be prompted to give the configuration a title (as shown in Figure 12.14), and you'll be able to recall this configuration at any time, from any score.

Figure 12.14 Save and name your Playback Configuration.

Playback Configurations are saved within your score, so once you switch them on, they stay active each and every time you work on that score, unless you decide to make a change.

The Sound Set Column

Within the Playback Devices window, you'll see three columns in the Active Devices list (as shown in Figure 12.15).

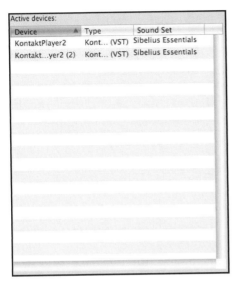

Figure 12.15 Active Devices.

The first two columns are fairly straightforward. The left column simply prints the name of the MIDI interface or plug-in. The type denotes whether it's an AU or VST plug-in, a MIDI interface, or a KONTAKT type (the plug-in used to host Sibelius Sounds Essentials and others). The last column is for a sound set, which is the pivotal concept here.

A sound set tells Sibelius where all the sounds are in a particular device (either a plug-in or a hardware-based instrument) so Sibelius can play back your score with the appropriate sounds. When you look at a configuration for Sibelius Sounds Essentials, you will see that the Sound Set column has automatically chosen Sibelius Essentials as its sound set. Sibelius does not have a sound set for every plug-in made; it only ships with a selection of very popular plug-ins to which it can speak directly. If you add a plug-in into your configuration that does not have a sound set, you'll want to skip to the "Manual Sound Sets" section, found later in this chapter. In the case of MIDI devices, you can use General MIDI or General MIDI 2 if your device adheres to the General MIDI standard.

Think of a sound set as a detailed set of operating instructions for Sibelius. If Sibelius has a sound set for the device or plug-in that you are currently using, you'll have to do nothing more than press Play to hear your scores in full glory. Without a sound set, you'll need to do some work to teach Sibelius about the particular details of your playback device and how to best use it. A sound set equals automatic playback.

Sound Set List You'll see a different listing of available sound sets based on the type of active device you have. If you insert a KONTAKT-type plug-in, such as KONTAKT PLAYER 2, you'll see a very different list of sound sets than if you add a AU or VST plug-in—Sibelius knows the difference between the plug-ins and acts appropriately.

Not every plug-in currently has a sound set, but that does not mean you can't use them. To find out all about using any plug-in with Sibelius, check out the "Manual Sound Sets" section later in this chapter. The next way to extend Sibelius is to use one of the optional sound libraries that *does* have a sound set, either from Sibelius itself or from one of its close partners, such as Garritan or Tapspace.

Adding Optional Plug-Ins

There is a collection of plug-ins that you can purchase for Sibelius that work perfectly out of the box. This means that the plug-ins have a full sound set, and to utilize them, all you have to do is make a Playback Configuration and press Play. This is the reason why sound sets are so very important. A proper sound set is truly transparent and requires no effort to make Sibelius's playback even better than it is currently. Here is a listing of some libraries that work seamlessly with Sibelius 5.

- Sibelius Sounds Rock and Pop

- Sibelius Sounds Choral

- Sibelius Sounds World Music

- Garritan Personal Orchestra

- Garritan Concert and Marching Band

- Garritan Jazz and Big Band

- Tapspace Virtual Drumline 2.5

This particular listing of instruments is grouped together because they all use the same KONTAKT PLAYER 2 plug-in that Sibelius Sounds Essentials uses. These instruments can be controlled by Sibelius, including automatic sound loading. Let's use Virtual Drumline 2.5 as an example.

Because all of the instruments listed use the KONTAKT PLAYER 2, we need to learn how to switch sound sets. Let's start by making a new Playback Configuration in Play > Playback Devices and adding a single KONTAKT PLAYER 2. To make this into VDL, simply change the sound set from Sibelius Essentials to VDL 2.5. If you're using one of the other sound libraries listed, simply change to the proper sound set, and Sibelius will take care of the rest.

Preferred Devices

What is a preferred device? If you head back to Play > Playback Devices, you'll see that there are four tabs across the top of the window: Active Devices, Manual Sound Sets, Preferred Sounds, and Effects. We will cover all of the sections in this chapter, but let's switch over to the Preferred Sounds tab, as shown in Figure 12.16.

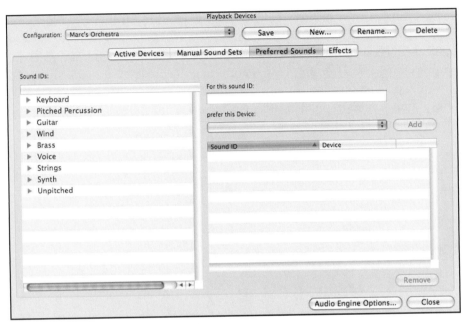

Figure 12.16   Preferred Sounds tab.

Now, the sound set rules all. In Sibelius, that tells the playback engine which sounds to load and why. When you combine several sound libraries together, you'll want some control over which sounds get played back from which library. For example, you have both Sibelius Sounds Essentials and VDL loaded into your configuration, and you'd like to use the percussion from VDL and everything else from Sibelius Sounds Essentials. How do you make Sibelius use one or the other? By default, Sibelius will choose what it wants to play back with, and this depends on a variety of factors, including the order in which you added the plug-ins to your Playback Configurations. If you want to have control over playback, this is where a Preferred Sound comes into play.

Optional Preferred Sounds are optional. You never have to deal with them if you just want to allow Sibelius to deal with playback. The minute you want Sibelius to use one sound over another, you have to use Preferred Sounds. Also, if you're using multiple playback devices together, you'll probably want to use them as well.

I'm going to absolutely glaze over the topic of soundIDs in Sibelius. Sibelius has a rather new system of identifying sounds, called soundIDs, which you can read about in the Sibelius reference for all the details.

In each family of soundIDs, there are huge trees of data, huge lists of possible percussion instruments. There is no reason why you need to deal with the intricacies of this. To make all of the percussion play back with VDL, from the Preferred Sounds window, simply select Pitched Percussion in the left-hand listing of instrument families. Don't expand the listing by hitting the arrow. As long as you select Pitched Percussion, it will create the following text in the For This SoundID field: Pitched Percussion.*. The "pitched.percussion.*" is a computing term, where * means "and everything else after it." This is convenient because you're not interested in the hundreds of possible percussion sounds; you want all of them. So what you're saying is this: Anything and everything related to pitched percussion sounds in Sibelius should play back with a certain device (see Figure 12.17).

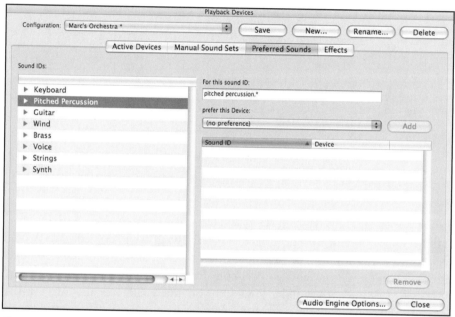

Figure 12.17 Preferred Sounds: Percussion.

In the same window, there is a Prefer This Device drop-down menu with a listing of all the available devices. One of them says VDL because I renamed that instance of KONTAKT PLAYER 2 to VDL so it would be easier to find. Once I select VDL and click the Add button, Sibelius will route all percussion playback to the VDL KONTAKT PLAYER and everything else to Sibelius Sounds Essentials. When it's all set up properly, it will look like Figure 12.18.

Here is one more example to get your head around. I recently got the Synful Orchestra plug-in from www.synful.com. It's an outstanding orchestral plug-in using a combination of synthesis and samples to provide realistic playback. It has no percussion, synth, brass, or guitar, so I'll need to use it in conjunction with Sibelius Sounds Essentials or another library for my playback. Look at Figure 12.19 to see how I set it up.

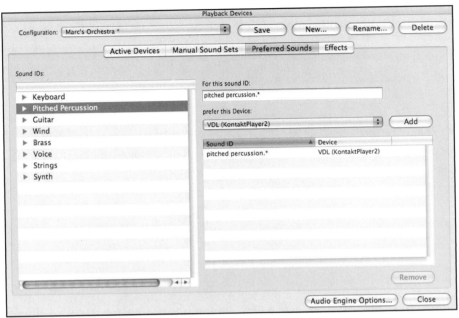

Figure 12.18   VDL and Sibelius Sounds Essentials. For most users, Preferred Sounds works well when you tell Sibelius to choose by family of instrument.

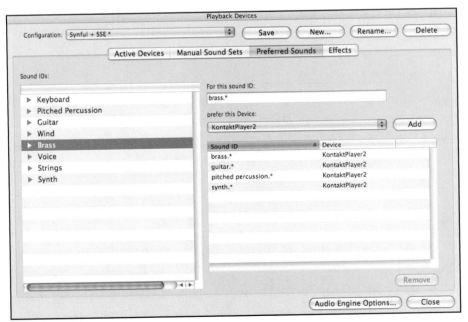

Figure 12.19   Sibelius Sounds Essentials and Synful.

As you get deeper into the soundIDs, you can assign a Preferred Sound for a specific soundID if you want to closely control how Sibelius makes the choices it does. At this point, you probably know quite enough about Preferred Sounds to utilize other plug-ins in your Playback Configurations and choose which sounds go to which plug-ins.

SoundID Want to better understand which stave gets which soundID? Go to House Style > Edit Instruments > Edit Instrument, and you will see the soundID listed in the Playback Defaults section.

Now that we can control how Sibelius loads sounds, let's look at how the Mixer can be used to change sounds as well.

The Mixer

Using Preferred Sounds was the first instance when we could start to override Sibelius's default behavior of choosing sounds. Preferred Sounds is still best when choosing one device over another. If you want to start making changes to which instrument is played back for a particular stave, you'll want to get into the Mixer in a bit more detail, because you can change sounds there as well. Let's start with Figure 12.20, which points out all the elements of the Mixer. (It's worth saying that changes you want to make in all scores are best done in Preferred Sounds; changes you only want to make once, in one score, are best done in the Mixer.)

Expand All If you'd like to expand all the Mixer strips at once, rather than clicking their triangles one at a time, you can hold down Ctrl (PC) or Command (Mac) while you click a single Mixer strip to toggle all your strips to the expanded view. Alternatively, you can Shift-click on the Mixer strips to expand all the strips of the same type.

Changing Sounds from the Mixer

Earlier in this chapter, we looked at exposing the Mixer strips by clicking the small triangle at the left side of the Mixer to expose additional details, as shown in Figure 12.21.

When Sibelius 5 shipped, every dialog that referred to sounds showed the soundIDs. So, if you haven't updated to Sibelius 5.2 yet, you will see the readout shown in Figure 12.22 in your expanded Mixer strip.

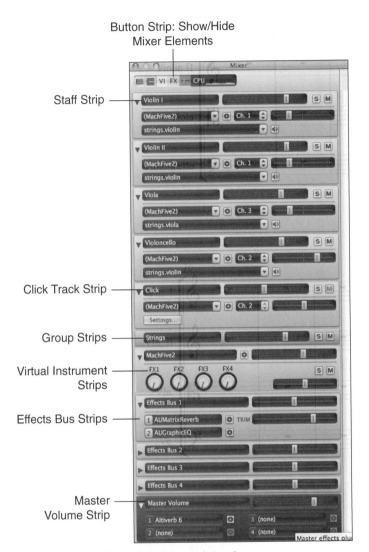

Figure 12.20   Mixer elements explained.

Figure 12.21   Expanded Mixer strip with program names.

Figure 12.22   Expanded Mixer strips with soundIDs.

This shows the initial soundID used by the staff. That's important to note because if you add a performance indication, such as pizzicato, it will change the soundID used, but the Mixer will still reflect the original as defined by House Style > Edit Instrument.

On the Playback page of the Preferences dialog, you'll find a choice to view either soundIDs or program names. As mentioned earlier, Sibelius 5.2 now shows program names by default, although you can change this.

Program Names A program name will only show up if you have a defined sound set for your playback device. Otherwise, the soundID will show anyway.

So, what can you do from these Mixer strips? To start with, you can choose a different patch for your stave. For example, if you create a score with a piano grand staff instrument and Sibelius Sounds Essentials is your playback device, it will choose Acoustic Grand Piano (Gold) as the default choice. However, this is not the only piano that ships with Sibelius Sounds Essentials. If you click on the arrow directly to the right of the patch name, you will get a listing like the one shown in Figure 12.23.

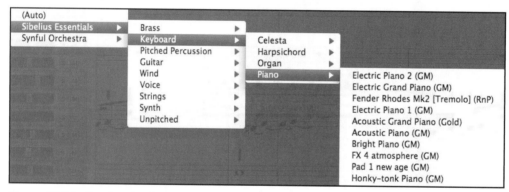

Figure 12.23 Patch selection.

Auto will always revert back to the automatic choice as prescribed by the sound set, which is good in case you change it and you want it to go back to the original sound. You can also navigate through the entire list of Sibelius Sounds Essentials patches and hone in on the choices for Keyboard > Piano, changing from the default Acoustic Grand Piano to either Honky-Tonk Piano or even Electric Piano. From this menu, you can change the playback of any stave in your score to any sound you choose.

Almost Never Change the Device You should almost never change the device from the Mixer. It's okay to pick a different sound from the Mixer, but if you want a different playback device, that's what Preferred Sounds are intended for.

Virtual Instruments

On the Mixer, there is a row of buttons that we started to detail in this chapter. One of the buttons across the top toggles the volume control for the virtual instrument, or VI for short. If you click on the VI button (as shown in Figure 12.24), you will expose a volume control for the virtual instrument with which you're playing back.

Figure 12.24   Virtual instrument strip.

For each virtual instrument you add to your Playback Configuration, you'll see a Mixer strip so you can control volume, solo, and mute for that instrument. This is handy when you're trying to balance the sounds between contrasting virtual instruments. You'll also see a small cog or gear directly to the right of the virtual instrument name. Clicking this will show or hide the interface for the virtual instrument you're working on, so you can change aspects of the plug-in directly.

You will also see a triangle at the left-hand side of the virtual instrument strip; this exposes more detail about the virtual instrument, including access to the four effects buses (or *FX buses,* as they are called in Sibelius). We'll talk about effects and routing in the section entitled "Level Three" at the end of this chapter.

Slots/MIDI Channel

When you expand a Mixer strip, you'll also notice a readout for a slot or MIDI channel (see Figure 12.25). The slot is something that Sibelius works out when using KONTAKT PLAYER 2, and it isn't something you have to worry about. If you're using a MIDI device as a part of your Playback Configuration, you'll be able to change MIDI channels directly from the Mixer by clicking on the up/down arrows next to the slot/channel number and choosing a MIDI channel.

Figure 12.25   Slot/MIDI channel.

The CPU Meter

The last important aspect of the Mixer is the CPU meter (see Figure 12.26). When playing back virtual instruments and effects, you always need to be mindful of how taxing playback can be on your computer. The CPU meter will give you a display indicating how you're doing. The readout scrolls from left to right and has vertical bars to indicate CPU load. Bars with lower height will display in green, indicating that you're doing okay. Higher vertical bars in red show that you're

Figure 12.26 Mixer CPU meter.

overloading your CPU (which you can likely hear as dropouts in the audio stream). Don't forget that you can make your CPU much happier during playback if you go to Play > Playback Devices, then click Audio Engine Options and change the buffer to a higher value if you experience dropouts.

Level Three

As a level-three user, you're prepared to get the most out of Sibelius's playback system, including adding instrument and effect plug-ins of any type, and you're prepared to use manual sound sets or actually dive into the separate Sound Set editor application to make your own. You have a vast knowledge of MIDI and effects, and you'll be tweaking lots of parameters under the hood of Sibelius to get your playback sounding exactly as you want it. You have experience with audio and sequencing programs. In short, you're a power user.

Using Any Plug-In

By now, you've heard me extol the virtues of sound sets in Sibelius; they are essential to transparent playback. However, not every MIDI device or virtual instrument has a sound set right now. Does this mean you can't use these instruments? No, but you'll have to get your hands slightly dirty to do so. Welcome to the world of manual sound sets.

The concept of a manual sound set is pretty simple: You're going to configure your own virtual instrument, setting up slots and channels as you need, and then you're going to tell Sibelius which device to play each soundID you're using in that score back with and which MIDI channel and program/bank it needs to be on. Once you teach Sibelius what to do and save your Playback Configuration, you'll be able to access your plug-ins. To make this work, you'll need a good understanding of MIDI and how your particular playback device operates. No matter how you slice it, having a true sound set is always better than having a manual sound set.

Not Automatic Remember that only KONTAKT PLAYER 2 is able to load sounds automatically through Sibelius. For all other virtual instruments, you'll have to load your own sounds in the Playback Configuration.

Manual Sound Sets

Let's look at how to set up a simple manual sound set using a third-party device. In this example, I'll be using Mach 5, which is a nice sampler plug-in from MOTU. Honestly, it doesn't matter much what the sound is, because the procedure is pretty much the same for any device when you are using a manual sound set.

I'll need to make a list of the soundIDs needed in my piece, and the best way to do that is to go to the Mixer, expand all the strips, and take a look at the soundIDs called for by this ensemble (which is a string quartet). The Mixer shows me the soundIDs shown in Figure 12.27.

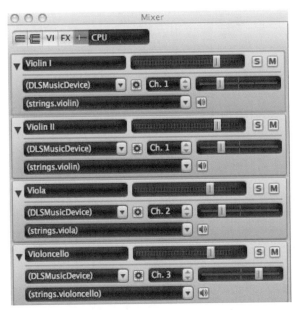

Figure 12.27   Mixer showing soundIDs.

At the very simplest terms, I'll need to add four entries to the Manual Sound Sets page, one for each of the soundIDs listed here. We'll start there and take a look at things such as soundID changes (for pizz. and other performance terms) in a few minutes. I've made a list of the soundIDs on a piece of paper, and now I'm ready to start making this configuration.

The first thing I need to do is add Mach 5 to my Playback Configuration and set its sound set to None, as there is no proper sound set for Mach 5 (see Figure 12.28).

I'm now going to set up Mach 5 to host four sampled instruments—one for each sound I want to load—each on its own MIDI channel. After I've done that, I'll save the Playback Configuration.

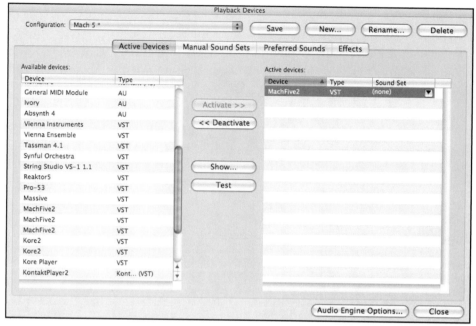

Figure 12.28 Playback Devices: Mach 5.

Now I can navigate to the Manual Sound Sets page and start building my manual sound set. For each sound in the score, I simply have to tell Sibelius which soundID should be routed to which MIDI channel on my Mach 5 plug-in. It doesn't have to be any more complicated than that. Let's look at the completed interface, and I'll explain what I did (see Figure 12.29).

To start with, I made the number of channels four because I'm addressing four sounds right now. (Even though Mach 5 can do more, I didn't want to muddy the waters for us.) Inside Mach 5, I assigned the following sounds to the Mach 5 plug-in:

- Violin assigned to MIDI Channel 1
- Violin assigned to MIDI Channel 2
- Viola assigned to MIDI Channel 3
- Cello assigned to MIDI Channel 4

I did this by loading up individual samples and programs into the interface and assigning them to listen to MIDI input on those channels.

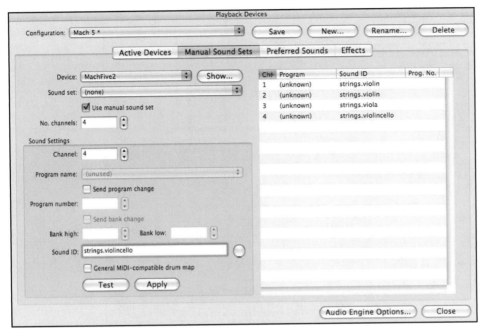

Figure 12.29 Completed Mach 5 manual sound set.

Next up, I selected each individual channel on the right side of the Manual Sound Sets page, and in the SoundID field on the left, I typed in the name I had written down. For Channel 1, I typed in strings.violin, and then clicked Apply to make the sound stick. I repeated this step for each of the four channels, using the proper soundID names the Mixer told me. In the end it looked like this:

- Channel 1 = strings.violin

- Channel 2 = strings.violin

- Channel 3 = strings.viola

- Channel 4 = strings.violincello

I saved my Playback Configuration, closed the window, and came back to my score. When I pressed Play, everything sounded good! There was one catch: There was a section of pizzicato that wasn't playing back. In the case of Mach 5, the samples I loaded up were arco sounds only, so if I wanted the pizzicato, I'd need to load up four more sounds into Mach 5—four more sounds for each of the strings pizzicato sounds. I went back to the Manual Sound Sets page and made it look like Figure 12.30.

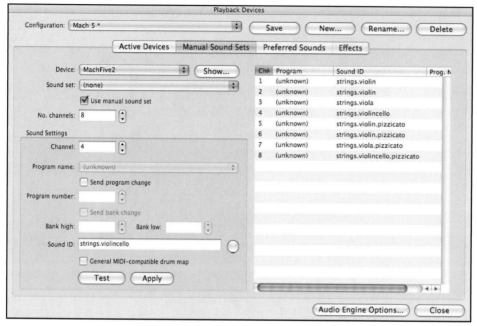

Figure 12.30 Expanded manual sounds.

I changed the number of channels to eight and assigned channels 5–8 to the following soundIDs:

- Channel 5 = strings.violin.pizzicato

- Channel 6 = strings.violin.pizzicato

- Channel 7 = strings.viola.pizzicato

- Channel 8 = strings.violincello.pizzicato

I applied the changes, saved and closed, and that was all I needed.

That's really all you have to do. Just define for Sibelius that when it sees a particular soundID, it should talk to a particular device on a certain channel. That's really it.

Now, does every device use separate MIDI channels like Mach 5 did? No, some instruments respond to bank and program changes to switch sounds, and that is also included in the Manual Sound Sets page, as shown in Figure 12.31.

If you know how your plug-in or MIDI device responds, you can program the appropriate messages in manual sound sets, and off you'll go. We'll get into this in more detail in an online addendum that will ship after the book has published. Check out Course Technology's website (www.courseptr.com/downloads) for all the details.

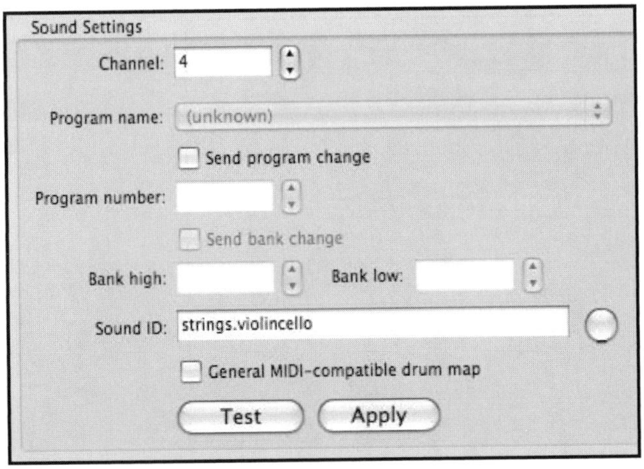

Figure 12.31   Program and bank changes.

Sound Set Editor Rather than doing all the work in the Manual Sound Sets page, you can download the separate Sound Set editor application from www.sibelius.com and make your own sets for all of your plug-ins. This is not for the faint of heart, but if you have MIDI chops, you can define a sound set and share it with the world. Make the sound set once, and you'll never have to touch it again!

Understanding Effects Buses

Effects buses can be terribly confusing, especially if you don't have a ton of experience with audio. My goal is to make them a whole lot simpler to understand. A *bus* is a path audio can take. We use buses in Sibelius specifically for audio effects. If you'd like to take your KONTAKT PLAYER 2 and send it to a beautiful reverb, you'll need to get the audio from KONTAKT PLAYER 2 somehow. In a studio, you'd likely use audio cables or patch cables to do this. In Sibelius and other modern programs, you can do this inside the computer, and you do it with buses. Buses are just ways to connect audio from one spot to the other. Now, we'll look at adding some effects to Sibelius and using buses to send audio back and forth. Let's look at effects.

Audio Effects

Sibelius can host any type of audio effect, from a lush reverb to the most aggressive guitar distortion plug-in. As mentioned earlier, Sibelius can host VST and AU plug-ins on the Mac and VST plug-ins on the PC. To add an audio effect, you have to navigate to Play > Playback Devices > Effects, as shown in Figure 12.32.

There are two types of audio effects you can add: master inserts and bus effects. I'll define those now.

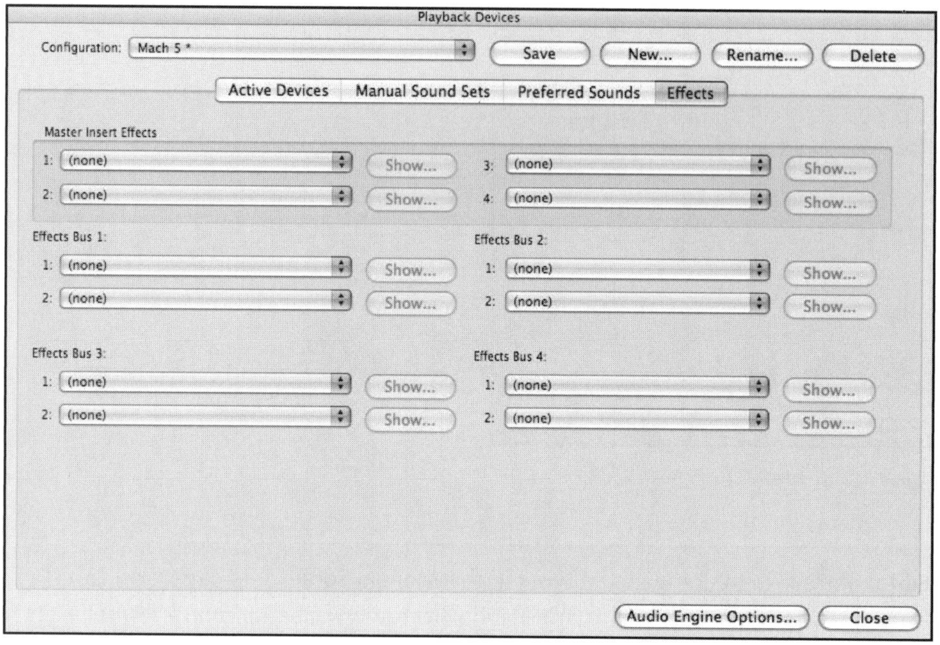

Figure 12.32   Effects.

A *master insert* is an effect that all the audio on your computer has to pass through. You use master insert effects when you want all of your sounds and all of your virtual instruments to pass through the effect. Elements such as compression and other dynamics processing and sometimes reverb work best on a master bus because you want all of your sounds treated equally.

A *bus effect* is used when you want to select which virtual instrument should get which effect and how much signal it should get. Simply put, when you want control, you use a bus effect.

There is one single master section where you can add up to four different plug-ins. The plug-ins are set up in a chain, one after the other. The effects are in series, so the sound of the first effect gets poured into the sound of the second and so on; thus, the order in which you place them is important!

There are four different effects buses, and they can hold two different effects, which are also in series. The effects buses are like chains. You could set up Effects Bus 1 with some guitar effects, Effects Bus 2 with some compression and limiting, Effects Bus 3 with some reverb, and Effects Bus 4 with delay and echo. Then, through the Mixer, you can choose which virtual instruments you want to send to which bus and how much of that signal to send to the bus.

Effects are part of a Playback Configuration, so make sure that you save your configuration when you're finished. Now I want to further define the difference between a master effect and an effects bus.

Master Effects

Honestly, master inserts are much easier to deal with because you have very little control over them. You add them, and all your sounds pass through them; the only control you have is over the plug-in itself. For example, if you're adding a reverb, such as Altiverb (probably the best reverb available), you'll want to show the plug-in interface (see Figure 12.33) and set up the plug-in to sound good. You may choose a different reverb emulation, tweak the wet-dry mix, and off you'll go. As a master insert, all of your sounds will filter through this plug-in.

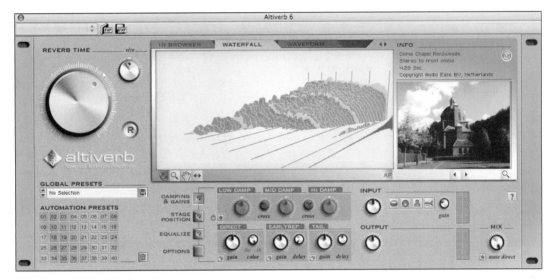

Figure 12.33 Altiverb.

Bus Effects

You have four effects buses (think of them as cables or connections) that you can use. Suppose you have three virtual instruments in your score—KONTAKT PLAYER 2, Ivory, and Mach 5. You'd really like the KONTAKT PLAYER 2 to grab a bit of guitar amp simulation (since that virtual instrument is hosting some guitar sounds), but you don't want it to affect Ivory or Mach 5. If you used a master insert, you'd be out of luck because there's no way to choose which effect goes to where—this is exactly why you want to use a bus effect.

Once you've added these to your Playback Configuration and saved it, you can exit out of the Playback Devices window and return to your score.

Using the Mixer Sends

It's critical to note that you can only send virtual instruments (as a whole) to a bus. You won't be able to send external MIDI devices to a bus because these buses live inside your computer, and Sibelius has no way of getting audio in, only audio out.

When you open the Mixer, click the VI button at the top of the Mixer interface to expose the virtual instrument strips. Now expand the virtual instrument strips, as shown in Figure 12.34; this will show you four rotary knobs, which are your send knobs.

Figure 12.34   FX send controls.

What do the send knobs do? Think of them like water spouts. When at zero, they send no signal to the bus, so they send no audio to the effects to process. As you open the spout, you allow more signal to get effected. At the maximum value (all the way to the right), you are sending all the signal to the bus, which will give you the most dramatic (wet) effect. Because you can configure four different effects buses, there are four effects sends knobs (labeled FX). If you wanted to send KONTAKT PLAYER 2 to Effects Bus 1, you'd turn the knob labeled FX 1 in the KONTAKT PLAYER 2 strip up until you got a sound you liked. If you wanted Ivory to send to Effects Bus 2, you'd turn FX 2 up on its VI strip. For each virtual instrument, you'd tweak the FX sends (1 though 4) to open the water valves and send audio to those buses. That's really all there is to it. When it comes to editing the effects themselves, you can do that right from the Mixer now.

FX Mixture The FX send knob is saying the following: How much of my signal do I want to send to the effect, and how much do I want to be unaffected? So if you set it to halfway, you'll get half the signal sent to the effect, and the other half will not change, so you'll always get a mix of true sound and effects. It's pretty important to note that you're not going to use 100-percent wet that often, if it all, and if you are using 100-percent wet, you should think about using a master insert effect instead.

Showing Effects Interfaces

If you want to edit the plug-in effect—for example, to change the type of reverb or delay—you don't need to go back to Playback Devices. You can do it right from the Mixer. If you click on the FX button at the top of the Mixer, it will expose all four effects buses, showing all of your inserted effects (see Figure 12.35).

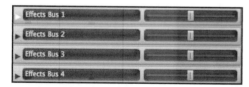

Figure 12.35   FX buses.

Now, let's expand each FX strip by clicking on the left-side arrow to show some additional controls. Next to each inserted effect, you'll see the familiar cog or gear that you can click to show the plug-in's interface. Once it is shown, you can edit the parameters as you see fit.

Mix When adding a plug-in on an effects bus that contains a wet-dry mix, always set it to 100 percent because the effects sends from the virtual instruments are acting as wet/dry mixes themselves.

There are two other controls on the Mixer section for effects (see Figure 12.36).

Figure 12.36   Effects strip controls.

- **Bus output gain.** This sets the overall level of the bus when added to the final output.

- **Input trim.** This sets how loud the inputs to the bus are. Most of the time you don't need to touch this, but some effects don't give you the control for overall loudness (gain), so it is provided here for those instances when you need to change the input gain.

Saving/Loading Presets

As you can see from Figure 12.37, when you show a plug-in interface, there are buttons for saving the current preset and loading saved presets. When modifying your effects settings, make sure that you save your presets for easy recall later.

Also for Instruments If you show the plug-in interface for your virtual instruments, you'll see the same Save and Load buttons, allowing you to save and load your virtual instrument presets as well.

Master Insert Controls

You might have noticed that the master insert effects are missing from the FX tab. That's because master insert effects live on the master fader. Click on the Show/Hide Master Volume button on the top of the Mixer to expose the master volume. Once it is shown, expand the master volume's Mixer strip to see the four possible master effects (see Figure 12.38).

From there, all you can do is show the plug-in interface by clicking on the gear/cog, since you can't control how much level goes into a master effect; it's either all or nothing.

Open Preset   Save Preset

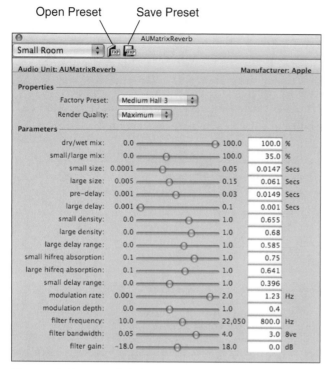

Figure 12.37 Save/load preset.

Figure 12.38 Master insert effects.

Final Cheat Sheet

Here is a nice listing of effects types and where you will want to add them:

- Reverb: Master inserts

- Dynamics (compressors, limiters): Master inserts

- EQ: Master inserts

- Modulation (chorus, flanger): Can be either, but only really works on a single instrument at once

- Distortion: Can be used on either, but best on a single instrument

Now, where do you get effects? If you're on a Mac, OS X ships with a nice complement of effects that you can use without doing a thing. For Windows users (and for Mac users wishing to expand their effects), you can check out www.vstplanet.com for some great free plug-ins or just Google "free VST plug-ins."

The Playback Dictionary

As you know, Sibelius can interpret words, symbols, lines, and other score markings and convert them to playback controls. This is done in the Play > Playback Dictionary window, as shown in Figure 12.39.

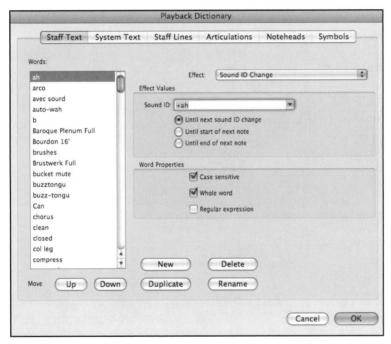

Figure 12.39   Playback Dictionary.

This window sets up a translation from visual symbol to SoundWorld soundIDs and MIDI messages. Sibelius does an excellent job of defining most of what you'll need in the Playback Dictionary. The Playback Dictionary is well documented in section 4.8 of the Sibelius Reference (Help > Sibelius Reference), but let's go through defining one new word in the Playback Dictionary so you can get the hang of how it works. It you study the preexisting Dictionary, you can get a great idea of how to make your own custom symbols if you want them. Let's define the word "softly" as another way to express a dynamic (because not all scores use the typical piano and forte derivations). From within the Play > Playback Dictionary dialog, follow these steps:

1. Press the New button and name it Softly. The word will be added to the list of staff words on the left side.

2. Deselect the Case Sensitive option so it won't matter whether you type the name with a capital letter.

3. Select the Whole Word option so Sibelius will look for the whole word. (It's not an abbreviation.)

4. From the Effect drop-down menu, select Dynamic because we're defining a dynamic change.

5. In the Dynamic field, change 95 to 50. (I'll explain why in the next paragraph.)

6. In the Attack field, change 95 to 45.

Your screen should look like Figure 12.40.

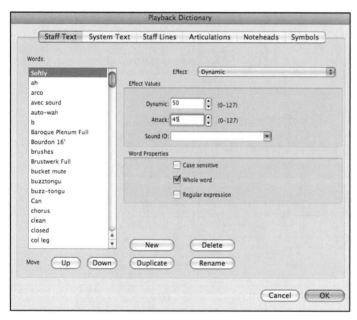

Figure 12.40 Softly defined.

At this point, you can click OK and return to your score. Now add the staff text of Softly to your score and listen to the result. Pretty cool, huh? Now, let's define what the numbers mean.

In MIDI speak, you can have a value from 0–127, and in terms of volume, 0 is off and 127 is full blast. If you check out the Dictionary, you'll see that Sibelius defines "p" (or piano) with a dynamic of 61/127, so I choose 50 to make Softly a softer dynamic. That's really all there is to it. Sibelius lets you define a whole bunch of things to Dictionary words, from simple dynamic changes to full-blown soundID changes. This should get you started with the Playback

Dictionary, even though many users will find little need to touch it—it's still good to get your head around some simple changes.

Rename You'll probably also find that many of the words you are going to custom-define already have the desired effect on playback, just with different names. Use the Duplicate and Rename functions to change the Dictionary to suit your own terms.

MIDI Messages

Did you know that you could write in MIDI messages, such as control changes, continuous controller messages, and many more, into your score, and Sibelius will play them back? You can! You just have to follow the right syntax. All MIDI messages should be written as a staff text style (system text will not work). You really do need to know a good deal about MIDI to make these work, and 99.9 percent of folks will not use these, but if you fall into this category and you really want to tweak things (especially pitch bend for microtonal playback), you can type them into your score.

Here's how it works: All MIDI messages start with the prefix of ~, which is directly followed by the following list of possible suffixes:

- Program changes: ~PX (Program number) For example, ~P1.

- Program change/bank: (Program number,bank) ~PX,X. For example, ~P20,36.

- Control changes: (Control change number,value) ~CX,127. For example, ~C10,127.

- Pitch bend: ~B0,X (X = 1/32 of a half step. Values at 64 are in tune. 65–127 are sharp, and 1–63 are flatter.)

- Aftertouch: (Channel aftertouch, polyphonic aftertouch) ~AX,X.

When you enter a MIDI message with the ~, it automatically hides in your score. To view it, make sure you have View > Hidden Objects on.

Microtones If you want to use a plug-in for microtonal playback, check out Plug-Ins > Playback > Quarter-Tone Playback, which will add the MIDI messages automatically!

Killer Plug-Ins

I want to provide a list of absolutely killer plug-ins that are shipping now that have sound sets (or don't need them) for Sibelius 5. If you want to take Sibelius 5 to the next level for playback, you might want to look at these exciting plug-ins:

- **VSL SE.** This is the Vienna Symphonic Library Special Edition. You'll need a fast computer to run this, but if you want to be amazed by quality, you'll be hard-pressed to find anything better.

- **Synful Orchestra.** This is a physical modeling orchestra, and it plays back very expressively. Because it's not completely sample-based, it won't hit your CPU too hard. (Note: It does not contain percussion sounds yet.)

- **Jeux.** This is a pipe organ SoundFont that you can actually download free (Google "Jeux: SoundFont"). It's actually pretty amazing, and it's free! Play it back in SFZ (Windows-based SoundFont player) or DLSMusicDevice on OS X. (Sibelius.com/helpcenter has an article on this; just search for it at the help center.)

- **Ivory.** The best sampled piano I've ever heard. It does not have a sound set, but it does not need it. Just add it with General MIDI as the sound set, and it will play back beautifully. You'll need a big hard drive and a fast computer for it, but it doesn't get much better than this.

Is That All?

Is that really all you have to say about playback, Marc? No. We could spend a ton more time, especially on the inner workings of SoundWorld and the Sound Set editor for making custom sound sets, but that will have to wait for the web. Please check the Course Technology webpage (www.courseptr.com/downloads) for this book to see extra materials related to playback and the Sound Set editor after the initial publication. When in doubt, grab the Sibelius reference or post at the Sibelius chat page. Now go write some great music!

13 Composing to Video in Sibelius

Essential Tips for Chapter 13

1. You can add video files and sync them to any score. The video will play back within the Sibelius score so you can easily compose along with it.

2. You can add Hit Points to your score to help you line up musical events with events in the video. The Hit Points can contain labels to help you remember what's going on at any particular spot.

3. Video is a great way to get students involved with film- and game-score composition.

4. Using the Fit Selection to Time plug-in, you can have a selection of music fit to a specified piece of video.

5. Sibelius provides example videos on the Sibelius 5 installation DVD. I've also included one on the resource CD that you can use to practice.

6. A great repository for open-source videos is www.archive.org. You can use these to practice your film scoring.

7. You can load audio files and MP3s into the Video window, and with a bit of tweaking, sync it up so that your score plays back the *real* audio file, not the virtual instrument (which is really impressive).

The video features in Sibelius 5 allow you to score to picture in the most practical way: You see the video in the score, it plays in sync with your score, and you can add Hit Points to make sure that important events in the video are easily synced to musical events in your score. For students learning about film composing or for professional composers, this feature is nothing short of revolutionary. You've been able to work with sequencers and video files for years, but never with the ability to create a professional-looking score like in Sibelius. Most composers worked in a sequencer, and then worked in Sibelius. Now, you can do all your work in a single application. Originally created in Sibelius 4, it has been extended in Sibelius 5 with the use of a few new plug-ins, which help make keeping video and audio in perfect sync that much easier. Even cooler is the fact that you can use the Video feature to load in real audio files and have them play back with your score!

Adding Videos

The first thing you need to do is add in your video files. You can add video files that will play in either QuickTime on a Mac or Windows Media Player on a PC. Practically all movie formats will work, although the standard in the film industry are .mov files.

To add your video, choose Play > Video and Time > Add Video. Doing so will bring up the Video window shown in Figure 13.1, which locates the file on your computer.

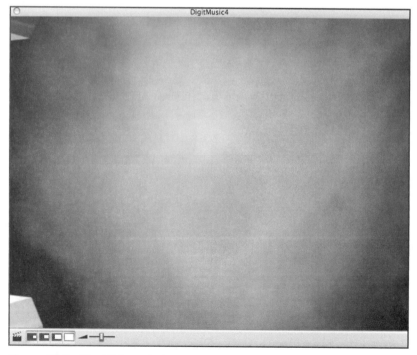

Figure 13.1 The Video window.

CD: If you want to follow along, you can add the digit.mov file to your Sibelius score and stay in sync with the text. (You can even compose your own music to it.) You'll find this file in the Chapter 13 folder on the CD that came with this book.

Once you've added the video into your score (by selecting the appropriate file and clicking Open), you'll see that the Video window now appears to float across the top of your score.

The Video window has several controls that are worth explaining. Figure 13.2 details what each of the buttons on the Video window does.

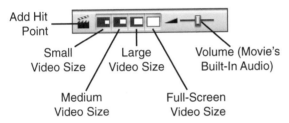

Figure 13.2   The Video window controls.

You'll want to resize the video to a comfortable size, so that you can see your work and still see enough of the video to work accurately.

I Can't See! If you make the video full-screen, you won't have any controls to get you back to your score. Don't worry, all is not lost—just press Escape, and you'll be taken back to your score.

Here are a couple of important things to know about your newly implanted video:

- Your video is now playing along with your score. Use the Playback slider on your Playback window to shuffle back and forth in your video.

- To see where your video is at any point in your score, select the note and press the Y key (Move Playline to Selection), and the video will snap to the current spot in your score.

- If your score is longer than the length of your video, your video will stay frozen on the last frame for the duration of any extra measures. Don't worry; you can trim the score exactly.

- Many movie files contain audio (dialogue or sound effects). They will play along with your score. Remember to set their volume on the Video window—there is no slider for video sounds in the Mixer.

Now that you have your video in, you'll want to see about adding Hit Points into your score to help line up important musical events in it.

Adding Hit Points

A Hit Point is a visual marker that you can place in your score. Its purpose is to mark important events in the video so you can see them as you compose your score. This helps line up important events in the video with musical events, such as dynamic changes, key changes, or changes in orchestration.

Before you go adding any Hit Points, though, you'll need to navigate your video with precision. The Playback slider on the Playback window can move pretty fast—maybe too fast for you! Here are some great key commands to help you navigate through your video with precision.

- The [ ] (brackets) will rewind and fast-forward your score 0.02 seconds in either direction.

- If you hold Shift+[or Shift+], Sibelius will rewind or fast-forward your movie frame by frame.

The normal brackets move in 0.02-second increments, while pressing Shift+bracket moves one frame at a time. A frame is much smaller than a second—there usually are 29.97 frames in a second—so it's a much finer resolution.

Using the key commands, I'm able to find some exact spots I'd like to mark in the score. The video file I have is only 12 seconds long, so I'm only picking one spot! If you watch the video, you'll see that when the .net comes into the picture (at 5 seconds, 11 frames), there is a visual effect of a "ripple" in the video. At that moment, I'll want something to happen musically to make it stand out. For everything else, I can just compose music that follows along, but that doesn't have to follow the video too closely. However, this particular moment is really important.

Once I've located my desired spot in the video, I'll want to add a Hit Point. The Add Hit Point button is located on the Video window (in the left corner); I'll click it to add a Hit Point. The Hit Point shown in Figure 13.3 appears on my empty score.

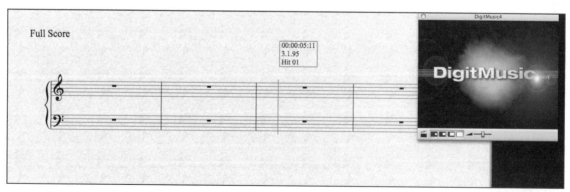

Figure 13.3 The Hit Point.

The Hit Point shows me the following information:

- **00:00:05:11.** This is the timecode of the Hit Point. The event happens at 5 seconds and 11 frames.

- **3.1.95.** This is the measure and beat information: The Hit Point occurs at Bar 3, Beat 1.95. (This information will change if I change the tempo of the piece.)

- **Hit 01.** This is the default name, which I can and will edit.

I'm also going to create a Hit Point at the end of the movie so I can make sure there are adequate bars in the piece. (This will also make it easier when I use the Fit Selection to Time option, which you'll learn about shortly.) I'll fast-forward to the end of the video and add a Hit Point there as well.

Next I want to show you how to edit your Hit Points and give them more meaningful names.

CD: On your CD, use Example 13.1 to add a Hit Point to the video provided. Instructions are in the Sibelius file.

Editing Hit Points

You can manage your Hit Points by going to Play > Playback and Video > Hit Points, which brings up the Hit Points dialog box shown in Figure 13.4.

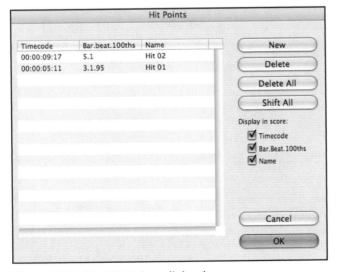

Figure 13.4 The Hit Points dialog box.

Hiding and Moving You cannot drag or move Hit Points as you can other text elements, because they are locked to events in your film. You also can't hide them in the normal Sibelius way by choosing Edit > Hide or Show > Hide.

In this dialog box, I can add new Hit Points, remove existing ones, and, most importantly, rename the ones I already created. Figure 13.5 shows the score with named Hit Points.

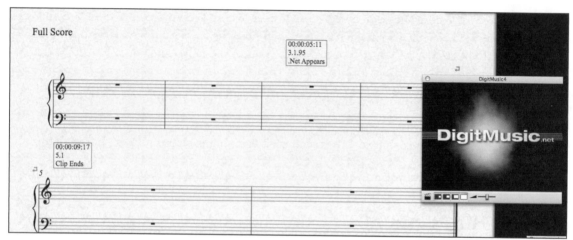

Figure 13.5 The score with named Hit Points.

Hit Points Move It's a good time to note that Hit Points are always in sync with video, which plays at a constant rate, but as you change tempo—either globally or by rit. and accel. markings—the Hit Points will move around your score as you'd except them to.

CD: Example 13.2 will teach you to rename Hit Points in a Sibelius file.

Now it's time for me to compose. Because this is a fast clip, I'm hearing some string chords (built up instrument by instrument, possibly with a tremolo) with a string quartet and some sort of hard chord at the important Hit Point: ".Net Appears." I'll need some help because the Hit Point falls at a difficult spot to line up. Sibelius includes a new plug-in called Fit Selection to Time, which will help me line up some preexisting music within the video.

I'll change my instruments from piano to a string quartet so I have the right instruments in my score, and then I'll start adding music to get an idea of what I want to do next. Figure 13.6

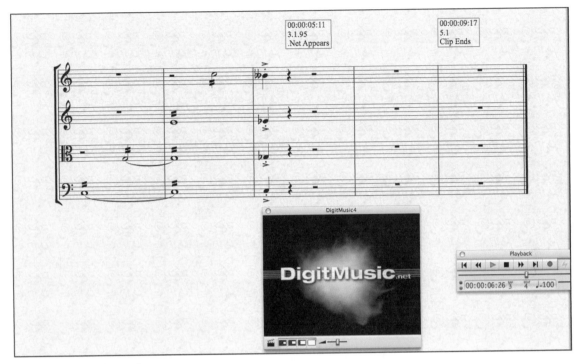

Figure 13.6 Basic scoring.

shows some basic ideas in my score, along with the Hit Points. Notice how I didn't try to line up the music with the first Hit Point yet; I'll leave that for Sibelius to help me.

Sharing Files with Movies If you are going to send your Sibelius score with a video file to someone, remember that you need to send the .Sib file and the associated movie file. Sibelius will look for the movie file in the same folder as the score was saved in. If it can't find the movie file, Sibelius will ask you to locate the file.

Fit Selection to Time

I want that chord to line up exactly! To do this, I have to change the tempo to match the video because the video won't speed up or slow down. Using the new Fit Selection to Time plug-in, I'll work on each Hit Point separately. Here's how to do it:

1. Select the music that will end at the first Hit Point. Because you want the chord at the third bar to stay aligned with the Hit Point, you don't want to select the chord. Only select the music in the first two bars by Shift-clicking. (Select everything that comes before that chord.)

2. Go to Plug-Ins > Composing Tools > Fit Selection to Time. The Fit Selection to Time dialog box will open, as shown in Figure 13.7.

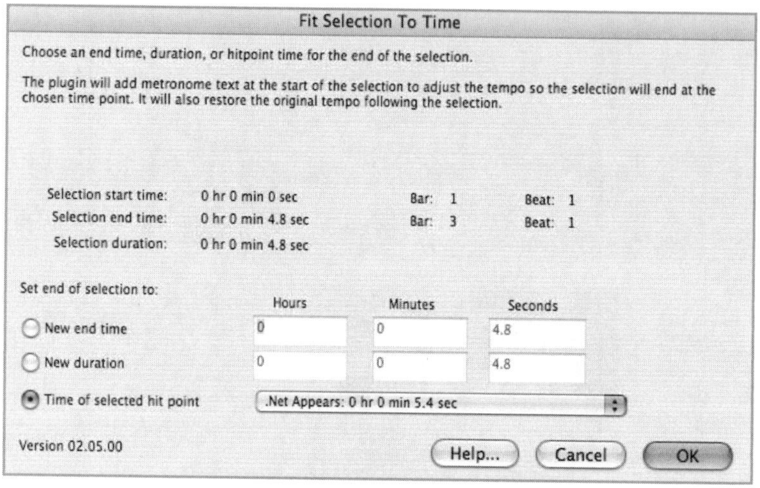

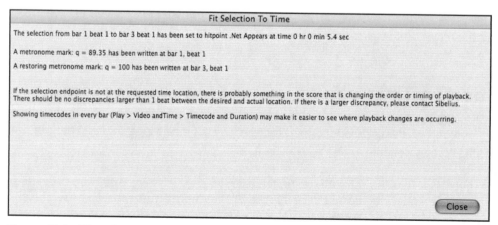

Figure 13.7   The Fit Selection to Time dialog box.

3. Choose the Time of Selected Hit Point option at the bottom of the screen and select the first Hit Point: .Net Appears.

4. Click OK.

5. You'll see one more Fit Selection to Time window that explains what happened (see Figure 13.8).

Figure 13.8   Hit Points explained.

CD: Use Example 13.3 to select the music that you'll use with the Fit Selection to Time plug-in.

The plug-in has calculated how fast the tempo needs to be (exactly) to get your music to fit. It does this by adding metronome marks so that the first two bars are the correct speed to line up the downbeat of Bar 3, which has the Hit Point. It's an absolutely incredible thing! The plug-in knows what your prevailing tempo is and tries to stay as close to that as possible, yet still line up your music to the Hit Point. You could add manual metronome marks from the Create > Text menu to manually line up your music (and nothing is stopping you from doing that), but for precision, the plug-in mathematically lines up everything.

I'm going to fit the rest of the music so that the last bar of my piece lines up exactly with the end of the video clip (which has a Hit Point). The final Hit Point in my score as it stands ends at 4.4.05, so it's close to the end of the fourth measure, but I'll use the plug-in to make it line up exactly on 5.1, which is the true completion of the fourth bar. Figure 13.9 shows the result of running the plug-in on the last few bars.

CD: Use Example 13.4 to fit the final bars of music using the Fit Selection to Time plug-in.

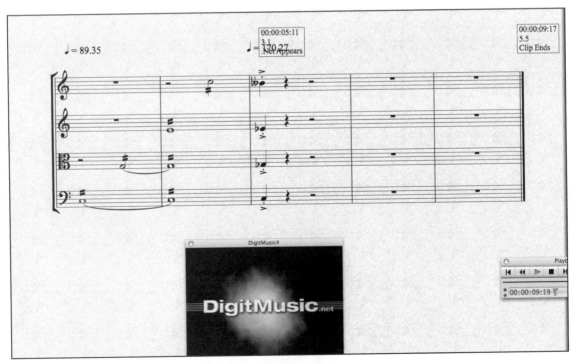

Figure 13.9 Final Hit Point lined up.

There are a couple of things I want to do now. First, I want to hide the metronome marks by selecting them and choosing View > Hide or Show > Hide.

I also want to hide the Hit Points by going to Play > Video and Time > Hit Points and deselecting all the Show in Score options. This will clear out the Hit Points—I don't need to see them right now. (I can always bring them back at a later time by revisiting the same window and re-selecting the options.) Remember: You can't manually hide Hit Points—you must do it by this method.

Now that everything is lined up, I can start to orchestrate this example by adding additional instruments, composing more interesting music, and possibly using some cool third-party sound effects via virtual instrument plug-ins. What's important is that we have the important elements lined up, and Sibelius made the proper tempo changes in the score to allow me to work and compose without having to worry about the timing.

Creating a Hit Point Stave

One thing that might make your life as a composer easier is creating a Hit Point staff, which is a single-line staff that contains the Hit Points and rhythmic information showing you exactly where the Hit Points line up musically within the current tempo. Sibelius does this automatically as a plug-in through Plug-Ins > Composing Tools > Add Hit Point Staff. Figure 13.10 shows the automatically created Hit Point staff.

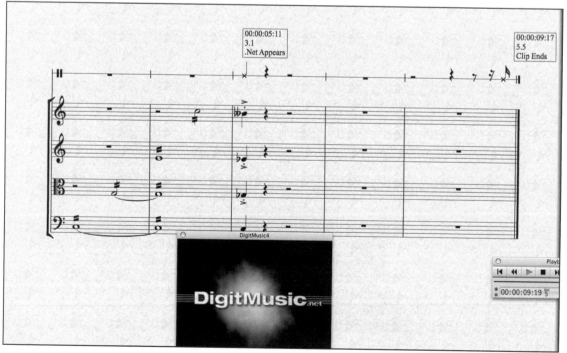

Figure 13.10 Hit Point staff.

Example Movies Don't forget that your Sibelius 5 installation CD has many other examples of videos within Sibelius scores. Take a look through the examples and see what else you can do!

Exporting and Merging

When you've composed to your heart's content, you'll want to merge your work so you can present a single video file with your score embedded in it. To do so, you'll have to export audio to bounce your music to a stereo audio file. You can do this by choosing File > Export > Export Audio or by clicking the Export Audio button (which resembles a CD) on the toolbar.

To merge the audio and video, you'll need a third-party application. At present Sibelius can't do this, but we're all hopeful that their acquisition by Avid will mean that these sorts of things will happen in future versions of Sibelius. For now, to merge your audio and video into one file, you'll need iMovie (if you're on a Mac) or Windows Movie Maker (if you're on a PC), both of which are free. Please refer to the documentation for each program to learn how to do this, but don't fear—it's not difficult!

Video Settings

There are some options that you'll want to know about with regard to how Sibelius handles and displays the video files. Professional composers who have dealt with video scoring use something called *timecode*, which is a way to keep the video and audio perfectly in sync for the final picture. Sibelius also adheres to timecode. Go to Play > Playback and Video > Timecode and Duration to open the Timecode and Duration dialog box, which is shown in Figure 13.11.

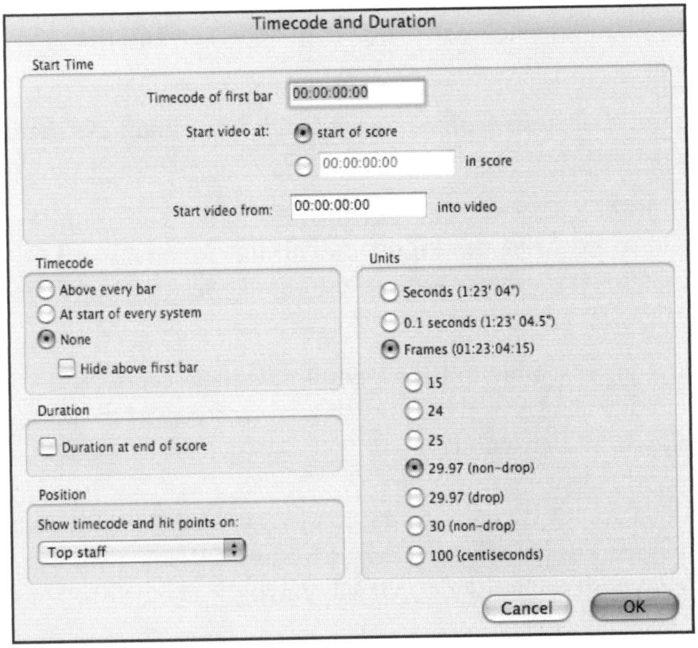

Figure 13.11 The Timecode and Duration dialog box.

This impressive dialog box boasts too many options to detail here, but one critical part is the Units section, which allows Sibelius to display different frame rates for different videos. In the video industry, there are multiple frames-per-second formats used (from 15 FPS to 100 centiseconds). To ensure that you're looking at the correct format in the Playback window and Hit Points, you'll set this to the frame rate of your video (which is something you'll know about beforehand).

Video Frames If you get a video and you're unsure of its frame rate, you can use Quick-Time (a free download from apple.com) and choose Window > Movie Inspector to tell you the frames per second, which is listed as *FPS* in the dialog box that appears.

The Timecode and Duration dialog box also lets you control which stave shows the Hit Points, as well as other advanced features, such as the ability to set a custom timecode for the first bar. (This is very important if you're working on cues for movies in which you'll be composing to clips in the middle of the movie.) There's more detail in the Sibelius Reference on advanced video techniques in Sibelius.

Adding Audio Instead of Video

One particularly impressive Sibelius attribute that isn't often discussed is the ability to use the Video feature as a host for audio files. That's right—you can load a .WAV, .AIFF or .MP3 file into the Video window, and although there won't be any video, you'll have a perfect audio file playing back with Sibelius. This is an amazing feature, and here are just a few uses for it:

- **Transcription.** Have your source audio play back with your score as you transcribe the music—this is great for jazz students!

- **Ear training.** Give your students aural skills tests with embedded audio files and have them notate on the score using Sibelius.

- **Mock-up.** If you have a good recording of a piece you composed, add it to the Video window so it plays back with your score. Go to the Mixer and mute the Sibelius sounds, so all you hear is the perfectly recorded audio. (You might have to use the Fit Selection to Time plug-in to keep the score in sync.)

- **Rehearsal.** Another great use is for your ensemble to hear a good reference recording linked to the score. It's very cool that Sibelius keeps the ability to go to any part of the score, and the audio will catch up and play from that point.

There are so many possibilities with this feature! If you're trying to sync up the audio file to a score so that it plays back in sync, you'll use Hit Points and the Fit Selection to Time plug-in to make the rubato sections of music line up with the fairly mechanical playback in Sibelius. Let's go through the process and do a sync together.

Syncing an Audio File to a Score

If you open the Chapter 13 folder on your CD, you'll find two files: Blood of the Lamb.sib and Blood.mp3. "Blood of the Lamb" is a piece composed by Sibelius Eastern manager (and good friend) Robin Hodson, who graciously donated his work for this book. (If you live on the East coast of America, you may have run into Robin at Sibelius events.) In any case, we're going to line up the audio and the score, and it won't be hard at all! I'll take it step by step so you can follow along.

1. Open the score, choose Play > Playback and Video, and add Blood.mp3 into the score using Add Video.

2. Rewind the score and have a listen. Make sure to watch the Playback bar and see how well they're in sync. Clearly, they won't be right in line together. Now, rewind the score again and listen to the tempo of the opening phrase. Rewind it a few times if you can, and get the beat in your head.

3. Select the first note of the piece and go to Plug-Ins > Other > Set Metronome Mark, which will open the Set Metronome Mark dialog box shown in Figure 13.12.

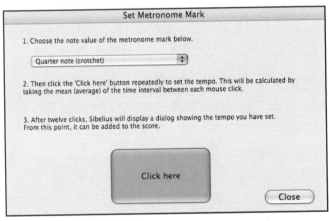

Figure 13.12 The Set Metronome Mark dialog box.

This clever plug-in does exactly what you'd think: You tap with your mouse, and it figures out what tempo you're using. When I did it, it gave me an initial tempo of 125. A quick playback proves that it's spot-on for the opening! The first two bars line up almost exactly, but at Measure 3, when the other voices enter, the speed is too fast.

1. Play back the score starting at Measure 3, and get the tempo in your head for that section. Click the first note of Measure 3 and run the Set Metronome Mark plug-in again. In my score, it set a metronome mark of 112 at the start of the third bar, which now makes the score play back very well up until the repeat. Now, listen back from the

beginning and watch the green Playback bar. It follows! This is not a film score, so I don't need mathematical precision. However, if I click on any spot in the score and play from there, I want the audio file to start in time.

2. Keep listening, and you'll notice that the second time it repeats, it's not playing back at 125 as it did the first time—it's a bit slower. I didn't actually use the plug-in to fix this; I just copied the initial metronome mark by clicking on it and pressing Ctrl/Command+C to copy it and Ctrl/Command+V to paste it right on top of itself. I used the arrow keys to move it above so I had two versions of quarter note = 125. Just by ear, I can hear that the tempo Robin took at Measure 3 is very close to the tempo on the second verse, so I edited the upper metronome mark to 112.

3. Now, I have to tell Sibelius to use the bottom metronome mark the first time it repeats and the upper metronome mark the second time it repeats. To do this, I need to choose Window > Properties.

4. Remember when we talked about Sibelius's ability to set certain musical elements to only play on certain repeats? This is called the *Play on Pass* feature, and we'll use it to tell Sibelius to listen to the lower metronome mark on the first repeat and the upper metronome mark on the second time through.

5. Click on the lower metronome mark, and in the Properties window, make sure Playback is shown. If it's not, click the word Playback to open the menu, as shown in Figure 13.13.

Figure 13.13 Playback.

6. Where it says Play on Pass, there are eight checkmarks. I only want this metronome mark to play the first repeat, so I'll deselect the marks for 2 through 8. (In other words, 1 should be checked, and 2, 3, 4, 5, 6, 7, and 8 should be unchecked.)

7. Click on the higher metronome mark in the Properties window (which is still open). We want to deselect all but the second check box. (In other words, 2 should be checked, and 1, 3, 4, 5, 6, 7, and 8 should be unchecked.) This tells Sibelius to listen to those metronome marks only on the proper repeats. With that set, I can listen back and see how well the parts line up. On my score, when Robin repeats, the 112 marking is too fast by a touch (the playback line is ahead), so I manually edit the metronome mark by guessing 110, which happens to work. I now get in-time playback up until Measure 9, when the refrain starts.

8. At Measure 9 it's ever so slightly out of sync again, so I listen only to Measures 9 through 11 to grab the tempo, and I use the Set Metronome Mark plug-in again with the first note of Measure 9 selected. Sibelius places a metronome mark of 113 at Measure 9, which sounds fine. (Robin was only one beat per minute off, but it made enough of a difference.)

9. Now I listen back to the piece from the beginning and grin because it has all worked out! Everything is playing back really nicely.

10. The last thing I want to do is hide those metronome marks. I select them and choose Edit > Hide or Show > Hide, and they go away!

Faster than you Think Writing these directions took me about 30 minutes, but actually doing the work took me about 3 minutes! It's not difficult, and the plug-in is an amazing tool to help you. The reason I had to tweak things a bit is that, as you know, natural musical performance is not mathematically metronomic. Music ebbs and flows, and my very simple changes (usually hovering between 110 and 112) made it all work out.

Try this with some other pieces you have; maybe download a MIDI file of Bach and use an MP3 of a performance to line up. Or simply practice on Robin's piece as provided on your CD. It's always amazing to see the score play and hear "real" audio play along. Thanks, Robin!

14 | Scanning and the Arrange Feature

Essential Tips for Chapter 14

1. Scanning is not an exact science.

2. A lower-resolution scanner often outperforms a higher-resolution scanner in PhotoScore.

3. Sibelius ships with PhotoScore Lite for free, and you can upgrade to PhotoScore Ultimate for a fee.

4. If you do a great deal of scanning, PhotoScore Ultimate is completely worth the price because it tackles more advanced functions than PhotoScore Lite does.

5. PhotoScore Ultimate is now able to do handwritten music, but you have to follow a style guide when you write, so it's not for everyone.

6. Scanning is a great way to get music from an old software program that no longer runs on current computers. Print the music out and scan it into Sibelius. *Remember that you can always print to a PDF and import into PhotoScore.*

7. The Arrange feature uses pre-built styles for orchestration and chord voicings. If you don't like them, you are free to create/edit and save your own Arrange styles.

8. Arrange is a copy-, cut-, and paste-based action, so to make it work you have to have something copied to the Clipboard first.

9. Professionals and students alike can use Arrange to teach some fundamentals of orchestration, but its strength lies in its ability to create quick reductions and explosions for a wide variety of instruments.

10. Arrange will not make you an arranger, but it will save you time on certain things.

We spent considerable time early in this book getting you familiar with the various ways to input music into Sibelius. One of the ways that we spoke about, but didn't look at yet, is scanning. Sibelius includes the Lite version of Neuratron's PhotoScore application, which allows you to scan in printed sheet music and have it recognized, edited, and then sent to Sibelius. PhotoScore is a separate application that you install with Sibelius, so if you don't see it on your computer, check your original Sibelius 5 installation DVD; you'll find it in a folder called Optional Installs. Another feature is the Arrange feature, which lets you take music and either arrange it from big to small (piano to larger groups/ensembles) or make reductions. The Arrange feature has built-in styles that automate the process for you, and coupled with traditional note entry and now scanning, the Arrange feature may come in handy.

Using PhotoScore Lite

PhotoScore Lite is a third-party application developed by one of Sibelius's partners in Europe, Neuratron software. PhotoScore allows you to take music, read it with a scanner (or via a graphics file), and have it converted from bits of data into a Sibelius score. That's right; you can scan into PhotoScore and send to Sibelius. It's an amazing tool that has evolved over many years. If this is your first experience with scanning, you're joining the party at a really good time—it has never been this easy to scan in music. And for the first time, you can scan in handwritten music, assuming that you are good with the pen. PhotoScore comes in two flavors, Lite and Ultimate. Let's break down the differences between the programs.

Lite versus Ultimate

PhotoScore Lite reads the following musical elements:

- Notes, chords, and rests

- Basic accidentals (sharp, flat, and natural signs)

- Treble/bass clef, key, and time signatures

- Five-line staves, six-line tab staves, and standard barlines

- The page layout, including staff size, margins, and all that good stuff

Now for most folks, that's an absolutely incredible feat. Better yet, it even works! Now, if you upgrade to PhotoScore Ultimate, you add the following:

- Text (lyrics, dynamics, instrument names, titles, fingerings)

- The rest of the clefs that Lite leaves out

- More advanced accidentals

- Tuplets

- Guitar chord diagrams/frames

- Codas, segnos, ornaments, repeat/endings, and other score lines

- Handwritten music

As you can see, Ultimate does a bunch more things. I give you this bit of advice: If you do a good deal of scanning, you should get Ultimate. It's worth it, and it reads symbols and text that you'd likely have to put in by hand.

Getting into PhotoScore

When you start up Sibelius, go to the File menu and choose Scan, which will automatically launch PhotoScore for you. If you already have PhotoScore Ultimate installed (which is an optional upgrade), this process will launch PhotoScore Ultimate for you. You'll be taken to PhotoScore (as seen in Figure 14.1).

From the File menu within PhotoScore, choose Scan Pages to take you to the control center for your scanner. Alternatively, if you don't have a scanner, PhotoScore will read graphics files (BMP, TIFF, and PDF files), so you can use PhotoScore to open files of your choosing. Use the File > Open command for PITC, BMP or TIFF files, or use File > Open PDF to read a PDF. Before we actually get into scanning, let's talk a bit about scanners.

Are You Compatible? On Windows, it's pretty easy to press the Scan button and expect PhotoScore to talk to your scanner. This is because the vast majority of scanners use a driver called TWAIN, which is a standard driver protocol on Windows that PhotoScore is compatible with. On the Mac, you'll find that fewer and fewer scanner manufacturers are supporting TWAIN. This means that you might not be able to scan from directly within PhotoScore. No worries—just use the included software that came with your scanner, save the resulting scan as a TIFF file, and open it in PhotoScore.

Talking about Scanners

So you got a nice scanner? Scans magazines and photos really well, huh? For PhotoScore, that doesn't matter at all. Music is black and white (the last time we looked), and high detail is not going to help. That's right—the $50 scanner from your local office supply will do. That's not to say that having a killer scanner will hurt you; it's just overkill. Now that that's out of the way, here are some tips for scanning:

- Never scan in color; always use black and white or grayscale.

- Make sure the lid of the scanner can close; unwanted light leads to bad scans.

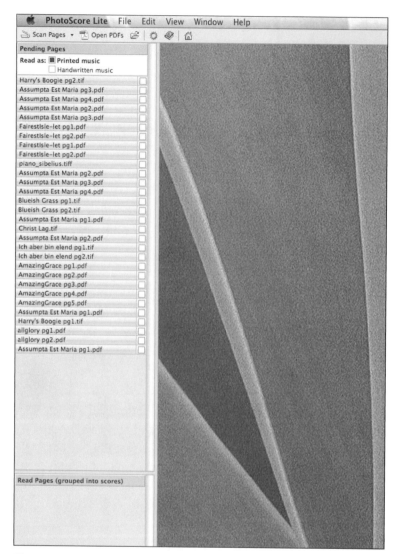

Figure 14.1 PhotoScore first run.

- Scan at a low resolution, typically between 200 and 300 dots per inch (DPI). Higher resolutions will only lead to errors.

- Music that has been photocopied too many times won't scan well. Try to get first-generation copies.

- Only scan one page at a time. Multi-page smaller scores with a crease never scan properly. You can scan scores that are longer than one page! Scan them, correct the mistakes, and send them to Sibelius, and Sibelius will reconstitute them as one large score.

Your scanner has a glass plate that it reads from—please keep it clean! A little Windex goes a long way.

Your First Scan/File

To help you follow along, you'll find a PDF in the Chapter 14 directory on the accompanying CD that you can use to work with PhotoScore, even if you don't have a scanner. If you *do* have a scanner, use the principles we work with here and adapt them to your own score.

You can either copy the file from the CD to your hard drive or other storage center, or simply read it from the CD. Choose File > Open PDF, navigate to the Chapter 14 folder, and open Scan .pdf (as shown in Figure 14.2).

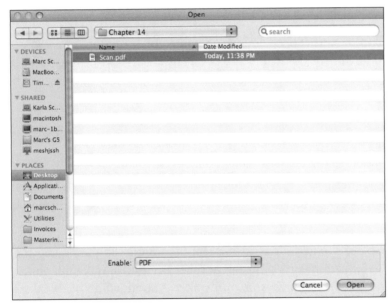

Figure 14.2 Opening a PDF.

Figure 14.3 shows the next screen that comes up. The screen asks you to pick a resolution for the scanned PDF. Most of the time, you simply won't know what the resolution of a PDF is; in these cases, pick 300 DPI. If it's reading terribly, you can always reopen it and choose a different resolution. By terribly, I mean with a great number of errors. If you see too many problems, before you go to correct them, try a different resolution setting and see whether you get a better reading.

After you press OK, PhotoScore will start to read the page, doing its magic to figure out what you've fed it. On the left side of PhotoScore's interface, you will see a listing of the pages that

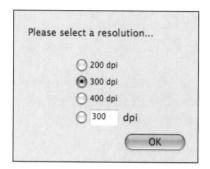

Figure 14.3 Pick your resolution.

have been scanned and read, along with your new file, which will have a green progress bar showing you the reading progress (see Figure 14.4).

When that's finished, you'll see PhotoScore's split window, showing you a mixture of the pure scan on the top and the converted document on the bottom (see Figure 14.5). At this point, you can start to compare the original PDF to the result of the PhotoScore process for editing, which we'll look at in our next section.

Alto Clef PhotoScore Lite will not read the alto clefs (or other clefs besides the treble and bass clefs). So, if you're reading in music for viola, PhotoScore will mess up the clef. No worries, you can fix this in Sibelius.

Source and Destination

When you read a file into PhotoScore, you get a look at the real file (in the top pane), and the bottom pane shows you what PhotoScore has read. In many other programs, including video and audio programs, this is referred to as a *source/destination model*. Although PhotoScore does not use this term, I will use it here for clarity. Figure 14.6 shows where the source and destination are.

Zoom Don't forget that you can zoom in on your score in PhotoScore either by using the magnifying glass found in the main toolbar or by choosing View > Zoom. Alternatively, the same key commands work from Sibelius: Ctrl/Command++ will zoom in, while Ctrl/Command+− will zoom out.

When you hover your mouse or select a note in the destination panel, PhotoScore will highlight the corresponding note in the source panel (as shown in Figure 14.7).

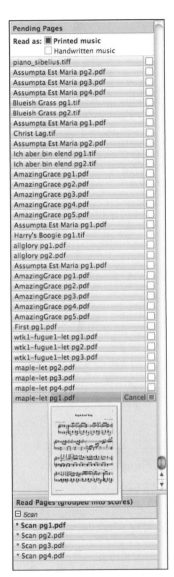

Figure 14.4   Read pages and progress.

As you continue to look through the score, always look at the source and make sure that Photo-Score did a proper job of translating from the scan to the file. If anything is wrong, it's very easy to fix. Just click on a note and change it using the same tools and methods you learned in Sibelius. You'll see your familiar keypad, voicings, and Create menu. When looking at voices, you'll also notice that PhotoScore conforms to the same colors that Sibelius does (blue for Voice 1, and so on).

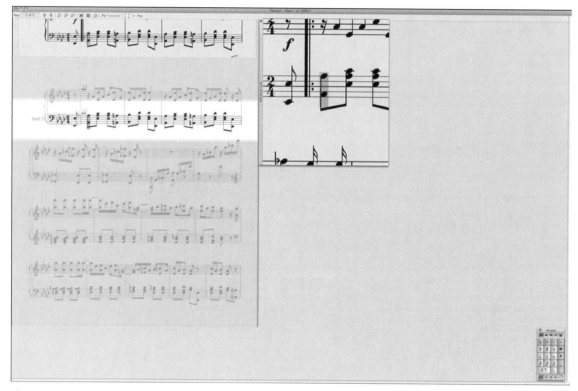

Figure 14.5 First PhotoScore reading.

Key Commands Although Sibelius and PhotoScore share the keypad and Create menu, they do not share the key commands for common tasks, such as key signatures, time signatures, lines, and symbols. To change these, you still need to go to the Create menu within PhotoScore.

If you're working with a multi-page PDF or scanned file, you'll need to toggle the viewable page to see the rest of your score to continue editing. You can toggle pages using the up and down page arrows on the main toolbar. The currently viewed page number will be displayed to the left of the arrows. You can't scroll from page to page—you must use the arrows to toggle the visible page.

Paste You can copy and paste in PhotoScore, just like you do in Sibelius, by selecting an object and holding down the Alt/Option key when you click the mouse. This can really speed up copying objects, such as incorrect clefs and other repeating inaccuracies.

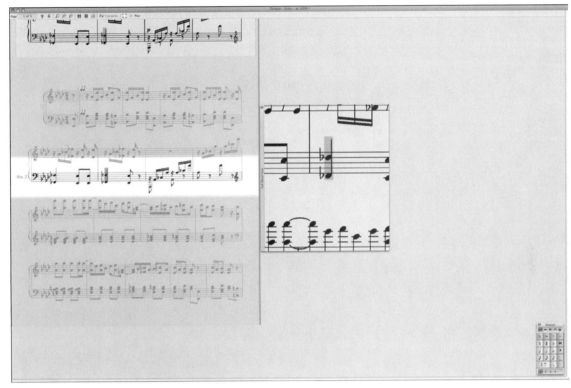

Figure 14.6 Source and destination.

Error Checking

You don't need to get your files absolutely spot-on perfect in PhotoScore, even though Photo-Score allows substantial editing. However, there are certain errors that you should fix. When editing in PhotoScore, I make sure that the following things link up before I export to Sibelius.

More Room and Detail Don't forget that you can hide the pages you've scanned by select-ing View > Toggle Pages Pane to give you more room. If you need even more detail, switch on View > Full Detail to get a real pixel-by-pixel preview of any note that you're editing in PhotoScore.

- Key signatures
- Time signatures
- Clef and clef changes

Figure 14.7 Highlighting a note in PhotoScore.

- Correct number of beats in the bars

- Correct voices

In PhotoScore, errors in key signatures, time signatures, or clefs may not be clearly seen. When the number of beats in the bar does not line up with the current time signature, PhotoScore lets you know onscreen with the symbol shown in Figure 14.8.

Figure 14.8 Beat error: Check your math.

> **Arrow > Error** Use your right arrow key to advance to the next object that may need to be fixed!

Fix the errors by selecting the rhythms that are incorrectly notated and fixing them with the keypad. When the measure lines up properly, the red notation in the score indicating a measure discrepancy will disappear. When you have all your clef, key, and time issues cleared up, you can send to Sibelius.

> **What about Text?** Why not correct the text-based errors in PhotoScore Ultimate (as Lite does not do much in the way of text reading)? Simply, Sibelius has far more robust facilities for editing and filtering text than PhotoScore does. Let PhotoScore do the magic of translating the notes for you. You should make sure the rhythmic elements line up, and then do the rest in Sibelius. Of course, this only applies to PhotoScore Ultimate, as PhotoScore Lite does not read text!

Scanning into PhotoScore

Opening a PDF is a neat trick, but most folks are indeed more interested in scanning actual music into PhotoScore from a flatbed scanner. To do so, you need to ensure that you have a scanner properly set up for use in your system, and that includes installing any drivers and software from the manufacturer. When that's finished, you can click the Scan Pages button on the main toolbar or go to File > Scan Pages (Ctrl/Command+G). Your scanner will load up its software interface, and you'll be able to scan as many pages as you need into PhotoScore. When you're finished scanning, you'll see all of the pages available for use on the right side of PhotoScore, in the Pages pane.

At this point, PhotoScore has not done any reading; it has simply read the scanned pages into memory. Clicking on any of the scanned pages in the Pages pane will load the raw scan into PhotoScore. First, PhotoScore tries to figure out what kinds of staves you have. It does so by placing small blue lines over the staves to count the number of lines. This is the most critical step before you read the pages. If PhotoScore can't find the staves or has a hard time due to low resolution, you might be instructed to fix the error by dragging the blue overlay to the proper spot. Usually, stave detection errors are indications of a problem with the scan, the resolution, or the angle of the page. If you get too many errors, try to rescan your page and see whether you have better luck. (You can do this easily by choosing Edit > Rescan.)

> **Orientation** The Edit menu lets you readjust the scanned image, which is especially useful if you've scanned it upside down or if it has been turned on its side!

When you're in good shape, click the Read Pages button on the main toolbar or choose File > Read Pages. After the page has been read, you can go through the same process as outlined with PDFs for cleaning up your music and then sending it to Sibelius, which is outlined in the next section.

Sending to Sibelius

When you've edited the score and you're pleased with the results, you can have the score sent to Sibelius automatically. This is achieved by choosing File > Send To > Sibelius, pressing Ctrl/ Command+D, or pressing the small Sibelius icon on the main toolbar. When you press the button, PhotoScore will launch Sibelius (if it's not already launched) and start the process of importing the file for you. Figure 14.9 shows the first window you'll see.

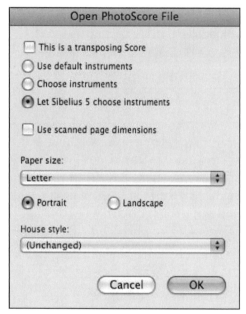

Figure 14.9 Send to Sibelius.

The Open Photoscore File screen has some important options that you'll want to know about to ensure that your file goes into Sibelius as smoothly as possible. Let's look at the options:

- **This Is a Transposing Score.** If you're scanning in music with transposing instruments, you'll want to select this check box. Sibelius will ask you for the correct instruments in the next step.

- **Use Default Instruments.** When this option is selected, it opens the file without assigning a particular instrument to a stave. This would be suitable when playback and transposing instruments are not concerns.

- **Choose Instruments.** This option lets you choose the instruments that will be present in your new score in the same way you'd choose when setting up a new score or adding instruments.

- **Let Sibelius 5 Choose Instruments.** Sibelius will read the staff names from the PhotoScore file and try to assign those staves to the proper instruments.

- **Use Scanned Page Dimensions.** When this option is selected, Sibelius will read the paper size and dimensions from the scanned output in PhotoScore.

- **Paper Size.** If you want Sibelius to ignore the scanned dimensions, you can set a new size here.

- **House Style.** If you want Sibelius to use a custom House Style for your score (such as ink pen or reprise fonts), you can change the House Style here.

After you have made the appropriate changes to suit your score, press OK, and Sibelius will open the file. When you are in Sibelius, you can start to make any large changes you want to, including adding instruments; copying, cutting, and pasting to other instruments; adding chord changes; and more. That's the beauty: It becomes a full-fledged Sibelius score, and you already know how to do thousands of things in Sibelius.

When Your Scanned File Looks Bad
After you have sent to Sibelius, you still might not love the layout and look of your score. Here are a few tips to help you out:

- If the staves aren't detected properly in PhotoScore, they will be totally messed up in Sibelius. You need to get staves and time correct in PhotoScore. PhotoScore is far more flexible for fixing rhythmic issues than Sibelius is!

- If your file has a ton of mistakes, make sure that you're not being limited by PhotoScore Lite's limitation on clefs and note durations!

- If the instruments are not detected properly in PhotoScore, no worries—use Create > Other > Instrument Change in Sibelius and click the instrument change at the start of the first measure to correctly identify the instruments.

- If your lyrics are in the way of the notes, choose Edit > Select All and Edit > Filter > Lyrics, and move them down with the arrow keys.

- If the staves are too close together, adjust the distance between staves in the Staves page of House Style > Engraving Rules.

■ If PhotoScore missed the pickup measures, you can always add them later using Create > Time Signature in Sibelius.

■ If the layout is completely messed up, you can Edit > Select All, then Layout > Format > Unlock Format, Layout > Reset Space Above Staff, Layout > Reset Space Below Staff, and Layout > Reset Position.

Start Small One of the best ways to learn PhotoScore is to start simple. If you throw dense scores at PhotoScore at first, you might have too many errors to deal with from translation errors to really learn the program. I'd recommend that you start small, and as you get more comfortable, starting upping the ante!

PhotoScore Ultimate

PhotoScore Ultimate is a pretty substantial upgrade from Lite. Many people ask me whether it's worth it, and I think I have some guidance. First, Ultimate advertises that it now does handwritten music, which is true, but you have to print your music to their "style" guide, so it's not truly handwritten. Now, this is not a knock on the software, as some people actually *do* write music close to their guidelines. This is the first version to do anything besides professionally printed music, so it's clearly an achievement for Neuratron.

So, who is PhotoScore Ultimate right for? Anyone who scans more than one piece of music a month or anyone who deals with lyrics and text on a regular basis. If you scan often, the extra features in Ultimate pay for themselves very quickly. If you scan in clefs other than treble or bass, you'll need Ultimate! Also remember that Lite stops reading note values at sixteenth notes. So any value of notes or rests faster than a sixteenth note will not be read. Lite is absolutely meant to get you started with scanning, but if you scan often, you'll want PhotoScore Ultimate.

Getting Started with Arrange

Why put the Arrange feature in a chapter on scanning? I think they fit together quite well! Arrange was designed to help students and professionals arrange and orchestrate music. It takes preexisting music and copies it to other staves using a set of rules, which Sibelius refers to as an *Arrange style*. These styles dictate which notes go to which instruments based on criteria such as the speed of passages, and they make sure that range considerations are followed when copying from instrument to instrument. Arrange is not going to make you Rimsky-Korsakov, but when used well, it can provide some really nice results. In addition to the included Arrange styles, you can modify and even create your own. Section 5.1 of the Sibelius 5 reference has a great deal of information on the Arrange feature. I'll show you how to get started using Arrange!

Reduction and Explosion Even though you'll find Explode and Reduce listed as styles in the Notes > Arrange window, Sibelius has released along with Sibelius 5 two new plug-ins that do the job of exploding and reducing better than Arrange, which was first introduced in an older version of Sibelius. You can find these new plug-ins by choosing Plug-in > Composing Tools.

Copy and Paste

To start, we need to get on the same page about how to use Arrange. Arrange is a really clever copy and paste. For Arrange to work, you must have something copied to the Clipboard using Edit > Copy, and then you have to select the destination staves. Arrange does the pasting for you, but it does it with some flair. To help with this, we'll use a score that I've worked on for you —just a wee bit of Mozart piano that we'll arrange for a group of instruments. Let's go step by step.

1. Open Example 14.2 on your CD. You'll see just the two staves of piano music present. Now I'd like you to add some extra instruments—it really doesn't matter what you add, as long as you make sure you have four or more instruments. If you're not feeling creative, just go for a string quartet (two violins, viola, and cello). Do this by selecting Create > Instruments. Figure 14.10 shows the properly formatted score.

2. You need to copy the entire piano part to the Clipboard. To do so, triple-click on the right hand of the piano to select all of the measures. Then hold down the Shift key and press the down arrow, which will extend your selection to the lower stave. You'll now have all the measures of the piano part selected.

3. Copy the music to the Clipboard by choosing Edit > Copy or pressing Ctrl/Command+C. Note that you get no feedback from Sibelius as to whether you've copied the music correctly, and no feedback as to when there is music on the Clipboard.

4. You now need to select the destination staves where you want Arrange to place your music. Select the first measure of your first instrument and hold down Shift while hitting the down arrow to extend your selection to grab as many staves as you need. When they are highlighted (and you don't need to grab anything more than the first measure), go to Notes > Arrange, which brings up the Arrange Styles window shown in Figure 14.11.

5. Select Standard Arrangement, which is a good pre-built Arrange style that will work well. Click OK, and let Sibelius do its thing. Figure 14.12 shows you the final result.

Now, take a look at the piece, and you'll see that Sibelius spread all the notes out across the ranges of each instrument properly. For down and dirty work, you can't get better than this! Now that you know a bit about how Arrange works, go ahead and try the different styles. You'll

Figure 14.10 Score waiting to be arranged.

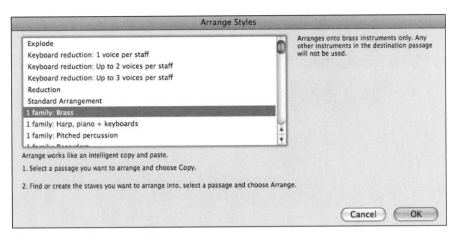

Figure 14.11 Arrange styles.

see that Sibelius ships with a good number of styles to get you started, across a wide variety of genres, groups, and textures Some of the basic ones are Explode and Reduce, which work well for a wide variety of things, as does the Standard Arrangement that we used before.

It's possible that the Arrange style you choose won't work because of the number of instruments you have selected. If this happens, Sibelius will give you an error, and you can select another style that is more suitable to the size of your arrangement.

Editing an Arrange Style

You can also edit the preexisting Arrange styles or create your own. In this section, you'll learn how to edit the Standard Arrangement style. We're going to change this one is because it allows a maximum of two voices on each stave, and for most instruments, we will want only one. Thankfully, this is an easy change. To edit the Arrange styles, go to Notes > Edit Arrange Styles, which will bring up what's shown in Figure 14.13.

Navigate to Standard Arrangement and click the New button on the lower left of the window. Sibelius will ask you, "Do you want the new style to be based on the currently selected style?" Say yes. Doing so will bring up what you see in Figure 14.14.

This window shows not only the name and description of the style, but also the groupings of instruments. From this window, you can control the groupings of instruments and their ranges, and you can instruct Arrange how it should do its magic. In this Arrange style, there is only one group of instruments. If you highlight Group 1 in the lower pane and click the Edit button, you'll be taken to the screen shown in Figure 14.15, which is a familiar window. (It looks like the Add/ Remove Instruments screen.)

Figure 14.12   After Arrange.

The instruments assigned to this group are listed on the right side of the window, while the available instruments are shown to the left using Sibelius's standard grouping of ensemble and family classifications. For what we're doing, you don't need to change anything, but you will come back to this window if you want to create a custom Arrange style.

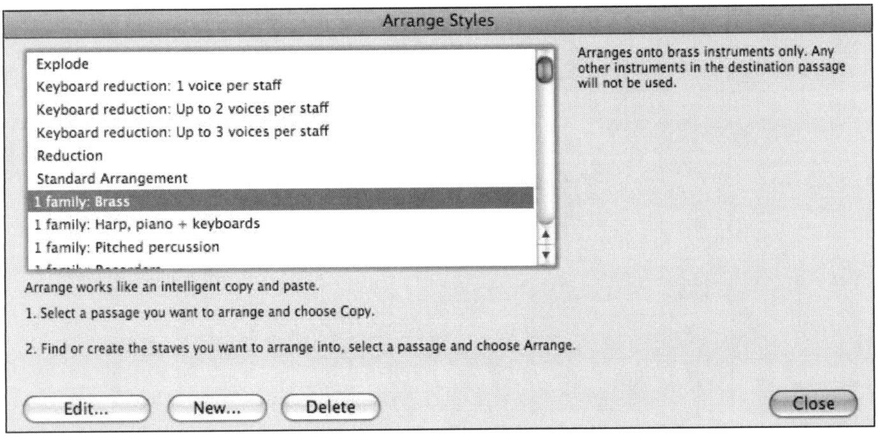

Figure 14.13 Edit Arrange styles.

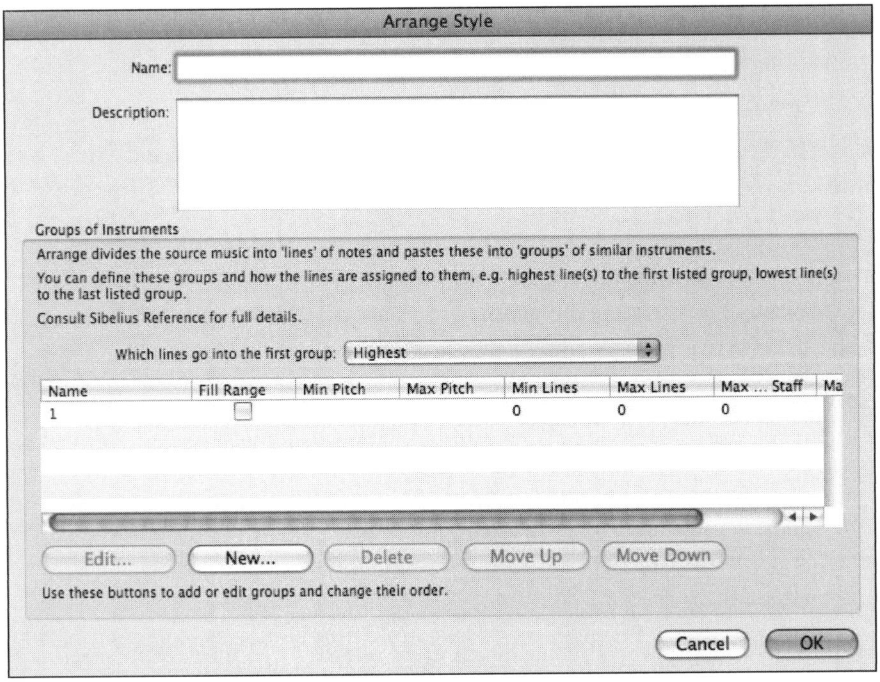

Figure 14.14 Deeper editing of Arrange styles.

To leave that window, click Cancel. You'll be taken back to the Edit Arrange Styles window, which has a bunch of controls and parameters you'll want to know about (refer to Figure 14.14).

- **Name.** Here you can name your instrument group.

- **Fill Range.** This is useful when you have a preset range of notes and you'd like Sibelius to arrange those notes for the given group. The range is set by the next two controls for Min Pitch and Max Pitch.

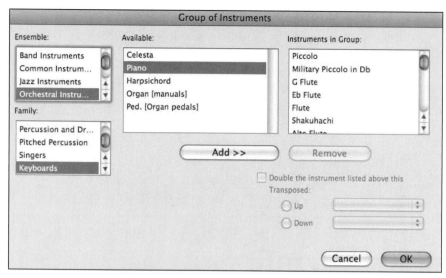

Figure 14.15 Group of instruments.

- **Min Pitch + Max Pitch.** These are only used when you're defining a range used with the Fill Range control listed above. They set the minimum and maximum pitch of the given group, respectively.

- **Min Lines.** This sets the minimum number of notes that the given group will play at any given point. Setting it to zero ensures that the group gets a break and doesn't have to play all the time. Most of the time, Arrange styles have this left at zero.

- **Max Lines.** This sets the maximum number of lines that can be played by any group. If you set it blank, it means that *any* number of lines can be played. Why would you want to set a number? If you specifically wanted doubling or another texture.

- **Max Lines per Staff.** When arranging, this is the greatest number of lines Sibelius is allowed to place on any given stave within the group. (Sibelius won't put multiple lines on a stave unless it has no other choice.)

- **Max Voices per Staff.** When arranging, this is the greatest number of voices that Sibelius is allowed to place on a single staff (even though it will only add a second voice when it absolutely has to).

In the given Arrange style, we're going to change the value of Max Voices per Staff from two to one. Right now, if it runs out of room, Sibelius will add a second voice to some staves, and for most arrangements, which are just groupings of solo instruments together, we want them to have only one voice each. When that's finished, change the name of the style to Standard Arrangements: One Voice so you can keep track of what's going on in your Arrange Styles list. Then, go ahead and run that style on some other music that you want to arrange, and look at how it arranges your music.

Really Getting into It If you're really interested in making your own Arrange styles and learning how to edit them, you'll want to study the included styles and look at Section 5.1 in the reference manual, paying close attention to the controls for "which lines go into the first group" so you understand how Sibelius will sort the groupings that you create based on either pitch or speed/texture.

Some Points about Arrange

Here are some valuable tips about Arrange and how to get the most out of it:

- When you're dealing with long sections of music, you might be told by Arrange, "We recommend that you arrange no more than a few bars at a time." It's a nice precaution, but one you can almost always ignore—Arrange can be undone with Edit > Undo.

- Arrange works slightly better when you have a similar number of voices in each staff. This may mean going through your music and changing the voicing of certain notes (especially in piano music).

- Arrange ignores the 8vs and 8vb lines, so if you have them in your source music, you should take them out and transpose the relevant sections.

- Arrange will copy all objects associated with your score. This is good in the case of dynamics and not so good when it comes to pedal markings and other instrument-specific notations.

- Arrange tries to keep music in the acceptable ranges, but it's not perfect. Make sure you have View > Note Colors > Notes out of Range turned on as a precaution, especially if you're not intimately familiar with ranges.

Arrange can be a great way to experiment with instruments and groups you've never worked with before. If you're learning about arranging, you can learn a ton from the pre-built styles. If you often work to a system when you arrange, you may find that investment in a custom Arrange style will pay off in spades.

15 Worksheets and the Worksheet Creator

Essential Tips for Chapter 15

The Essential Tips for this chapter were provided by Mary Elizabeth, the planner and designer for all the international content of the Worksheet Creator. (She researched, organized, and created or supplied content for more than 98 percent of the included worksheets!)

1. Because the worksheets were planned and designed based on five countries' music curricula—USA, UK, Australia, Canada, and New Zealand—you might find some material that is new to you. This is an opportunity to see different approaches and repertoires and incorporate them as appropriate into your own instruction. It is not meant to be complete, but it is a useful sampling.

2. If you want to make your own worksheets, check out the templates. These boilerplate scores allow you to add your own material quickly and easily. For Orff, Kodály, and Dalcroze instruction, there is a Stick Notation template, which can be combined with notehead type 25 to make it easy to prepare suitable scores. You can also take an existing worksheet and change the contents.

3. There are hidden goodies in the Worksheet Creator. The Posters section not only has the Circle of Fifths and other basic music elements suitable for wall display, but dozens of instrumental graphics that you can reuse on worksheets of your own creation. You can use the repertoire not only for performance, but also for score analysis, listening exercises, and so on.

4. Sometimes it's easier to find a score by going into File > Edit Worksheets than by going into File > Worksheet Creator.

5. If you make frequent use of worksheets, consider using File > Edit Worksheets to create new folders that suit your needs. You can do something as simple as create a My Scores folder and move it to the top of the list, or you can create a folder for each of your classes or even individual students. Any additions

you make to the folder hierarchy will appear when you go to File > Worksheet Creator.

6. If you like a particular worksheet, you'll want to save it as a Sibelis score; otherwise, you'll have to go through the worksheet search each time, which takes time.

7. The worksheets are expertly formatted; if nothing else, you can learn a thing or two about formatting a score by looking at one of the templates provided. (Before Sibelius 4, worksheets and their formatting remained one of the most difficult tasks for educators.)

What Is the Worksheet Creator?

The Worksheet Creator function was built into Sibelius 4, and it made Sibelius the first notation program to come with educational content. Simply put, Sibelius contains more than 1,700 different premade worksheets, assignments, songs, posters, and materials meant to enhance your teaching. There is a wealth of information contained within the Worksheet Creator that you might not know even exists! In addition to the premade materials, there are templates, which are preformatted worksheets that you can adapt to your individual teaching.

It's All Sibelius The best part about the Worksheet Creator is that each and every worksheet is simply a Sibelius file. This means that if you want to change any part of the worksheet and adapt it for yourself, you're free to do so and edit it just like any other Sibelius document.

To access the Worksheet Creator, go to the File > Worksheet Creator, which brings you to the Worksheet Creator dialog box shown in Figure 15.1.

From this dialog box, you can choose from more than 1,700 teaching and learning materials or explore the templates. Let's choose the 1,700+ teaching and learning materials. On the right side of the screen is a group of options under Add to Worksheet—information that will be added automatically to the student and answer sheets. You can check these off however you want. Then click the Next button (at the lower-right), which brings you to the second page of the Worksheet Creator dialog box, as shown in Figure 15.2. Here, you can start to zero in on the type of material, since there are so many worksheets. (The first time you use the Worksheet Creator, it takes a long time to search. Subsequent launches will be shorter.)

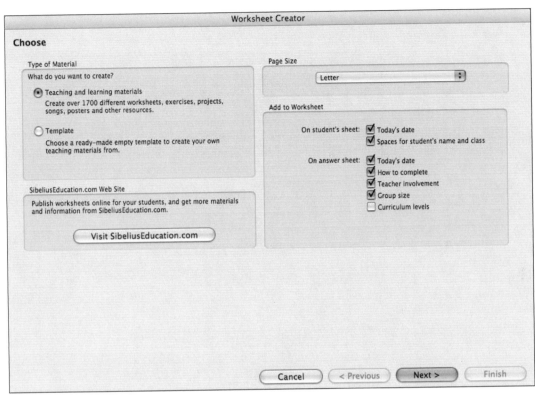

Figure 15.1   The Worksheet Creator dialog box.

This page of the dialog box allows you to narrow down the search through the worksheet database. In the Type of Material section, there are two main options:

- **Size of Group.** You can choose Any to see the full list, or you can limit the choices to individuals, small groups, or groups of any size.

- **How to Use.** You can choose Any to see the full list, or you can specify whether the worksheet should be completed on paper, at the computer, or by performing.

Additionally, if you've used the Worksheet Creator before, you can search for a specific worksheet by name in the Or Specific Worksheet section.

Size=Time Realize that as you search through the database of worksheets, Sibelius will take a bit of time when looking if you choose the Any option in your search criteria. The more help you give Sibelius (by limiting the search criteria) to help you find material, the faster it will load. With that said, if you want to see and explore all the worksheets, you'll need to select Any for both parts.

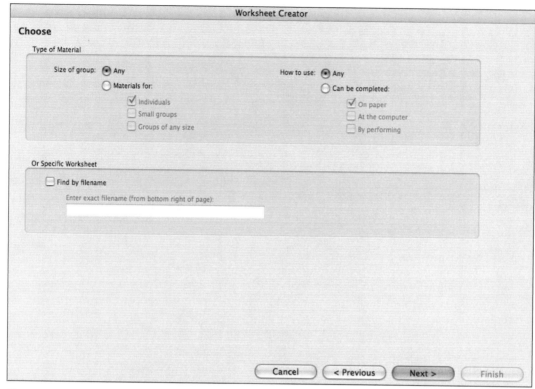

Figure 15.2 Choose the type of worksheet.

For now, we'll search for Any under both options in the Type of Material section to show the full list of worksheets. Doing so will bring up a progress bar (see Figure 15.3) as Sibelius searches through the available worksheets. Depending on the speed of your machine, you might have to wait a few moments.

When that's finished, you'll be taken to the next page in the Worksheet Creator, shown in Figure 15.4, which displays the results of your search and shows you how the material is organized.

How Is the Material Organized?

The Worksheet Creator is organized into the following six categories:

- **Elements of Music.** This includes music theory, musicianship, sight reading, and rhythmic training.

- **Writing and Creating Music.** This includes activities for creating, transposing, arranging, and improvising music.

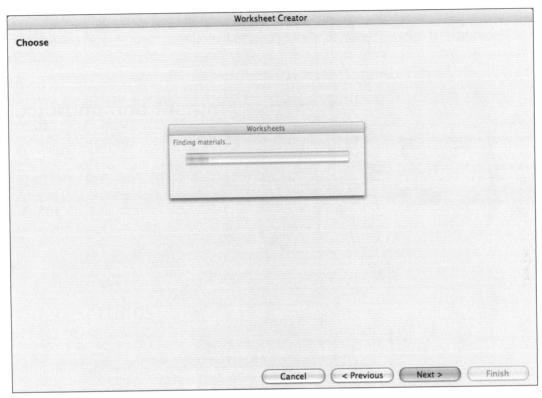

Figure 15.3 Search progress.

- **Selected Repertoire.** This contains more than 400 works for a wide variety of instruments, songs in multiple languages, more than 50 Bach works, and even poems for students to set to music.

- **Reference.** This is a complete reference library, complete with scales and modes, instrumental ranges, a full chord library, and a listing of U.S. and British music terms compared.

- **Posters, Flashcards & Games.** This contains more than 200 posters, flashcards, and games for teaching music to younger students.

- **UK KS3 and GCSE Projects.** This contains UK-specific programs for composition, listening, and composing based on national standards particular to the United Kingdom.

At this point, you'll want to pick one of the six elements into which you can dive a little deeper.

Number of Elements The number of worksheets contained in any one area can be found in the title of the six worksheet categories; it is always shown in parentheses. For example, if you view all of the Elements of Music category, you'll be able to view

465 different worksheets. As you limit your material in further searches, you'll always see the number of relevant results in a listing next to the category name (for example, 210/465).

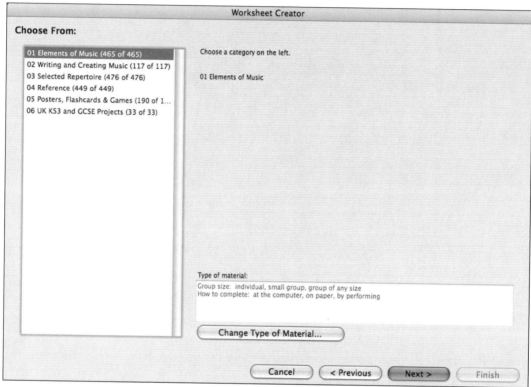

Figure 15.4 Search results.

Before you dive deeper, there's one last screen element I should let you know about—the Change Type of Material button. This button is found at the bottom of your screen and allows you to change your selections at any point. Figure 15.5 shows you what happens when you click the Change Type of Material button.

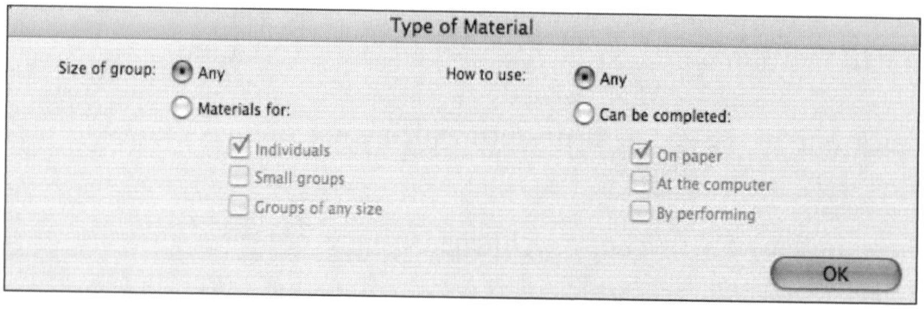

Figure 15.5 Changing the type of material.

This familiar dialog box lets you change the search parameters for your worksheet search. If you make a change here, when you come back to the Worksheet Creator dialog box, you'll have a different number of available choices. This effectively limits your search terms.

Of course you'll want to explore worksheets on your own, but for now we should look at one category and explore it in the text. Let's look at the Elements of Music section. I'll highlight that category in the list and click Next, which takes me to the Worksheet Creator page shown in Figure 15.6.

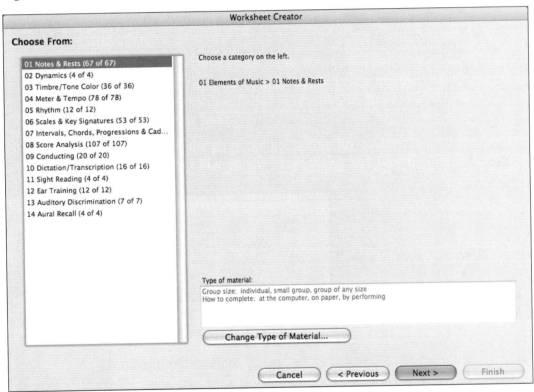

Figure 15.6 Elements of Music choices.

Now I'm one level deeper and I need to choose from one of the subcategories listed in Figure 15.6. Notice that each subcategory shows the number of worksheets it contains. I'm going to look at the Scales & Key Signatures subcategory, so I'll click on that and click Next to take me to the screen shown in Figure 15.7.

Changing the Type of Material Notice that you can always change the type of material via the button of the same name on the Worksheet Creator interface. This way, you can always find the correct worksheets for you.

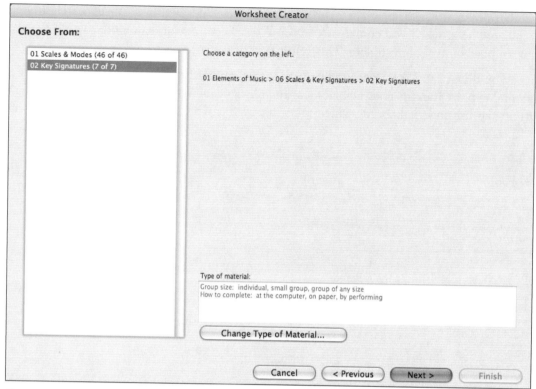

Figure 15.7 The Scales & Key Signatures subcategory.

Once again, I get another list of choices! You can see how much organization and material went into these worksheets. I'm going to choose Key Signatures, which takes me to the screen shown in Figure 15.8.

I have to choose another subcategory—this time the options are Naming Tonics for Key Signatures or Complete Circle of Fifths. I'm going to choose Complete Circle of Fifths, which is a difficult thing to produce in Sibelius. (I did one for a book of mine years ago, and it was a ton of work; I'd have killed for a pre-made one.) Doing so takes me to yet another level of the Worksheet Creator (see Figure 15.9).

Thankfully, I'm now at the last step—the step where I'll see the available worksheets!

This particular screen gives us much more information than the other ones we've seen thus far—we're looking at individual worksheets now. The right side of the screen lists the following information:

■ **Name.** This is the name of the worksheet, which is really handy if you want to search for an individual worksheet without having to go through all of the sub-steps to get there.

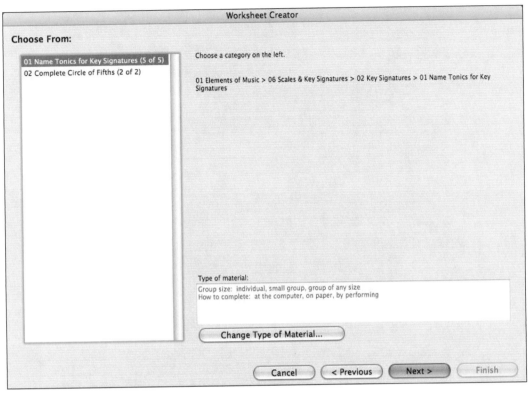

Figure 15.8 More detail: the Key Signatures subcategory.

- **Category.** This is the path you took to find the worksheet. (You might want to make a note of this in case you ever want to edit the worksheet later.)

- **Description.** This provides some more information about the specific worksheet you're looking at.

There are other fields (Size of Group, Can Be Completed, Teacher Involvement, and Curriculum Level) that may be present depending on which worksheet you've selected.

At the bottom of the screen is a very important section, shown in Figure 15.10.

The worksheet I've selected does not support the Number of Questions option, but worksheets that are based on quizzes and exercises will allow you to toggle the number of questions that the worksheet will contain. (Sibelius has a database of questions and will pick from that pool at random to create the questions.) You can choose to include a box of possible answers and create an answer sheet too (an option that is switched on by default).

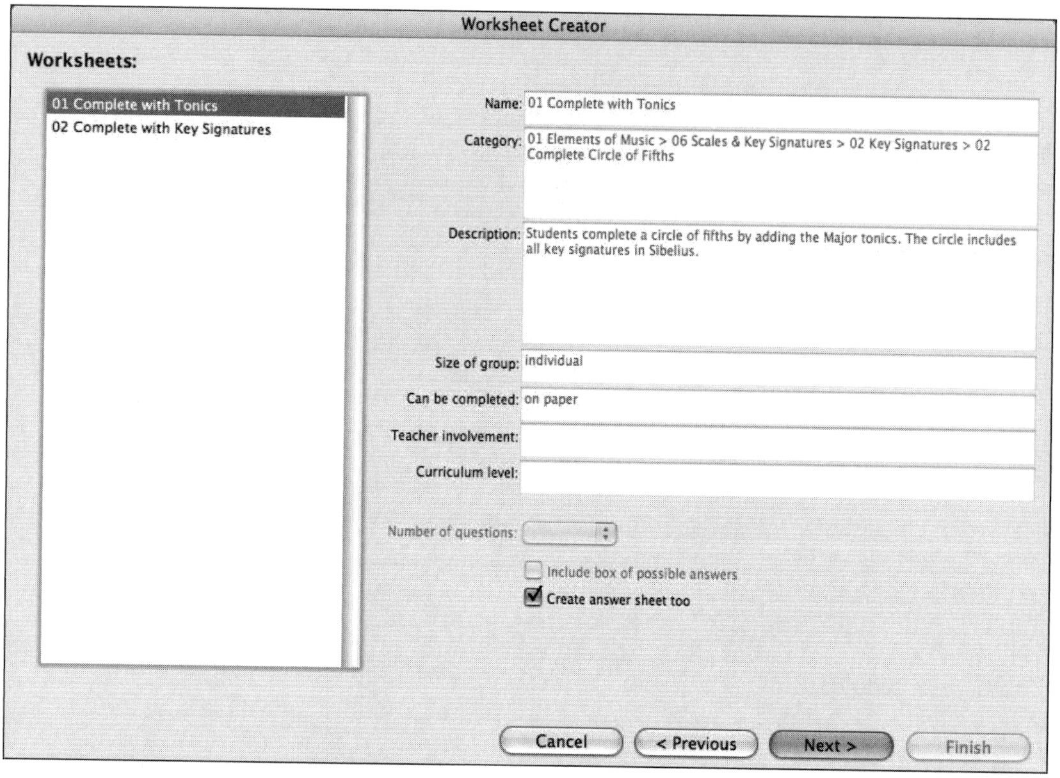

Worksheet Creator
Worksheets:
01 Complete with Tonics
02 Complete with Key Signatures
Name: 01 Complete with Tonics
Category: 01 Elements of Music > 06 Scales & Key Signatures > 02 Key Signatures > 02 Complete Circle of Fifths
Description: Students complete a circle of fifths by adding the Major tonics. The circle includes all key signatures in Sibelius.
Size of group: individual
Can be completed: on paper
Teacher involvement:
Curriculum level:
Number of questions:
Include box of possible answers
Create answer sheet too
Cancel
< Previous
Next >
Finish

Figure 15.9 Choose your worksheet.

Number of questions:
Include box of possible answers
Create answer sheet too

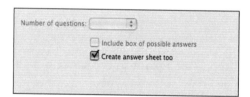

Figure 15.10 Worksheet data.

Answers and Questions When you open a worksheet that contains both answers and questions, Sibelius will create two worksheets for you, one on top of the other. Make sure to go to the Window menu to see both open scores and switch between the answer and student sheets.

Getting back to the worksheets at hand; there are two to choose from. I'll choose Complete with Tonics, a worksheet in which the students will see all the key signatures and have to name them. Clicking the Next button will bring you to a preview, showing both the student sheet and the answer sheet (see Figure 15.11).

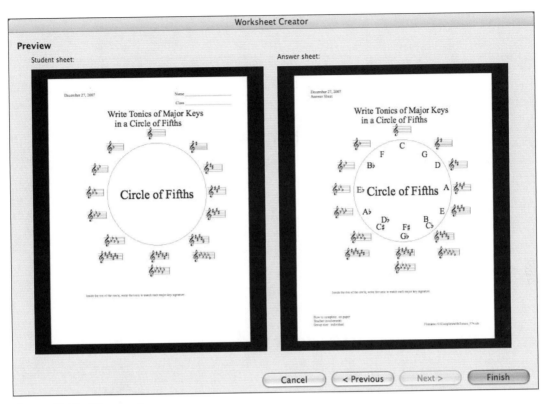

Figure 15.11   The preview.

Last Chance to Back Up   The preview screen is your last chance to back up and change your worksheet search. Once you click Finish and create your score, you'll have to go through the *entire* Worksheet Creator again to change your worksheet search.

If everything looks good, you'll be taken to Sibelius, where the worksheets have been created for you in Sibelius format. Figure 15.12 shows you what Sibelius creates for you.

Sibelius has created two scores for you—the answer sheet and the student sheet. The answer sheet is sitting on top of the student sheet, so you're only seeing the answers. (This is also indicated by the words "Answer Sheet" on the score itself.) Go to the Window menu, and you'll see all of your open scores at the bottom of the menu (see Figure 15.13). There, you can toggle between the answer sheet and the student sheet. (The student sheet doesn't contain the answers, of course.) Now you can print, save, and distribute these Sibelius documents. Feel free to modify them as you see fit—that's the beauty of the Worksheet Creator!

At this point you've created your first worksheet. I selected the Circle of Fifths because it's a commonly used sheet in music classes, and it's very tough to make one by yourself. Remember,

Figure 15.12   A created worksheet.

this is only one of more than 1,700 worksheets, so you owe it to yourself to explore the worksheets and see what's available.

Save If you like the worksheet you find/create, make sure to save it in your normal score folder so you can retrieve it quickly. Otherwise, you'll have to go through the entire Worksheet Creator again to find it.

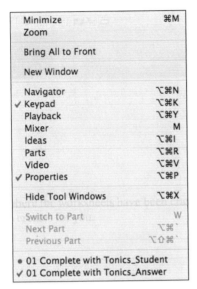

Figure 15.13   Open scores.

How Are Templates Different?

Another area of the Worksheet Creator consists of the templates. The templates are different from the worksheets in that they hold no pre-made musical material. There is simply a list of predefined and preformatted templates for you to work with and add your own musical material to. Figures 15.14 and 15.15 show all of the templates available in the Worksheet Creator:

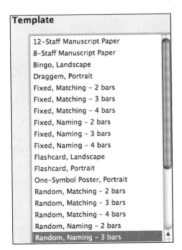

Figure 15.14   Templates.

All of the templates are preformatted and ready for you to add music into and save. Figure 15.16 shows an example of the Worksheet, Numbered template.

Figure 15.15   More templates.

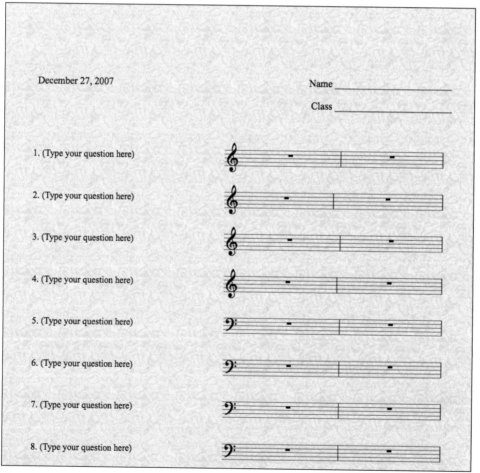

Figure 15.16   The Worksheet, Numbered template.

This particular template is perfect for the following purposes:

- Changing the text to reflect test/quiz/handout headings.

- Changing the clefs of the examples to suit your exercises. (Remember to hide the cautionary!)

- Adding the appropriate music.

As you can see, the templates take the hardest part of the worksheet process (formatting) and quickly let you build up your own personal library of examples and worksheets.

Save Templates You can always save the templates, too. If you make a template that you'll keep coming back to, you can save it and even add it to the list of templates! (See the following section.)

Can I Add My Own Worksheets?

Yes, you can add your own worksheets! If you create a worksheet with a template or otherwise modify a preexisting worksheet, you can add it into the main Worksheet library so it can be searched and easily retrieved. To do so, simply create your score/worksheet as you see fit and go to File > Add to Worksheet Creator, which brings you to the Add to Worksheet Creator dialog box shown in Figure 15.17.

From this dialog box, you can choose how your worksheet will be displayed in the Creator search, along with its name, description, instructions, and other relevant information. Most importantly, you can choose in which category your worksheet will appear.

Reference If your score will be a test/quiz type of worksheet, you should check out Section 5.22 in the Sibelius Reference (Help > Reference) for instructions on how to set up your score for an answer sheet and format it to randomly pick questions.

Once you've added to the Worksheet Creator, you'll want to know how to edit the content in it.

How Do I Edit Worksheets?

You can edit worksheets either by changing/removing existing worksheets or by adding other categories not present in the default Worksheet Creator. To do this, go to File > Edit Worksheets, which brings up the Edit Worksheets dialog box shown in Figure 15.18.

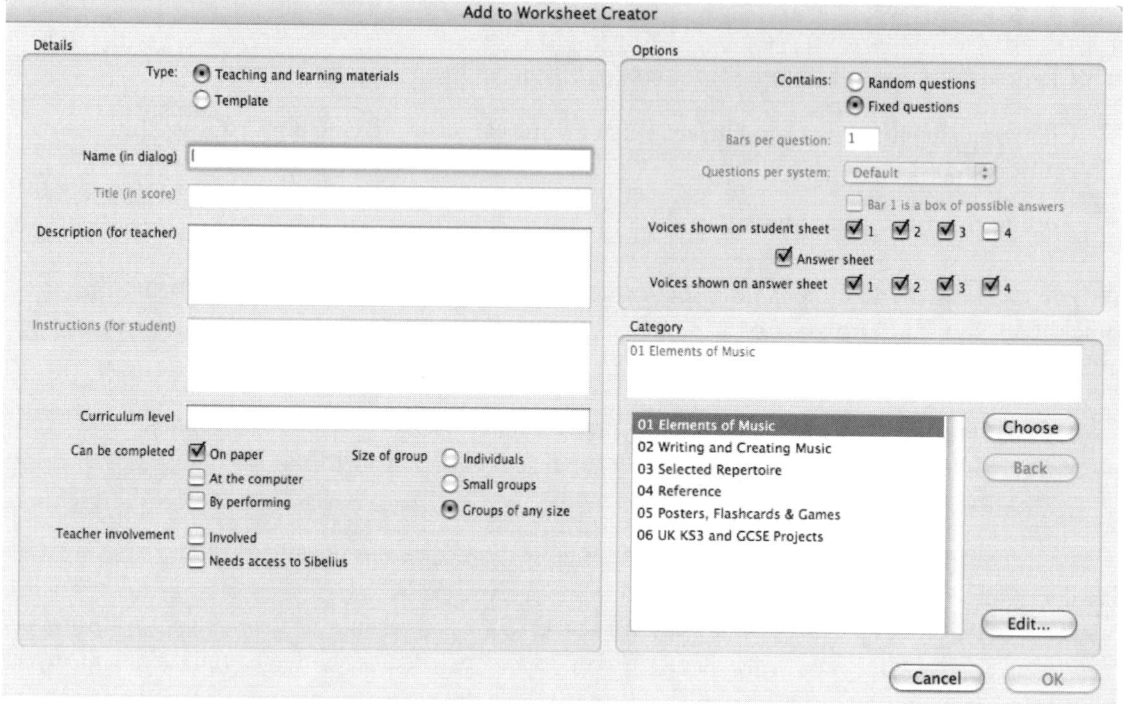

Figure 15.17　The Add to Worksheet Creator dialog box.

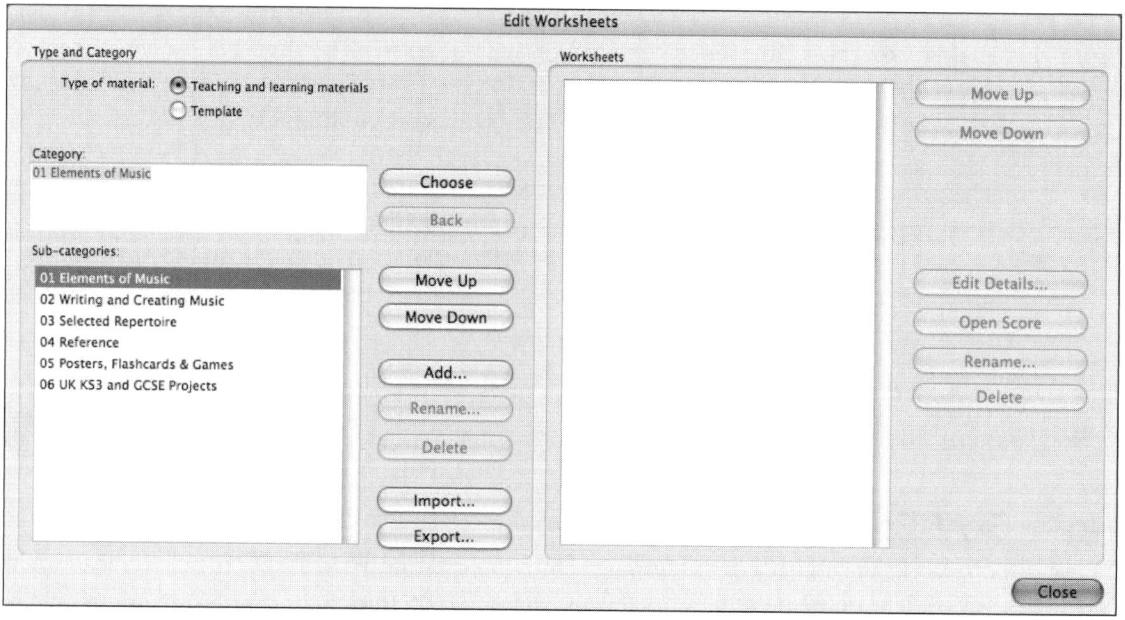

Figure 15.18　The Edit Worksheets dialog box.

As you can see from Figure 15.18, you can add or remove any of the categories (of the built-in six), change their order, rename them, and import/export them. Importing and exporting is important because you can share your own personal worksheets from this window. In the next section, I'll show you how to grab worksheets from the Internet, and you'll need to import them through this dialog box.

Share The only place you can share your worksheets through the Worksheet Creator by importing/exporting is through the Edit Worksheets dialog box.

From this dialog box, you can quickly look inside the subcategories that make up each individual section and do the following:

- Edit the details of any preexisting worksheet.

- Open the score to edit it and make changes. Once you close the score and save your changes, they will be reflected automatically in the Worksheet Creator.

- Rename any worksheet.

- Delete any worksheet.

If you're using the Worksheet Creator frequently, you'll definitely find yourself inside this dialog box often.

Pro Tip You can access all the scores in the Worksheet Creator by choosing File > Edit Worksheets. The benefit is that you don't have to wait for Sibelius to search! I often use File > Edit Worksheets to explore the content of the Worksheet Creator because it's faster for me.

Where Can I Go to Find More?

If the 1,700 built-in worksheets aren't enough for you, you'll be pleased to find out that Sibelius has set up a community at www.sibeliuseducation.com. This website is a repository for teaching and learning materials and contains a wealth of information, including additional worksheets that you can download and import into the Worksheet Creator. (Remember, to import worksheets into the Worksheet Creator, you must go to File > Edit Worksheets.)

The www.sibeliuseducation.com site contains the following content:

- Free worksheets created by professional musicians, pedagogues, and educators

- Links to curricula and curricular development

- Additional free videos for the Score-to-Video feature in Sibelius

- An online forum for users to discuss relevant educational issues

Make frequent use of the site—it's a great resource that grows every day. To help it grow, you'll want to share your own worksheets! Another Sibelius website, www.sibeliusmusic.com, may also contain music that you can download for free and use in your teaching as well. Check it out!

Sharing Worksheets

Sharing your worksheets is really easy in Sibelius. Follow these simple steps:

1. Create your worksheet and save it to disk.

2. Go to File > Publish on Sibeliuseducation.com.

3. When your web browser loads, either sign in or create your account.

4. Go to the My Work section of the site and follow the directions for uploading your worksheets.

The more you share, the more the community grows, so become active!

More Worksheets For more worksheets from Mary Elizabeth, check out http://stores.lulu. com/patternsforlearning.

---

16 Using Plug-Ins

Essential Tips for Chapter 16

1. The term "plug-in" is thrown around the computer world often—even in Sibelius, it has two meanings. For this chapter we are talking about the plug-ins accessible through the Plug-Ins pull-down menu.

2. A plug-in is anything that does an automated task for you in Sibelius. Think of plug-ins as helpers—things that make your life easier.

3. There's no way we're going through all the included plug-ins. They are covered in detail in the Help > Reference PDF included with Sibelius. I'll highlight a selection of cool plug-ins that will make your life easier.

4. There will be a CD example for each plug-in so you can run it immediately to see how it works.

5. If you don't like what a plug-in did, you can undo it in Sibelius 5. (This is something you couldn't do in earlier versions of Sibelius.)

6. Plug-ins can finally affect tuplets or selections that contain tuplets!

7. If you use a plug-in often, you can assign it to a key command/shortcut.

8. You can request new plug-ins! There is a vibrant community of plug-in developers who love to help out others.

9. There are many extra plug-ins online that you can download and use for free.

10. If you have programming chops and experience with general computer programming, you can even learn how to make your own plug-ins.

What Is a Plug-In?

The term "plug-in" has been around since the early 1980s. A plug-in is something that you can use to enhance a software program in some way. What's a bit confusing is that plug-ins have taken on different meanings in different contexts (even within Sibelius). Here is an example:

- Sometimes a plug-in can produce a sound. A virtual instrument is a plug-in that produces sounds based on MIDI input. The KONTAKT PLAYER 2 you learned about in Chapter 12 is a virtual instrument plug-in.

- Sometimes a plug-in can produce an effect on an audio signal. An example of an effects plug-in is a reverb or a delay. You also learned about these in Chapter 12, when you dealt with insert effects.

- Sometimes a plug-in does some sort of automated task in Sibelius. For example, there are plug-ins that will name all of the notes in your score and add text below them. There are plug-ins that will look for parallel fifths and octaves in your voice leading. Plug-ins can name your chord voicings. There's a plug-in for almost anything in Sibelius. These plug-ins are found in the Plug-Ins pull-down menu.

While each definition of plug-in is valid, for the purposes of this chapter, a plug-in is an automated task within Sibelius. Plug-ins are designed to make your life easier!

When Should I Use a Plug-In?

When should you use a plug-in? When shouldn't you?! There are so many plug-ins available on a wide variety of topics that it's difficult to imagine a score or other project in Sibelius that wouldn't be enhanced by using a plug-in. Plug-ins also save you some energy and time. They are great for doing a single action automatically and applying it to the whole score. Plug-ins also have an amazing way of making Sibelius do things you didn't think it could do.

Undo A major new feature in Sibelius 5 is that you can undo plug-ins by choosing Edit > Undo (or by using Ctrl/Command+Z or the toolbar icon). In earlier versions of Sibelius that was not the case, and you had to save a copy of each score before you ran the plug-in.

In each of the forthcoming examples, I'll show you when you should use the particular plug-in and how it can enhance your workflow in general!

Some Included Plug-Ins

We're going to look at 10 plug-ins that are included in the Sibelius 5.2 package. The plug-ins described here are only 10 out of a total of 115 included with Sibelius, so you'll definitely want to check out the reference (Section 5.11) for descriptions of all the included plug-ins.

Alternatively, since plug-ins are undoable, why not just check out the Plug-Ins pull-down menu and try some out yourself? With Undo, you can't hurt a thing!

Selection-Based Like so many other things in Sibelius, plug-ins (usually) require you to pre-select some music for the plug-in to work. There are some plug-ins that don't require any selected music (these plug-ins typically work on a full score), but nonetheless, you'll get a warning from the plug-in about whether you'd like the operation to apply to the entire score.

The Plug-Ins pull-down menu is organized into subcategories. Here's how they are organized (along with brief descriptions of what each category does):

- **Accidentals.** These plug-ins deal with the addition or removal of accidentals within a selection.

- **Analysis.** These plug-ins deal with analysis of musical material within a selection.

- **Batch Processing.** These plug-ins apply an operation to an entire folder of scores at once.

- **Chord Symbols.** These plug-ins deal with adding or changing chord symbols within a score.

- **Composing Tools.** These plug-ins deal with tools to help you compose music.

- **Notes and Rests.** These plug-ins deal with operations to notes and rests (such as splitting rests, rewriting note values, and so on).

- **Other.** These plug-ins don't fall into an easily defined category. You'll find some of the coolest plug-ins in this category.

- **Playback.** These plug-ins deal with manipulating Sibelius's playback in some way.

- **Proof-reading Plug-ins.** These plug-ins check your scores for musical mistakes. (I wish I'd had this when I was a student.)

- **Simplify Notation.** These plug-ins simplify the notation in your score in different ways.

- **Text.** These plug-ins deal with the automatic addition of text (fingerings, note names, rhythmic notation) or the appearance of text (exporting or aligning lyrics, changing dynamics, finding and replacing text).

- **Tuplets.** A special category! This set of plug-ins deals with the complex task of tuplets in Sibelius.

Tuplets Before Sibelius 5, plug-ins were unable to operate on selections that contained tuplets. The new Tuplet subcategory in Sibelius 5 is a welcome addition!

Now it's time to look at the plug-ins we've selected. Grab the CD-ROM that came with your book, because you'll want to try each of these plug-ins out to see what they can do!

Composing Tools: Add Simple Harmony

This plug-in is pretty amazing: It looks at a melody and adds a simple harmony appropriate for the given melody! It will add diatonic harmony for either guitar or piano by adding a new instrument to your piece. This is a great plug-in for teaching very young students to compose and also for doing harmonic analysis. Figure 16.1 shows the plug-in interface.

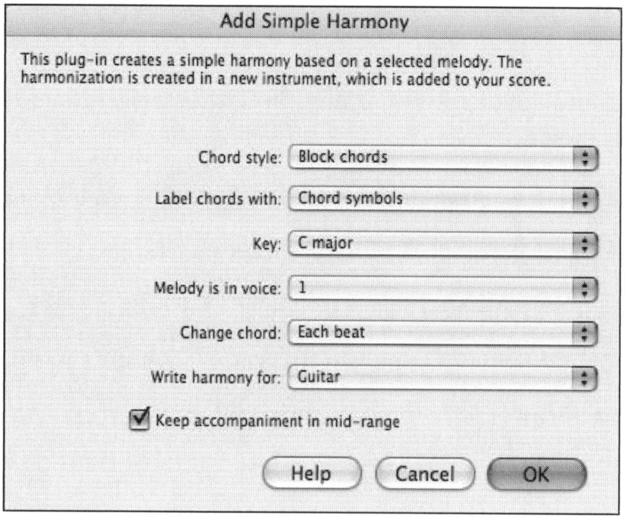

Figure 16.1   Add Simple Harmony plug-in.

CD: Open Example 16.1, which contains a simple melody to which you can add some simple harmony!

To make this work, all you have to do is start with a single-line melody, select those bars, and run the plug-in. When you've done that, the plug-in gives you a few options from which to choose:

- **Chord Style.** This drop-down menu lets you choose how the harmony is presented. You can choose a range of styles from block chords to arpeggiated styles (even Alberti bass).

- **Label Chords With.** After your harmony is created, you can have chord symbols, Roman numeral analysis, or no chord symbols created for you.

- **Key.** This sets the key of the melody to be analyzed and its resulting harmony (major and harmonic minor).

- **Melody Is in Voice.** Selects which voice the plug-in should analyze as your melody.

- **Change Chord.** This sets the frequency of the harmony that Sibelius will add for you. You can set it by beat group, bar, or beat.

- **Write Harmony For.** You can choose the instrument for which the harmony is written. Currently, piano, guitar, and guitar tab are supported.

- **Keep Accompaniment in Mid-Range.** You can keep the accompaniment figures away from the melody.

On your CD, run the plug-in as described in the example instructions. Be aware that the plug-in makes some very intelligent decisions, but it doesn't always make the decisions you might have!

When the plug-in comes across notes outside of the diatonic key, it is able to harmonize those notes as well, using typical common chords from neighboring keys. Melodies with tons of accidentals may have mixed results. You'll have more success when the key signature of the piece matches the key you set within the plug-in.

Composing Tools: Explode/Reduce

This set of two plug-ins is designed to either explode music onto a larger number of staves or reduce the music from a larger number of staves to a smaller number. Both plug-ins are found in the Plug-Ins > Composing Tools subcategory. Let's start with the Explode plug-in.

Single Explode The Explode plug-in only works on single staves. If you want to explode from more staves, you'll want to use Sibelius's Arrange feature.

The Explode plug-in has a couple of clear uses. For one, it can take multi-voiced music on a single stave and extract those parts to new staves (much like the Arrange feature). This is great for taking a divisi part and separating it to individual parts or for quick arrangements of any multi-voiced piano music. Figure 16.2 shows the Explode screen.

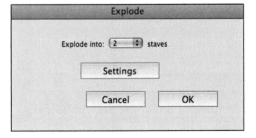

Figure 16.2 Explode.

The first screen you see isn't too impressive—it just wants to know the number of staves onto which you'd like to explode. (The maximum is four.) You can see further settings by clicking the Settings button, as shown in Figure 16.3.

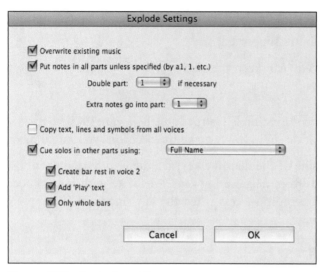

Figure 16.3   Explode settings.

When you've decided on the correct settings, click OK to run the plug-in. You still have one more screen to look at—the Explode Destination screen (see Figure 16.4).

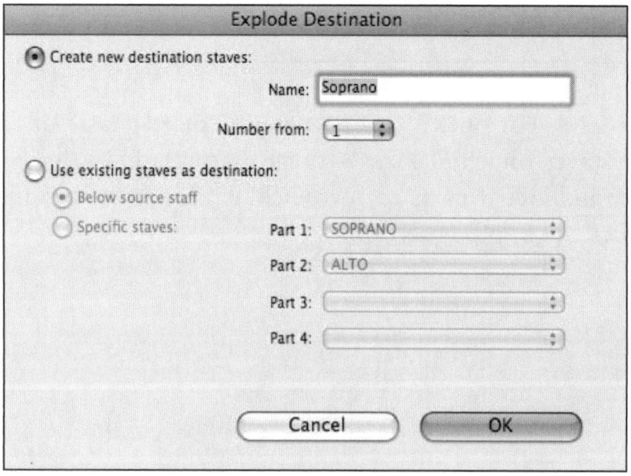

Figure 16.4   Explode Destination.

From this dialog, you can choose whether you want the exploded music created on new staves (and if so, how you'd like those staves named and what their location is) or you'd like to use existing staves.

CD: Example 16.2 is a great model that you can use with the Explode plug-in.

Explode You'd typically use the Explode plug-in to separate a divisi section into multiple staves or to orchestrate some counterpoint.

Now let's look at the Reduce plug-in, which takes music from a larger number of staves and reduces it to a single stave. You'll also find Reduce in Plug-Ins > Composing Tools. Because Reduce works on multiple staves at once, you'll have to select the multiple staves you want to reduce before you run the plug-in. When you've done so, run the plug-in, which brings up Figure 16.5.

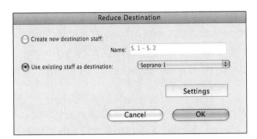

Figure 16.5   Reduce Destination.

You also have a Settings button in this dialog, which is shown in Figure 16.6.

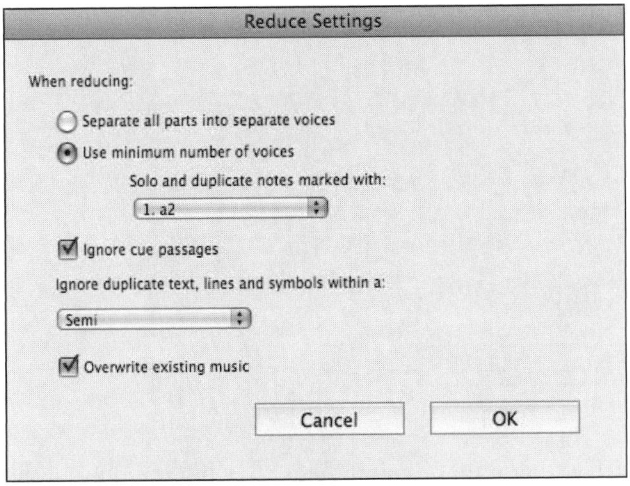

Figure 16.6   Reduce Settings.

Choose your options and run the plug-in to automatically reduce your selected staves to a single stave.

CD: Example 16.3 is a great model (with music) for you to practice using the Reduce plug-in.

Reduce You'd typically use the Reduce plug-in to arrange music for several instruments to a piano reduction or for a simple harmonic analysis.

Composing Tools: Fit Selection to Time

The Fit Selection to Time plug-in from the Composing Tools subcategory is an incredible plug-in for composers who write for film and TV. You used this plug-in extensively in Chapter 13, so you might want to review that chapter if you need a refresher. In short, Fit Selection to Time takes any selection of music and calculates what the tempo needs to be to have the selection fit into an exact time. For example, if you're composing for a commercial and you need your piece to be exactly 60 seconds, you can have the plug-in calculate the overall tempo for the music you already have to make it work.

Because we covered this plug-in in such detail in Chapter 13, I'll refer you to that chapter and the included example on your CD to try it out. Figure 16.7 shows the Fit Selection to Time plug-in dialog.

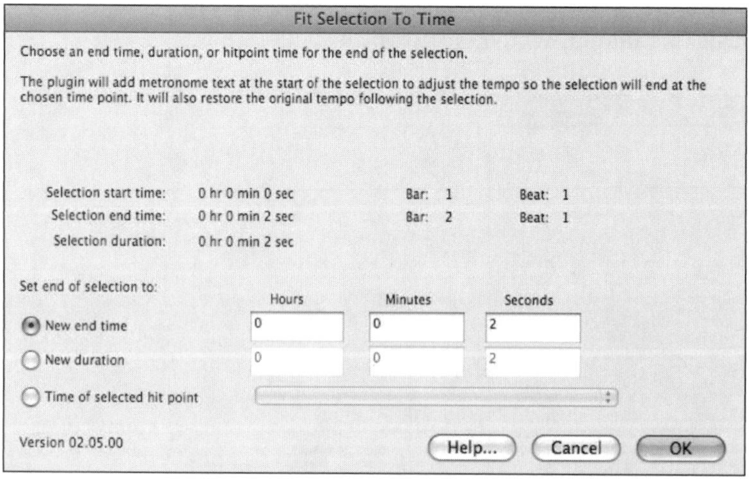

Figure 16.7 Fit Selection to Time.

After you run the plug-in, you're greeted with a dialog that explains exactly what the plug-in did (which is handy). See Figure 16.8.

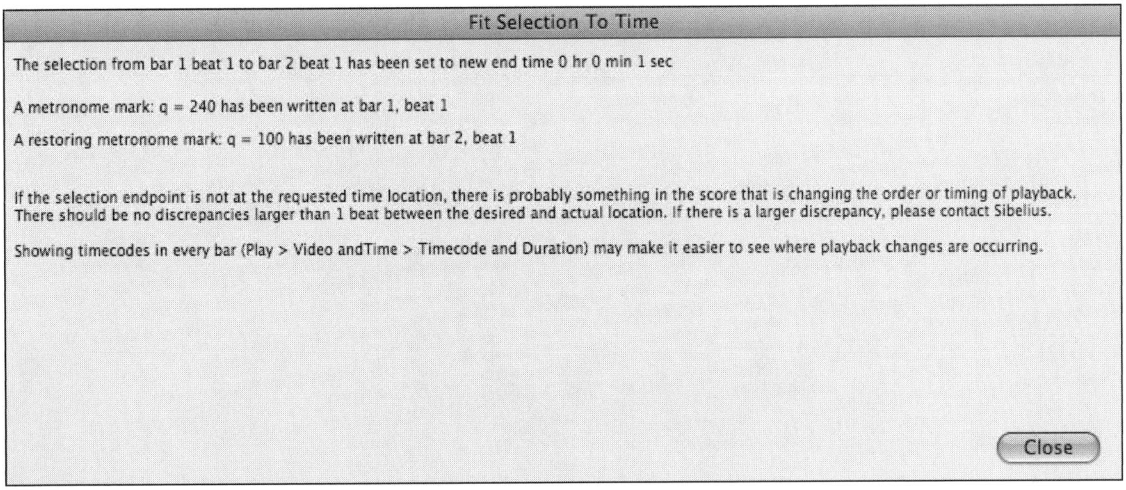

Fit Selection To Time

The selection from bar 1 beat 1 to bar 2 beat 1 has been set to new end time 0 hr 0 min 1 sec

A metronome mark: q = 240 has been written at bar 1, beat 1

A restoring metronome mark: q = 100 has been written at bar 2, beat 1

If the selection endpoint is not at the requested time location, there is probably something in the score that is changing the order or timing of playback. There should be no discrepancies larger than 1 beat between the desired and actual location. If there is a larger discrepancy, please contact Sibelius.

Showing timecodes in every bar (Play > Video andTime > Timecode and Duration) may make it easier to see where playback changes are occurring.

Close

Figure 16.8   Fit Selection to Time results.

CD: Look at Examples 13.3 and 13.4 for examples of Fit Selection to Time.

Notes and Rests: Add Slash Noteheads for Parts

Here's a great plug-in! When you add slash noteheads in jazz improvisation, they are typically on the middle space of your stave to indicate that time is passing for an improvisation. When you use transposing instruments, the parts always make those slash noteheads transpose as well, and you are left with slash marks on the wrong notes in the staves. The Add Slash Noteheads for Parts plug-in very easily corrects this by creating a second voice that is hidden from the score with the slash noteheads on the correct lines. It works extremely well! Figure 16.9 shows the plug-in's dialog.

CD: Example 16.4 has a score that is perfect for learning about when to use the Add Slash Noteheads for Parts plug-in.

If you're writing jazz music, big band music, or any music that has improvised sections delineated by slash marks with transposing instruments, you'll need to run this plug-in—it's really invaluable.

Other: Add Note Names to Noteheads

If you're a music educator, you're going to love this next plug-in: Add Note Names to Note-heads. A picture is worth a thousand words, so look at Figure 16.10.

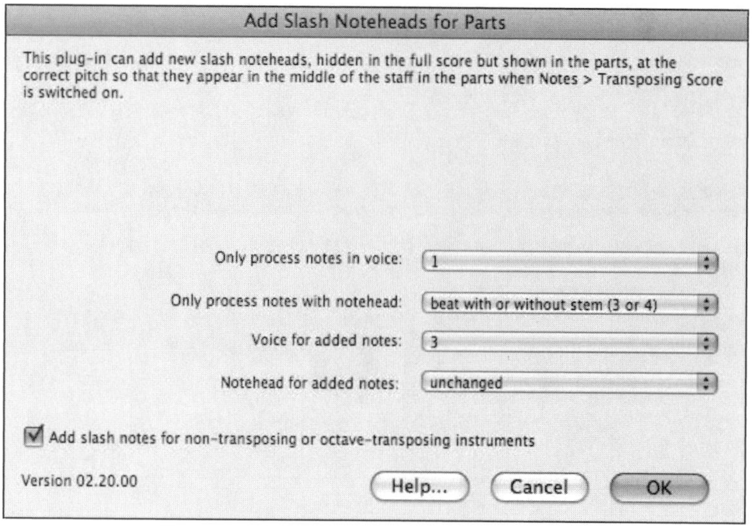

Add Slash Noteheads for Parts

This plug-in can add new slash noteheads, hidden in the full score but shown in the parts, at the correct pitch so that they appear in the middle of the staff in the parts when Notes > Transposing Score is switched on.

Only process notes in voice: 1

Only process notes with notehead: beat with or without stem (3 or 4)

Voice for added notes: 3

Notehead for added notes: unchanged

☑ Add slash notes for non-transposing or octave-transposing instruments

Version 02.20.00   Help...   Cancel   OK

Figure 16.9   Add Slash Noteheads for Parts.

Figure 16.10   Add Note Names to Noteheads.

Because it's difficult to see in a printed book, I've added the names of the notes above the noteheads as well. But in your program, you will see the names in the noteheads. This is an absolutely invaluable tool for teaching students to read music and for early method books. Running the plug-in couldn't be simpler: Select the music to which you want to add the noteheads and go to Plug-Ins > Other > Add Note Names to Noteheads.

CD: Example 16.5 will let you practice using the Add Note Names to Noteheads plug-in.

Size When you run this plug-in, you might notice that the notes are a touch small. In published educational music, it's not uncommon for the notes and the staves themselves to be a bit larger. If you'd like to increase the size of your staff and notes, go to Document Setup from the House Style menu and increase the staff to a suitable size to allow for easy reading of the new noteheads.

Other: Set Metronome Mark

Another simple but infinitely useful plug-in is the Set Metronome Mark plug-in. This lets you set a metronome mark by clicking with your mouse to an exact beat. Sibelius then figures out how fast you clicked and adds the appropriate metronome mark. Figure 16.11 shows the plug-in's dialog.

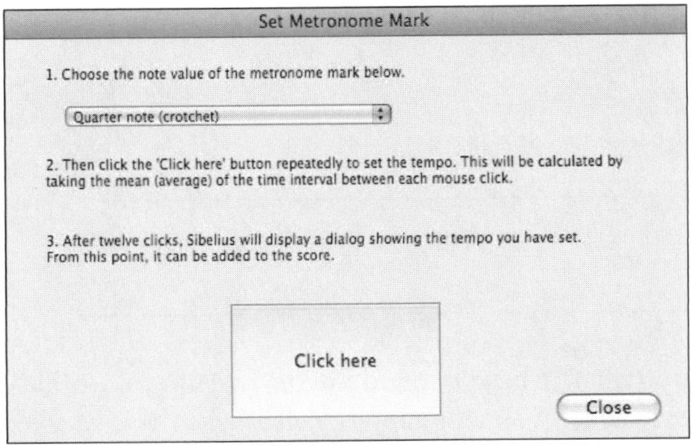

Figure 16.11 Set Metronome Mark.

First, use the drop-down menu to set the note value for the metronome mark. Then, click in the box that says Click Here, and Sibelius will get your exact tempo. (You'll have to click a number of times for Sibelius to get your exact tempo.) This is an invaluable tool for playback when you want the tempo exactly as fast as you tap. After you've tapped your tempo, Sibelius will give you the option to use your exact tempo or the closest rounded tempo mark on a metronome. You can choose either option from the window that appears.

Because this plug-in can apply to any score, I won't put an example file on the CD; just try it on any score.

***

Attachment When you run this plug-in, it will attach the metronome mark to a selected note. If you want this to apply to the whole score, make sure that no notes are pre-selected. Selecting a note will apply the metronome mark from that note onward.

***

Proof-reading: Check for Parallel 5ths/8ves

This is the plug-in that we all wished we had in college—a plug-in that checks for parallel fifths and octaves in a voice leading! The plug-in does what it says: It finds voice leading mistakes and marks them with text, showing you where the error is. It won't fix the errors for you, though—that's just cheating. Figure 16.12 shows the plug-in's dialog.

Check for Parallel 5ths/8ves
Check parallel and hidden 8ves
Check parallel and hidden 5ths
Check selected passage only
Check whole score
Ignore parallels between rests
Cancel
OK

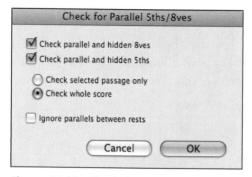

Figure 16.12 Check for Parallels.

CD: Example 16.6 is a four-part voice leading. Use the Check for Parallels plug-in to check for mistakes.

If you're lucky, the plug-in might just report that it hasn't found any errors! If you *do* have errors, it will mark the score with plain text, which you can happily delete when you've fixed the errors.

Simplify Notation: Change Split Point

A *split point* is the point in grand stave music (piano, harpsichord, harp, and others) where the notes get distributed to each staff. When you use Flexi-time or import a MIDI file, you can either choose a fixed split point or let Sibelius choose one for you. This plug-in resets the split point between staves and spreads the notes based on the split point you give. Figure 16.13 shows the plug-in's dialog.

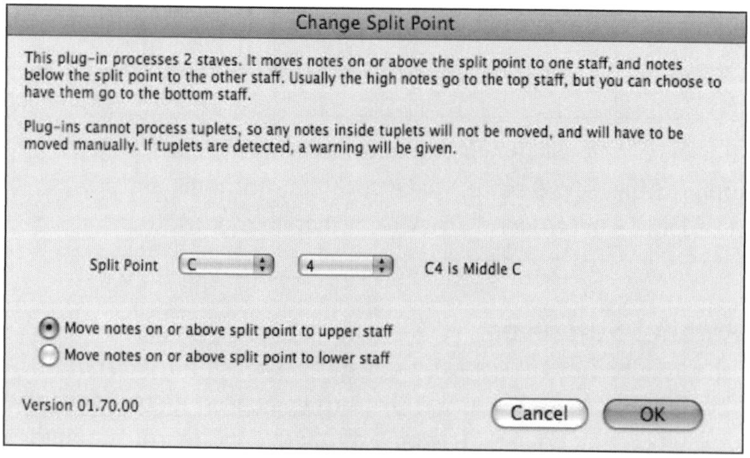

Change Split Point
This plug-in processes 2 staves. It moves notes on or above the split point to one staff, and notes below the split point to the other staff. Usually the high notes go to the top staff, but you can choose to have them go to the bottom staff.
Plug-ins cannot process tuplets, so any notes inside tuplets will not be moved, and will have to be moved manually. If tuplets are detected, a warning will be given.
Split Point
C
4
C4 is Middle C
Move notes on or above split point to upper staff
Move notes on or above split point to lower staff
Version 01.70.00
Cancel
OK

Figure 16.13 Change Split Point.

You Need Two Staves When you use the Change Split Point plug-in, you need to select two staves (no less, no more) to run the plug-in.

You can use this plug-in not only with Flexi-time or imported MIDI files, but any time you want to change the split point between two staves.

Step-Time In Step-time entry, you can't currently record into two staves at once. With the Change Split Point plug-in, you can enter your music into a single stave, and then have the plug-in move the notes below your selected split point to the lower staff!

CD: Example 16.7 has a few examples for you to practice with the Change Split Point plug-in.

Simplify Notation: Renotate Performance

One of the frustrations with Flexi-time or MIDI import is that the settings you choose in the Note Input page for Sibelius's own quantize settings can't be changed after the fact. If you've chosen the wrong minimum duration during Flexi-time, you have to either play it again or fix the notation manually. Along comes the Renotate Performance plug-in, which does just that—it tries to make a selection of music simpler to read by re-quantizing the original data. Figure 16.14 shows some music that I played in using Flex-time. As you can see, it has a few issues.

Figure 16.14 Flexi-time notation in need of some help.

Rather than re-recording this, I'll use the Renotate Performance plug-in to fix it. Figure 16.15 shows the resulting dialog box when I invoke the plug-in.

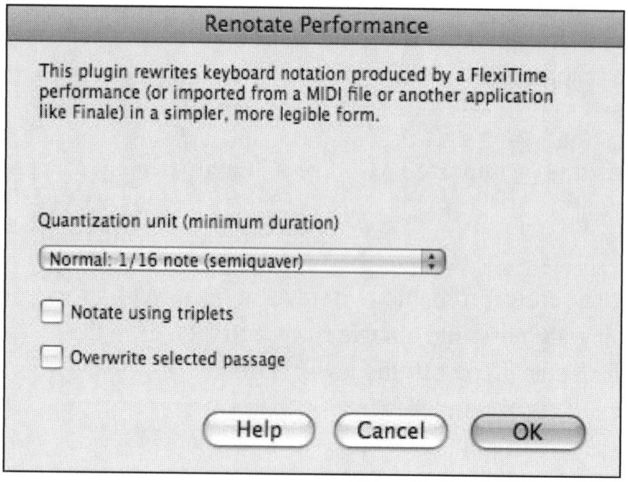

Renotate Performance

This plugin rewrites keyboard notation produced by a FlexiTime performance (or imported from a MIDI file or another application like Finale) in a simpler, more legible form.

Quantization unit (minimum duration)

Normal: 1/16 note (semiquaver) ⬍

☐ Notate using triplets

☐ Overwrite selected passage

(Help)   (Cancel)   (OK)

Figure 16.15 Renotate Performance.

The plug-in interface is simple enough—the drop-down menu simply lets you choose a new quantization value.

> **Overwrite** The Overwrite Selected Passage check box is very important to understand. If you select it, the plug-in will renotate your performance and overwrite the old notation. With the Overwrite Selected Passage option deselected (unchecked), the plug-in will copy the newly notated music to a new stave. That way, you can compare the old to the new.

When I run the plug-in (choosing for it not to be overwritten), you can see how the plug-in has successfully simplified the notation and made it more legible (see Figure 16.16).

Figure 16.16 After Renotate Performance.

If you use Flexi-time or MIDI import, you'll definitely want to explore this powerful plug-in.

CD: Example 16.8 has some music that was input with Flexi-time and can benefit from the Renotate plug-in. You can also experiment with your own music and the plug-in.

Text: Add Note Names

The final contender in our sampling of Sibelius plug-ins is the simple Add Note Names, which (wouldn't you know?) adds the names of the notes automatically! All you have to do is select some music and invoke the plug-in, which brings up the dialog shown in Figure 16.17.

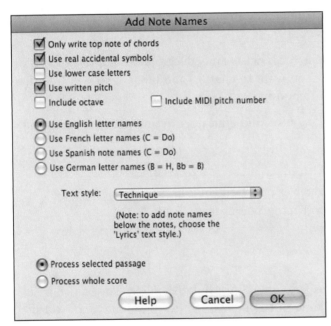

Figure 16.17   Add Note Names.

CD: Example 16.9 will allow you to practice using the Add Note Names plug-in.

This plug-in has a multitude of uses for:

- Music instruction books in which new notes are introduced

- Translation into French, Spanish, and German pitch names

- Listing the MIDI pitch number

- Showing the octave of each note

This plug-in is really part of the larger family of text-based plug-ins that you should be aware of. Because of space considerations, I'll just list some other amazing plug-ins within the Text subcategory.

- **Add Brass Fingerings.** You guessed it: You specify which brass instrument, and Sibelius adds the appropriate fingerings.

- **Add String Fingerings.** Same as Add Brass Fingerings, except with string fingerings. (You can even choose the position.)

- **Add Tonic Sol-Fa.** This adds the proper Curwen/Kodaly Sol-Fa symbols to your score. If you teach with this system, it's a huge timesaver.

- **Change Dynamic.** This adjusts all written dynamics up or down a step. Make all your piano to mezzo forte adjustments in one fell swoop.

- **Find and Replace Text.** This is a huge one for lyricists and educators. Search for a word or phrase that you may have misspelled or you want to change, and the plug-in will find that word and replace it with a word of your choosing.

- **Number Beats.** This is a boon for percussionists and educators. It automatically adds the beats and numbers them below the stave!

CD: Example 16.10 has a number of examples on which you can run plug-ins from the Text subcategory. The instructions are within the Sibelius file.

Online Plug-Ins

In addition to the included plug-ins, there are other plug-ins available online. To see a complete list of all the third-party plug-ins available for Sibelius, go to the following website: www.sibelius.com/download/plugins.

This will bring you to the plug-in site. You'll want to look at plug-ins for Sibelius 5, so make sure to select Find Plug-Ins by Version and then select Sibelius 5 to see the new plug-ins available for Sibelius 5. When you've done that, you can see a listing of the new plug-ins and you can easily click on any of the plug-ins to download them.

Installing Plug-Ins

After you've downloaded the plug-ins, you'll need to install them to the proper location on your hard drive. There are different instructions for Windows and Mac, so here are the Windows instructions first:

1. Open a My Computer or Windows Explorer window and choose Tools > Folder Options.

2. Choose the View tab and make sure Show Hidden Files and Folders is switched on, then click OK.

3a. On Windows Vista, navigate to C:\Users*username*\AppData\Roaming.

    OR

3b. On Windows XP/2000, navigate to C:\Documents and Settings*username*\Application Data.

4. If there is a folder called Sibelius Software in this location, double-click it to open it; if not, create one (choose File > New > New Folder) and then open the folder.

5. You should see a folder called Sibelius 5. Double-click it to open it. If it's not present, create a folder called Sibelius 5 and open it.

6. You should see a folder called Plugins. Double-click it to open it. If it's not present, create a folder called Plugins and open it.

7. Create a folder into which to install your new plug-in. Call the folder From the Web or any other relevant name you'd like.

8. Copy the plug-in you downloaded into your newly created folder.

Here are the instructions for the Macintosh users:

1. Use the Finder to navigate to Hard Drive/Users/*username*/Library/Application Support.

2. If there is a folder called Sibelius Software in this location, double-click it to open it; if not, create one (choose File > New Folder) and then open the folder.

3. You should see a folder called Sibelius 5. Double-click it to open it. If it's not present, create a folder called Sibelius 5 and open it.

4. You should see a folder called Plugins. Double-click it to open it. If it's not present, create a folder called Plugins and open it.

5. Create a folder into which to install your new plug-in. Call the folder From the Web or any other relevant name you'd like.

6. Copy the plug-in you downloaded into your newly created folder.

Check back often, as new plug-ins are being written all the time!

Reboot When you add a new plug-in to Sibelius, don't forget to quit and relaunch Sibelius in order to see the newly installed plug-in.

Where to Request a Plug-In

Where do you go to request a plug-in? Many of the plug-ins have been created by a very small number of people who monitor the Sibelius chat page. If you hang out there (which you should because it's an amazing resource) and bring up topics and plug-in requests, you'll find that you may just get a plug-in written for you. The address for the chat page is www.sibelius.com/helpcenter.

Once on that page, you'll see Chat Page as a link below; there you can sign in and become part of the Sibelius chat community.

Chat to Learn The chat page is populated by some of the masters of Sibelius, including the grand master of them all, Sibelius's Senior Product Manager Daniel Spreadbury, who takes great pride in answering as many questions as humanly possible. If you did nothing more than just read his answers to technical issues, you'd learn a great deal about Sibelius.

Learn to Write a Plug-In

If you'd like to learn about writing plug-ins, I'll point you to two resources.

- On your Sibelius installer DVD, inside the Extras folder, is a PDF file detailing Manuscript. Sibelius's own plug-in creation language. This will serve as a guide to the knowledge you need to start writing your own plug-ins. (There may be an updated PDF guide available at anytime at the Sibelius plug-in download page.)

- The plug-in developers list is an invaluable resource for anyone who wants to develop his own plug-ins and learn from master plug-in developers. To subscribe to the list, go to www.sibelius.com/download/plugins and click on Write Your Own Plug-Ins. Then click on Join Our Plug-In Developer Mailing List. This will send an email to Sibelius with a request to join the email list.

As a last word on plug-ins: Use them! They greatly increase the power and efficiency of Sibelius. There's always some gem in the Plug-Ins menu to make your life better!

17 Customizing Sibelius

Essential Tips for Chapter 17

1. You can make custom manuscript paper (with any House Style and instrument groups) that shows up in your New Score window.

2. It's vital that you get your preferences set up for your working style.

3. Make sure that auto-saving is activated and saving at a regular interval.

4. Make sure you deselect the Restore Original Item after Single-Bar Selections option in the Note Input Preferences.

5. Make sure you select Program Names, rather than SoundIDs, in the Playback Preferences.

6. You don't have to watch Sibelius load up all your sounds when you open each score!

7. You can change the default key commands in Sibelius.

8. You can assign a key command to any function in the program. This is especially important, for example, if you use a text style that's several levels deep in the Create > Text menu.

9. You can turn off the intro music before it drives you crazy.

10. You probably could use Focus on Staves more than you are now.

11. You have a great deal of control over how Sibelius does almost anything; you just have to know how to change it.

As we're nearing the end of this book, it's clear that Sibelius 5 is a robust program. One of the great hallmarks of a powerful program is its ability to mold and adapt to a wide variety of users. In this chapter you'll learn how you can take some key aspects of Sibelius and change them to better suit you. You'll learn this through text examples only (there won't be CD examples), but if you like what you see, you can make these changes instantly in your version of Sibelius. I'll also show you some of my favorite tweaks and explain why you might consider adopting them yourself.

Saving Custom Manuscript Paper

Several times throughout this book, I've mentioned that you can customize manuscript paper so whatever instrument groups you'd like to have will show up in your New Score window. I've also talked about the way to save a House Style into a manuscript paper so you can have your House Style changes load up in future scores. This is a simple task—one that you can learn in just seconds and that will be a great benefit to your working speed in Sibelius.

To save your own custom manuscript paper, follow these steps:

1. Open a blank score that represents as closely as possible the type of score on which you want to work.

2. Add or remove instruments from the Create > Instruments window so your manuscript paper contains the correct instrument groupings.

3. Manually adjust any elements of the House Style that you need to.

4. Import a custom House Style if you've already predefined one.

5. Don't add any music.

6. Save your score (blank) with a suitable title (one that reflects the manuscript paper). (If you want it to appear at the top of the list in the New Score window, save it with a name that starts with _aaa, such as _aaa(name).

7. From the File menu, choose Export > Manuscript Paper.

8. That's it! Your score is now exported as manuscript paper.

Now, when you start a new score, your list of manuscript papers will contain your newly created entry. As for the file you saved, don't worry about keeping it; you can throw it out because Sibelius made a copy elsewhere as soon as you exported to manuscript paper.

Too Many? If you only work with a small number of manuscript papers, you can always go in and delete the paper that you never use, thus leaving yourself with a small list of papers.

Setting Up Preferences

Within Sibelius 5 there are a multitude of preferences that you can set to make the program easier to use. Preferences are just that—options—and the default set might not be right for you. I'm going to take you through the relevant parts of the Preferences dialog box and show you what you might want to change and why.

Many Preferences There are a total of 15 different categories of preferences with Sibelius 5. We won't talk about all of them in this chapter (some of the preferences are outside of the scope of this book), but don't let that stop you from exploring the additional aspects of Preferences as a whole.

Display

Let's start with the Display section of the Preferences dialog box (see Figure 17.1).

There are a few minor things to tweak here.

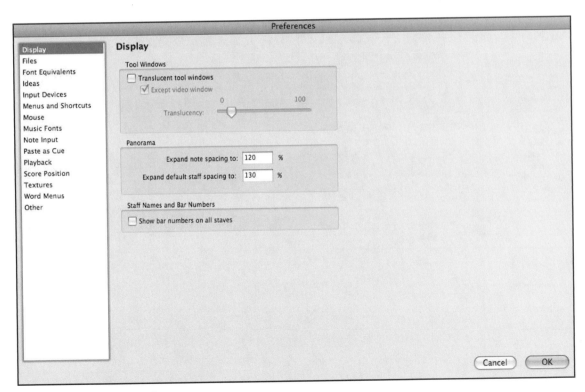

Figure 17.1 Display preferences.

- **Translucent Tool Windows.** By default, any of the floating tool windows (Keypad, Navigator) are slightly transparent by default. There is a Translucency slider to control how transparent they are. I actually make my windows quite transparent because I know the contents by heart now, and my laptop has a small screen, so squeezing as much as possible on the screen is very important to me. You might not feel the same way, and in fact you can deselect the Translucent Tool Windows box to make them not transparent at all, if you wish. Many experienced users don't even use their floating windows—they rely on the key commands.

- **Except Video Window.** No matter how transparent or nontransparent you make your tool windows, the Video window should not be transparent. The Except Video Window option is selected by default (meaning that it won't be transparent) because video should be seen in all its glory.

I would leave the Panorama section alone in this window because the defaults are quite nice, but do tweak them as you see fit.

Files

In the Files section of the Preferences dialog box, there are a few changes you can make. In fact, this section includes probably one of the most critical changes you can make in Sibelius: Enable Auto-Saving. Figure 17.2 shows the Files Preferences page.

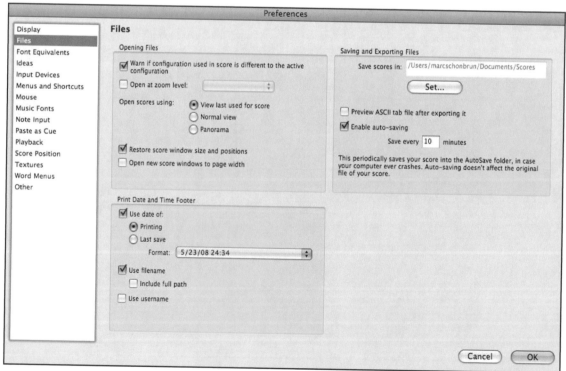

Figure 17.2 Files preferences.

Here's what you might want to tweak:

- **Open Scores Using.** If you can't get enough of Panorama view, you have the choice to open a score in any view that you like—Normal view, Panorama, or whatever the score was saved in. Because I'm a huge Panorama fan, I switch this on by default by clicking the Panorama radio button.

- **Save Scores In.** Yes, you can change the default save-to location. The default is always the Scores folder inside of your main Documents folder, but some folks do not keep their scores there. If you're sick of having to choose a different folder each time you save a file, click the Set button and choose a different location.

- **Enable Auto-Saving.** Thankfully, this option is on by default, and Sibelius saves back-up scores for you every x minutes in a folder called AutoSave. The default is 10 minutes, but you'll want to change that to something more frequent. I set mine to every one minute, just in case.

Open Score Settings Just because you set the Open Scores Using setting to either Panorama or Normal, that doesn't mean you can't change it the second you open a score. So if you think you'll want Panorama 80 percent of the time, choose that as your default and change the display back to Normal by pressing Shift+P.

Mouse

I'm pretty picky about this part of the Preferences because the mouse is your main gateway to moving around the interface. Even though I use a ton of key commands, it's still important to set the mouse up. Let's take a look at the Mouse preferences and see what is set and why it's set the way it is (see Figure 17.3).

- **Dragging the Paper.** By default, Sibelius lets you drag the manuscript paper when you click and drag on it. I change my Dragging the Paper option to Hold Command and Drag, so I can now grab multiple objects by drawing a selection box with my mouse, instead of dragging the paper.

- **Show Shadow Note.** If you're doing mouse entry, it's good to have this option on because it tells you where your notes will enter. If you're not doing mouse entry, then I recommend turning it off because it can be a visual distraction.

- **Snap Positions.** The default position your mouse snaps to in mouse entry mode is a quarter note, meaning that when you go to click in a measure with your mouse, your mouse can only access quarter-note divisions of a measure. I almost always advise folks to change this to an eighth note, even if they don't use mouse entry often. When I *do* use mouse entry, it's to start mid-measure, and without being able to access the eighth notes, it's just not very practical.

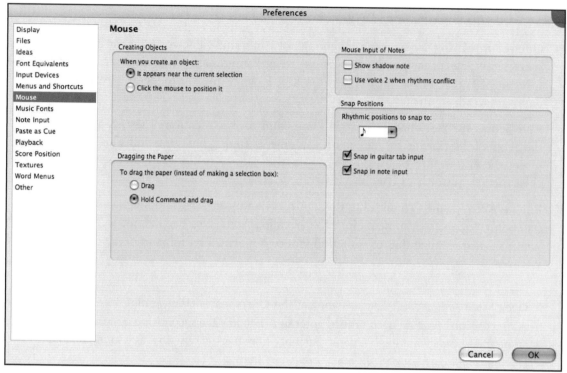

Figure 17.3   Mouse preferences.

Note Input

The preferences for note input are vital to working in Sibelius. I'm often amazed that many users never come here. I come here all the time to change things around, and I'll show you why! Figure 17.4 shows the Note Input preferences.

- **Accuracy When You Input Chords.** This slider governs how loosely (or tightly) Sibelius interprets chords when you enter them in Step-time. Being a somewhat sloppy piano player and frequent MIDI guitarist, I needed to tweak this. How do you know whether yours needs adjusting? When you input a Step-time chord, do you end up with one chord or two? If you're getting two, set the slider toward Loose.

- **Transposing Staves.** This governs how you'll enter MIDI notes onto transposing staves. Suppose you're copying music from an existing printed, transposed score using a MIDI keyboard. Wouldn't it be faster just to read the notes on the score you're copying and play them as written into the score? Yes, it really would be, but that won't work unless you tell Sibelius to input written pitches. Otherwise, Sibelius will transpose the incoming MIDI data, no matter which Score view you have turned on (transposing versus non-transposed Score view).

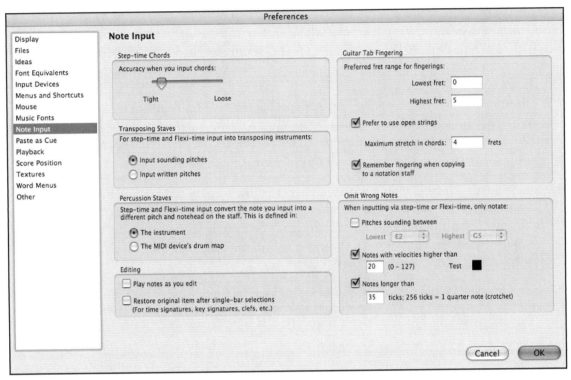

Figure 17.4   Note Input preferences.

- **Percussion Staves.** This was covered in detail in Chapter 6, so refer back to that chapter for more information. Almost all of the time, you want percussion staves hearing MIDI input from the instrument. The other choice—the MIDI device's drum map—is only when you're playing on a General MIDI keyboard and you're playing the sounds you hear, not what will be notated. Your particular preference depends solely on what you're used to: If you're adept with the General MIDI key map, than choose that option. If you're more comfortable with the staff notation, then go with that.

- **Play Notes as You Edit.** If you click on a pitch, do you need to hear it? This is a choice you'll want to decide because it pertains to another upcoming preference—loading sounds when you start your score. If you don't need to hear while you edit, go ahead and deselect this option. (Notes will still play back when you actually play.) This is quite handy to have off if you have sounds *not* loading when scores open. When you click on a note, it would force Sibelius to load all of your sounds at that point, which takes time.

- **Restore Original Item after Single-Bar Selections.** This is huge, especially for past users of Sibelius. If you select a single measure and make a key signature change, Sibelius will only change it for that one measure by default. Because most music doesn't make use of single-bar changes in time, key, or clef, it's best if you turn off this option by unchecking the box.

Older versions of Sibelius didn't do this by default, and for most folks, being able to select a single measure and have their clef, time, or key change appear there is a better way to work. I tell every class I teach to turn off this setting as soon as they start the program.

Playback

The settings in the Playback preferences are another aspect of Sibelius that I tell new users to look at immediately. If you're only using Sibelius as an engraving program, you can happily skip over this section, but because most users are taking advantage of the new playback system in Sibelius 5, this section is particularly relevant. Figure 17.5 shows the Playback preferences.

- **Load Sounds When Opening Scores.** Ever get really bored watching Sibelius load up all your sounds when you open each and every score? Granted, this process is much faster than it was in the past, but it's no less annoying if you're only going in to edit a few things. Uncheck the check box! Now, to be clear, this doesn't stop Sibelius from loading sounds; it just waits to do so until you press Play!

- **Allow Manual Sound Sets.** Turn this option on by selecting the check box. If you ever decide to dive deeper into the world of virtual instruments and SoundWorld, you'll need to have

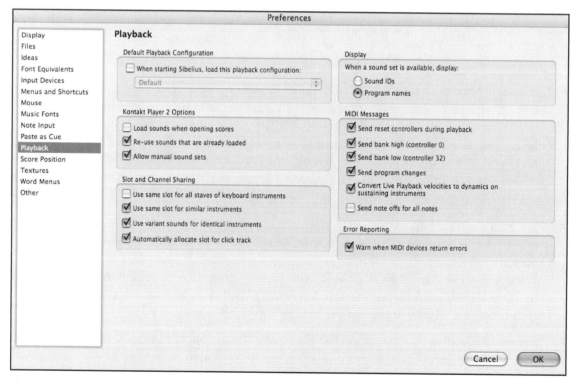

Figure 17.5 Playback preferences.

this checked. And even if you never get into sounds, it won't harm anything to have this option turned on.

- **When a Sound Set Is Available, Display.** For your own sanity, please change this setting from the default SoundIDs to Program Names. What's the difference? SoundIDs are something that Sibelius uses internally for its sound engine (which is quite brilliant). SoundIDs classify all sounds into IDs, such as strings.piano.grand for piano sounds. This is all well and good, but it can be very confusing to see such long names, such as my personal favorite: unpitched.exotic.silence. If you turn on the Program Names option, you'll see the names of the patches, so you'd see Steinway Grand instead of strings.piano.grand.

Textures

The Textures preferences refer to how Sibelius draws your music paper and desk onscreen. It's purely an aesthetic/visual thing, and you can live your whole life without ever coming to this part of the Preferences dialog box, but hey—why not? Figure 17.6 shows the Textures preference.

What would you tweak here? Surprisingly, there aren't that many choices, with the exception of an important tip from the layout chapter: You can change the paper from the default white linen

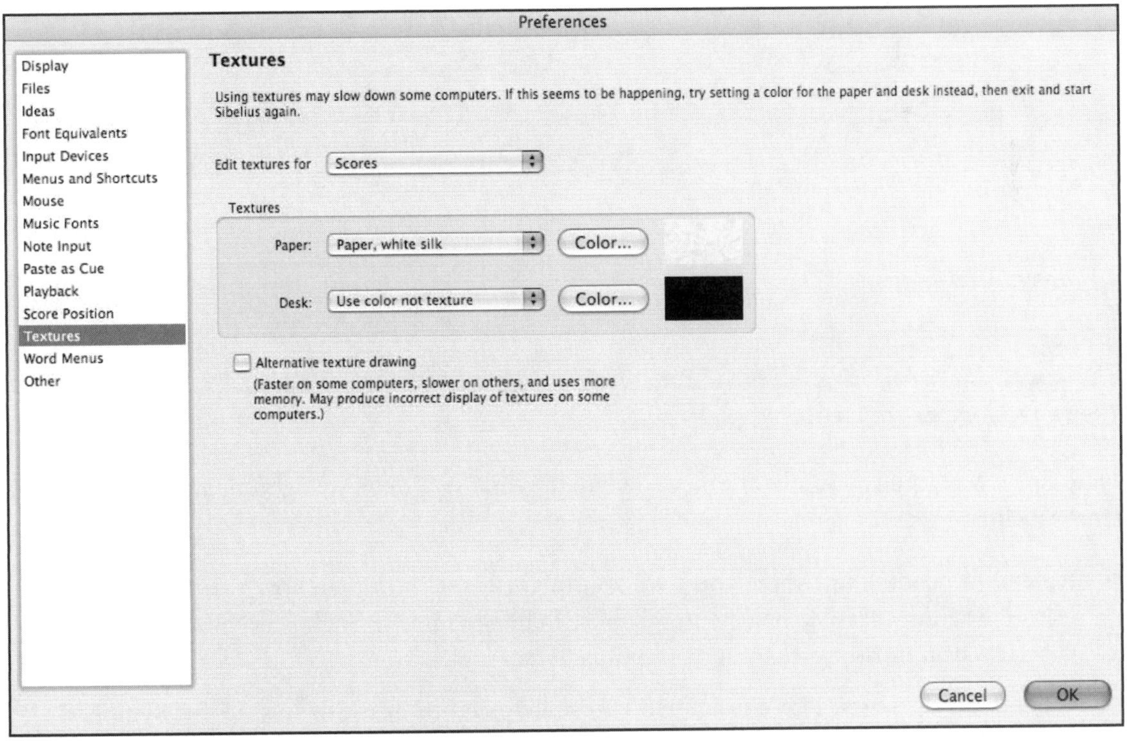

Figure 17.6 Textures preferences.

to graph paper, which is great for laying out a score and aligning objects. You can also change the color of the desk you write on, if that makes life easier for you in any way. (I change mine to gray because it shows up better on a laptop.)

Other

The last spot in Sibelius's preferences is the Other screen of the Preferences dialog box. This window covers a hodgepodge of preferences that otherwise would be too small to warrant their own categories, and there are a few important gems in here as well. Figure 17.7 shows the Other preferences.

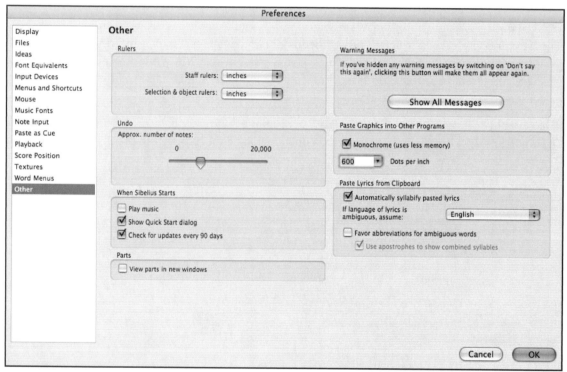

Figure 17.7   Other preferences.

Here are a few things you might want to change while you're enjoying your newfound power over Sibelius.

- **Rulers.** Depending on where you live, you might want to change how the different rulers in the program measure objects in Sibelius. I change mine to inches because I live in the U.S. and deal mostly with American publishers.

- **When Sibelius Starts.** Play music? Do you really need to hear Sibelius's Fifth Symphony again? True story, I was in the car, and Sibelius's Fifth was on the radio, and I wondered how my laptop had started up from my backpack.... You can turn this off by unchecking the box.

- **View Parts in New Windows.** If you have multiple monitors or a really big monitor, you might want to have your parts open in their own windows, rather than toggling the view with the main score.

- **Paste Graphics into Other Programs.** If you're using the Copy and Paste to Word features, you'll want to know that you can change the resolution of the music you copy. The default is 300 dpi, which is fairly standard in print but can look grainy. I changed mine to 600 for a sharper view. The only tradeoff is that my files are larger, but they look better so it's a fair trade.

Views

Sibelius offers you multiple ways to look at your music, and you'll want to know about all of them because they're designed to improve your workflow. Some of the view options I've clearly covered before and I won't rehash them, and some are just too important not to mention again. We'll start out with Focus on Staves.

Focus on Staves

Focus on Staves isn't a new feature. It was introduced in Sibelius 4, but it's still a very cool feature—one you should probably use whenever you can. The basic premise is this: You're working on a large score with many instruments, and you're perpetually scrolling around your score, especially when you write for only a few different groups of instruments at once. Wouldn't it be nice to hide the staves you're not working on? That's exactly what Focus on Staves does. To make it work, you have to select the staves you want to work on. Then, if you click on the toolbar icon (which resembles a five-line stave) or choose View > Focus on Staves, Sibelius will hide all but the staves you've selected. You can now work as you need to, making the most of your precious screen real estate. Remember, this is *not* the same as Dynamic Parts! This is just another way to look at multiple staves at once while composing, not while preparing parts.

Tip to Focus On One final tip: You don't have to work on instruments that are in order. You can just as easily work on noncontiguous instruments. For example, if you're writing a section for winds and strings, you'll want to be able to select just the winds and just the strings. If you try to Shift-click to select the staves, you'll end up selecting all the staves in between. Remember that if you want to select noncontiguous staves, you'll need to Ctrl-click (Windows) or Command-click (Mac) and select each stave individually, and then invoke the Focus on Staves feature. You only need to select a single measure of a stave, not the entire instrument (all measures) before invoking Focus on Staves.

Panorama

When you're entering music, you have two choices in Sibelius 5 regarding how you view your pages. You can use the Page view, which is the normal view, or you can use Panorama view. Why do I keep bringing up this feature? If you're a true veteran Sibelius user, you had Panorama view back in Sibelius 7, on the original Acorn system. If your first version of Sibelius was on a Mac or a PC, you've only ever had Page view, and Panorama is new in Sibelius 5 so you may not be used to it.

Panorama view is great for composing when you don't want to deal with page breaks and other layout changes (because you can't view them in Panorama). Page view is best suited for laying out music after you've composed it. Is this a hard-and-fast rule? No, of course not. If you're working on a lead sheet, it might be best to work only in Page view because it's a single line, and you can see more than you can with Panorama. Just know the views are there and you can toggle them by pressing Shift+P whenever your little heart desires. In addition, you can use Panorama in conjunction with Focus on Staves, and you can certainly use Panorama if you're engraving modern "linear-style" scores that might use unusual or long "free-time" time signatures.

Rulers

When you're working with layout and things must line up, there's nothing better than rulers. Please remember that you can turn rulers on and off at will. Here are the types of rulers you can show by choosing View > Rulers:

- **Selection rulers.** When switched on, these rulers tell you how far the selected object(s) are from their anchor point (which is usually a stave).

- **Object rulers.** When switched on, these rulers tell you how far any object is from its anchor point. Object rulers are like selection rulers, but they're always on (you don't have to select them).

- **Staff rulers.** When switched on, these rulers tell you how far each stave is from one another and how far each stave is from the margins (in all directions). These rulers are absolutely critical for score layout.

Rulers are there to help you; use them when necessary!

View Memory The settings in your View > Rulers menu are saved when you save a score. If you're going to send someone a .sib score, make sure you have the proper views enabled.

Keyboard Shortcuts

As you can tell at this late chapter, I'm a big proponent of keyboard shortcuts. I think you work faster when you know a good number of them. It's also something I've witnessed when working with really great Sibelius users; the best ones know the keyboard shortcuts, and the really, really fast ones know them all.

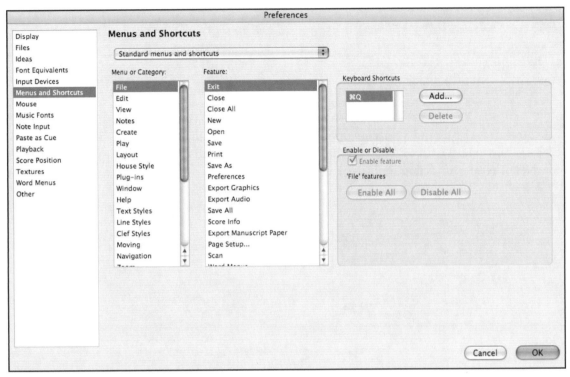

Figure 17.8 Menus and Shortcuts preferences.

One thing you might not know is that you have complete and total control over the shortcuts. The shortcuts you've learned are the default ones in the program, but in truth you can make anything a shortcut. You can do this back in Sibelius's Preferences (which you know how to get to already). Figure 17.8 shows the Menus and Shortcuts preferences.

From this window, you can view all the current key command shortcuts, assign your own custom ones, and even disable items from the drop-down menus. (I'm not sure why you'd want to do that, but you can.)

School Set The School Features set of shortcuts is very useful because it limits students' access to menus and program functions that they don't need to deal with, or ones that might get them into trouble.

If you want to edit shortcuts, the first thing you need to do is create a new set of shortcuts. At the top of the window, you'll see a drop-down menu that reads Standard Menus and Shortcuts, which is the standard set of shortcuts with which Sibelius ships (see Figure 17.9).

Figure 17.9   Menu and shortcut presets.

The Standard Menus and Shortcuts option is a read-only file that you can't edit. You'll need to create a new one. To do so, click on the drop-down menu and choose Add Feature Set to open the New Feature Set dialog box (see Figure 17.10).

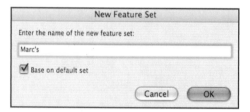

Figure 17.10   Add a feature set.

Once you've named the feature set (make sure you leave the Base on Default Set option selected), you can start making changes. What kinds of things are you going to change? Well, the only reason you'd go into this dialog box is if you were using a feature in Sibelius that currently doesn't have a default shortcut, and you're using it often enough that a shortcut would save you considerable time.

Here's a personal example: I often use Boxed Text from Create > Text > Other Staff Text in my work. I think it's clear, and the box draws attention nicely to the text within it. Unfortunately, there isn't any default shortcut assigned, so I'd have to choose Create > Text > Other Staff Text each time I wanted to use it (which is often). Instead, I'll create my own feature set, and then I'll navigate to the Text Styles menu on the right side of the window and find the Boxed Text option (see Figure 17.11).

As expected, there's no default key command associated with this. I'd like to assign Ctrl+B (Windows) or Command+B (Mac). Right now, Command+B is adding a single bar at the end of my score—a feature I don't ever use—so I'm willing to let that shortcut reassign to adding boxed text. From the Preferences dialog box, you can assign any key combination you want by clicking the Add button under the Keyboard Shortcuts section. Doing so brings up the Add Keyboard Shortcut dialog box shown in Figure 17.12.

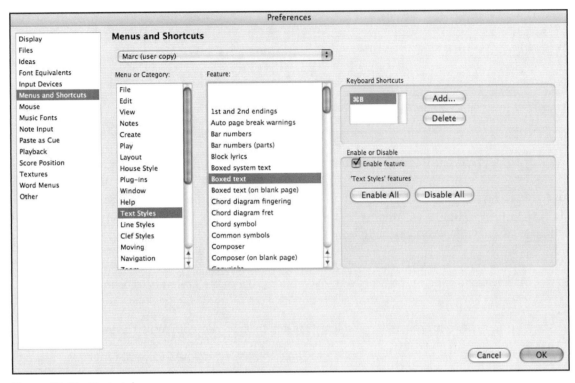

Figure 17.11   Text styles.

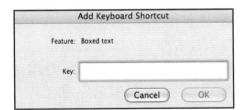

Figure 17.12   The Add Keyboard Shortcut dialog box.

New Keys There are few unused keys in Sibelius. O and U are unassigned, so use those first. Also, the J key is for guitar bends, so if you're not a guitarist or engraving guitar music, you can use that one as well. All other shortcuts will need an extra modifier (Shift or Option).

From this dialog box, I can type in the desired shortcut. When I click OK, Sibelius will respond with a warning, as shown in Figure 17.13.

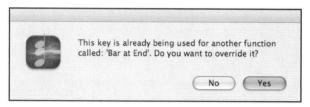

Figure 17.13 Overwrite the key command?

Rightly so, Sibelius has informed me that this key is taken (which I knew, but you won't remember every one, so it's good to have the reminder) and allows me to cancel the remapping or override it. I want to override it, so I click Yes. That's really all there is to it. You can go through and assign shortcuts to commonly used items this way, and save your own feature sets for different uses (which you can toggle in the Preferences whenever you want).

Disable Commands In the Menus and Shortcuts page of the Preferences dialog box, you have the ability to disable a shortcut completely. Here are some possible uses:

- In a school environment, disabling features that are not applicable to students.

- Disabling the regular Save option to force the use of Save As to create multiple redundancy backups. I use the Save As trick often because incremental saves are a great idea for very important work that you absolutely can't afford to lose.

Editing Word Menus

Remember those wonderful word menus? If you don't, that's okay. Here's a refresher: When you're adding text (of any sort), you can right-click (two-button mouse owners) or Control-click (Mac folks) and bring up a list of pre-built words like the ones in the Tempo text style (see Figure 17.14).

The contents of the word menu are supplied by Sibelius, but you can change them and add additional entries yourself. To do so, go back to Sibelius Preferences, this time looking at the Word Menus page, as shown in Figure 17.15.

In this page of the Preferences dialog box, you have the list of word menus on the left side of the screen. Select the one you want (in this case, Tempo Words), and the right side of the screen will show you the available list of words. In this screen you can add new words, delete unused ones, and change the order of the words as they appear in the menu. If you find yourself using word menus often, it's probably a good idea to tweak them and make sure that the words you use most often are shown and moved to the top for easy access.

Figure 17.14 The Tempo word menu.

Word Menus Look Different on PCs and MACs If you're using a PC, when you use a word menu, the words are displayed horizontally across the screen, making it easy to look at large list of word menus. On the Mac, word menus look different (due to how the OS codes these lists)—they scroll vertically, and you can't see huge menus without scrolling. If you're a Mac user, editing the word menus you use might make your life much easier— you can ensure that your most frequently used entries are toward the top of the list and always visible. Even if you don't intend to add words, you still might want to change the order of the words.

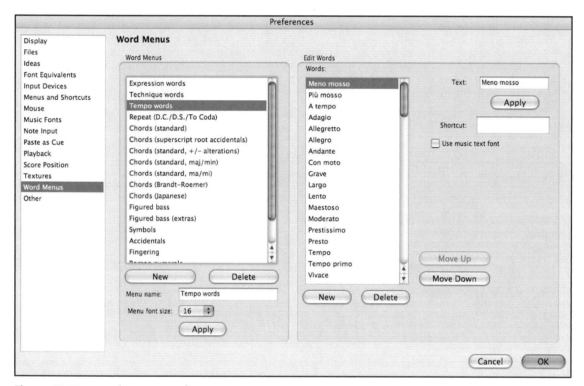

Figure 17.15 Word Menus preferences.

And that's all I have to say about setting up Sibelius! Sure there's more, but now you know where to look. So have no fear, and start poking around the Preferences and making Sibelius your own.

18 Importing and Exporting

Essential Tips for Chapter 18

1. You can import MIDI files into Sibelius. Better still, there are millions of free MIDI files on the web, including almost everything Bach, Beethoven, and Mozart ever wrote (and many more).

2. You can open files from other music notation programs, such as Finale, using MusicXML.

3. You can export your scores to Finale using MusicXML with the optional Dolet plug-in.

4. You can export your scores as graphics files (TIFF, EPS, PDF) for use in professional publishing.

5. You can copy selected bits of your score and paste them into Microsoft Word (or other programs).

6. You can make an audio file of your score and burn it onto a CD.

7. You can save your score as a Scorch webpage, and others can see, play back, and print your score without having to own Sibelius. And, Sibelius gives you free web space to host the files!

8. Almost every possible export in Sibelius can be executed in batch through the Plug-In > Batch Processing menu option—explore it!

You've done it! You're at the last chapter, and we're going to look at the final little bits of the program—getting music into and out of Sibelius using various types of import and export styles. You'll learn about everything from MIDI to Scorch webpages.

MIDI Import

MIDI is one of those things that strikes fear into the hearts of musicians everywhere, which is a shame because MIDI is an amazing, free resource. Why is it often disliked? For starters, MIDI is old (more than 25 years old at this point), and many musicians' experience with MIDI hasn't been favorable, to say the least. Most think of MIDI as poor-sounding computer music.

Whatever the case, for notation programs, MIDI files are pretty cool. For those of you who don't know, a MIDI file is a small document that contains the "instructions" for music. It's not notation; it's just a set of commands so that a computer can play back the file and make it sound like something. Think of it as the modern-day equivalent of the player piano reel.

What's cool about MIDI is that there are millions of MIDI files out there. Literally every major classical work has been saved as a MIDI file. There are rock and pop MIDI files as well, but there are legal issues with regard to copyright, so it wouldn't be appropriate to link you to illegal files. The classical stuff is definitely legal; just remember that the copyright rule extends 70 years after the death of the composer.

You can import MIDI files into Sibelius. The clarity of the transfer from MIDI to Sibelius is the real trick.

Before we get into anything about MIDI files, you have to know that the majority of MIDI files are not professionally done; most MIDI files are made by folks just like you and me. The main difference between MIDI and notation is that MIDI simply has to sound acceptable, whereas notation has to look right. MIDI files often will play back fine, but when converted into notation, they sometimes look really bad. This is the trick to dealing with MIDI files: Some import very cleanly, and others do not.

Here is a list of a few sites from which you can grab MIDI files:

- **www.classicalarchives.com.** This is a good source for classical MIDI files of all types.

- **www.midiworld.com/midifile.htm.** This is another smattering of good files.

- **www.musicrobot.com.** This is a search engine for locating pop music MIDI files on the web.

- **www.cpdl.org.** This is an excellent choral music public-domain site with 9,000 files. These are not MIDI files, but rather PDFs that you can import using PhotoScore (refer to Chapter 14).

- **www.cyberhymnal.org.** This site contains thousands of hymn tunes and lyrics, all free to download. These are avaliable as MIDI, PDF, Sibelius, and Finale files, so there are many from which to choose.

Alternatively, you can just Google "free MIDI files," and you'll see thousands of links.

In any case, let's import a MIDI file together. On your CD, you'll find a MIDI file for "Sheep May Safely Graze" by J.S Bach. This one was obtained online and should meet our needs nicely.

CD: On your CD, locate the Sheep.mid file inside the Chapter 18 folder. You'll need it to follow along with the next steps.

Even though we're importing this MIDI file, you'll get to it by choosing File > Open. Navigating to the file gives you the Open MIDI File dialog box shown in Figure 18.1.

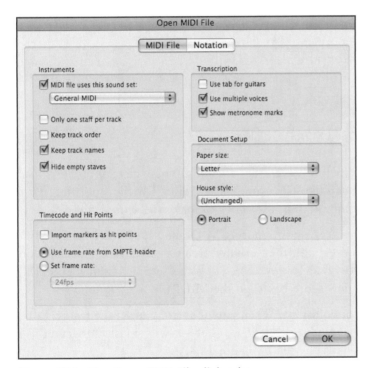

Figure 18.1   The Open MIDI File dialog box.

Because MIDI files vary wildly, Sibelius needs to know a bit about this file in order to proceed. Since there's more to talk about than space allows, copy the settings from Figure 18.1. You'll find more detail about MIDI file import in the Sibelius Reference.

There are actually two pages in this dialog box—we're looking at the MIDI File page, and you can switch to the Notation page to show you some more options (see Figure 18.2).

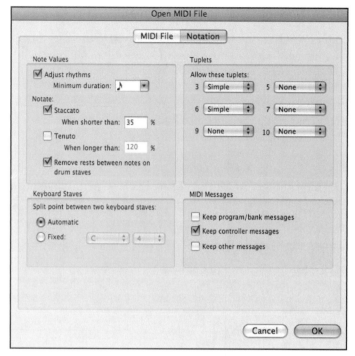

Figure 18.2 The Notation page of the Open MIDI File dialog box.

This page is pretty important. As I said before, MIDI files are built to play nice, not to look nice, so a bit of rhythmic help is needed (much like Flexi-time). The Adjust Rhythms portion of this window is key. Sibelius will clean up the rhythms as it goes to make the score legible.

One final note: Sibelius has options for keeping or ignoring MIDI messages. Most times, MIDI messages are there for playback purposes, and they usually aren't needed in a Sibelius score because Sibelius does the playback for you. In any case, copy the settings from Figure 18.2 and click OK. You'll be taken into a new score based on the MIDI file (see Figure 18.3).

The trick with a MIDI file is to look for collisions. When you quantize you set the fastest value, and if there's something faster, Sibelius won't just make it faster—it will smash it together as a dyad. It would look something like what you seen in Figure 18.4.

This is a clear spot where our choice of a sixteenth note as the minimum duration wasn't correct. Close the file without saving. (Don't worry, it's okay not to save.) Reopen it, and this time, from the Notation page, choose the Adjust Rhythms option and change it to a thirty-second note. You'll now open the score correctly.

Now that you've made that change, play the file back. There are a few things left to do, and here's a list of things you might want to change:

■   Find all occurrences of notes in other voices that don't belong and get rid of them.

Figure 18.3 The imported score.

Figure 18.4 A dyad.

- Run the Change Split Point plug-in on the harpsichord part to clean up the distributions to clefs.

- Add some new instruments and expand the arrangement.

- Work on the layout and formatting.

- Ponder all the time you just saved and will save in the future.

I'm being brief intentionally about MIDI, and that's not because it's not important. The beauty of Sibelius is that you don't have to know a ton about MIDI files to import them and use them in your scores and arrangements. Just look at what you did: This saved you many hours of inputting. All you have to do is clean up a few things, and you are good to go. Just think of the possibilities for arranging music—there really are millions of files out there.

Clean MIDI To be honest, I chose this particular MIDI file because it imports pretty well. Not all MIDI files import perfectly, and you'll definitely have to tweak the settings on the Notation page of the Open MIDI File dialog box to get things right. Don't be afraid to open a score several times to get it right.

Renotate Another option for MIDI files is to use the new Renotate Performance plug-in. If your MIDI comes in with the wrong note values (typically it's too short), you can run the Renotate Performance plug-in and have it clean up things. Although watch out: Renotate tends to remove dual voicing and put all notes into the same voice, which may not be what you want! It might be better to fix the errors by hand if it's just a few errors.

MusicXML Import

Let's face it—the music notation world has two major players: Sibelius and Finale. You have this book because either you're in love with Sibelius already or you want to learn more about it. No matter which one you like, there will be times when you'll need to open work from Finale. The best way to do this is through MusicXML.

Older Finale Some older Finale files that were created before MusicXML may be able to open in Sibelius, through Sibelius' built-in Finale converter, which only works on .mus or .etf scores.

What Is MusicXML?

Let's start with XML: XML is a free text-based database language developed specifically to make sharing data easier, without the need for any proprietary file formats. Music software companies encrypt their formats, so Sibelius can't open Finale files and vice versa—this is done to protect intellectual property. Then along came a company called Recordare (www.recordare.com), founded by Michael Good, who decided to take the initiative and create a MusicXML language—a nonproprietary way for any and all music software to share files. It has been very successful, used by music scanners, sequencers, electronic music stands, and many other types of music programs. Both Finale and Sibelius have adopted MusicXML (to a certain degree). Here's the rundown:

- Finale can export and import MusicXML for free.

- Sibelius can import MusicXML for free. To export from Sibelius, you have to buy an optional plug-in called Dolet (rhymes with *Chevrolet*).

Sibelius 5 can't export files in MusicXML directly because the third-party Dolet plug-in is available from Recordare for those users who need it.

Thankfully, most Sibelius folks open Finale files and rarely have to export to Finale, so it's not a huge deal. If you do end up needing to export MusicXML to Finale, the plug-in is available from store.recordare.com and is worth its weight in gold. Without MusicXML, Sibelius and Finale would have a very difficult time communicating.

Other XML MusicXML is supported in more programs than just Finale and Sibelius. Cubase and Notion have adopted MusicXML, and the list of other companies to do so is growing daily. Check out www.recordare.com/xml.html for a complete list of programs that support MusicXML.

Opening MusicXML

Once you've obtained your MusicXML file, all you have to do is choose File > Open. Sibelius will greet you with the Open MusicXML File dialog box shown in Figure 18.5. (A sample .XML file is in your Chapter 18 folder.)

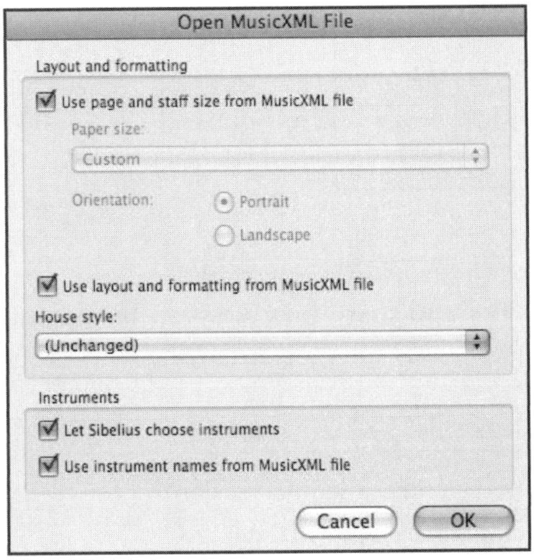

Figure 18.5 MusicXML import settings.

The default settings are fine; just click OK and take a look at Figure 18.6, which is pretty impressive considering this score started in Finale!

Figure 18.6 Imported MusicXML.

Amazingly, everything is there! MusicXML is clearly the way to share files between Finale and Sibelius. MusicXML is almost like scanning music in—it retains all the formatting and other important elements that MIDI leaves out.

Evolutionary MusicXML is undergoing an evolution and has now released version 2 (free upgrade). Thankfully, Sibelius 5.2 supports the new capabilities of MusicXML 2.0.

Exporting XML

If you need to export scores from Sibelius to other software programs, you'll need to purchase the Dolet for Sibelius plug-in (available at store.recordare.com), which allows you to export MusicXML. It's never fun to have to buy additional software, but if you need to deal with the Finale world, the plug-in pays for itself in very short order and is completely worth it. When installed, it shows up in the Plug-In window within Sibelius.

There's actually nothing to show you about the Dolet plug-in! It just does its thing and saves the MusicXML file to a location that you specify. There's even a plug-in that will convert a folder of scores at once, saving you a great deal of time if you have to send a score and parts to Finale. Does it seem too easy? It's only that easy because it's so well implemented. Well done, Recordare!

MIDI Can't you just use MIDI instead of MusicXML? Isn't MIDI free? Although it's true that you can use MIDI to send music from computer to computer, MIDI leaves out a lot of things. MusicXML carries the notes, formatting, lyrics, dynamics, chord diagrams, guitar tabs, and other score-specific features. MIDI only gives you the notes, and without the formatting it's not a great solution, especially when MusicXML exists and is so widely supported.

Exporting as Graphics

In the world of publishing, Sibelius scores aren't used to publish the final music. Programs that create books (such as InDesign and Quark) don't read scores—what they do read are graphics files, such as EPS and PDF files. Sibelius gives you options to export your scores to graphics files in a variety of formats. From the File menu, go to File > Export > Graphics to bring up your options. Figure 18.7 shows you all of the various options for exporting graphics from Sibelius.

It's a pretty simple workflow. You select the application to which you're exporting on the left side of the dialog box, and the options relevant to that selection will appear on the right side of the dialog. I have personally published many music books using this feature, and it produces camera-ready art for all publishers. It's also a great way to get around the "we only use Finale" publishing houses: Tell them you'll give them an EPS file, which is what they'd export out of Finale in the end anyway.

Batch Through the use of Sibelius's plug-ins, you can export a whole folder of scores and convert them to graphics. Just choose Plug-Ins > Batch Processing > Convert Folder of Scores to Graphics to convert a folder of scores in one shot. You can do hundreds of files at once!

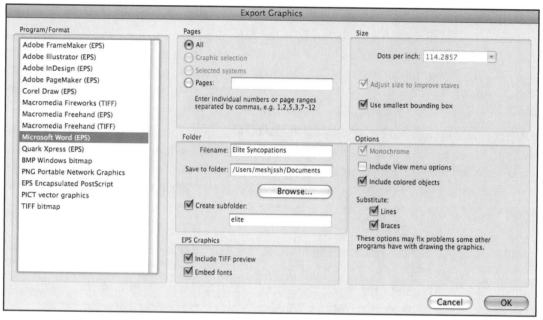

Figure 18.7 The Export Graphics dialog box.

PDF Export

Sibelius doesn't provide direct support for PDF export, but that doesn't mean you can't do it easily. The technique is different for Mac and PC, so here are the things you'll need to know to export scores to PDF.

- On the Mac, you create PDFs by choosing File > Print and clicking the PDF button in the Print dialog box. You'll see a Save to PDF option, and you'll have a perfectly created PDF. This is so because Mac OS X provides the PDF functionality within the system.

- On a PC, you'll need to install a free PDF printer driver. The software takes the place of a printer, and you invoke a normal print operation. However, instead of choosing your [*insert printer manufacturer here*] printer, you choose the PDF printer, and out comes a PDF. Because the web changes its links from time to time, do a Google search for "PDF creator" to find the necessary link. Install the free software and follow the directions provided. One PDF printer is the free CutePDF Writer that many users like and have reported success with.

PDFs are the best way to send scores to folks who don't have Sibelius. The files are small and easy to email.

Scorching Hot Although PDFs are a good way to share files, they don't play back. You could send MIDI, but there is another way: Scorch. The final section of this chapter deals with Scorch, a Sibelius technology with which people can see and hear the score without owning Sibelius.

Copy and Paste to Word (or Other Programs)

How many times have you tried to enter text into Sibelius, only to be frustrated that Sibelius isn't a word processor and it doesn't have spell check? What about when you need to write a paper that includes a snippet of a score? In the old days, you had to use some screen-capture utility, carefully grab a snippet of your Sibelius score, and import it into Word (or whichever document-creation program you were running). In Sibelius 4, a new option was created—Copy and Paste to Word—that does exactly what you think. Here's how it works:

1. Prepare your score so it looks exactly as you need it to. (This can include zooming in and turning off rulers and other objects, because the Copy function will grab all visible screen items. This could also include adjusting your margins to match your Word document.)

2. Choose Edit > Select > Select Graphic (or use the shortcut Alt/Option+G).

3. A small cross-hair will appear. Use your mouse to click and drag a selection box around the music you want to copy. A dotted blue line will appear to show you your selection. You can click the corners to resize the box.

4. Copy your selection by choosing Edit > Copy or pressing Ctrl+C (Windows) or Command+C (Mac).

5. In Word (or another document processor), navigate to the spot where the music should be pasted, and choose Edit > Paste or press Ctrl+V (Windows) or Command+V (Mac). Your music will appear there.

It's important to get the size of your selection correct because the minute you paste it into Word, it becomes a bitmapped image and won't scale larger without looking grainy, so you might end up re-pasting. Copy and Paste to Word is a simple but very useful feature, especially to students (of all levels) who integrate musical examples into text. Take a look at the results in Figure 18.8.

Resolution You set the resolution of the music you paste into Word by choosing Preferences > Other and going to the Paste Graphics to Other Programs option. The default is 300 dpi, and you can increase that for a sharper, more detailed image. Keep in mind that most printers don't exceed 300 dpi, so regardless of how good it looks onscreen, it will print at a lower resolution.

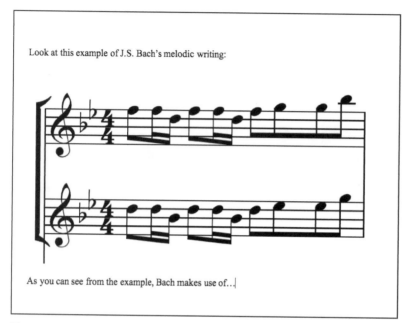

Look at this example of J.S. Bach's melodic writing:

As you can see from the example, Bach makes use of...

Figure 18.8 Copy and Paste to Word.

Export as Audio

Being able to export your score as an audio file is even more relevant now with the new playback system in Sibelius 5. When you export as audio, Sibelius will include all of the VST or AU instrument plug-ins in your score, along with any effects plug-ins, and bounce to a single stereo audio file. It's a very simple procedure; let's talk about how to set it up.

1.   Make sure your score plays back as you want it to in your final version.

2.   Adjust the levels on the mixer so everything sounds balanced.

3.   Rewind your score to the beginning using the Playback window.

4.   Select File > Export > Export as Audio or click the Export Audio button on the toolbar (it looks like a small CD).

5.   Name your file in the resulting dialog, give it a save location, and click OK. Sibelius will render your audio into a single stereo audio file.

Once you start, Sibelius will show you the Export Audio dialog box, shown in Figure 18.9, which shows you the length and size of the file you're going to create.

When Sibelius is finished, you'll have an audio file that you can burn. There's a bit more to talk about, so I want to break down a list of important things to consider.

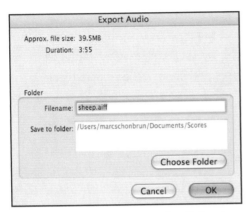

Figure 18.9   The Export Audio dialog box.

End Silence Sibelius allows a gap at the end of the exported audio file to allow room for the reverb to die out naturally. The default is four quarters (crotchets) of silent gap. If you find that this isn't the right gap, choose Play > Performance and change the setting. If you have audio-editing chops, you can always get the free Audacity wave editing software (or use other software you might already have, such as Pro Tools) and manually fade out your recordings for that final polish.

- If you're using external MIDI gear for playback, the Export as Audio option won't contain those sounds. You'll want to switch to the Sibelius Sounds Essentials playback configuration, or default, so you can hear sounds in your bounced file.

- The audio file created is optimized for burning to a CD. It is full-sized, uncompressed audio, which is perfect for burning a CD. However, due to file size, a full-sized audio file is not great for posting online or emailing. (See the following MP3 note for more information.)

- Starting with Sibelius 5, you can now export audio even if you don't have the Sibelius Sounds Essentials library installed—Sibelius will use the DLS music player (built into the Mac) and the MS Wavetable Synth (built into Windows) to generate playback.

- In Sibelius 5, when you export to audio, Sibelius will take however long it needs to ensure that your audio file is free of any defects. On a modern, fast computer, it might export faster than real time, and on a slower computer it might take longer. This is a good thing because it ensures that scores that won't play back properly in real time will always bounce correctly.

MP3 The audio files generated by Sibelius are full-quality AIFF (Mac) and WAV (PC) files, which sound great but are a bit too big for emailing or posting online. The best way to convert to MP3 is to use iTunes. Import your audio files into iTunes, select the relevant score(s), and from the Advanced menu, choose Convert Selection to AAC, which will convert the audio to a smaller, compressed format. The default codec for iTunes is the Apple Advanced Audio Codec (AAC). If you really want to have a plain ol' MP3, you'll need to go to iTunes Preferences > Advanced > Import and change the Import Using option from AAC Encoder to MP3 Encoder.

Once you've run the Convert Selection to AAC/MP3 procedure, you'll see a second file with the same name, but that file will be much, much smaller—perfect for distribution or posting online. To get that file out of iTunes, just drag it to your desktop.

Export to Scorch

The final way you can export scores out of Sibelius is by using Scorch. Scorch is a technology that embeds a Sibelius score inside a web page. Using the free Scorch plug-in, any user can do the following things to the Sibelius score:

- View the score on a Mac or a PC with a small, dial-up-friendly transfer size

- Play back the score from his or her own computer

- Play back from a third-party sound device (if installed)

- Change the playback speed

- Save the Sibelius score to a hard drive (if allowed)

- Change the instrument playing back

- Transpose the music

- Print the score (if allowed)

This is a very cool technology that Sibelius has had for a number of years. It's very easy to make your scores into Scorch web pages; all you have to do is choose File > Export > Scorch Web Page, which will first request a Save location. When that's selected, it will bring up the Export Scorch Web Page dialog box, shown in Figure 18.10.

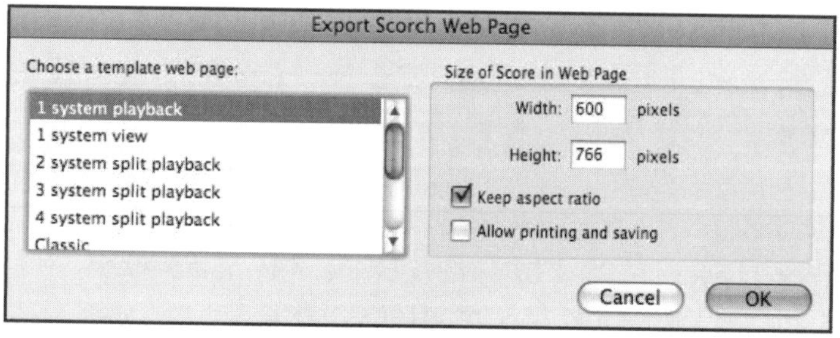

Figure 18.10 Export to Scorch options.

Score Info When you export to Scorch, it will take the Score Info information to construct and name your Scorch document. Make sure to go to File > Score Info and fill out all of the fields. If you don't, Sibelius will alert you!

In this dialog box, you can select the appropriate template for the web page, which is based on the number of systems you want on the page. (More systems make the music smaller.) If you'd like to specify the exact size of the score, you can do so by setting an exact range of pixels for the width and the height.

The most important feature in this dialog box is the ability to control whether the user can save and print the score. You can toggle this by selecting (or deselecting) the Allow Printing and Saving option.

Why would you disallow printing and saving? For starters, if you were planning to sell your score and you wanted to use Scorch to provide a preview, you wouldn't want to allow printing and saving. No matter what your intention is, you have the power to control saving and printing.

Publishing Online

After you export your score, Sibelius saves two files. The first file is the score itself, in .sib format, and the second file is a web page in .htm format. To place these scores online, you'll need to have both the .htm and the .sib file present.

Speaking of posting these online, if you're new to this whole concept, Sibelius makes it very easy for you to publish online. Just go to www.sibeliusmusic.com and sign up for a free account. You'll be able to upload your scores for free, and Sibelius will host them for you, creating a webpage automatically. Even better, if you're interested in selling your scores, Sibelius will do all of the e-commerce for you, and you can start making money from your music right away! If you use SibeliusMusic.com, there's no need to convert to Scorch; you can just send the Sibelius file, and Sibelius will do the rest.

As an alternative, you can create your own web pages with Scorch documents. (Just make sure you upload both the .htm and the .sib file to the same directory on the server.) When someone navigates to the page, they will encounter one of two things. If they don't have Scorch installed, they'll see the warning message shown in Figure 18.11.

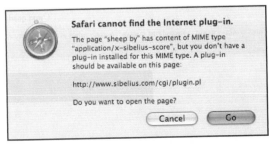

Figure 18.11 Missing plug-in: Scorch.

At this time they'll be asked whether they'd like to go to grab the free download. Once that's installed, they'll see what a user who has Scorch installed sees (as in Figure 18.12).

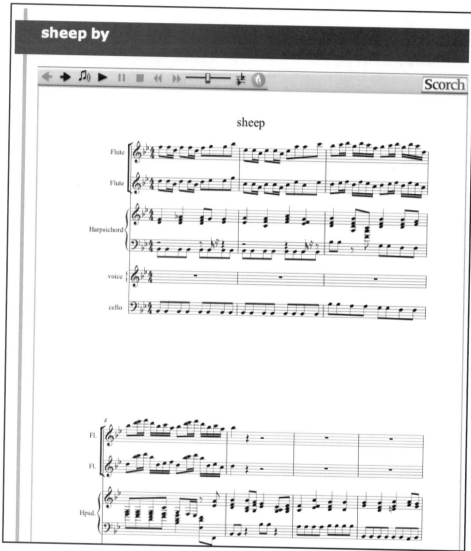

Figure 18.12 A Scorch web page.

From there, they can take advantage of all that Scorch has to offer: playback, transposition, printing, and saving (if enabled).

Here are some obvious uses for Scorch technology:

- Sharing your music with colleagues

- Distributing parts to musicians so they can not only see, but also hear, their parts
- Preparing practice music for your students to play, listen to, and print at home
- Selling your scores online
- Providing interactive, educational websites for theory and aural skills training

---

Heard But Not Seen I use Scorch with my students on a daily basis to prepare ear training and dictation examples. I write an example on Page 1 and hide the notes in Sibelius. On Page 5 (intentionally far away), I copy the music and show it so the students have an answer reference. When the students play Page 1, they can hear the music but they don't see anything. It's a great tool for ear training and dictation.

Index

A

accent new notes, filtering, 221–222
accessing
    Create menu parameters, 68
    Dynamic Parts, 288–294
    keypads, 29
    plug-ins, 421
accidentals, 202–203, 421
    ordering, 38
    spelling, 65
accuracy, chords, 52–53
Acoustic Grand Piano (Gold), 346
Active Devices, 339
Add Harp Pedaling dialog box, 190
adding
    audio instead of video, 374
    augmentation dots, 40–42
    bars, 70
    breaks, 254–256
    chords, 48
    clefs, 82–85
    effects, 358–359
    features, 450
    flutes, 16
    Hit Points to video, 366–367
    Ideas, 305
    Ideas feature to scores, 315–316
    instruments, 89–92
        to manuscript paper, 14–15
    intervals, 43–44, 48
    keyboard shortcuts, 448–452
    key signatures, 74–77
    measures, 69–72
    metronome marks, 18
    note names, 427–428
    plug-ins, 340
    simple harmony, 422–423
    staccato, 59
    tab instruments, 172
    technique text to scores, 112
    tempo text, 18
    text, 215
    time signatures, 78–80
    titles, 245
    tuplets, 48
    video, 364–366
    worksheets, 415

additional verses to lyrics, 130–131
Add Keyboard Shortcut dialog box, 451
Add Note Names plug-in, 433–434
Add to Worksheet Creator dialog box, 416
adjusting rhythms, 59. *See also* modifying
Advanced Filter, 134, 219–226
aligning
    chord symbols, 247
    expression markings, 108–111
    hairpins, 116
    House Styles
        Default Positions, 245–248
        System Object Positions, 243–244
        Text Styles Vertical Positions, 244–245
    lyrics, 259
    objects, 258–260
    Recent Position command, 261
    staves, 262–264
    text, 259
    titles, 246
Align Staves dialog box, 263
alphabetic (computer) keyboard input, 47–48
anacrusis bars, 17
analysis, 421
appearance
    Dynamic Parts, 294–299
    of rehearsal markings, 124–125
applications
    Arrange, 392–399
    cross-platform, 2
    PhotoScore Lite, 380–392
    PhotoScore Ultimate, 392
    Scorch, exporting to, 468–469
    Word, copying and pasting to, 465–466
    Worksheet Creator, 402. *See also* Worksheet Creator
applying Flexi-time recording, 61–62
arpeggios
    guitar indications, 167
    non-arpeggio brackets, 188–191
Arrange, 392–399
    copying, 393–395
    editing, 395–399
    optimizing, 399
    pasting, 393–395
    styles, 395
arrow keys, 37
articulations, 201–202

License Agreement/Notice of Limited Warranty

By opening the sealed disc container in this book, you agree to the following terms and conditions. If, upon reading the following license agreement and notice of limited warranty, you cannot agree to the terms and conditions set forth, return the unused book with unopened disc to the place where you purchased it for a refund.

License

The enclosed software is copyrighted by the copyright holder(s) indicated on the software disc. You are licensed to copy the software onto a single computer for use by a single user and to a backup disc. You may not reproduce, make copies, or distribute copies or rent or lease the software in whole or in part, except with written permission of the copyright holder(s). You may transfer the enclosed disc only together with this license, and only if you destroy all other copies of the software and the transferee agrees to the terms of the license. You may not decompile, reverse assemble, or reverse engineer the software.

Notice of Limited Warranty

The enclosed disc is warranted by Course Technology to be free of physical defects in materials and workmanship for a period of sixty (60) days from end user's purchase of the book/disc combination. During the sixty-day term of the limited warranty, Course Technology will provide a replacement disc upon the return of a defective disc.

Limited Liability

THE SOLE REMEDY FOR BREACH OF THIS LIMITED WARRANTY SHALL CONSIST ENTIRELY OF REPLACEMENT OF THE DEFECTIVE DISC. IN NO EVENT SHALL COURSE TECHNOLOGY OR THE AUTHOR BE LIABLE FOR ANY OTHER DAMAGES, INCLUDING LOSS OR CORRUPTION OF DATA, CHANGES IN THE FUNCTIONAL CHARACTERISTICS OF THE HARDWARE OR OPERATING SYSTEM, DELETERIOUS INTERACTION WITH OTHER SOFTWARE, OR ANY OTHER SPECIAL, INCIDENTAL, OR CONSEQUENTIAL DAMAGES THAT MAY ARISE, EVEN IF COURSE TECHNOLOGY AND/OR THE AUTHOR HAS PREVIOUSLY BEEN NOTIFIED THAT THE POSSIBILITY OF SUCH DAMAGES EXISTS.

Disclaimer of Warranties

COURSE TECHNOLOGY AND THE AUTHOR SPECIFICALLY DISCLAIM ANY AND ALL OTHER WARRANTIES, EITHER EXPRESS OR IMPLIED, INCLUDING WARRANTIES OF MERCHANTABILITY, SUITABILITY TO A PARTICULAR TASK OR PURPOSE, OR FREEDOM FROM ERRORS. SOME STATES DO NOT ALLOW FOR EXCLUSION OF IMPLIED WARRANTIES OR LIMITATION OF INCIDENTAL OR CONSEQUENTIAL DAMAGES, SO THESE LIMITATIONS MIGHT NOT APPLY TO YOU.

Other

This Agreement is governed by the laws of the State of Massachusetts without regard to choice of law principles. The United Convention of Contracts for the International Sale of Goods is specifically disclaimed. This Agreement constitutes the entire agreement between you and Course Technology regarding use of the software.